Hard Target

The *Studies in Asian Security* book series promotes analysis, understanding, and explanation of the dynamics of domestic, transnational, and international security challenges in Asia. The peer-reviewed publications in the Series analyze contemporary security issues and problems to clarify debates in the scholarly community, provide new insights and perspectives, and identify new research and policy directions. Security is defined broadly to include the traditional political and military dimensions as well as nontraditional dimensions that affect the survival and well-being of political communities. Asia, too, is defined broadly to include Northeast, Southeast, South, and Central Asia.

Designed to encourage original and rigorous scholarship, books in the Studies in Asian Security series seek to engage scholars, educators, and practitioners. Wide-ranging in scope and method, the Series is receptive to all paradigms, programs, and traditions, and to an extensive array of methodologies now employed in the social sciences.

Hard Target

SANCTIONS, INDUCEMENTS,
AND THE CASE OF NORTH KOREA

Stephan Haggard and Marcus Noland

STANFORD UNIVERSITY PRESS
Stanford, California

Stanford University Press
Stanford, California

Printed in the United States of America on acid-free, archival-quality paper

Library of Congress Cataloging-in-Publication Data
Names: Haggard, Stephan, author. | Noland, Marcus, author.
Title: Hard target : sanctions, inducements, and the case of North Korea / Stephan Haggard and Marcus Noland.
Other titles: Studies in Asian security.
Description: Stanford, California : Stanford University Press, 2017. | Series: Studies in Asian security | Includes bibliographical references and index.
Identifiers: LCCN 2016031455 (print) | LCCN 2016032208 (ebook) | ISBN 9781503600362 (cloth : alk. paper) | ISBN 9781503601994 (ebook)
Subjects: LCSH: Economic sanctions—Korea (North) | Korea (North)—Foreign economic relations. | Korea (North)—Foreign relations. | Nuclear disarmament—Korea (North)
Classification: LCC HF1602.6 .H34 2017 (print) | LCC HF1602.6 (ebook) | DDC 327.1/17095193—dc23
LC record available at https://lccn.loc.gov/2016031455

Cover photo: A North Korean soldier looks at the south side through a pair of binoculars at the Panmunjom truce village. Reuters.

Typeset by Newgen in 10.5/13.5 Bembo

Contents

Figures and Tables

TABLES

Preface and Acknowledgments

This book addresses the debate over economic sanctions and inducements in the context of North Korea's nuclear weapons and missile programs. Its focus on the country's external economic relations can be regarded as a complement to our previous work, *Famine in North Korea: Markets, Aid and Reform* (2007) and *Witness to Transformation: Refugee Insights into North Korea* (2011), which centered on the country's internal political economy.

Methodologically, the latter work was built on surveys of North Korean refugees undertaken with the support of the Smith Richardson Foundation. We were fortunate that the foundation was willing to support further activity in this vein. In this book, we extend our analysis of the political economy of North Korea by surveying Chinese and South Korean businesses operating there. Our thanks to the Horizon Group and Milward Brown for their respective conduct of the Chinese and Korean surveys.

From the surveys, which make up the backbone of Chapter 5, our focus subsequently widened to encompass North Korea's broader foreign economic and political relations with the other five parties to the Six Party Talks (South Korea, China, Japan, Russia, and the United States). Al Song, our interlocutor at Smith Richardson, was endlessly patient as we reformulated what we were doing and delayed drawing the story to a conclusion. Workshops convened at the Asia Society by Chuck Kartman and Susan Shirk in 2009 (Asia Society 2010) and by Etel Solingen (Solingen 2012) at the Woodrow Wilson International Center for Scholars in 2010 sharpened our focus on the logic of sanctions and engagement.

In addition to his affiliation with the Peterson Institute for International Economics, Marcus Noland is a senior fellow at the East-West Center. Stephan Haggard benefited from a POSCO Fellowship at the center in 2015; thanks to Denny Roy for his support. The center graciously provided support during joint residencies and published a monograph (Haggard and Noland 2011b) that was a test run for some of the ideas here.

One reason for the delay in bringing the book to a conclusion was that we simply started to learn more. At the time our refugee book was published, we launched the *North Korea: Witness to Transformation* blog at the Peterson Institute for International Economics (http://blogs.piie.com/nk/). Initially tied to the theme of refugees and the humanitarian and human rights issues surrounding them, the blog ultimately became a site where we analyzed current events, published interim findings of various sorts, and kept up with other research and writing on the Koreas. We consider it a kind of repository that pursues many issues that we address in more detail than we can provide in this book. We would like to thank the Peterson Institute for International Economics for graciously supporting our work on North Korea. Special thanks are due to its publications department and web team for their support in hosting and promoting the blog.

Needless to say, given the long gestation and wide-ranging nature of this project, we have benefited from interaction with innumerable colleagues, students, and conference and seminar participants. Like breathless Academy Award winners, we would like to thank everyone for everything, particularly the numerous colleagues from both academia and the policy world where we have presented our work over the years. We will surely forget some and not get to others before the exit music starts playing. Instead of even trying to go down that road, we will keep things short and sweet and recognize some of the people without whom this book would not exist.

At the Peterson Institute, research analysts Erik Weeks, Jennifer Lee, Alex Melton, Kevin Stahler, and Kent Boydston all contributed to various aspects of this project. It should be noted that all are alumni of the Graduate School of Global Policy and Strategy at the University of California, San Diego, where Stephan Haggard teaches. Dan Pinkston, Dave Kang, and Chung-in Moon deserve particular mention, as they are founts of useful analysis and information on the peninsula as well as good friends; all three commented on various aspects of this evolving project over time. Stephan Haggard would also like to thank colleagues and former students from the Graduate School at the University of California, San Diego, including TaiMing Cheung, Luke Herman,

Jihyeon Jeong, Euijin Jung, Miles Kahler, Eddy Malesky, Barry Naughton, Jaesung Ryu, Susan Shirk, and Yu Zheng.

Once a manuscript exists, it takes yet another team of dedicated individuals to turn it into the book that you hold in your hands. We are particularly grateful for the efforts of Jenny Gavacs and the staff at Stanford University Press.

Finally, our biggest debts are owed to our families, who sometimes endured life with what must have seemed like absentee husbands and fathers. This book is little recompense for that lost time, but it is the best that we can do.

Note on Romanization

For purposes of Romanization of the Korean language, we rely on a combination of transliteration conventions in our own style. In general, for specifically South Korean or neutral Korean words, we use the South Korean government's Revised Romanization method. For names of people, we follow the spelling most commonly used for the specific individual, as will be familiar to readers. We also use a hyphen in between the first and second syllables of given names (e.g., "Park Geun-hye" and "Kim Jong-un"). For names, places, or concepts specific to North Korea, we use a Revised McCune-Reischauer Romanization in accordance with standard use in the DPRK. We should also point out that Korean names are written in their traditional order, with the surname preceding the given name.

Hard Target

1

Introduction

The Political Economy of Engagement

North Korea is routinely ranked among the most economically distorted, closed, and politically anachronistic authoritarian systems in the world. If it were located elsewhere, interest in the country would be limited to its chronic humanitarian problems: its pervasive human rights abuses, food shortages, and even outright famine. But North Korea's geographic position and nuclear ambitions have forced the major powers in Northeast Asia—China, Japan, South Korea, Russia, and the United States—to pay attention.

Most analysis of the extended nuclear crisis that first broke in 2002 has focused, quite legitimately, on high politics: the diplomatic and military strategies of the contending parties and their consequences (for example, Cha and Kang 2003; Funabashi 2007; Pritchard 2007; Chinoy 2008; Bechtol 2010; Pollack 2011; Cha 2012). What has driven North Korea to acquire nuclear weapons? What role do security concerns play in the regime's calculations? What military or political pressures might be brought to bear on it? What are the risks of war?

However, the course of the crisis and the prospects for reaching a durable settlement have rested in no small measure on economic issues. Could economic engagement and side payments moderate North Korean behavior? Are sanctions a more effective way to capture North Korea's attention? To what extent do economic inducements or constraints affect the North Korean leadership one way or another?

These questions are ultimately tied to a host of important domestic political economy issues that have received far less attention than they should. How

willing is the North Korean leadership to continue to pay the tremendous opportunity costs of autarky? Can the regime be induced onto a reform path that
would also push the country toward a settlement of the nuclear issue? Or is a
settlement of outstanding security issues a political precondition for coaxing
North Korea out of its economic shell?

In *Famine in North Korea* (Haggard and Noland 2007a), we took a first cut
at the political economy of the post-1990 period, focusing on the economic
and humanitarian consequences of North Korea's isolation. Highly dependent
on support from Moscow, claims of self-reliance notwithstanding, the North
Korean economy experienced a full-blown collapse following the demise of
the Soviet Union. The country experienced one of the great famines of the
twentieth century, a tragedy in which, we estimate, between 600,000 and 1
million people died. Although external shocks and adverse weather played a
role in the calamity, at root it was the manifestation of profound state failures
that included not only lack of accountability and unequal distribution of food
but also the unwillingness of the regime to tap foreign sources of food supply.
We showed that with relatively minor adjustments to its economic strategy,
the regime could have largely avoided catastrophe.

The famine had wide-ranging economic and social consequences; we focused on two. First, the central planning system effectively collapsed, causing
the North Korean economy to undergo a largely unplanned and unintended
process of marketization and privatization from below. Small-scale social
units—households, work units, local government and party offices, and even
military units—adopted entrepreneurial coping strategies to secure food and
survive. Farmers took advantage of the dramatic shift in relative prices to work
on private plots and engage in market-related activities as well.

As we show in Chapter 2, the regime's reaction to these new economic and
social forces was ambivalent at best. The leadership initially acquiesced in the
marketization process, decriminalizing coping behaviors, ratifying the changes
taking place on the ground, and even initiating tentative reforms in 2002. Following the onset of the second nuclear crisis in October 2002, the government
oscillated between stricter controls on market forces and periods of relaxation
and pilot reforms. At no point, however, did it openly signal a willingness to
undertake the types of reforms that China had pioneered in the Deng era.

The second effect of the economic crisis of the 1990s was a fundamental
change in North Korea's foreign economic relations. Throughout the Cold
War, the country's trade, investment, and aid ties centered largely on the
socialist countries. Tentative forays into Western product and capital markets
were limited in part by sanctions but more fundamentally by North Korea's

autarkic economic strategy. Many contacts ended in mutual disappointment and recrimination (Cornell 2002).

The crisis of the mid-1990s did not result in a liberalizing shift in foreign economic *policy*, but the country did see substantial changes in its foreign economic *relations*. The famine triggered a massive international aid effort, at its peak feeding more than one-third of the population (Haggard and Noland 2007a). In addition, the famine triggered slow but steady growth in foreign trade and an effort to diversify trading partners and exports. These developments sprang in part from new diplomatic initiatives and in part from efforts to secure foreign exchange through both licit and illicit means. But this growth, particularly in ties with China, also reflected spillover from the process of de facto marketization triggered by the famine. An array of actors sought out commercial opportunities—and foreign exchange—in the interstices of the great wall that the regime had constructed around the country. Cross-border exchange, in turn, further fed the domestic marketization process.

In this volume, we draw on a growing theoretical and empirical literature on economic statecraft to connect marketization processes, changing foreign economic relations, and the strategic interplay around North Korea's nuclear program. The ultimate objective is not only to understand North Korea but to address the debate about sanctions and the merits and demerits of "engagement" with adversaries.

As we show in Chapter 3, it is no simple matter to document North Korea's external economic relations; even the simplest national accounts information is treated as a state secret, and information on foreign trade and investment is similarly controlled. Moreover, the country has been engaged in a variety of illicit activities, from drug smuggling to counterfeiting. Export revenue derived from the sale of weapons and associated consulting services has also played a critical role in the economy.

However, North Korea's external relations leave at least some traces with foreign partners. Economic forensics allow us to reconstruct its growing economic relations with major trading partners, particularly South Korea and China, and a broader balance-of-payments accounting as well. We assess the extent to which North Korea is becoming more open, and we identify the public and quasi-private North Korean entities engaged in cross-border trade and investment and the nature of their activities, both and illicit and legitimate. In Chapter 5, we explore these issues at the firm level by drawing on two original surveys of Chinese and South Korean firms doing business in North Korea.

This book is not simply about North Korea. It also seeks to address the broader theoretical and empirical question of how and whether "engagement" with adversaries—and economic engagement in particular—can mitigate security dilemmas, induce cooperation, and even transform recalcitrant states. The question first became salient in US foreign policy with the efforts of the Nixon administration to reach détente with the Soviet Union, building on ideas pioneered by West Germany's *Ostpolitik*. These same ideas were subsequently appropriated by Kim Dae-jung's "Sunshine Policy," by Roh Moo-hyun and by Park Geun-hye's *Trustpolitik* as well. The debate with respect to US foreign policy has continued in discussions about China (for example, Shinn 1996) and the other so-called rogue regimes with which the United States has had to deal, including Cuba, Iraq, Libya, Iran, and Myanmar (Littwak 2000; Rotberg 2007; Nincic 2005, 2011; Solingen 2012a).

The issues debated are nested in the larger question of how economic statecraft, including both sanctions and engagement, work. As David Baldwin (1985) notes in his classic work on the topic, sanctions have multiple objectives that range from outright denial of economic gains to controls on prescribed and illicit trade to signaling third parties of intent. Yet they are typically undertaken with the strategic objective of linkage: changing the behavior of the target state.

In contrast to the voluminous literature on sanctions, less has been written on the political logic of positive inducements or "engagement" (exceptions include Baldwin 1971, 1985; Crumm 1995; Long 1996; Drezner 1999, 2000; Brooks 2002; Kahler and Kastner 2006; Solingen 1994, 2007, 2012b; Nincic 2010, 2011; Verdier and Woo 2011). Clearly the logic of engagement is by no means limited to the economic sphere (Haass and O'Sullivan 2000). For example, engagement entails the commitment to talk and negotiate in the first place, and this theme comes up repeatedly in the North Korean case. Yet economic inducements play a central role in engagement strategies. We thus define engagement as the promise or extension of economic exchanges—including trade, investment, aid, and other transfers—as an instrument of foreign policy.[1] How and to what extent might such engagement work, both in general and with respect to North Korea and other nuclear proliferators in particular?

We begin in this Introduction with an outline of the core theoretical issues before turning to the complications posed by humanitarian considerations for economic statecraft, including both sanctions and inducements. We then set the stage for the chapters that follow with a brief political history of the post–Cold War period on the Korean peninsula, focusing on the so-called second nuclear crisis that starts in 2002; we conclude our story in 2016. We close with an outline of our empirical strategy and a description of the contours of the book.

The Political Economy of Sanctions and Engagement I:
Economic Statecraft as Linkage

There are two distinct conceptions of how engagement affects the behavior of a target state (Nincic 2010, 2011). First, engagement can be modeled as a chip in a bargaining game in which inducements are offered in exchange for policy quid pro quos. Keohane (1984) has called such exchanges narrow or specific reciprocity. In this model, engagement, like sanctions, "works" by changing the cost-benefit calculus of the leadership of the target state. But economic engagement has also been theorized to have broader transformative effects (Solingen 2007), such as strengthening political coalitions with more moderate foreign policy preferences or socializing the target's political leadership to new opportunities and norms. At the extreme, engagement may result in fundamental changes in domestic politics, a stated objective of Kim Dae-jung's Sunshine Policy. We take up each of these models in turn.

Theoretically, the logic of inducements as a quid pro quo should not differ fundamentally from the logic of sanctions. Both involve the manipulation of costs and benefits in the context of a bargaining game. In fact, however, there are a number of potential differences between the logic of imposing constraints and that of extending rewards. These include psychological differences in how individuals—and presumably countries—view the prospects of gains versus losses (Kahneman and Tversky 1984; Levy 1997). Sanctions and inducements also have quite different signaling effects: sanctions are more hostile and threatening than rewards.

At the same time, there are a number of similarities in the use of economic inducements and sanctions that have been overlooked in the highly polarized policy debate over the merits of engagement. For example, inducements no less than sanctions can be undermined by coordination and bargaining problems. And while it is widely noted that sanctions are much less likely to have their desired effect if leaders can impose their costs on the citizenry with relative impunity, domestic political factors may also influence the efficacy of inducements. Imagine, for example, the efficacy of promises of greater trade and investment with a state that is wary of economic engagement to begin with.[2]

As the sanctions literature shows, it is highly doubtful that we can reach a blanket judgment on the efficacy of sanctions and inducements. The early debate on whether or not sanctions worked (for example, Pape 1997; Elliott 1998; Baldwin and Pape 1998) has rightly given way to a more nuanced discussion of the conditions for success, and more careful consideration of what "success" even means. We follow a similar line here, focusing on three central parameters that have been shown to influence the efficacy of sanctions but which we show can also affect engagement strategies. These are the domestic political economy of the target state, problems of coordination, and credible commitment problems that emerge in quid pro quo negotiations. We take up the first issue in more detail in Chapter 2 and the other two in Chapters 3, 6, and 7.

North Korea as a Hard Target

Early theoretical papers modeled sanctions as a bargaining game between sender and target (Eaton and Engers 1992), but such models quickly gave way to a consideration of the domestic political economy of the target (particularly Kirshner 1997; Kaempfer and Lowenberg 1988, 1992). Sanctions can work via *direct* economic costs on the leadership of the target state—for example, by freezing government or personal assets—or *indirect* political costs that affect the welfare of constituent groups or broader publics, such as through trade embargoes. These costs are in turn presumed to induce political leaders to cooperate.

One of the more robust findings in the literature is that the target's regime type is an important determinant of sanction success (Brooks 2002; Kahler and Kastner 2006; Allen 2005, 2008a, 2008b; Letzkian and Souva 2007; Hufbauer et al. 2007; Escriba-Folch 2012). Because authoritarian regimes can repress and impose costs on their populations—and may even be incentivized to do so by sanctions (Allen 2008a, 2008b; Wood 2008; Escriba-Folch and Wright 2010; Escriba-Folch 2012; Major 2012)—they constitute "hard targets," vulnerable only under highly specific circumstances. Needless to say, this observation is highly germane to North Korea. The North Korean regime survived a famine that likely killed between 3 and 5 percent of the population in the mid-1990s. It is doubtful that the major parties could coordinate actions that would be nearly as consequential or, if they could, that the North Korean government would necessarily respond. Sanctions are only likely to work in such a setting if they can be targeted quite narrowly at the leadership, a recurrent preoccupation in the broader sanctions literature (e.g., Cortright and Lopez 2002).

However, we must consider whether the domestic political characteristics of the target state also constrain the efficacy of inducements. Sanctions have impact through their adverse welfare effects; inducements operate by providing welfare gains. Advocates of engagement argue that inducements influence internal decision making in favor of "doves" (for example, Harrison 2001; Moon and Bae 2003 on North Korea). But it is by no means clear that authoritarian decision making can be modeled as the result of interest group politics (although a number of accounts have tried; see, for example, McEachern 2010 on North Korea). The stylized quid pro quo envisions prospective economic benefits flowing to reformers, enterprises, and individuals that stand to gain from greater openness. The political leadership reaps some political gain from the welfare gains of these groups and is thus either induced or constrained to behave in a cooperative way. Concessions are made by those opposed to cooperation, presumably including some portions of the military.

Yet as we show in Chapter 2, the evidence that Kim Jong-il and Kim Jong-un saw major economic or political gains from expanded trade and investment relations is mixed at best. The hesitancy of the government with respect to "reform and opening" is clear and, at least to date, stands in contrast with the more openly reformist paths taken by the communist parties of China and Vietnam. Moreover, the forms that North Korea's "engagement" with the world economy has taken include illicit activities, money laundering and weapons sales, hardly the type of activities that would have transformative political and social effects of the desired type.

Indeed, the main lesson that Kim Il-sung, Kim Jong-il, and Kim Jong-un appear to have learned from the collapse of European communism is that it resulted from political and economic opening. Following the collapse of the Soviet Union, the regime redoubled its emphasis on ideology and leadership, particularly the latter's dynastic features (Quinones 2002). Kim Jong-il's main ideological innovation after taking office from his father in 1994 was "military first" (*songun*) politics, which sees the military as the exemplary institution of the revolution and by implication a key pillar of the regime's support. Military and national security tropes continued to play a central role in governance under Kim Jong-un, most notably in the articulation of the so-called *byungjin* line of 2013, which emphasizes the simultaneous pursuit of economic development and nuclear weapons. To the extent that Kim Jong-un relies on the military or is constrained by it, marginal inducements are unlikely to result in a wholesale shift in political alignments or public policies in favor of reform.

Paradoxically for advocates of engagement, positive economic inducements are most likely to have an effect in authoritarian regimes when they mirror the structure of "smart sanctions"; that is, they directly pay off the leadership and its core supporters. The problem, of course, is that paying off objectionable dictators and their cronies and tolerating illicit forms of engagement is politically unpalatable. As we see repeatedly, the nature of "engagement" that the North Korean leadership favors is heavily skewed toward transfers that it can directly control; it is at best lukewarm toward engagement that has wider social effects.

Coordination

In addition to the domestic political context, the international environment plays a crucial role in the success or failure of sanctions. It is an often repeated finding in the literature that sanctions are more likely to be effective when coordinated (Martin 1992; Hufbauer et al. 2007).[3] But a simple and obvious point is that engagement can be undermined by failure to coordinate as well. In the course of the nuclear crisis, and even before, those parties that sought to engage the North—South Korea, China, and Russia—found themselves in conflict with a US strategy that emphasized constraints. As we show in Chapter 6, on the political economy of the Six Party Talks, there was at least somewhat greater progress in negotiations when North Korea was facing economic distress. However, the regime never simply capitulated to sanctions; rather, progress typically hinged on combining constraints with offers of some quid pro quo in return for North Korean cooperation.

We also find evidence of what we call a "dynamic" coordination problem. There is a growing body of empirical work examining how sanctions change patterns of trade away from the sanctioning country (Caruso 2003; Kaempfer and Ross 2004; Haidar 2017). Differences across trading partners in the extent to which they use economic inducements also have a bearing on the direction of trade. Ceteris paribus, target countries should gravitate toward partners that place the least restrictions on trade, are least demanding with respect to policy quid pro quos, and offer more in return. As we show in Chapter 3, this is exactly what happened: North Korea increasingly focused on the most proengagement of its partners, particularly China and, at least during certain periods, South Korea.

The implications for the debate about sanctions and engagement are crucial. On the one hand, it is frequently claimed that sanctions against North Korea "don't work." Yet sanctions vis-à-vis North Korea did not fail only because of the willingness and capacity of the North Korean regime to absorb their costs. They failed also because sanctioning states did not have the effective leverage to impose them when others sought to engage. Put most bluntly, we need to continually ask whether sanctions failed to work or whether they were not tried.

Second, engagement no less than sanctions faces a "weakest link" problem. Open-ended engagement with targets can easily generate moral hazard problems, with the behavioral quid pro quo never being realized. Moreover, these moral hazard problems are dynamic. Targets will orient their trade precisely toward those partners who are less demanding that policy quid pro quos be enforced, generating second-order enforcement problems: how to control the behavior of states that enable the target in evading sanctions.

Engagement Bargaining and Bargaining Failure

A second and closely related international policy problem has to do with important issues of time inconsistency and credibility in the quid pro quo model of engagement. These constraints can easily generate bargaining failures (Fearon 1995, 1998). The realization that sending states can both threaten and impose sanctions drew attention to important strategic issues in sanctioning games as well as to possible selection effects in any empirical analysis (Drezner 1999, 2003; Nooruddin 2002; Lacy and Niou 2004; Y. Li and Drury 2004; Drury and Li 2006). Once sanctions are actually imposed, however, there are immediate costs for the target whether it complies or not.

Sequencing in inducement games operates somewhat differently. If the inducements are offered and granted first, the target state may subsequently have little incentive to cooperate. Critics of North Korea have long focused on the moral hazard problems associated with engagement (Downs 1999; Eberstadt 1999; Bolton 2007). In his 2010 memoir, George W. Bush draws an analogy between Kim Jong-il and a spoiled child throwing food on the floor: "The United States is through picking up [Kim Jong-il's] food." He also recounts a March 2001 meeting where he decided that the basic mode of dealing with North Korea would change: "From then on, North Korea would have to change its behavior *before* we made concessions" (emphasis in the original).

The opposite problem also exists, however: if economic inducements are made conditional on some action and promised only in the future, the initiating or sending state has the credibility problem. Will it deliver on its promises? Will it have incentives to deliver on promises if the target state takes actions that are not easily reversible, such as dismantling its nuclear capability?

Such time inconsistency or sequencing problems can generate a very narrow conception of reciprocity that in turn creates second-order bargaining problems. In the favored terminology of the North Koreans, negotiations require "words for words, actions for actions." The result, however, is that the goods to be exchanged are sliced into finer and finer tranches. Exchanges may be made more comparable and less time inconsistent, but, as in Zeno's paradox, the ultimate goal to be achieved can easily recede. One result is the periodic attraction of "grand bargains" that cut through these sequencing issues with large deals that put everything on the table at once. Because these various goods cannot be delivered on similar schedules, however—in part for physical reasons, such as the time to build a light-water reactor—the bargaining problems remain. To date, grand bargains have had no greater success than more incremental and phased approaches.

The Political Economy of Sanctions and Engagement II: Engagement as Transformation

The idea that interdependence can have transformative effects is an offshoot of the liberal tradition in international relations (Schumpeter 1919; Polachek 1980; O'Neal and Russett 1997; Russett and O'Neal 2001; Morrow 1999; Mansfield and Pollins 2003; Copeland 2014; for a theoretical and empirical critique, see Barbieri 1996, 2002). Regardless of the initial intentions of the political leadership in the target state, the very expansion of economic interdependence raises the cost of conflict, bolsters interests that are more amenable to international cooperation, and provides opportunities for credible signaling (Gartzke, Lie, and Boehmer 2001).

However, the openness of the economy and the level of trade are at least partly endogenous to politics and policy. Etel Solingen, following Gourevitch (1986), gives the fundamentally economic argument of the liberal peace a co-alitional foundation. She argues that the chances for regional stability (1998), the nature of grand strategies (2001), and even the pursuit of nuclear weapons (2007) are related to the strength of what she calls "statist" or "backlash" as opposed to "liberalizing" coalitions. She summarizes the logic in a passage with obvious relevance to understanding North Korea:

> Backlash grand strategies seek to preserve state entrepreneurship and military-industrial allocations, resist external pressures for economic liberalization and intrusions on sovereignty, and target internationalizing adversaries at home and abroad. Regional insecurity and competition is a natural side-effect at best, and a dominant requirement at worst, of this grand strategy. Regional cooperation threatens backlash coalitions because it scales back military imperatives, erodes statist privileges, and devalues nationalist and confessional myth-making as a political currency (2001, 524).

Despite the claim that grand strategy is partly endogenous to politics, Nincic (2010, 2011) and Solingen (2012a) argue that external inducements may have political effects, at least over the long run. It is worth walking through the mechanisms of such transformation as they are central to the empirical tests that the book offers.

We begin with a closed economy and therefore with a political leadership that pays little economic cost—except an ongoing opportunity cost—for aggressive or bellicose foreign policy positions. The initiating state offers to lift sanctions and thereby permit expanded trade, investment, and aid relations with the target. These new economic relations create stakeholders in the target state who now risk losses from bellicose behavior and thus act as a political constraint on the government. Interdependence can then gradually shift the overall political balance—the ruling political coalition—in favor of reform. Unless this scenario be thought far-fetched, consider China, where a nominally Communist party not only opened its economy but subsequently moderated its foreign policy and even welcomed capitalists into its ranks. International ties can also have socializing and learning effects. Individuals, firms, officials, and even high-ranking politicians reassess their grand strategies in light of new information delivered via increasing political and economic integration.

It is worth underlining that this transformative conception of engagement was clearly central to Kim Dae-jung's Sunshine Policy and appears to be a staple of the current Chinese approach to North Korea.[4] Beijing has not hidden its preference for the leadership in Pyongyang to pursue a more reformist route (Snyder 2009; International Crisis Group 2009; Szalontai and Choi 2013; Reilly 2014a, 2014b). Yet the conditions necessary for this benign circle to operate may be more restrictive than proponents of engagement suggest. An ample theoretical and empirical literature shows that sanctions have the effect of creating rents that leaders in the target country can exploit, thus offsetting sanctions' adverse effects on core constituencies (Kaempfer and Lowenberg 1988, 1992; Andreas 2005; Gibbons 1999 on Haiti; Rowe 1999 on Rhodesia; Niblock 2001 on the Middle East). However, it is wrong to believe that economic integration through engagement necessarily takes place in a way that dissolves rent-seeking opportunities. While governments intent on reform may provide opportunities for such engagement strategies, partial reforms provide opportunities for rent seeking and corruption that are no different from those associated with sanctions. Moreover, this partial reform path may constitute a political equilibrium (Hellman 1998).

A particularly important empirical issue is whether foreign transactions are effectively captured by state- or military-controlled enterprises in the target state. Think, for example, of a strategy of engagement with a country in which a monopoly is allowed to capture the rents from trade. Rather than inducing transformation, such a strategy empowers a strong, status quo force with limited interest in further economic opening. In Chapter 5, we use firm-level surveys to consider whether cross-border transactions between North Korea and China and South Korea resemble the kind of commercial relations postulated by the engagement model. As expected, the findings provide limited support for this proposition at best.

A final consideration has to do with the types of economic activity in which hard targets such as North Korea are engaged. In Chapter 3, we trace the country's long history of illicit activities and weapons sales. These are hardly the type of engagement that we associate with a moderate foreign policy, yet they are in fact quite typical of difficult regimes that pose challenges to the international community. Put differently, foreign economic ties reflect not only the inward orientation highlighted by Solingen but also types of "engagement" that other parties view as having negative rather than positive externalities.

Humanitarian Dilemmas

Were constraints on the success of an engagement approach not enough, we must also consider the humanitarian dilemmas that arise in dealing with hard targets. As sanctions grow in popularity, initiators must address the issues of collateral humanitarian damage. Sanctions against Iraq, Yugoslavia, and Haiti all raised these issues in stark terms. Moreover, their adverse effects not only were economic but extended to the risk that repressive governments would reap "rally around the flag" benefits and exploit external pressure to repress oppositions. A wide-ranging theoretical and empirical literature emerged around these potentially perverse effects (Kirshner 1997; Kaempfer, Lowenberg, and Mertens 2004; Wood 2008; Peksen 2009; Escribà-Folch and Wright 2010; Peksen and Drury 2010; Escribà-Folch 2012). Such concerns also had policy effects, giving rise to "smart" or targeted sanctions (Cortright and Lopez 2000, 2002; Drezner 2011).

However, engagement strategies, particularly those driven by humanitarian rationale, face their own distinctive policy dilemmas. The literature on foreign aid has long noted the so-called Samaritan's dilemma (e.g., Gibson et al. 2005). Knowing that the donor will continue to provide support on humanitarian grounds, there is little reason for the recipient to change its behavior, especially in ways that reduce support over the longer term. Similarly, increased access to foreign resources not only allows targets of engagement strategies to remain intransigent but has the larger effect of sustaining both the regime and the economic order that gives rise to conflictual behavior in the first place (Kalyvitis and Vlachaki 2011; Ahmed 2012). These issues have been raised forcefully by critics of extending humanitarian aid to North Korea (for example, Hill 2014).

As we showed in some detail in *Famine in North Korea*, the international community responded generously to North Korea's food shortages. Donors also periodically sought to use humanitarian assistance for political ends, a phenomenon we label "food for talks." Precisely because of the compelling quality of the humanitarian concerns, however, and the coordination problems that surrounded a multiplicity of donors, the North Korean leadership was able to maximize aid while gaining substantial leverage over the terms on which it was offered.

Over time, an opposite set of risks emerged which parallel quite closely the humanitarian dilemmas associated with sanctions. Impatience with North Korea's nuclear ambitions and diversion of aid generated political backlashes among donors. Donors either explicitly linked humanitarian assistance to progress on the nuclear issue or established much tougher ex ante conditions with respect to humanitarian access and monitoring. We show that this was true of not only the United States but South Korea and possibly even China. Given the failure of the regime to adequately prioritize commercial imports, the predictable result of recurrent backlashes was a failure of the international social safety net. From 2007 to 2012 in particular, North Korea reverted to chronic food insecurity, with shortages equal to any since the famine of the mid-1990s.

The Political Economy of Engagement: A Reprise

The debate on sanctions has clearly evolved toward more conditional statements of their effects, and similar caution is required with respect to the use of inducements and engagement. Our review suggests that engagement as a source of leverage or transformation is also subject to limiting conditions and is less likely to be effective.

- With respect to authoritarian regimes.
- With respect to statist economies, and coalitions, that directly control production and trade, including illicit activities and weapons.
- Where the beneficiaries of any inducements are state or military as opposed to private actors.
- Where humanitarian problems induce outside parties to extend unconditional or less conditional aid and subsidies.
- Where "engagement" must be coordinated across countries with different strategic and economic approaches to the target state.

All of these constraints have pertained with respect to North Korea. The processes of marketization have clearly spilled over into the foreign sector, but have nonetheless taken place in an authoritarian state-socialist context. At least through 2016, the leadership had not openly embraced reform in the same way that China or Vietnam did at similar stages in their development, or that Myanmar and even Cuba and Iran have more recently. De jure reforms have been halting at best, with the state retaining substantial control. As for South Korea—and even China—the government has shown a penchant for an "enclave" strategy at sites such as the Kaesong Industrial Complex (KIC) and the Rason Special Economic Zone, in which foreign firms are isolated from the domestic economy in ways that limit the "spread" effects of commercialization and marketization.

Thus the evidence on transformation is mixed. Although we do see signs of commercial and quasi-commercial cross-border activities, we need to consider very carefully whether investment, trade, and aid channeled through central government and state-controlled enterprises will have the transformative effect postulated by the engagement-as-transformation approach.

In addition to these political constraints on engagement strategies, we have also noted several acute bargaining problems with engagement. First, no less than with sanctions, engagement faces coordination problems and is less likely to have an impact when countries with strategic interests in the target state have divergent preferences. In addition, engagement faces the same credible commitment problems that sanctions do. On the one hand, moral hazard problems abound where engagement is extended prior to compliance. On the other hand, the target may see promised inducements as lacking credibility, particularly where compliance involves measures that are irreversible. We elaborate on these bargaining dynamics in Chapters 6 and 7.

The stage is set for the remainder of the book with a brief overview of the military, strategic, and political setting on the peninsula and the broad role that economic statecraft plays in it. We begin with the period from 1990 to the onset of the second nuclear crisis in 2002, which encompasses the first nuclear crisis and the conclusion of the Agreed Framework. We then divide the second nuclear crisis in two: from 2001 to 2009, during the first and second Bush administrations, which correspond almost exactly with the onset of the crisis and the rise and fall of the Six Party Talks (Chapter 6); and the period from 2009 to mid-2016, the bulk of the Obama presidency, when the Six Party Talks were in abeyance (Chapter 7).

The Korean Peninsula 1990–2016: A Brief International History

From the End of the Cold War to the Second Nuclear Crisis

Prior to 1990, North Korea's foreign economic relations were a function of the Cold War system, although complicated by the Sino-Soviet split (Chung 1978). Socialist patrons provided exports and aid and absorbed North Korea's export offerings—sometimes reluctantly (Szalontai 2005, 46–52). The United

States maintained an effective embargo through a complex, multitiered sanctions regime (Kim and Chang 2007; Lee and Choi 2009), as did its alliance partners in the Pacific (Noland 2000, 87–132). Japan permitted somewhat greater interaction because of the historical artifact of its large Korean community, but it did not enjoy diplomatic relations with North Korea. Neither did Western Europe, whose interest and engagement with the country was, with a few interesting exceptions (Cornell 2002), sporadic at best.

The waning of the Cold War held out the promise of fundamental political and economic changes in Northeast Asia. South Korea underwent a democratic transition in 1987–1988. President Roh Tae-woo's *Nordpolitik* sought to use economic inducements to de-escalate tensions on the peninsula. In late 1991, Seoul and Pyongyang signed the benchmark Agreement on Reconciliation, Nonaggression and Exchanges and Cooperation between the South and the North, which became known as the Basic Agreement. This was a crucial document foreshadowing virtually all elements of the Sunshine Policy, including

- Mutual recognition of each other's political systems and a promise to forego interference and subversion.
- A promise to forego the use of force and to transform the armistice system into a more durable peace regime.
- The initiation of economic and social exchanges.

The Basic Agreement was followed closely in 1992 by the Joint Declaration of the Denuclearization of the Korean Peninsula, in which both sides foreswore nuclear ambitions.

Nevertheless, the very dynamism of the South Korean economy made it more and more difficult, and costly, to maintain military parity. Newly declassified documents suggest that Kim Il-sung was well aware of this fact by the 1980s (Weathersby 2005). Moreover, the success of the South posed the ideational and legitimation challenge of justifying a system that by all objective metrics underperformed its neighbor.

The Soviet Union normalized relations with South Korea in January 1991, and China followed suit in less than a year. These important diplomatic breakthroughs were political, but they also reflected reform processes in both China and Russia as well as the desire to trade more extensively with South Korea and to transform economic relations with their North Korean client. Following normalization, both countries sought to shift from the "friendship prices" and implicit subsidies that had characterized their exchanges with North Korea to trade based on convertible currencies at world market prices.

These events, and the revolutions in Eastern Europe, were deeply unset-
tling for the North Korean regime (Moltz and Mansourov 2000). The end of
the Cold War spelled the demise of fraternal Communist regimes in the Soviet
Union and Eastern Europe. And although Soviet and Chinese recognition of
South Korea did not imply political abandonment or external pressures for
political reform—to the contrary, both countries proved exceedingly toler-
ant of the Kim dynasty and made efforts to provide assurances—as we show
in Chapter 3, the shift to market prices in trade with its two most important
socialist partners was a tremendous shock.

Given its extraordinary level of militarization, the end of the Cold War and
the olive branch extended by the South offered North Korea a larger peace
dividend than any other country in the world (Noland, Robinson, and Wang
2000; Noland 2000). However, a significant shift in the regime's grand strategy
was required to exploit the new geostrategic terrain. This challenge proved
too great for a leadership in transition. By evading its commitments under
the Non-Proliferation Treaty, North Korea triggered the first nuclear crisis of
1992–1994.

The most obvious explanation for North Korean behavior is a classic re-
alist one: a nuclear program provided a relatively inexpensive hedge against
the manifold insecurities associated with the end of the Cold War. However,
because of a central analytic problem we confront throughout this volume,
nothing is simple: the predictions of different theories about North Korean
behavior are often observationally equivalent and thus difficult to adjudicate.
The sharply conflicting lines of interpretation with respect to the first nuclear
crisis and its aftermath make this point clear and have persisted to this day.

One group of scholars has focused on North Korean insecurities and argued
that tough US and International Atomic Energy Agency (IAEA) responses to
North Korean derogations exacerbated the crisis (Harrison 2005; Cha and
Kang 2003, chaps. 2 and 4; McCormack 2004). An extensive body of analysis
by Sigal in particular (1998, 2002, 2005, 2009, 2010, 2016) concludes that
Pyongyang was driven by insecurity and so more responsive to inducements
than hawks believed (even if the regime's effort to extort resources from the
concerned parties is acknowledged). In effect, Sigal argues that the country
was playing a tit-for-tat game.

On the other hand, both new historical materials and alternative theoretical
approaches have suggested that the pursuit of a nuclear option was politically
hardwired and thus more impervious to either external sanctions or inducements. It is now clear that North Korea had long sought a nuclear option
(Szalontai and Radchenko 2006; Clemens 2010). Some, including prominent

US policy makers (Bolton 2007), drew the inference that the country never had any intention of giving up its quest for nuclear weapons. The sources of this pessimism are ultimately to be found in the North Korean political system, including the core family-party-military coalition at the heart of the regime (Solingen 2007; Smith 2015), its authoritarian political structure (Haggard and Noland 2007a, 2011a; Lind and Byman 2010), and ideological constraints and strategies of legitimation that relied on mobilizing against external enemies (Hymans 2006; Myers 2010, 2015; Habib 2011).

Whatever the source of the bargaining failures of the early 1990s, the result was a prolonged crisis in 1992–1994 that came dangerously close to war and was avoided largely by the unscripted intervention of former president Jimmy Carter (Oberdorfer 1997; Witt, Poneman and Galucci 2005; Creekmore 2006). The subsequent negotiation of the Agreed Framework included a number of important quid pro quos, including economic ones. The North agreed to freeze and eventually dismantle its nuclear program in return for inducements that included two light-water reactors (LWRs), the interim supply of heavy fuel oil, some relaxation of sanctions, and, above all, progress in normalizing political relations with the United States.

Progress on normalization—the political lynchpin of the deal from North Korea's perspective—quickly stalled. The Korean Peninsula Energy Development Organization (KEDO) orchestrated early work on construction of the LWR and, with occasional delays, the United States met its commitments with respect to heavy-oil shipments and the partial easing of sanctions. But the Clinton administration and the Agreed Framework came under increasing pressure from Republican hawks in Congress after the midterm elections of November 1994 (Hathaway and Tama 2004).

North Korea's internal problems were even more profound, including the political transition following the death of Kim Il-sung in July 1994 and the extreme economic conditions that characterized the peak famine period. Once these immediate challenges had passed, Pyongyang dragged its feet on negotiations that would have institutionalized a final settlement to the Korean War (the so-called Four Party Talks in 1997–1999) while engaging in a string of conventional military provocations, most notably the failed attempt to place a small satellite into orbit in August 1998 (Michishita 2010, 117–137). Pakistani intelligence uncovered through the A. Q. Khan network suggests that it was almost certainly during this period, well prior to the election of George W. Bush, that North Korea also moved to acquire technology and equipment for enriching uranium—in direct violation of a number of its international commitments (Albright 2010).

The missile launch of 1998 triggered a wide-ranging review of US policy conducted by former Defense Secretary William Perry (1999). Perry reiterated the engagement logic, but nested it in what was subsequently known as a two-track approach (2015, 103–109, 160–171). The United States was willing to trade security guarantees and the economic benefits associated with normalization for denuclearization, but it was also willing to ramp up sanctions if North Korea proved recalcitrant.

The key factor in pushing toward a more forthcoming US policy toward North Korea was clearly the election of South Korean President Kim Dae-jung in December 1997 and his articulation of the Sunshine Policy. Although subsequently diminished by revelations of illicit payments, the June 2000 North-South summit between Kim Dae-jung and Kim Jong-il marked the high point of a common engagement strategy between the United States and South Korea, capped by a visit to Pyongyang by Secretary of State Madeleine Albright. Economic inducements, a diffuse conception of reciprocity, and a belief in the transformative effects of engagement were the hallmarks of the Kim Dae-jung era. But time had run out on the outgoing Clinton administration, and American policy subsequently took an altogether different course that severely complicated Kim Dae-jung's chosen approach. It is this subsequent period that is the focus of this volume.

The Contours of the Second Nuclear Crisis I: The Rise and Fall of the Six Party Talks (2001–2008)

The Bush administration quickly backed away from the Perry approach well before 9/11, but the terrorist attacks of that day had important implications for the Korean peninsula. In rapid succession, North Korea was dubbed a member of the Axis of Evil and the United States outlined a new counterproliferation strategy that justified preemption, showing that the threat was not empty by confronting Saddam Hussein over weapons of mass destruction and ultimately going to war.

The second nuclear crisis that is the focus of this book broke in October 2002 when the United States confronted North Korea with evidence of a clandestine uranium enrichment program that violated a number of North Korea's international commitments. North Korea quickly escalated the crisis through a series of calculated steps, including the expulsion of IAEA inspectors from Yongbyon and threats to reprocess plutonium. While escalating the crisis, the regime was relatively consistent in stating its preferred terms for a settlement. In return for addressing the nuclear question, Pyongyang sought a negative security guarantee from the United States, an end to Washington's "hostile policy," and a normalization of relations. The quest for aid—euphemistically referred to as "economic cooperation"—was a persistent leitmotif as well.

Influenced both by Bush's own personal priors on North Korea (Bush 2010) and by the post-9/11 environment, the new administration was in no mood to negotiate with North Korea, let alone offer additional inducements. In this context, China brokered a face-saving solution for both countries by hosting three-party talks, which gelled into the Six Party Talks in August 2003 with the addition of South Korea, Japan, and Russia.

A salient feature of these negotiations from their inception through their collapse in 2008 was divergence in strategy *among* the five parties—a classic coordination problem. In the first Bush administration, the United States saw the Six Party Talks as a means of reaching a common stance and a coordinated set of constraints on North Korea; they were designed to line up the five against the one. The United States did not even table a meaningful proposal through the Six Party Talks until June 2004. Japan's policy went through numerous oscillations, but increasingly converged around a relatively hard line. South Korea, by contrast, was on a completely different political cycle during the 1998–2008 period of progressive governments, pursuing an open-ended strategy of engagement with the North. China and Russia also consistently expressed doubts about the wisdom of using sanctions to bring North Korea to the bargaining table, leaving US strategy floundering.

During its second term, the Bush administration shifted course. A combination of multilateral pressure and economic inducements brought the North Koreans back to the negotiating table in July 2005 and produced a statement of principles in September—the so-called Joint Statement—that contained many of the quid pro quos that had been implicit up to that time: a promise to dismantle the nuclear program in return for security guarantees, future steps toward normalization, and economic assistance.

At almost exactly the same time, the United States began to target North Korea's illicit economic activities, focusing on a small Macau bank called Banco Delta Asia (BDA). North Korea responded to US actions against BDA by walking away from the talks and ultimately by conducting missile and nuclear tests in July and October of 2006. Nonetheless, the two countries resumed bilateral talks surprisingly quickly, and the Six Party Talks generated a pair of implementation agreements in February and October 2007 that outlined a road map for denuclearization. In addition to longer-term promises of normalization, short-term economic assistance and the lifting of some sanctions played a role in reaching these agreements. The positive movement was reinforced by a highly ambitious joint statement following a second North-South summit between Kim Jong-il and Roh Moo-hyun in October 2007 that out-lined a wide array of economic cooperation projects.

The year 2008 proved fateful and disappointing. Conflicting interpretations of the ultimate breakdown of the Six Party Talks abound (Chapter 6). North Korea failed to produce an accurate accounting of its nuclear activities, new information on proliferation activities emerged, and by the end of the year the country was preoccupied by Kim Jong-il's health problems. The Bush administration remained internally divided over strategy and faced unexpected diplomatic constraints on engagement because governments and public opin-ion had changed in both South Korea and Japan. When the two sides failed to reach agreement on a verification mechanism at the very end of the Bush administration, the Six Party Talks effectively collapsed.

The Contours of the Second Nuclear Crisis II:
"Crisis" Without End? (2009–2016)

Barack Obama came into office facing the worst financial crisis since the Great Depression and ongoing wars in Afghanistan and Iraq, and expressed a will-ingness to extend an olive branch to adversaries. Yet, before the new admin-istration could settle on the details of a new engagement strategy, the North Koreans attempted a long-range missile test in April of 2009 and a second nuclear test in May. The tests were a clear setback for the new administration's engagement approach, and the Obama administration quickly orchestrated support for a new Security Council sanctions resolution.

From this point forward, the US approach, dubbed "strategic patience," involved a combination of both constraints and inducements, with the lat-ter largely prospective, contingent on North Korean behavior. Sanctions were deemed necessary not only to signal displeasure and move North Korea back to the negotiating table but also to protect the United States and its allies from missile and nuclear proliferation. At the same time, the United States more than once repeated its willingness to reengage through the Six Party Talks. The par-ties began to circle back to negotiations in late 2009 and early 2010, but progress was interrupted by another round of provocations in 2010, including the sink-ing of a South Korean naval vessel, the *Cheonan*, in March and the shelling of a South Korean island in November. New South Korean sanctions, known as the May 24 measures, quickly followed. From these two crucial incidents until the death of Kim Jong-il in December 2011, the Six Party Talks were foreclosed by tensions on the peninsula and North Korean preoccupation with the succession.

During the first year of the Kim Jong-un government, domestic politi-cal imperatives and a defensive posture toward potential threats drove North

Korean foreign policy. The period was marked by long-range missile tests configured as satellite launches in April and December 2012, the collapse of an aid deal with the United States, and a third nuclear test in February 2013 followed by a period of particularly tense relations on the peninsula. Despite, or perhaps in response to, a new round of sanctions, the North Korean regime rolled out its *byungjin* line, enshrining in its constitution the simultaneous pursuit of economic development and nuclear weapons. These moves did not appear tactical. The cycle of nuclear and missile tests, new sanctions, and escalation of tensions was repeated in January and February 2016 in advance of a crucial Korean Workers' Party Congress in May that reiterated the regime's commitment to the *byungjin* line. Following an acceleration of missile tests that reflected a push for altogether new capabilities, including road-mobile and submarine-launched missiles and missiles of longer range, the regime undertook its fifth nuclear test in September 2016.

We fill in important details of these last two periods in Chapters 6 and 7, examining particular offers and counteroffers in much more detail and seeking to disentangle their effects. However, two simple points already emerge from this brief narrative. First, balancing the instruments of economic statecraft—sanctions and inducements—has been a recurring issue both within and among the five parties. Second, neither set of instruments, at least as deployed, has succeeded in securing a more lasting settlement of either the nuclear question or the longer-standing political-military issues on the peninsula. Had strategy gone wrong or were advocates of both sanctions and engagement overestimating their effects?

Empirical Strategy: An Outline of the Book

It seems difficult if not impossible to test conditional claims about engagement strategies using a single case—at best, it appears, we can use details of the case only to confirm or modify broader theoretical arguments previously advanced or to provide anecdotal support. In fact, however, this assumption about the limits of case studies is not true. An analysis of the crisis provides ample opportunity for comparisons. First, five major powers have had to reach decisions on North Korea, and the alignment, and misalignment, among them has varied over time. We focus particularly on the United States, China, and South Korea. Second, the policy instruments deployed by these actors—the mix of inducements and sanctions and the types of each used—have also shifted over time, allowing us to consider whether different strategies worked and in what way.

Third, there have been important if subtle variations in North Korea's stance over time. The famine of the mid-1990s gave way to a brief reformist

moment from 1998 through the onset of the second nuclear crisis. There is
at least some evidence that during this period the regime was contemplat-
ing an alternative strategy, but this crucial window was not fully exploited.
In the wake of the first nuclear test in 2006, another promising window of
negotiation opened and then shut, as it did again immediately following the
inauguration of Barack Obama in 2009. Following Sigal (1998), but reaching
somewhat more pessimistic conclusions, we exploit within-case comparison of
diplomatic moves in Chapters 6 and 7, showing the extent to which sanctions
and inducements generated cooperative or uncooperative responses.

Finally, we exploit data that are typically not used in the study of sanctions
and inducements, at least not at the country level. Most econometric work on
sanctions has been cross-national. Typically case studies have neither recon-
structed the shifting political economy of statecraft in the target country nor
empirically modeled the effects, and noneffects, of sanctions on the target. We
undertake both in Chapter 3 by looking more closely at North Korea's trade
with China and South Korea. We also use novel firm-level surveys in Chapter
5 to provide insight into what we call the microeconomics of engagement:
the cross-border exchanges that have emerged between Chinese and South
Korean firms and their North Korean partners and the extent to which these
relationships confirm or disconfirm the transformative engagement logic.

We approach the issue in a number of discrete, overlapping steps. In Chapter 2, we start with the domestic political economy of North Korea. We consider formal political institutions and what they tell us about the composition
of the ruling coalition, the coercive apparatus, and the economic strategies
that the country has pursued over time. That North Korea is authoritarian and
capable of extraordinary control and repression is not surprising. What is surprising is the extreme narrowness of the ruling coalition. A highly personalist
regime, the top leadership has relied to an extraordinary extent on the military
and security apparatus, even at the expense of the party. The succession crisis
of 2008–2011 only exacerbated these tendencies, but problems of consolidation persisted into 2016. The implications of this political configuration for
sanctions are obvious: this is not a regime that is likely to fold under pressure.
The coalitional and ideological foundations of the regime also cast doubt on
the prospects for effective engagement.

Chapter 2 also addresses the country's economic policies. The leadership
failed to prevent the famine and showed extreme ambivalence toward the
marketization processes that followed in its wake. Nonetheless, the country
did undergo a brief reformist moment in 1998–2002. Although the lines of
causation are no doubt mutual, we show an association between the reforms

and a marginally more accommodating shift in the country's foreign policy. Not coincidentally, the onset of the nuclear crisis was associated with an assault on the market, culminating in the disastrous currency conversion of November 30, 2009. It is impossible to tell whether this "right turn" can be attributed to external pressures—which could have vindicated the advocates of engagement—or simply reflected a return to a longer-standing political equilibrium. Despite policy experimentation, however, strong ambivalence about reform clearly persisted into the Kim Jong-un era. Moreover, the regime embraced a strategic concept, the so-called *byungjin* line, that appeared to reject any trade-off between pursuit of nuclear weapons and economic development.

Chapter 3 reports our efforts to reconstruct North Korea's direction of trade and balance of payments. During the 1990s, the country diversified its foreign economic relations, normalizing them with most European countries and deepening them with South Korea following the inauguration of Kim Dae-jung in 1998. The direction of trade changed dramatically after 2000, with the varied sanctions and engagement strategies of the five parties playing a central role in this process. Economic relations with Japan dropped sharply, and trade with China and South Korea increased equally dramatically.

We then report on our effort to reconstruct North Korea's balance of payments through the end of the Kim Jong-il era. This exercise in economic forensics requires estimating the relative magnitude of the influence of unconventional activities on North Korea's external relations, including weapons exports, illicit drug trade, and counterfeiting. Even taking into account such estimates, several important conclusions emerge. First, the country consistently ran current account deficits throughout the entire Kim Jong-il period, implying sources of foreign financing that were difficult to determine but almost certainly came mainly from China. This finding comports with the trade data, but is a reminder of the additional coordination problems that arise as a result of capital flows.

Second, as illicit activity and aid shrank, the country adjusted by pursuing new commercial activities. These included exporting and hosting foreign direct investment in extractive industries, which raised the question of whether North Korea's political economy should be seen through the lens of the resource curse (Ross 2013). Not surprisingly, this particular pattern of commercialization, including reliance initially on aid and illicit activities and then on extractive industries, was not associated with any significant modification of North Korea's foreign policy.

In Chapter 4, we analyze the country's recurrent food shortages during the nuclear crisis and the humanitarian dilemmas that they posed, and continue to pose, for donors. We show that as aid flowed in at the end of the famine period, commercial imports fell. Rather than contributing to improved food security, aid was used as implicit balance of payments support, freeing up resources for other expenditure priorities. Aid continued to generate substantial moral hazard problems for donors thereafter as well. During the Kim Dae-jung and particularly Roh Moo-hyun governments, the North Korean regime enjoyed substantial food and fertilizer aid from the South along with sustained support from the World Food Program. Yet humanitarian aid failed to achieve the political objectives to which it was often linked, and it did not fully mitigate ongoing humanitarian stress in the country, particularly during the international price shocks of 2012–2013. We track increasing aid fatigue as the regime sought to limit the monitoring of aid distribution and persisted in its bellicose foreign policy.

Chapter 5 shifts to the microlevel and reports on the results of two firm-level surveys of Chinese and South Korean firms doing business in North Korea. These unique surveys provide information on what we call the "microeconomics of engagement," which are directly germane to arguments about the transformative effects of increased economic interdependence. First, we find that at the time of the surveys, state-owned enterprises played a dominant role as the counterparty to Chinese investors and traders.

Second, we find that Chinese and South Korean firms operated in quite different environments. Chinese firms appeared to receive little support from official sources and thus operated in an environment characterized by weak institutions. The surveys provide ample evidence that formal dispute settlement mechanisms did not work, interfirm trust was low, and bribery was pervasive. That these arrangements were suboptimal is clear. Institutional weakness deters integration and investment relative to trade, and it inhibits normal trade finance quite apart from the uncertainties created by the larger political milieu.

In contrast, until 2016 many South Korean firms operated in the relatively institutionalized export-processing zone at Kaesong, which protected them to some extent from the political risks Chinese firms faced. But this protection was bought by confining firms to an enclave over which North Korean authorities exercised substantial authority and from which they extracted significant rents. If anything, the potential for transformation arising from South Korean investment seemed even more limited than that associated with the Chinese presence. Moreover, the apparently insulated enclave of Kaesong did not prove immune to the vagaries of the broader political setting; it was closed temporarily by North Korea in 2013 and shuttered more permanently in 2016 by South Korea following the fourth nuclear test, showing clearly how deeply trade and investment with North Korea are politicized.

Chapters 6 and 7 focus on the quid pro quo elements of engagement with North Korea since the onset of the second nuclear crisis, giving particular attention to the United States, China, and South Korea. We divide the narrative into two parts: the rise and fall of the Six Party Talks (2001–2008) and what we call the period of "permanent crisis" following their collapse (2009–2016). As noted, these two periods correspond almost exactly to the presidential terms of George W. Bush and Barack Obama.

In general, the evidence provides little support for the claim that hardline policies or sanctions "worked," at least in the sense of generating negotiations or making enduring progress on denuclearization. On the contrary, they tended to generate escalatory responses from North Korea. Previously we noted the coordination problem in orchestrating commercial sanctions and the political imperviousness of a target regime even if they are successfully coordinated. The narrative account confirms the econometric analysis of DPRK trade with China and South Korea presented in Chapter 3: multilateral sanctions had scant effect on Chinese trade and investment and thus on the willingness of the North Korean regime to negotiate.

So-called "smart sanctions" (Cortright and Lopez 2002), particularly the financial measures undertaken in 2005 against Banco Delta Asia, fared somewhat better in gaining the regime's attention and overcoming the coordination problem. However, the economic effects of these measures did not automatically translate into the desired political response; they only influenced the negotiations when coupled with a willingness to negotiate, including on inducements. Moreover, a new round of targeted sanctions in early 2016 did not even have that modest effect and was followed by sustained escalation.

These skeptical findings with respect to sanctions do not imply, however, that inducements worked either. Coordination problems plagued efforts to offer inducements throughout the history of the Six Party Talks, albeit with shifting alliances depending on the partisan identity of the governments in office in South Korea, the United States, and Japan. In contrast to the United States, South Korea under Kim Dae-jung and Roh Moo-hyun provides textbook examples of a "diffuse reciprocity" approach to engagement in which quid pro quos were sacrificed in favor of trust building and hopes for transformation. These hopes were dashed in part by coordination problems; both governments were at odds—sometimes very pointedly—with the Bush administration over engagement with North Korea.

But South Korean engagement also faced a number of the moral hazard problems that we outlined previously. We focus particular attention on how the North Korean regime successfully manipulated the terms of engagement with the South to maximize transfers over which the regime had the greatest discretion while both limiting their transformative effects and minimizing policy concessions. These problems spilled over into efforts to extend inducements in the context of the Six Party Talks.

North Korea exhibited many of the behaviors that its critics have catalogued: inducements were periodically demanded simply to talk; inducements were offered in exchange for declaratory statements of intent; or the regime only acceded to actions that were easily reversible, most notably a freeze on existing activities. North Korea also sought discrete payments for highly disaggregated actions—a variant of the "salami" tactic—with the effect that important stages in the denuclearization process were effectively put off into the distant future. In the interim, the leadership retained its nuclear deterrent.

Yet we also show that the United States faced recurrent credibility problems during the Bush era as the administration wrangled internally and with its allies over the appropriate course of action. When the United States did seek to negotiate, progress was at least partly affected by political constraints in the United States, South Korea, and Japan as well as by North Korean behavior.

When talks broke down in 2008, the incoming Obama administration shifted back toward "strategic patience," in which it held out the promise of negotiations and future benefits but only on the condition that North Korea undertake concrete steps signaling its intent to denuclearize. Neither this approach, which might be called "prospective engagement," nor more direct inducements (most notably in the failed Leap Day Deal of 2012) had any more success in steering North Korea back to the bargaining table than the Bush administration approaches had. Nor did similar strategies of prospective engagement yield much fruit for the Lee Myung-bak or Park Geun-hye governments.

China's increasingly explicit focus on fostering closer commercial ties after 2009 is a cautionary tale with respect to engagement. Its strategy toward North Korea during the late Hu Jintao era mirrored the long-term transformative approach of South Korea's Sunshine Policy. Whatever the longer-term transformative effects of the Chinese approach—and they may ultimately prove great—China's diplomacy toward North Korea has to date provided little evidence for the political benefits of engagement. Running out of patience following the fourth nuclear test of January 2016, China finally appeared to tire of its old approach and supported a more wide-ranging UN sanctions resolution. But implementation quickly faltered, in part because of a recurrence of coordination problems with the United States and South Korea over the appropriate approach to the country, coordination problems that as in the past played to North Korea's advantage.

In the Conclusion, we undertake a more prospective analysis. First, what might happen if domestic political and economic conditions in North Korea were to change? Would the country be more vulnerable to the effects of sanctions or inducements? Second, what might happen if the five parties were to pursue somewhat different sanctions and engagement approaches than they have to date—for example, coordinating more effectively on commercial sanctions, multilateral economic inducements, or negotiations on a peace regime? Our conclusions are that economic statecraft may simply be less effective than its proponents think, depending most centrally on future developments within North Korea itself.

2

The Political Economy of North Korea

The Paradigmatic Hard Target

As we argued in Chapter 1, one of the more robust findings in the sanctions literature is that sanctions' effectiveness depends on political and economic characteristics of the target state. Ceteris paribus, sanctions are less likely to be effective against authoritarian regimes, particularly those with narrow political support coalitions and the capacity to repress. If leaders do not face significant domestic audience costs from broader publics or if they can ignore or repress dissent, sanctions are unlikely to have much bite (Brooks 2002; Kahler and Kastner 2006; Allen 2005, 2008a, 2008b; Letzkian and Souva 2007; Hufbauer et al. 2007; Escribà-Folch and Wright 2010; Major 2012; Solingen 2012a; Escribà-Folch 2012). Indeed, sanctions may even have perverse political effects (Peksen 2009; Peksen and Drury 2010; but see Marinov 2005).

From a political economy perspective, economic policy is endogenous to the political order just described (Solingen 1998, 2007, 2012a) and we consider the actual extent of economic openness in Chapter 3. Nonetheless, we expect targets to be more accommodating in the face of sanctions to the extent that they show an interest in economic reform and opening. The pursuit of more outward-oriented strategies in particular should create vested interests both in a more open economy and in a more accommodating foreign policy. Sanctions are less effective against countries pursuing inward-oriented and more autarkic economic strategies and that are therefore less exposed (Letzkian and Patterson 2015).

The central argument of this chapter, however, is that these political and economic characteristics not only are relevant to understanding the likely

effect of sanctions; they affect target states' sensitivity to economic inducements as well (Brooks 2002; Milner and Kubota 2005; Kahler and Kastner
2006; Solingen 2012b). Indeed, if inducements empower groups outside the
regime's core supporters or foster unwanted reform and opening, they can
pose obvious political challenges.

How can we measure these mediating political and economic conditions
that affect the responsiveness of target states to sanctions and inducements?
In authoritarian systems, both the nature of political institutions and the
identity of the "selectorate" (Shirk 1993; Bueno de Mesquita et al. 2003;
Solingen 2007)—the coalition to which the leadership is accountable—can be
used to identify the interests that leaders must take into account. Authoritarian
regimes vary in institutional design.[1] Some rely on control and repression; others permit limited pluralism and even submit to controlled elections. Authoritarian regimes have also rested on a wide variety of coalitional foundations,
from mass publics in populist regimes, such as Chavez's Venezuela, to more
narrow constituencies of economic elites, narrow ruling parties, state elites,
and militaries.

As for economic policy, some authoritarian regimes have undertaken economic reform and opening, widening the scope for the market and for private
actors. China and Vietnam are the most relevant Communist comparators in
this regard. Others have suppressed markets and private actors and pursued
more autarkic policies. In theory, open economies, more so than closed ones,
are vulnerable to sanctions.

Where does North Korea sit in this distribution of authoritarian regimes?
We show that it constitutes the virtually paradigmatic "hard target" on virtually all of these dimensions. At the formal political level, the regime has shown
no interest in the institutional reforms, such as legislatures or other representative bodies, that would widen its accountability; it has relied instead on an
extraordinarily narrow ruling coalition. An analysis of core political institutions in North Korea reveals a hybrid authoritarian structure, part personalist, part single party, and part military (Gause 2015; Smith 2015). Yet close
analysis of membership in these institutions shows that they overwhelmingly
represent the personal and familial retinues around the ruler, the military, the
security apparatus, the military-industrial complex, and the control-oriented
party functionaries. The representation of these groups comes at the expense
of the cabinet, the economic and social ministries, and those with technocratic or diplomatic backgrounds. In such a political system, key bases of political support either are indifferent to economic constraints and inducements
or have strong material as well as policy interests in uncooperative foreign

policies—including weapons programs—that such sanctions and inducements are designed to mitigate. Increased trade, investment, and even aid can pose risks—for example, by threatening existing rents, empowering competing factions and constituencies that would benefit from a more open political economy, and increasing the flow of independent information.

Given this coalitional foundation, sanctions can work if narrowly targeted at the leadership and these core groups of supporters (Cortright and Lopez 2000, 2002; Drezner 2011). In Chapter 6, we document an important episode—the freezing of assets in the Macau-based Banco Delta Asia (BDA) in 2005—that directly targeted foreign exchange under the leadership's control and appears to have had at least some effect. Subsequent targeting of luxury goods trade and particular entities and secondary sanctions were also designed to have this effect. However, the current autarkic nature of the regime's economic strategy and its reliance on China have made the top leadership less vulnerable to such targeting.

Perversely, this analysis of the coalitional foundations of the state suggests that inducements, like sanctions, are more likely to be attractive to such authoritarian regimes when they are targeted as well, that is, when they provide material benefits or rents directly to the leadership and core constituencies. In Chapters 6 and 7, we show a strong revealed preference on the part of the regime for direct side payments, which for quite obvious reasons are not politically appealing to the external parties seeking to change North Korea's behavior.

This analysis of North Korea as a hard target is confirmed if we look at the instruments of social control. The North Korean regime is legendary in this regard. As we noted in the Chapter 1, the regime survived a famine that probably killed between 600,000 and 1 million people. Not even Pyongyang and the lower levels of the military and party were spared.[2] The regime survived by maintaining a complex system of surveillance down to the household level, exercising control over all social organizations, and maintaining an internal security apparatus and prosecutorial, judicial, and penal systems capable of swift and harsh punishment of even the most modest infractions (Haggard and Noland 2011a, chap. 4; Gause 2013, 2015; Lankov, Kwak, and Cho 2012). These controls are not limited to political activity but extend to economic activity, movement, including that across borders, and flows of information. Given this capacity to repress and control, outside pressures are not likely to generate parallel domestic political pressure on the regime. On the contrary, they are likely to generate more repressive responses (Peksen 2009; Peksen and Drury 2010).

The very apparatus of social control also tends to limit the appeal of certain types of economic inducements, particularly those that might decentralize economic decision making, increase the independence of firms and households, or loosen the regime's control over the flow of information. Just as the greater economic openness associated with economic inducements threatens the integrity of ruling coalitions at the top, so it poses challenges for the capacity of the regime to control civil society.

North Korea's claims to self-reliance (*juche*) have always had a fictive component. As Myers (2015) shows in detail, the nominally reigning ideology has had surprisingly little influence on actual policy, which has always involved substantial dependence on outside actors. Nor is the economy entirely autarkic. As we show in Chapter 3, informal marketization has extended across the Chinese border and the economy has become decidedly more open since 2000, potentially increasing its vulnerability to both sanctions and inducements.

However, a review of the country's flirtation with reform suggests that the leadership's interest in it has been halting at best, subject to political reversal and repeatedly subordinated to the dictates of the country's confrontational military and foreign policy. A detailed consideration of the regime's efforts to attract foreign direct investment shows a fundamental failure to understand the basic policy, property rights, and credible commitment issues involved in integrating into global production networks.[3]

Moreover, the fashion in which the economy has internationalized— including through illicit activities, weapons sales, and complex strategies designed to evade sanctions—is hardly indicative of Solingen's (1998, 2002, 2007) outward-oriented coalition. In 2013 the government demonstrated this with an exclamation point by promulgating a strategic line (*byungjin*) that explicitly sought to combine economic reconstruction with the maintenance and development of a nuclear arsenal. Whether or not such a strategy is ultimately sustainable is debatable, but it suggests strongly that the regime does not see the trade-off between the two objectives that proponents of transformational engagement do.

The Political System

The Political Foundations of Personalist Authoritarianism: Identifying the Ruling Coalition

North Korea routinely falls at the extreme authoritarian end of cross-national codings of regime type,[4] although such rankings do not fully convey the hybrid nature of the regime or its coalitional base of support. The personalist features of the North Korean system and the cult of personality have been well documented and are often portrayed, with good reason, as its defining feature (for example, Cheong 2000; Martin 2006; Lim 2009; Jang 2014). From virtually the outset of the regime, Kim Il-sung designated himself as the leader (*suryong*), and subsequent propaganda work emphasized that the political system was leader dominated (*suryongje*) and monolithic (*yuil cheje*). The system was cemented by ideological innovations combining residual Marxist-Leninism with familialism and even outright racism in the form of myths of national purity (Myers 2010). Although these formulations underwent subtle shifts following the two successions (Kim, S. 2006; Kim, K. 2008; Lim 2009; Gause 2015; Myers 2015), the emphasis on the leader as the center of the system remained intact and references to the familial nature of the regime became if anything more explicit.

However, no dictator, no matter how much discretion he wields, can rule alone. As a result, authoritarian regimes differ significantly in their institutional form and in the size of their selectorate and its constituent base. We consider each in turn.

As in other Communist systems, the core institutions of government, particularly the Supreme People's Assembly (SPA) and the cabinet, were subordinated to the party shortly following independence and then quickly declined into irrelevance.[5] As the formal channel of representation, the SPA has become the proverbial rubber stamp: voting is compulsory, but the party nominates single candidates for each seat and SPA sessions, lasting only a few days, serve as a channel for disseminating information on the party line, not as a deliberative body. The cabinet has not wielded much influence either, being subjected not only to control by the party but to a leadership preference for managing government though different and often ad hoc organizational channels around the leader.

What is peculiar about North Korean communism is that party organs also atrophied as contending factions were purged in the late 1950s and early 1960s and the base of the regime narrowed. Power was increasingly concentrated in the hands of Kim Il-sung and the faction around him: a group of guerillas who had fought in Manchuria during the war and subsequently assumed the leadership of core military and security positions (Suh 1988; Buzo 1999; Lankov 2002, 2007; Szalontai 2005). Following the 4th Party Congress in 1961 (and an ad hoc Party Conference in 1966), for example, only two more formal party congresses were held, in 1970 and 1980, and not until the succession of Kim Jong-un were these organs tentatively revived.[6] In December 1993, six months prior to Kim Il-sung's death, the last Central Committee Plenum was held. Power in the party was exercised by narrow bodies chaired by Kim Il-sung,[7] by the party Secretariat, but also by the leader's personal secretariat and by informal institutions and networks that Bermudez (2004) calls "close aide rule." By the time of the first hereditary succession from Kim Il-sung to Kim Jong-il in 1994, key features of the North Korean political order were in place: centralization of political power in an exalted and even deified leader; an extremely narrow ruling elite with strong military and security representation; an increasingly hierarchical as opposed to deliberative party structure; and a weak cabinet and even weaker legislature.

The challenges in orchestrating hereditary successions are not trivial (Brownlee 2007); in Korea they generated ample analysis as the second succession began in 2009 (Lim 2009, 2012; Gause 2011, 2012, 2015; Mansourov 2013, 2014; Haggard, Herman, and Ryu 2014). Could Kim Jong-il, and later Kim Jong-un, ensure that the bases of support and lines of command and compliance that Kim Il-sung had constructed would hold up? The short answer is that they could not: both institutional innovations and personnel changes were required to build independent bases of support for the new leaders.

In a 1992 constitutional revision, the National Defense Commission (Chapter 3, Articles 111–117) was dramatically upgraded and placed under Kim Jong-il's control, allowing him to assume formal, independent control over the military apparatus from his father while providing an institutional instrument for building a base of support.[8] Control over a powerful Organization and Guidance Department, one of the most crucial institutions in any communist system, solidified his personal dominance over the party and military by allowing him to use both purges and appointments to build loyalist networks (Lim 2009, 67–69; Jang 2014). Kim Jong-un proved even more aggressive in turning over top personnel (Haggard, Herman, and Ryu 2014; Gause 2015).

Following his father's death, Kim Jong-il did not immediately assume the position of president or general secretary of the KWP but ruled through other bodies.[9] The most distinctive feature of the new political order was not its formal institutional arrangements; rather, it was the continued narrowing of the top leadership and the overt turn to the military and the security apparatus for support (Koh 2005; Lim 2009, 2012; Smith 2015). Heightened attention to the military not only guaranteed a smooth process of succession; it also deterred external challenges and compensated for the dramatic weakening of the state and party apparatus during the economic collapse of the 1990s. "Military-first" (*songun*) politics had important ideological implications as well, and Kim Jong-il ultimately promoted this concept as his distinct ideological contribution (Koh 2005). *Songun* elevated the military, and military-style discipline,

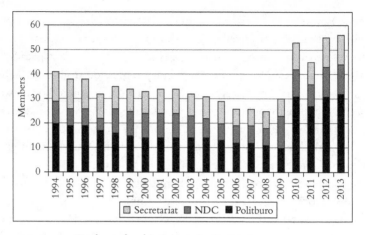

FIGURE 2.1   Total membership in core institutions

SOURCE: Haggard, Herman, and Ryu (2014), from *Korea Central News Agency* reports.

into the leading and exemplary social force that would achieve the new state doctrine of "building a strong and prosperous country" (*kangsong taeguk*). *Songun* institutions and doctrines were formally inaugurated at the first session of the 10th Supreme People's Assembly in September 1998, when yet another constitutional revision broadened the powers of the NDC chairman. This political order constitutes the immediate backdrop to the second nuclear crisis that began in the fall of 2002 and the period analyzed in this book.

In Figure 2.1, we show the number of members of each core political body—the NDC, the Politburo, and the party Secretariat—from the first familial transition in 1994 through the second in 2011–2013.[10] All of these bodies gradually shrank over the 2000s, becoming more and more gerontocratic over time. These main bodies bottomed out at only twenty-five members between them in 2008, with an average member age of eighty, before expanding as the succession went into full swing. Yet even these counts overestimate the size of the very top leadership, since many individuals held positions in all three bodies, including most obviously Kim Jong-il. Indeed, prior to Kim Jong-il's death "interlocking directorates" among top leaders increased as the system became more fused (Table 2.1).

The membership of the NDC, the Politburo, and the party Secretariat speaks not only to the breadth of the ruling coalition but to its social and professional composition as well. Again, it is important to emphasize that actual decision making may well have been concentrated in narrower bodies, including informal meetings of key personnel and the personal secretariat of

TABLE 2.1

Interlocking directorates during the transition

	2008	2009	2010	2011
Member of all three	2	2	1	1
Politburo and Secretariat	2	2	10	8
Politburo and NDC	0	0	8	6
Politburo only	7	6	12	12
Secretariat only	3	3	0	0
NDC only	6	12	2	2

SOURCE: Authors' calculations from Korea Central News Agency reports.

the leader. Still, these formal institutions together can be read as a proxy for the coalitional base of the regime.

We start with the NDC (Table 2.2).[11] Although designed to oversee core military issues, this body was granted much wider political authority in the constitutional revision of 1998, was nominally the platform from which Kim Jong-il ruled, and was also headed by Kim Jong-un following the actual succession. We consider NDC membership at three points in time that are of particular relevance to the second nuclear crisis: September 2003, a year after the onset of the conflict and following an SPA meeting that produced the first significant membership turnover since 1998; April 2009, when the NDC was significantly expanded during the early phase of the succession, a period also marked by the onset of the succession and a particularly confrontational external stance; and April 2012, following Kim Jong-il's death in December 2011 and immediately after the 2012 Party Conference that anointed Kim Jong-un as the successor. In each period, we note four mutually exclusive and exhaustive member categories: those in which the position and the person occupying it were unchanged from the previous period; the addition of new positions; positions that remained in the NDC but with changes in their occupants; and positions that were removed altogether.

Except for one provincial secretary, all of the personnel sitting on the NDC in 2003 at the onset of the nuclear crisis were connected with the military and the military-industrial complex (for example, the chairman of the Second Economic Committee, which oversees military production). Moreover, the one provincial secretary was from Chagang, where much of the military-industrial complex is located. The 2009 expansion brought in two high-ranking party officials, including Kim Jong-il's brother-in-law, Jang Song-thaek. In addition to the family connection, Jang headed the Administration Department of

TABLE 2.2

Membership of the National Defense Commission by position

	September 2003	April 2009	April 2012
Unchanged	• Supreme Commander (Kim Jong-il) • Director of KPA General Political Bureau (Jo Myong-rok) • Minister of the People's Armed Forces (Kim Il-chol) • Chief Secretary of Chagang Province (Yon Hyong-muk) • Chief of the KPA General Staff (Kim Yong-chun) • Secretary of Munitions and Industry (Jon Pyong-ho)	• Supreme Commander (Kim Jong-il) • Director of KPA General Political Bureau (Jo Myong-rok) • Secretary of Munitions and Industry (Jon Pyong-ho) • Chairman of the Second Economic Committee (Paek Se-bong)	• Director of KWP Administration Department (Jang Song-thaek) • Director of KWP Operations Department (O Kuk-ryol) • Chairman of the Second Economic Committee (Paek Se-bong)
Positions added	• Minister of People's Security (Choe Ryong-su)	• Director of KWP Operations Department (O Kuk-ryol) • Director of KWP Administration Department (Jang Song-thaek) • Deputy Director of KWP Military Industry Department (Ju Kyu-chang) • First Vice Minister of the People's Armed Forces (Kim Il-chol) • First Deputy Director of KPA General Political Bureau (Kim Jong-gak) • First Vice Minister of State Security (U Tong-chuk)	• Director of KWP Civil Defense Department (Kim Yong-chun) • Director of KWP Machine-Building Industry Department (Ju Kyu-chang) • Minister of State Security (Kim Won-hong)

Personnel replaced	• Chairman of Second Economic Committee (Paek Se-bong)	• Minister of the People's Armed Forces (Kim Yong-chun) • Minister of People's Security (Ju Sang-song)	• Supreme Commander (Kim Jong-un) • Director of KPA General Political Bureau (Choe Ryong-hae) • Minister of the People's Armed Forces (Kim Jong-gak) • Minister of People's Security (Ri Myong-su) • Secretary of Munitions and Industry (Pak To-chun)
Positions removed	• Deputy Commander-in-Chief of KPA • Guard Commander	• Chief Secretary of Chagang Province • Chief of the KPA General Staff	• Deputy Director of KWP Military Industry Department • First Vice Minister of the People's Armed Forces • First Deputy Director of KPA General Political Bureau • First Vice Minister of State Security
Share of personnel holding military positions and KPA rank	5/8 Marshal (1), Vice Marshal (4)	9/12 Marshal (1), Vice Marshal (4), General (3), Colonel General (1)	10/11 Vice Marshal (4), General (4), Colonel General (2)

NOTE: Ri Yong-mu, Vice Chairman of the NDC, is also a Vice Marshal and member of the Politburo, but holds no other position.

the party, which also had oversight of the Ministry of State Security and the Ministry of People's Security. The other new entrants held the number-two positions at three organizations that were crucial to the success of transition: the Ministry of the People's Armed Forces, the Korean People's Army General Political Bureau, and the Ministry of State Security. The transition was associated with substantial personnel turnover at the top of the military and security hierarchy, reflecting an interest on the part of Kim Jong-un in appointing a new retinue (Haggard, Herman, and Ryu 2014; Gause 2015). But despite these changes, the interests represented on this core body did not change fundamentally or widen to incorporate broader interests, such as those of technocrats. If anything, representation during the last period we analyze here was even more dominated by military and security personnel.

We would expect the Politburo to have a more diverse membership, but trends in its composition are surprisingly similar. We look over a longer time frame at representation from six mutually exclusive career backgrounds, recognizing that subjective assessments are necessary where individuals moved between categories over their career: the central party; officials with diplomatic backgrounds; officials with economic backgrounds; central state officials (excluding those with diplomatic or economic backgrounds); provincial officials; and the military (Figure 2.2). We also use a more expansive measure of the military by including officials in the internal security apparatus (who do not hold positions in the KPA) and officials in charge of the military-industrial complex.

Party officials and those with diplomatic backgrounds jumped in significance on the "transition Politburo" at the expense of those with economic and provincial backgrounds. By 2012, a total of fifteen top party members had entered the Politburo (compared with the composition before September 2010), including powerful figures such as Jang Song-thaek and virtually all heads of the Secretariat portfolios. Using the slightly expanded definition, however, the increase in military representation that began earlier is even more pronounced. This finding holds if we discount the fact that several high-ranking "military" officers were in fact civilians appointed laterally (Foster-Carter 2012; Mansourov 2012; Haggard, Herman, and Ryu 2014). Among the altogether new ministries represented in the Politburo following its expansion were the People's Armed Forces and State Security, and People's Security. Also included was the Chief of the KPA General Staff.

Although institutional representation can be a proxy for the ruling coalition, it does not fully capture the way in which the regime favored the military during the second familial transition. As Gandhi and Przeworski (2006) point

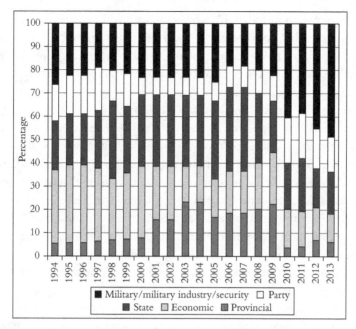

FIGURE 2.2   Politburo membership by career affiliation, 1994–2013
(percentage)

SOURCE: Haggard, Herman, and Ryu (2014), from *Korea Central News Agency* reports.

out, dictators secure support not only through institutional representation but through the distribution of rents and patronage as well. Indeed, in a nonmarket economy such as North Korea these career opportunities—controlled by the Organization and Guidance Department and ultimately by the top leadership—are even more crucial than they are in market economies where there are outside options. Between 1991 (when he took over as supreme commander) and 1998, when the SPA meeting was held, Kim Jong-il had promoted a staggering number of officers. According to South Korean assessments, 1,023 of 1,400 general officers were turned over during this period (Gause 2011). While the numbers do not appear as large since the succession to Kim Jong-un began in earnest, the regime nonetheless saw waves of military promotions (Gause 2015).

Several important conclusions emerge from our discussion so far with respect to the breadth and identity of the regime's coalitional base, an important domestic variable affecting the efficacy of both sanctions and inducements. First, however, it is important to note that there was substantial turnover in personnel as a result of the succession both before and after Kim Jong-il's death. Purges even included the surprising arrest and execution of Jang Song-thaek in December 2013 (Mansourov 2013). This turnover, representing the ups and downs in the occupants of particular positions, is a preoccupation of North Korea watchers and has been analyzed deeply for signs of waning and rising influence (for example, Park Hyeong-jung 2011; Mansourov 2013, 2014; Haggard, Herman, and Ryu 2014; and particularly Gause 2011, 2015).

Purges and new appointments did not mark a generalized reign of terror. Rather, they were calculated tools for building new networks of loyal supporters that extended from the bottom of the system to top party, military, and security personnel. Moreover, there is no indication that the fundamental organizational features of the regime that we highlight here—the narrowness of the ruling group and its sociopolitical foundation—fundamentally changed as a result of the succession. Rather, the system was effectively reproduced, with new occupants moved into existing offices. As Figure 2.1 shows, despite the churning of particular positions, the military appeared to be a major beneficiary of the expansion of formal institutions, matched by major promotions within the military itself. These persistent trends suggest a regime that was highly personalist and nominally party-dominant but nonetheless one that can be characterized by an unusual dependence on military interests. We would expect such a coalition to be particularly immune to both economic sanctions and economic inducements.

The Mechanisms of Social Control

Arguments about the effects of sanctions on a regime's stability or its propensity to respond to outside incentives hinge critically on the relationship between the state and its citizens. Two arguments are germane. The first is the claim that sanctions can generate political pressures in the target state and may even produce regime change. The second is the obverse: that inducements serve indirectly to loosen the bonds of social control by strengthening social forces that benefit from engagement.

Our review of a number of indicators, including the control exercised over civil society, the apparatus of repression, the penal system, and the criminalization of economic activity, casts strong doubt on the first proposition. Despite the famine of the mid-1990s, North Korea is by no means a weak or failed state. Rather, as numerous human rights studies have shown,[12] it maintains an extraordinary repressive apparatus.

The second argument is more complex, and we suggest in our conclusions in Chapter 8 how this claim for engagement based on fostering new social forces might work looking forward. Here we underline two major analytic points that are frequently missed in the engagement literature, however. First, authoritarian regimes often retain substantial control and discretion over market-oriented activity. When they do, such control typically extends to cross-border transactions and communication in particular. Second, even when controls are relaxed, such reforms do not necessarily have a politically subversive effect; to the contrary, they can strengthen elite and even mass support for the regime. As Dimitrov (2013) and his colleagues strongly argue, such adaptations help account for the resilience of the remaining communist systems.

We look first at so-called organizational life and the monopolization of social organization and then at the instruments of repression and control. We pay particular attention to how the government has managed the emergence of economic crimes, including border crossing, since these policies are directly relevant to our consideration of the possible effects of greater economic openness and at least some economic inducements, such as increased trade and investment.

"Organizational life" (OL) refers to a network of surveillance and indoctrination practices conducted under the aegis of five, top-down social organizations: the Korean Workers' Party (KWP) itself, the Youth Union, the Trade Union, the Farmers' Union, and the Women's Union (Hunter 1999 60–65; Sung Chull Kim 2006, 65–75; Lankov, Kwok, and Cho 2012). All adults are sorted into one, and only one, of these five organizations, which serve the purposes of indoctrination and surveillance.[13] Two features of these organizations are of interest. First, they are encompassing—no other independent civil society organizations exist. As our refugee interviews also attest, this pervasive, omnipresent, top-down organization has an atomizing effect, limiting the incentives or the ability to organize outside of the state (Haggard and Noland 2011a). Second, the OL not only indoctrinates and communicates directives; it also provides an ongoing means of surveillance. This system operates through the party and the OL—with their time-consuming indoctrination and self-criticism sessions—and through the so-called *Inminban* system, which reaches down to the smallest residential unit. The *Inminban*, consisting of thirty to forty households, link the head of each neighborhood with the security apparatus, permitting extraordinary monitoring of the population (Demick 2010; Gause 2013).

Social control is by no means limited to cooptive mechanisms. The state also maintains a large and highly elaborate internal security apparatus. The Ministry of State Security (MSS) is the equivalent of a secret police focused on the government's expansive conception of antistate activities and political and economic crimes. It has an estimated fifty thousand personnel and runs an elaborate network of informers. Since about 2000, the MSS has also conducted the first screening process of those apprehended for border crossing or repatriated by Chinese authorities, a reflection of how serious illicit border crossing is viewed. The Ministry of People's Security (MPS) conducts basic police functions, but is also responsible for internal security. With an estimated force of 210,000 personnel (Gause 2013, 11), it conducts surveillance that extends down to unannounced household visits.

The organization of the penal and criminal justice system provides a particularly useful indicator of the repressiveness of the regime. The most notorious component of the prison system is the massive *kwanliso* administered by the SSD and variously translated as political prison camps, labor colonies, or concentration camps (Kang 2005). Incarceration for standard criminal offenses, as well as economic crimes, is distributed through the remainder of the penal system. Of particular interest for our purposes is the explosive growth of *rodong tanryondae*, or labor-training centers, a network of local facilities dating to the 1990s that emerged as an ad hoc response by authorities to the fraying of socialist control during the famine and in its immediate aftermath, including unauthorized movement, black market activity, border crossing, and other economic crimes (Noland 2000). In the 2004 revision of the penal code, and as an indicator of what we call "reform in reverse," "labor-training sentences" were explicitly introduced as a new form of punishment, which institutionalized the *rodong tanryondae* (Han 2006; Yoon 2009; KINU 2009; B. Kim 2010; Haggard and Noland 2011a).

Labor-training centers have been particularly important in the management of those caught crossing the border or repatriated from China, given that unauthorized exit from the country is criminalized (Muico 2007; Haggard and Noland 2011a). It was initially considered equivalent to treason. The 1999 criminal law revision first distinguished defectors leaving for purely economic reasons and those engaged in subversive activities, including contact with South Koreans while in China or even exposure to South Korean propaganda, broadcasts, movies, or music. Since the onset of the Kim Jong-un era, however, there has been a sustained effort to crack down on illicit border crossing and communication, including cell phones (see, for example, Human Rights Watch 2015). As we show, this has occurred even as the border has become more open to trade, investment, and official cross-border movement.

Of particular interest to an understanding of economic statecraft is how the government dealt with the process of de facto marketization. Political authorities in fraying and marketizing state socialist systems face a number of challenges to the integrity of the state sector, including the outright theft or destruction of government property. As the regime's planning process collapsed, both acquisition of inputs and sale of final output increasingly took place through informal exchanges, making it more and more difficult for lower-level planning bodies to exercise effective oversight. Given the inefficiency of the planning process, managers could earn enormous rents by allocating resources more efficiently, engaging in trade, including foreign trade, and under-reporting earnings (Yang and Shepard 2009). Households and work units also engaged in income-earning activities that posed economic as well as political challenges. For example, individuals engaged in unauthorized private enterprise and trading do not show up at their work units and are difficult to tax. They also risk slipping through the OL and *Inminban*'s elaborate net of political surveillance and monitoring.

The evolution of economic crimes in North Korea exhibits a complex dialectic related to the government's tacking between reform and retrenchment that we outline in the next section (see Yoon 2009). In the 1998 revision of the constitution, the government took the step of recognizing income earned through legal economic activities as private property (Article 24). For a socialist system, this was potentially a major breakthrough (Frank 2005). Yet the combination of system fraying and the partial economic reforms themselves gave rise to a variety of activities that went beyond what the state allowed. In the 1999 criminal code, the "Chapter on Offenses against the Management of the Socialist Economy" included eight articles. In 2004 it was retitled "the Chapter on Offenses against the Management of the Economy" and included seventy-four offenses. If taken literally, these crimes represent a wide array of standard commercial activities.[14] Of interest is the fact that violations of trade and foreign exchange controls receive particularly detailed attention (Articles 104, 1065–107 116–117, 125–126). However, virtually all aspects of economic activity—commerce, financing, labor hiring, foreign trade, and foreign exchange acquisition—are potentially criminal. In 2007 a series of "additional clauses" (*buchik*) singled out a number of economic crimes, such as theft of state property, for more severe punishment, including fixed prison terms and even death.

Particular mention should be made of efforts to control information flows, both internal and external.[15] Increasing marketization from below was associated not only with economic activity and movement but with increasing access to outside media, both through broadcasting efforts from the South and elsewhere and trade with China in information technology (IT) and cultural products: USB drives, MP3 players, and CDs and DVDs of Korean music and films. Smuggled Chinese cell phones also permitted those close to the border to contact relatives, even in the South, and outside organizations to secure information. Yet the regime maintains its own closed intranet and, partly as a preemptive move and to ensure control, rolled out its own cellular network in 2008 with foreign investment from an Egyptian firm. This network has undergone significant although still limited growth.[16] Even as it introduced these controlled information flows, however, the regime has also sought to ensure that they not be used for subversive purposes, particularly with respect to the border. News reports note increasing surveillance in the Kim Jong-un era and even the use of new technologies to track cell phone use and identify and arrest those engaged in illicit border crossing and communication (Human Rights Watch 2015).[17]

In sum, not only is North Korea's ruling coalition incredibly narrow and skewed toward the military; it also has maintained a remarkable capacity to control and repress. The implications for economic statecraft are clear. First, as the economy becomes more open, sanctions potentially expose both elites and citizens to costs, which must be weighed against the capacity of the state to control and repress. Unless targeted at elites, sanctions in such a system can impose costs on the wider population without necessarily having the intended political effect. Second, however, many of the "inducements" on offer from the international community—in the form of trade, investment, and even aid—are not necessarily appealing to a regime that seeks to control economic activity, movement, and particularly foreign links. It is possible that "stealth engagement" may have subversive effects, and we return to it in our conclusions in Chapter 8. However, as with our analysis of the political system, consideration of the system of social control suggests constraints on engagement as well as sanctions strategies.

The Political Economy of North Korea

Our portrayal of the political system suggests a virtual textbook example of Solingen's (2007) inward-looking coalition exercising tight control over polity, society, and economy. This section extends this analysis and has several purposes. First, interest in reform, including reform of the foreign sector, is an important proxy for and even determinant of regime intent. Is the government emphasizing economic issues and growth? Or is it wedded not only to control but to an allocation of resources that favors the military? Second, reform and opening are of interest precisely because they can have the effect of making countries more vulnerable to sanctions and inducements, thus sending a costly signal to foreign audiences.

For the bulk of the period under review here, the North Korean stance on reform was ambivalent at best. A period of policy immobilism in the wake of the collapse of the Soviet Union contributed to the famine and was followed by a period of ad hoc crisis management in the immediate aftermath of Kim Il-sung's death (1994–1997). The famine was ultimately followed by a brief period of cautious economic reform in 1998–2002, but it was limited in scope and followed by a swing back in a more closed direction over much of the period considered here, roughly 2005 through the death of Kim Jong-il in December 2011. In back-and-forth fashion, the regime appears to have launched de facto if not de jure reforms under Kim Jong-un. However, these occurred in the context of a new ideological doctrine, the *byungjin* line, that explicitly repudiated any connection between reform and a moderation of foreign policy.

We undertake this review in four steps, beginning with a brief outline of the country's notoriously complex and fragmented economic structure, which includes both the formal planned economy rooted in state-owned enterprises and an emerging market economy, a "court economy" that services the personal and political interests of the top leadership and significant economic activity under military control as well. We then turn to the course of economic policy under Kim Jong-il and more recent developments under Kim Jong-un. Finally, we consider in more detail the country's stance toward foreign direct investment, a particularly interesting indicator of its ambivalence toward economic opening.

Economic Structure and Decision Making: The Multiple North Korean Economies

North Korea appears to have a highly orthodox state socialist economy dominated by the planning apparatus, state-owned enterprises, and agricultural collectives and cooperatives. To this, as we show, has been added a substantial shadow or market economy that grew up in the interstices of the famine. As both the state sector and the emerging private economy engage in cross-border transactions, North Korea's vulnerability to sanctions should increase, ceteris paribus.

However, it is important to note that the economy also includes at least two other distinct spheres which, while internationalized, have always operated in the international gray zone of black markets and illicit activity: the court economy and a complex of firms under control of the military and the military-industrial complex (Park 2009, Park and Walsh 2016).

Given the personalist nature of the North Korean political system, the lines between the public and private spheres are necessarily blurred. This is in some ways due to outright corruption in the maintenance of Kim family assets, in part because of the need for ongoing sources of revenue that can be used for the distribution of rents to the regime's inner circle. The notorious Offices 38 and 39 are charged with managing the Kim family's funds and ensuring that a share of all foreign exchange earnings are remitted to the direct control of the top leadership. Office 39 has been implicated in a variety of illicit activities that we document in Chapter 3 (see also Chestnut 2007, 2014; Bechtol, Kan, and Collins 2010; North Korea Leadership Watch 2012; Hastings 2015; Gause 2015). In addition, the military controls a variety of companies directly, including those involved not only in weapons sales and procurement but in more purely commercial activities (Park 2009; Pollack 2011; Park and Walsh 2016).

The activities of the court and military economy have quite naturally been the target of sanctions over the years. Yet both spheres have substantial experience in avoiding detection and possible sanction in part because of the political geography of North Korea's trade, which we take up in Chapter 3.[18] Moreover, the "openness" associated with these activities hardly reflects the coalition of interests that would see advantages from reform, opening, or a moderation of North Korea's foreign policy. To the contrary, these business activities are devoted precisely to circumventing sanctions activity in order to generate revenue for the regime (Park and Walsh 2016; Center for Advanced Defense Studies 2016). Put differently, it is quite possible for an economy such as North Korea's to "internationalize" in ways that are not only at odds with the logic of transformative engagement but actively hostile to it.

Reform and Reversal Under Kim Jong-il

The starting point for North Korea's reform efforts was an unusually orthodox command economy. In contrast to the Soviet Union and its Eastern European wards, the regime rejected the path of de-Stalinization following purges of more moderate factions in the period from 1956 to 1961. Rather, it pursued heavy industry, collectivized agriculture, and suppression of private production and trade. Claims of self-reliance notwithstanding, this development strategy relied on imported Soviet oil and other inputs, which proved a fatal vulnerability. Frustrated by North Korean unwillingness to repay accumulated debts, the Soviets began reducing aid in the mid-1980s and when the Soviet Union collapsed in 1990, North Korea was hit by a massive trade shock as a result. As the Eastern bloc disintegrated, access to subsidized inputs disappeared. At this critical juncture, and in the years that followed, the North Korean regime faced fundamental policy choices. Would it seek to defend or revive the command economy or loosen the reins of government and experiment with reforms, including those that would allow it to expand exports to finance imports, including food? The regime chose to maintain the broad contours of policy and suppress consumption, cutting rations delivered through the PDS and initiating a "Let's eat two meals a day" campaign. It was not until the spring of 1995, with the famine in full force, that the regime belatedly exploited floods and a natural disaster narrative to appeal for assistance.

One result of the famine was a considerable decentralization of the entire economy (Haggard and Noland 2007a). The marketization that had begun with food gradually encompassed a broader range of household goods, in part building on an official sanctioning of cottage industries for consumer goods begun in 1984 ("the August 3 campaign for people's goods") and in part a result of entrepreneurial activity. Marketization was not limited to households. Local government and party officials, enterprise managers, and military units also scrambled to survive. Entrepreneurs affiliated with SOEs or other institutions, including government agencies, used official connections to obtain political protection for quasi-private production, marketization of interfirm relations, and even direct sales to the public at noncontrolled prices.

Emerging from the famine with a mortally wounded planning mechanism and an economy and state marketizing beyond central control, the government belatedly began cautious reform around 1998. The 1998 constitution included provisions that nominally granted greater scope for private activity (Article 24), for incentives within the state sector (Article 33), and for foreign trade and investment (Articles 36 and 37). These measures were prelude to a package of reforms announced in 2002 that were substantial by North Korean standards (Frank 2005). Analyses of subsequent official economic discourse reveal an ongoing debate over economic strategy that persisted until middecade, when, as we will see, reforms were slowed down and reversed (Carlin and Wit 2006; Haggard and Noland 2010a; Choi and Lecy 2012).[19]

The 2002 reforms had four components: microeconomic policy changes, including alteration of administered prices and wages; macroeconomic policy changes, including the introduction of direct taxes; an effort to revive special economic zones as a source of scarce foreign exchange; and aid seeking. We focus here on the first of these and take up the reform of the external sector and aid subsequently and in Chapters 3 and 4. That the reforms were tentative, experimental, and somewhat incoherent is to be expected. Few state socialist systems went the route of "big bang" reforms, and those that did typically did so in the context of more fundamental political change toward democratic rule. But components of the reforms were motivated in part by an effort to reestablish rather than relinquish state control and by the middle of the decade the regime had started to reverse them.

The microeconomic reforms involved several distinct price changes, each with its own political-economic implications. Changes in relative prices and wages could be interpreted as an attempt to increase the role of material incentives, but these occurred in the context of a tenfold increase in price *level* and an ongoing inflation that exceeded 100 percent annually between 2002 and 2005. The engineering of a dramatic inflation appears to have had the objective of effective confiscation of cash holdings held by the newly emerging trading class or at least that portion of it lacking political connections.

In the industrial sphere, North Korean enterprises were instructed that they were responsible for covering their own costs; they would no longer receive state subsidies. But at the same time, the state administratively raised wage levels, with certain favored groups such as military personnel, party officials, scientists, and coal miners receiving supernormal increases. Despite some changes in relative prices, the state continued to maintain an administered price structure, which tended to lag the inflation in market prices. In sum, enterprise managers were told to meet hard budget constraints but were given little scope to actually manage. In the absence of any formal bankruptcy or other "exit" mechanism, enterprises remained in operation at extremely low levels of capacity utilization supported by a variety of state subsidies.

In the agricultural sector, finally, the government increased the procurement price of grains to incentivize farmers and increase the volume of food entering the public distribution system (PDS). It also engineered a dramatic increase in PDS consumer prices. However, procurement prices did not keep pace with rising market prices, and the policy was not successful in coaxing the local harvest back into the PDS system. Thus, agricultural reforms were some of the first to be explicitly reversed.

In sum, rather than "leading" the transition, the reforms of 1998–2002 were a rearguard response to de facto marketization. One can develop economic explanations for each microeconomic policy change, and the reform may simply have reflected a lack of knowledge about likely market consequences of government actions. However, the reforms clearly rewarded friends and punished enemies. Favored groups such as the military received supernormal wage increases, but incentives to managers, farmers, and traders had limited effect because of the failure to adjust prices and because of the government's lack of credibility. The enormous jump in price levels could even be interpreted as an assault on the class of traders and black marketers that had sprung up over the previous decade.

The timing of the reform proved highly inauspicious and raises an issue to which we return repeatedly: the ongoing tension between military and economic imperatives. Within months of the launching of the 2002 reforms, the second nuclear crisis had broken. The October revelation of a highly enriched uranium (HEU) program, the escalatory response to it, and the revelation that North Korea had indeed abducted Japanese citizens had the effect of cutting off possible sources of trade, investment, and aid. As a result, the regime was left with the problematic legacy of the partial economic reforms of July 2002 but without the complementary political and economic payoffs that were needed to make the reforms work.

A number of policy measures from 2005 forward suggest a reversal of reform (Haggard and Noland 2010a; Choi and Lecy 2012). During the 2005 harvest, the government engaged in confiscatory grain seizures, reneging on its commitments to farmers. Buoyed by support from China and South Korea—and demonstrating the perverse effects that engagement can have—the regime subsequently announced that it was banning private trade in grain, resuscitating the PDS, and expelling the World Food Program (WFP) and NGOs engaged in humanitarian operations.

The postreform effort to reassert state control by no means was limited to the food economy but included a wider assault on market activity and cross-border trade.[20] The reactionary tenor of government policy was vividly represented by a revival of the 1950s Stalinist "Chollima" movement of Stakhanovite exhortation and the initiation of "speed-battle" mobilization campaigns. In 2009 revisions to the planning law overturned reforms introduced in 2001 and 2002, codifying a more top-down planning process (Institute for Far Eastern Studies 2010a).

The culmination of the antireform drive came on November 30, 2009, with a surprise confiscatory currency reform aimed at crushing market activity and reviving orthodox socialism (Haggard and Noland 2010a). This move had a chilling effect on virtually all economic activity, both public and private, and ushered in a period of acute shortage and an enormous rise in prices—of food most importantly. The government was ultimately forced to accommodate itself to economic realities by acquiescing in the reopening of previously banned markets and allowing the use of foreign currency. It also sought to revive and deepen the China trade, which would have important implications for the Six Party Talks, as we show in Chapter 7. But currency reform was the last significant economic initiative of the Kim Jong-il years; as we will see, it corresponded with a more belligerent foreign policy stance from the start of 2009 as well.

Why reverse reforms? The government might have done so in a misguided effort to restore the social safety net or as an anti-inflation measure.[21] The onset of the nuclear crisis might also have provided an entry point for hardliners who were opposed to the reforms in any case. We pursue this possibility in Chapter 6. The alternative is that the regime was simply uncomfortable with the bottom-up marketization of the economy, particularly as the political system entered a highly uncertain transition. Whatever the cause, reversal clearly reflected the triumph of statist thinking in the regime over a reformist path.

Economic Policy Under Kim Jong-un

After the death of Kim Jong-il, there was hope that a more cosmopolitan outlook or simple desperation would lead Kim Jong-un to implement reform. In his first significant policy speech on April 15, 2012, against a backdrop of worsening economic conditions, the new leader stated, "It is our party's resolute determination to let our people who are the best in the world—our people who have overcome all obstacles and ordeals to uphold the party faithfully—not tighten their belts again and enjoy the wealth and prosperity of socialism as much as they like."[22] He also suggested that subtle institutional changes were afoot, most notably an elevation of the status of the cabinet. As we saw earlier, the weakness of the cabinet and the representation of technocrats were defining features of the system.[23] Even the purge of important military hardliners was read through both a "reform" and a "succession" lens.

Details of the reform effort were not publicly announced, however. Rather, analysts discerned pilot measures emanating from a 2012 directive, "On the Establishment of a New Economic Management System in our Own Way," which leaked out of the country via information channels and defectors. This directive came to be known as the June 28 measures for the date on which it was purportedly announced to party cadre (Park 2013; Noland 2013). Pilot policy changes were somewhat more clear in the agricultural sector, where the state planned to reduce the size of work teams on cooperative farms to approximate the household responsibility system introduced in China in the late 1970s; allow greater access to private plots; and allow cultivators to consume their surplus, barter it, or sell it back to the state at an administratively determined price. In 2015, in a potentially significant shift in policy, officials stated privately that the laws against selling grain in the market had been relaxed.

Similar though less specific reforms were vetted for manufacturing and services, where activity was dominated by state-owned enterprises. Under the so-called May 30 [2014] measures—again, named after the date on which they were purportedly introduced—enterprise managers would pay a fixed share of revenues to the state as a tax and would be able to keep the rest. State-owned enterprises would be permitted to purchase inputs at market prices from their suppliers of choice; hire and fire labor at prevailing wages; sell excess output not specifically dedicated under plan commitments; and enter into joint ventures with registered investors, including domestic partners. By providing a greater degree of freedom to SOE managers, the reforms, if fully implemented, would effectively recognize the role of an emerging class of private businesspeople capable of mobilizing cash and inputs, including through cross-border trade.[24]

The course of actual policy proved anything but straightforward and was influenced by broader political developments. Within weeks of reaching the so-called Leap Day Deal with the United States in February 2012, the regime blew up the agreement by announcing its intention to launch a long-range satellite (Chapter 7). This decision set in train a long cycle of confrontation that ran through a second satellite launch in December 2012, the third nuclear test in February 2013, and two fraught months of tension on the peninsula in the test's aftermath (Chapter 7). These external moves appeared to have internal political roots. Less than six weeks after Kim Jong-un's April 2012 speech, the May 30 *Rodong Sinmun*, the official newspaper of the Central Committee of the Workers' Party of Korea, reintroduced the idea of belt tightening in an editorial that explicitly tilted the "guns versus butter" trade-off in favor of guns: "Reinforcing military power, however . . . [requires] funds, as well as up-to-date technology. . . . The work of reinforcing the military power is one that cannot succeed without a firm determination and tightening one's belt." A much anticipated meeting, the 6th Session of the 12th SPA in September 2012, came and went with deafening silence on the June 28 measures dealing with agricultural reforms. By the end of the year, more systematic external assessments, most notably the Food and Agriculture Organization (FAO)/WFP 2013 crop assessment, pulled few punches on the absence of agricultural reform.

The overall policy direction of the new regime was clarified with the rollout of the *byungjin* line but in a direction that directly contradicted the theoretical expectation that a commitment to economic reform would go hand-in-hand with more moderate foreign policy behavior.[25] The new policy line—announced in the midst of the most significant crisis on the peninsula since the onset of the nuclear crisis in 2002—committed the country to *both* economic reconstruction and the pursuit of its nuclear program. There is little question that it reflected a major statement on the overall grand strategy of the new regime: a political compromise seeking to split the difference between a focus on economic issues and the *songun* approach.

However, while the economic components of the new line appear to have been undertaken on a pilot basis and by acquiescence to developments on the ground, the military component of the strategy was highly explicit. Nuclear weapons were never to be bargained away "as long as the imperialists and nuclear threats exist on earth." Moreover, "the DPRK's possession of nukes should be fixed by law and the nuclear armed forces should be expanded and beefed up qualitatively and quantitatively until the denuclearization of the world is realized." A separate edict committed the country to its space program and set up a Space Development Bureau, suggesting an institutionalized commitment to a long-range missile capacity as well.

As with the 2002 reforms, political economy factors may have limited the scope of the reforms in the short run in much the same way that they had after 2002 (Park 2013). Figure 2.3 traces the path of North Korean *won* prices for rice, the black market exchange rate, and the (resulting) dollar prices of rice in the aftermath of the November 2009 currency reform. The reform wiped out the savings and working capital of many North Korean households and businesses and damaged the credibility of the won as a currency. The result

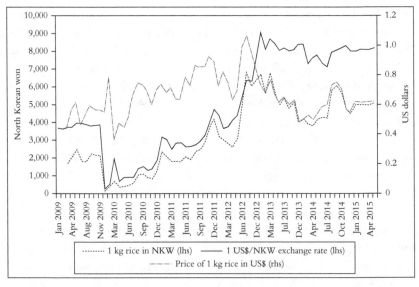

FIGURE 2.3   Price of rice and US dollar exchange rate in Pyongyang markets, January 2009–2015

SOURCE: Authors' calculations from *DailyNK* market prices.
NOTE: Points represent average values of all available data collected within a one-month period.

was steep depreciation and high inflation, as noted previously. But around the briefings on the reforms in mid-2012, trends in rice prices and won depreciation accelerated and did not moderate until 2015 after which they stabilized. As a result, when pilot reforms were rolled out in select cooperatives, they appeared to generate adverse short-term effects.[26] These problems were only compounded by institutional features of the cooperatives and collectives, which are top heavy with state and party personnel who have little interest in shifting incentives toward farmers (Park 2013).

Somewhat different problems emerged with enterprise reform. Sectors where there was effective demand for surplus output, such as cement, boomed, and wages rose sharply. However, the resultant increase in demand simply generated price increases for basic consumer goods and of course did nothing for sectors in which longer-term prospects were unfavorable. Moreover, the reforms faced fundamental supply constraints: even if factories could generate profits, they needed inputs. Social infrastructure—power, raw materials, intermediates, transport—remained in disarray as investment was poured into elite ventures in Pyongyang. These were white elephants such as the Masik Pass ski resort and continuing demands coming from the military. Yet despite these drains on state resources, the government was unable to establish an effective tax system and could not float bonds because the country had no real financial sector, or even a banking system, to speak of.

Viewed over the longer run, the *byungjin* line may prove a tactical concession that will permit reform to be pursued by stealth, by acquiescing to continuing marketization rather than undertaking de jure policy reforms, and we explore this possibility in our conclusions in Chapter 8. Whatever the future path of reform, the *byungjin* line cut directly against the expectation that a reformist impulse would moderate foreign policy behavior. Rather, the opposite occurred, with military and security concerns dominating economic ones and the leadership recommitting to the *byungjin* line at the May 2016 Party Congress.

The External Sector and the Quest for Foreign Investment

Opening to foreign direct investment is a particularly telling signal that the regime is willing to partially forego control over foreign transactions in order to reap the benefits of engagement. Integration into complex production networks has been a hallmark both of the capitalist economies in the region, including South Korea, but also of reforming socialist systems such as China and Vietnam. But attracting foreign investment requires credible commitments to investors, including with respect to the overall policy and political environment. How has North Korea's foreign investment policy evolved?

Our answer is simple. Although we can trace recurrent efforts to attract foreign investment—and an uptick in them under Kim Jong-un—such efforts have suffered from what might be called the "parchment illusion." The government has written numerous laws governing foreign investment that have repeatedly fallen victim not simply to infrastructure deficiencies or poor economic performance but to political and foreign policy risk, including outright default on foreign borrowing, effective expropriation of foreign assets, and recurrent crises in the country's weapons program. Rather than demand for investment driving foreign policy in a more moderate direction, foreign and domestic policy priorities have repeatedly undermined the credibility of the government's efforts to attract foreign investment, particularly in larger projects in which the holdup problem is most acute. The one exception to this finding proves the rule. North Korea has been able to attract large-scale Chinese investments in resource extraction, but precisely because such investments can generally secure high-level political protection. The result, however, is a pattern of specialization that looks more like that of a rentier state than that of the other small open economies in the region.

The regime's limited historical interest in attracting foreign investment initially reflected reliance on trade with the Soviet bloc. However, North Korea never even joined the Soviet-era Council of Mutual Economic Assistance and went so far as to time its central plans to frustrate linkage with the fraternally allied socialist states. During the 1970s, it followed a number of other developing countries in borrowing money from Western banks looking to recycle petrodollars, with some of this borrowing used to import turnkey factories (Cornell 2002). But the country subsequently defaulted on those loans, the only communist country to do so. In addition to market perceptions of risk, unresolved debt has effectively barred North Korea from international capital markets ever since.

The first expressed interest in attracting foreign direct investment came with the establishment of a special economic zone in the extreme northeast corner of the country, in Rajin-Sonbong, which was later rechristened Rason. However, the sheer isolation of the zone reflected the caution with which the government approached the project. The unwillingness to invest in refurbishing port facilities or transportation links between Rason and neighboring China and Russia initially prevented it from taking off (Noland and Flake 1997).

As documented in Chapter 3, the 1998 election of Kim Dae-jung in South Korea and the inauguration of his Sunshine Policy were accompanied by a growth in inter-Korean trade. Investments in a processing-on-commission business were small and did not face significant expropriation risk. However, the overwhelming share of total South Korean direct investment in North Korea came through a tourist project around Mt. Kumgang and particularly in the Kaesong Industrial Complex (KIC). The KIC was the result of a private political initiative by the Hyundai Group in the heyday of the Sunshine Policy, but ultimately involved substantial government financing. Partly because of subsidies and guarantees against political risk, it attracted investment from small- and medium-sized enterprises and began exporting in 2006.

As we show through firm-level surveys in Chapter 5, Chinese investment has a somewhat longer history, accelerating over the second half of the 2000s and particularly from 2009 to 2010 as a result of North Korea's opening up to raw materials investments. A series of political-cum-economic initiatives on the part of China (Chapter 7) and growing interest on the part of provincial governments and firms in the northeast of China drove this process. Exemplary of these initiatives was a commitment to build two export-processing and industrial zones on the islands of Hwanggumpyong and Wihwa with significant Chinese financing and joint project management.

Attracting foreign investment seemed to constitute one of the defining features of the late Kim Jong-il and Kim Jong-un regimes and even of the *byungjin* line. Between 2010 and 2013, the government established a State Development Bank, announced a decision to initiate a "10-Year State Strategy Plan for Economic Development" in which foreign investment played a prominent role, and tasked rival organizations with encouraging and screening foreign direct investment. In 2014–2015, the government made a series of announcements regarding the establishment of new special economic zones throughout the country, supported by detailed legal reforms and the suggestion that the zones would enjoy at least a degree of autonomy. These initiatives did result in a significant increase in foreign investment during the latter half of the nuclear crisis period, most notably in resource investments from China that could be collateralized through the underlying trade generated. Kaesong also continued to boom.

However, the regime's foreign and domestic policies continually served to undercut the effort to attract foreign investment outside of the mineral sector and the Kaesong and Rason zones. The Mt. Kumgang tourist resort was effectively shuttered following the shooting death of a tourist in 2008. North Korean unwillingness to issue security assurances stalled talks to reopen the project; these talks effectively ended when the zone was expropriated outright in an apparent bargaining ploy to secure South Korean concessions. Kaesong initially survived the sinking of the *Cheonan*, but South Korea imposed sanctions on all trade and investment outside of the zone, effectively putting an end to the processing-on-commission trade. Further expansion of Kaesong was also put on hold. Amid the spike in tensions on the peninsula in the spring of 2013, and in an apparent effort to show resolve, North Korea chose to withdraw all workers from the zone, setting in train a prolonged closure that was resolved only when the Park administration sent signals of a willingness to close the zone altogether. It finally did so following the nuclear and missile tests of January and February 2016.

Investment conflicts were by no means limited to South Korea. Even Chinese mining operations were not altogether immune.[27] Efforts to develop export-processing zones appealing to Chinese manufacturing or service firms yielded limited results as well. As of late-2016, the Hwanggumpyong and Wihwa islands projects remained fallow, following years of stalled negotiations over protections for investors.[28] An ongoing dispute with the Egyptian telecomm giant Orascom centered on the exchange rate for repatriation of capital, which tied up hundreds of millions of dollars and went to the very heart of the investment process.[29] And despite the conspicuous involvement of foreign advisors in Kim Jong-un's zone initiative, none of the zones had attracted any investment as of late 2016. Only Rason appears to have made sustained progress in integrating into regional production networks, a result of location, subtle differences in its management, and no doubt strong Chinese and Russian pressures associated with substantial zone infrastructure investments.[30] However even the fate of this enclave was threatened by the new rounds of sanctions imposed in 2016 following the fourth and fifth nuclear tests.

We look at North Korea's policy toward foreign investment as a proxy for its intent with respect to economic opening. The pattern that emerges is relatively clear and comports with the broader message of other indicators. Stated intentions to attract foreign investment have repeatedly run up against not only domestic political and policy risks but foreign policy risks as well. Whatever the intention of reformers in the government, the regime has never been able to close the gap between statements of intent, the "parchment institutions," and the complex of policy and ultimately political commitments required to secure robust foreign investment.

Conclusion

This chapter identified the political constraints that operate on both sanctions and engagement strategies in hard targets such as North Korea. Following the theoretical literature on the topic, we looked at the constraints posed by regime type and the capacity to exercise control, the breadth and composition of the regime's support base, and the country's economic, particularly foreign economic, policy. Using the composition of formal institutional bodies, we demonstrated that the core constituency of the regime, the selectorate, is both extremely narrow and biased in favor of the leader's court retinue, the military, the security apparatus, and the military-industrial complex. These groups command resources from the system and thus appear relatively impervious, if not outright hostile, to either sanctions or the many forms of economic engagement.

As for North Korea's broader civil society, the mechanisms of social control have been well documented and do not require extensive comment. The regime may face some constraints from the emergence of a quasi-independent civil society and market economy when compared with the all-encompassing control it exercised through the workplace when the planning system was more functional. We return to this possibility in our conclusions in Chapter 8 and consider the possible effects of more tightly coordinated sanctions negotiated in 2016.

To date, however, these constraints have been met not with political concessions but with innovations in the internal security system, including the expansion of economic crimes and the development of low-level labor-training camps that have been used to effectively intimidate and extort. Like other authoritarian regimes under threat of sanctions, North Korea's leadership seems more than willing to impose the costs of international isolation on a vulnerable domestic population (Peksen 2009; Peksen and Drury 2010). Indeed, as we show in more detail in Chapter 4, the regime was even able to turn domestic deprivation into a tactical advantage by extorting aid, at least for a while, from the international community.

Finally, we traced the course of economic reform and found strong reluctance to reverse economic course or to sustain reformist experiments. Even in the face of the extraordinary economic collapse leading to famine, the regime squeezed consumption rather than undertake relatively modest and simple reforms that would have altered its relationship with either society or the world economy. Although we do find important windows of experimentation in 1998–2002 and again in 2012–2015 (under Kim Jong-un), these reforms not only were partial but raised fundamental questions about whether they were aimed at relaxing state control or rationalizing it.

The separate analysis of the external sector is particularly revealing. The regime has shown a recurrent interest in attracting foreign direct investment, and the increasing integration with China is a theme we pick up in Chapter 3. But integration with a socialist mixed economy raises the important analytic question of whether deeper integration generates either leverage, in the quid pro quo model of engagement, or the liberalizing effects postulated in "transformative engagement" models. Any understanding of the political effects of growing economic openness must address a crucial point raised by Solingen (1998, 2012a): that statist political coalitions are perfectly aware of the potentially corrosive effects of market-oriented engagement and, precisely for that reason, seek to limit or control it. Thus, the apparent preference for a rentier strategy centered on raw materials over integration into global production networks that require surrender of control and credible commitments to investors.

This penchant for control imposes enormous economic costs. But the *byungjin* line should give pause both to advocates of sanctions and to those who expect that engagement will foster reform or moderate the country's foreign policy behavior. Indeed, in our conclusions in Chapter 8, we raise an important possibility that cuts strongly against transformative engagement models: that the pursuit of incremental reform, including in the external sector, may prove an adaptive response that increases support for the regime rather than exposes it to risk (Dimitrov 2013). Before turning to those issues and the foreign policy dimensions of the crisis, we turn to a closer examination of the effects of the policy choices pursued in the external sector. Does growing economic openness possibly expose the regime to greater vulnerability going forward? The answer to this question hinges on the geography of North Korea's foreign economic relations, the rapidly growing dependence on China and the coordination problems raised in Chapter 1.

3

North Korea's External Economic Relations, 1990–2016

Since the onset of the nuclear crisis in 2002, North Korea has been subjected to an array of multilateral and bilateral sanctions. Before we can assess the *political* effect of these sanctions, a task we take up in Chapters 6 and 7, we must first attempt to assess their *economic* effect on the country's trade, investment, and aid relations. Is North Korea constrained by the variety of sanctions it has faced, including those imposed since 2002? Or has it managed to limit the damage by courting new partners and diversifying its economic activities? Has the regime been able to finance imports with new streams of export revenues and capital inflows? Or has it become more vulnerable over time to foreign exchange constraints and, as a result, more likely to respond to sanctions or inducements? These questions go directly to the long-standing observation that effective economic statecraft hinges crucially on solving coordination problems (see, for example, Martin 1992).

Answering these questions is not straightforward. North Korea's external economic relations are astonishingly opaque, with even international trade statistics regarded by the regime as state secrets (Noland 2001; Eberstadt 2007). However, by using so-called mirror statistics collected from North Korea's trading partners and undertaking some financial forensics, not only can we reconstruct the magnitude and direction of North Korea's trade; we can provide estimates of its aggregate balance-of-payments position as well.

We begin with a simple, even naïve, test of the effects of sanctions by considering North Korea's merchandise trade since the onset of the nuclear crisis. A full understanding of the opportunity costs that North Korea pays as a result of sanctions, or as a result of its autarkic economic strategy and provocative foreign policy behavior, requires a more sophisticated counterfactual analysis, which we have attempted elsewhere (Noland 2014). Nonetheless, we can show through simple descriptive statistics, a statistical model of China-DPRK trade, and a case study of luxury goods that multilateral sanctions appear to have had surprisingly little effect on the country's commercial trade and have certainly not kept it from steadily increasing.

A consideration of the country's merchandise trade also permits a brief digression on the commodity composition of North Korea's trade, an analysis that reinforces our findings with respect to overall economic strategy and foreign direct investment in Chapter 2. North Korea's trade expansion since the onset of the second nuclear crisis has been driven to an underappreciated extent by extractive industries as opposed to the manufacturing industries that fueled Asia's rapid growth. These findings confirm the regime's inability to integrate with regional production networks, and they even raise the question of whether North Korea's political economy should be seen through the lens of the resource curse.

The third section offers an explanation for the puzzle of tightening multilateral sanctions and consistent trade growth by addressing coordination more directly in an examination of the political geography of North Korea's trade. We place economic developments since 1990 into a political context that begins with the collapse of the Soviet Union as well as the famine and the gradual and erratic recovery from it.[1] This analysis shows that North Korea diversified away from countries more likely to impose sanctions, such as Japan, and toward the developing world. But the most significant share of the country's trade growth came with South Korea during the engagement era and with China.

The analysis of observed merchandise trade ignores other sources through which North Korea can access foreign exchange, including not only services exports, foreign investment, and aid but also illicit activities. Providing a coherent estimate of illicit activities is a much more complicated task and requires that we construct, from the bottom up, a balance of payments for North Korea, which we do for the period from 1990 to 2011, the end of the Kim Jong-il period. This exercise is crucial for understanding exactly how North Korea earns foreign exchange and the nature of its vulnerability to external pressures, but it also provides critical evidence on the nature of the links that North Korea has established with the world economy. Of particular interest is the country's history of illicit activities—weapons exports,[2] drugs, and counterfeiting—that hardly conform with liberal arguments about trade's beneficent effects. Our account also underlines the extent to which aid seeking has been a central component of the country's grand strategy despite the regime's provocative behavior. This is an issue we take up more extensively in Chapter 4.

A number of estimates of North Korea's illicit activities exist, but none have been constrained to fit within a simple balance-of-payments accounting framework. A consistent framework generates the finding that reliance on such activities, although not trivial, is probably more modest than often thought. Moreover, these activities have probably been affected by sanctions and interdiction. An implication of this finding, however, is that the disruption of illicit trade, while justified on other grounds, is unlikely to have a decisive impact on the regime's behavior, in part because of a revealed capacity to adjust through new export activities and in part because of capital inflows.

North Korea appears to have historically run current account deficits. This finding is underappreciated because it implies that the country has been able to finance its deficits with capital inflows. We show that these deficits are almost certainly dominated by capital inflows from China, probably in the form of foreign direct investment (FDI) and perhaps implicit aid in the form of accumulated arrears on loans and cross-border transactions between state-owned enterprises. A critical question following the new round of sanctions in 2013 and 2016, which included new financial provisions, is whether such capital inflows will persist and how North Korea will adapt if they slow down. Preliminary evidence suggests ongoing experimentation with an array of adjustment strategies, from labor exports to deepening business ties with Chinese intermediaries.

Sanctions and North Korea's Foreign Trade

North Korea's observed licit merchandise trade from 1990 through 2014 is shown in Figure 3.1, in which vertical lines show the timing of multilateral sanctions efforts. As noted, the data are derived not from North Korean sources but from the "mirror statistics" of its trade partners.[3] The descent of the North Korean economy into the mid-1990s famine is reflected in the sharp decline in both observable exports and imports in the first half of the decade. But this decline continues thereafter, reaching a nadir in the late 1990s at less than 40 percent of 1990 values.[4] Despite the onset of the second nuclear crisis in 2002, North Korea's foreign commercial relations expanded during the 2000s and 2010s, even if it took over a decade for trade volumes to return to their prefamine levels. Not until 2015 did trade actually turn down, a result of the end of the commodity supercycle.

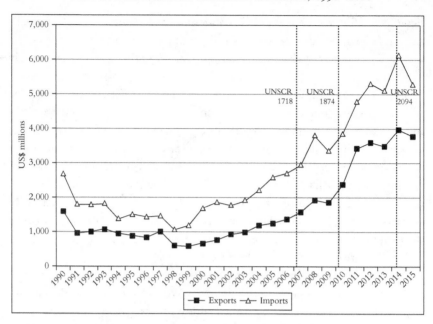

FIGURE 3.1   North Korea's observed commercial merchandise trade

SOURCE: Authors' calculations from Korea Trade-Investment Promotion Corporation data on North Korean foreign trade trends; Ministry of Unification statistics on inter-Korean relations; and IMF Direction of Trade statistics.
NOTE: Ten percent CIF/FOB conversion applied to values reported from partner countries. Excludes inter-Korean trade designated as "noncommercial" by Ministry of Unification.

From mid-2006 on, North Korea has been subject to a succession of ever tightening multilateral sanctions contained in a succession of UN Security Council resolutions: UNSCR 1695 of July 2006, UNSCR 1718 of October 2006, UNSCR 1874 of June 2009, UNSCR 2094 of February 2013, and, after the period covered here, UNSCR 2270 of March 2016 and preliminary responses to the fifth nuclear test of August 2016, which we take up in our conclusions in Chapter 8. We describe these earlier sanctions later in this chapter and their political context in Chapters 6 and 7. It is sufficient to note here that, because of the Chinese veto on the Security Council, the sanctions were initially defined relatively narrowly around WMD-related matériel and major weapons systems. As we show in the next section, there was also a weakly enforced ban on luxury goods exports to North Korea. The gradual introduction of complementary multilateral sanctions on financial flows in later resolutions was similarly tied to WMD and weapons-related activities and did not, in principle, affect the financing of commercial trade. Not until 2016, with UNSCR 2270, was commercial trade targeted directly for the first time, and as of this writing uncertainty about Chinese implementation of that resolution remains.[5]

Despite limits on their scope, there are several reasons that sanctions may have broader effect. First, the multilateral sanctions were accompanied by other forms of collective enforcement. Interdiction activities were conducted not only under the aegis of the UN resolutions but through the US-led Proliferation Security Initiative (PSI) as well. Examples of interdiction efforts, listed in Table 3.1, provide a sense of the range of proscribed activities. Second, a number of other countries not only imposed sanctions in line with the UNSC resolutions, but added further bilateral controls. Japan was particularly important in this regard, with its North Korea trade gradually falling to zero. Third, in addition to their direct impact on arms and luxury goods, sanctions may also drive up the risk premium on all exchange with North Korea by introducing uncertainty and deterring commerce in areas not directly subject to them.

However, multilateral sanctions quite clearly did not stop aggregate trade from expanding, as Figure 3.1 shows. After a downturn during the global financial crisis in 2009, when world trade contracted sharply, North Korea's trade continued to grow, particularly as a result of relations with China, as we will see, albeit moderating somewhat during the Kim Jong-un era.

We conducted a more sophisticated econometric test of the effect of sanctions by modeling China-DPRK trade from 2000 to the beginning of 2012, controlling for the level of economic activity, the exchange rate, and the seasonality of trade as well as period dummies for the introduction of sanctions (See the chapter appendix). The analysis failed to uncover any evidence that sanctions depressed Chinese exports to North Korea; indeed, we obtained the perverse result that the 2006 sanctions appear to have *increased* trade. In effect, China was consciously or unconsciously compensating for whatever losses might have occurred vis-à-vis other countries, including an initial decline in trade with South Korea following the imposition of new sanctions in 2010.[6] Of course, we could not assess what trade might have looked like in the absence of all sanctions. But the sanctions did not lead either directly or indirectly, through an increase in the risk premium, to a decline or even a pause in the regime's trade with China. As we detail later in this chapter and in Chapters 6 and 7, the noneffect of sanctions is related both to the design of the sanctions regime and to ongoing problems of nonenforcement and leakage that are a leitmotif even of official reporting on implementation.[7]

TABLE 3.1

Interdiction of shipments in relation to sanctions against North Korea

Date	Country of interdiction	Goods	Departure country	Destination country	Comment
December 2007	Austria	3 Steinway concert pianos	Austria	North Korea	
March 2008	Undisclosed UN member state	5,000 point detonating rocket fuses and related material	North Korea	Iran	Containers shipped from North Korea to Dalian, China, where transshipped by major maritime carrier unaware of origin
October 2008 and December 2008	Japan	Luxury goods, including 34 pianos, 4 Mercedes-Benz automobiles, and cosmetics	Japan	North Korea	
January 2009	Democratic People's Republic of Congo	Arms and ammunition	North Korea (alleged)	Democratic People's Republic of Congo	North Korean vessel *Birobong*
May 2009	Italy	2 luxury yachts	Italy	North Korea	
July 2009	United Arab Emirates	10 containers of munitions, detonators, explosives, and rocket-propelled grenades	North Korea	Iran	Vessel owned by an Australian subsidiary of a French company under a Bahamian flag; transshipped several times
July 2009	Italy	High-end electrical/electronic apparatus for recording and reproducing sound and images	Italy	North Korea	
August 2009	Italy	150 bottles of cognac, 270 bottles of whiskey	Italy	North Korea	
September 2009	South Korea	Chemical safety suits (dual use: military utility for chemical protection)	North Korea	Syria (alleged)	Panamanian vessel *MSC Rachele*; Syria denies being destination; transshipped in China
December 2009	Thailand	35 tons of arms, including parts of long-range missile Daepodong #2	North Korea	Iran (alleged)	Georgian cargo plane; Iran denies being destination

Date		Item			Details
November 2009	South Africa	Tank parts (Soviet-designed T-54 and T-55 tanks)	North Korea	Congo-Brazzaville (Republic of Congo)	French cargo vessel; transshipped in China and Malaysia
November 2010	France	Military use—specifically, brass discs and other items	China	Unknown	
Early 2011	Undisclosed	Submarine parts	Undisclosed European country	Undisclosed South-East Asian country	
May 2012	Japan	Luxury goods, including alcoholic beverages, tobacco, electronic items, automobiles, and cosmetics	Undisclosed	North Korea	Nine separate cases of luxury goods interdictions reported by Japan since May 2012
November 2012	N/A	Engines, spare parts, and scrap from 20 MiG-21 jets	Mongolia (alleged)	North Korea	Alleged contract signed by former Mongolian Air Force official to provide North Korea with parts; parts shipped but never reached destination
July 2013	Panama	240 metric tons of weaponry material, including disassembled missiles, two MiG-21 jet fighters, 15 engines, and antiaircraft missile complexes	Cuba	North Korea	Materials seized from North Korean ship *Chong Chon Gang*; Cuba alleges weaponry to be repaired in North Korea and returned
2013	Unspecified	Spare parts for Scud missiles	China	Egypt	
May 2014	Unspecified	Dual-use items	China	Syria	Consignee was Syrian company with military links

SOURCE: United Nations Panel of Experts (2010, 2013, 2015, 2016); "North Korean Ship Yields Worrisome Cargo," *Wall Street Journal*, July 17, 2013.

NOTE: In June 2009, a North Korean vessel, the *Kang-nam 1*, allegedly on its way to Myanmar, was tracked by American Navy vessels for weeks on suspicion of carrying illegal weapons. Inspection was not carried out, however, and the ship turned around and returned to Nampo port of North Korea.

Luxury Imports: A Sanctions Case Study

One small category of commercial imports provides an opportunity to consider the coordination problems in defining and enforcing sanctions; it also provides insight into the priorities of the regime. Following North Korea's October 2006 nuclear test, UN Security Council Resolution (UNSCR) 1718 banned both direct luxury exports and transshipment of luxury goods to the country; this second injunction is important given the substantial transshipment of goods across the Chinese–North Korean border that originate from elsewhere. However, the task of defining "luxury goods" was left up to individual member states. Some states developed relatively extensive and precise lists and then enforced them; South Korea, the United States, and Japan report no such trade. Other countries, such as Russia, defined them quite narrowly or, in the case of China, avoided a commitment to restrict this trade altogether. A significant number of states did not report to the UN Sanctions Committee at all.

In the absence of a Chinese list of sanctioned luxury goods, Figure 3.2 reports trends in Chinese exports of luxury goods to North Korea from 2000 to 2013 using three different product definitions.[8] It is clear from the figure that the Security Council resolutions have had no discernible effect on China's

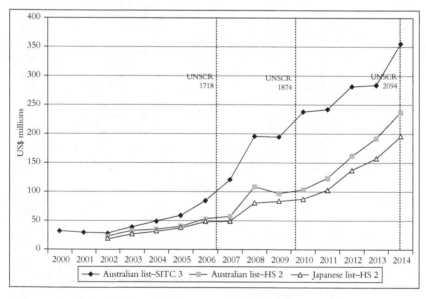

FIGURE 3.2   Chinese luxury goods exports to North Korea, 2000–2014
SOURCE: Authors' calculations from UN Comtrade database.

luxury good exports.[9] Despite the sanctions, China continued to export a variety of products that other countries defined as luxury goods, including certain electronic products, vehicles, food, and tobacco products. Indeed, China became the sole supplier of many of these products. The European Union is presumably the original source of many luxury products that do find their way into North Korea. We conducted a similar exercise for European luxury goods, and found that they were trending down even before sanctions were imposed and have since fallen to low levels.[10] In effect, the decline in direct European export of luxury goods may be offset in whole or in part by a substitution of Chinese for European luxury goods or, more likely, the transshipment of European luxury goods through China and to a lesser extent Russia.

In short, this simple descriptive analysis of merchandise trade shows that overall trade volumes do not appear to be greatly affected by the sanctions regime, in part because of the regime's design and enforcement. First, until UNSCR 2270 (2016), sanctions failed to penalize commercial trade. Second, despite multilateral sanctions on luxury goods, no common definition of these products emerged until UNSCR 2094, adopted following the third nuclear test in 2013. At Chinese insistence, 2094 was limited to an extremely narrow range of products (jewelry, yachts, luxury and racing cars). As a result, increasing volumes of luxury goods, largely electronics and vehicles, continued to enter North Korea from China. The luxury goods case is an example in microcosm of how China can undermine the efficacy of sanctions both by limiting their definition in the first place and then by serving as a transshipment point for goods that have been banned by other exporting countries.

The Commodity Composition of North Korean Exports

Besides North Korea's aggregate trade (Figure 3.1), the commodity composition of the country's trade is revealing of North Korea's foreign economic policy. As we noted in Chapter 2, North Korea has appeared unwilling or unable to integrate fully into the region's dense international production networks, in part because of the difficulties in providing credible commitments to investors. Although there is nothing in the composition of North Korean imports that is particularly striking, Figure 3.3 provides information on the commodity composition of North Korea's exports.

With respect to manufactured exports, we have noted how other economies in the region—Japan, South Korea, China, and Vietnam—got rich by tightly integrating into global value chains organized by multinational corporations and buying groups and by specializing in manufactured exports. An unusually detailed analysis of the performance of North Korean manufacturers in the

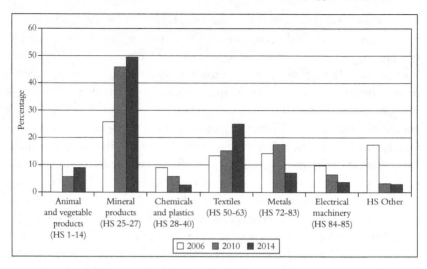

FIGURE 3.3   Composition of North Korea's exports, 2006, 2010, and 2014

SOURCE: Korea Trade-Investment Promotion Corporation data on North Korean foreign trade trends.
NOTE: Computed shares do not account for inter-Korean trade and economic cooperation.

Chinese, South Korean, and Brazilian markets (Jing and Lovely 2015) finds little evidence of indigenous manufacturing capable of meeting international standards and inadequate investment from or trade with multinational firms to compensate for this domestic weakness. In Figure 3.3, this is reflected in the continued decline in the export share of some intermediates and manufactures such as machinery. However, Jing and Lovely do show that North Korea has adjusted to external constraints by shifting into textile exports, probably from Rason and other processing-on-commission activities. How this activity will be affected by the 2016 closure of Kaesong and a tightening of sanctions on South Korean firms operating in China remains to be seen. To date, however, the fact that North Korea has shown an unwillingness or inability to engage in light, labor-intensive manufacturing speaks directly to the regime's reluctance to engage with the world economy and the corresponding lack of an export-oriented coalition, even if tacit or informal, that would offset biases in favor of autarky and statism.

At the same time, the figure shows that licit exports are increasingly concentrated in mining products: by 2014 natural resource–based products accounted for about 50 percent of North Korean's exports.[11] Several features of this development are striking. These resource exports are largely controlled by state-affiliated entities, an issue we address through firm surveys in Chapter 5. The dominance of natural resource exports also raises the question

FIGURE 3.4   North Korea's commercial exports and world commodity price indices, 1995–2016

SOURCE: Authors' calculations from International Monetary Fund (n.d.); Korea Trade-Investment Promotion Corporation data on North Korean foreign trade trends; and Ministry of Unification statistics on inter-Korean relations.

NOTE: Metal and LMIC price index plotted as monthly values; North Korea merchandise exports plotted as annual values.

of whether North Korea's political economy should be seen increasingly through the resource curse lens. As a wide-ranging literature has shown, resource dependence not only has potentially adverse economic affects; in the words of one recent study (Hendrix and Noland 2014), it has also "weakened domestic institutions, undermined democratic governance, produced corruption and enrichment of elites, and finally led in many cases to devastating violence and war" (vii).

The rise in export values appears to be driven not only by Chinese growth but by the rise in global prices during the period. Figure 3.4 shows trends in North Korean merchandise exports against two commonly used indices of world commodity prices. The close correlation suggests that North Korea's trade was driven by an increase in prices as much as in quantities, and that the rentier strategy pursued by the regime may be vulnerable as those prices fall. We revisit this possibility in our conclusions in Chapter 8.[12]

The Political Geography of North Korea's Foreign Trade

What accounts for North Korea's trade growth despite the imposition of sanctions? The answers can be found in the changing direction of North Korea's trade, which in turn has reflected pivotal changes in the diplomacy surrounding the Korean peninsula. We start with the profound shock of the collapse of the Soviet Union and subsequent relations with Russia. We then turn to an overview of North Korea's trade with the five parties—China, Russia, the United States, South Korea, and Japan—and its efforts to diversify its political and economic relations during the Kim Jong-il era. These overviews demonstrate clearly the centrality of South Korea and China to North Korea's foreign economic relations and go a long way toward explaining the coordination problems that sanctions have faced.

The Shocks of the Early 1990s: The Demise of the Soviet Union and the Re-Emergence of a Russian Card

Notwithstanding its pursuit of self-reliance, North Korea had long been deeply dependent on the Soviet Union and to a lesser extent on support from other Warsaw Pact countries in Eastern Europe. Not only did the Soviet Union effectively finance North Korea's continual current account deficits with a combination of loans and arrears—visible in the large bilateral trade deficits of the late 1980s in Figure 3.5—but Soviet pricing of coal and oil exports reflected additional subsidies (Eberstadt, Rubin, and Tretyakova 1995).

Facing economic constraints of its own and seeking to define a new foreign policy in the Asia Pacific, the Soviet Union under Gorbachev began to cut aid and reduce its support to North Korea beginning in 1986 (Noland 2000, table 3.13). In 1990 Moscow initiated a diplomatic breakthrough with South Korea and simultaneously demanded that North Korea pay world market prices, in foreign exchange, for Soviet goods.[13] This fundamental change in North Korea's external relations was a profound political shock (see Oberdorfer 1997, chaps. 9 and 10). But the end of barter and debt financing, and the subsequent collapse of the Soviet economy, constituted a profound economic shock as well. By 1993 imports from Russia were only 10 percent of their 1987–1990 average and subsequently declined to near irrelevance (Figure 3.5) (Eberstadt, Rubin, and Tretyakova 1995).

Following a Kim-Putin summit in 2001, and accelerating in the 2010s, Russia took new diplomatic initiatives with respect to the peninsula, raising the question of whether the Soviet-era relationship between Russia and North Korea might be at least partly revived (Vorontsov 2007; Zakharova 2016). One

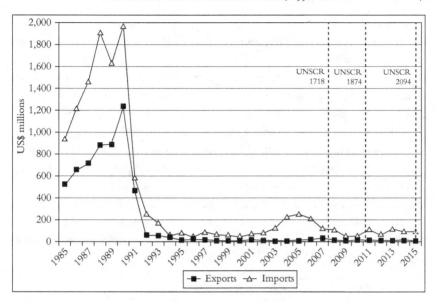

FIGURE 3.5   North Korea's trade with USSR/Russia, 1985–2015

SOURCE: Eberstadt (2003) and UN Comtrade database data.
NOTE: Ten percent CIF/FOB conversion applied to UN Comtrade values reported by Russian Federation.

barrier to closer cooperation was accumulated North Korean debt from the Soviet era, estimated at $11–14 billion, although this valuation seems somewhat
arbitrary since the debts were incurred in the form of nonconvertible Soviet
rubles. After years of failed attempts to resolve the debt issue, Russia and North
Korea came to an agreement that effectively wrote off the debt in 2012.[14]

In the early 2010s, a combination of economic interests and geostrategic
dynamics combined to boost Russian interest in North Korea. Gorbachev and
his successors all recognized the economic gains to be had from pivoting toward Asia (for example, Bauer 2009; Lee 2013; Federovskiy 2013; Zakharova
2016). These included the benefits of extending land transport and pipeline
networks, including through North Korea. President Putin's push for a more
prominent Russian role in the post-Soviet space may have also played a role
following growing tensions with the West over NATO expansion, Georgia,
the Crimea, and Ukraine.

The first concrete step in this cooperation was a €150 million joint venture
rail project reconstructing track between the Russian border and the port
of Rajin-Sonbong, or Rason. This project was accompanied by investments
in the port and the development of a land terminal for the transshipment of

Russian coal, which began in earnest in 2014, negotiation of an agreement allowing settlement in rubles, and the formation of a joint business council. However, these initial investments were to be only the opening wedge into a more ambitious cluster of projects dubbed *Pobeda* (Victory) that would include refurbishment of the entire North Korean rail network, investment in mining, and possible construction of oil and gas pipelines. These projects were accompanied by a stated objective of reaching $1 billion in two-way trade. This was an ambitious goal given the limited complementarities outside of raw materials trade, much of which took the form of Russian transshipment. High financing costs, constraints on Russian capabilities following the Crimean and Ukrainian crises, the collapse of oil prices, and high holdup risks all limited possibilities for growth. Despite declaring 2015 "The Year of Friendship," there is little reason to anticipate a sharp departure from the post-Soviet patterns visible in Figure 3.5.

Trade with the Other Five Parties: An Overview

In his memoir, George W. Bush recalls his response to revelations that North Korea was pursuing an enriched uranium program in 2002, offering his rationale for the Six Party Talks. "The United States was done negotiating with North Korea on a bilateral basis. Instead, we would rally China, South Korea, Russia and Japan to present a united front against the regime" (Bush 2010, 423–424). As we show in more detail in Chapter 6, this strategy was not successful. However, President Bush saw clearly that North Korea's economic as well as political relations with the five parties necessitated coordination.

Figure 3.6 is based on data taken directly from the Korea Trade-Investment Promotion Agency (KOTRA), South Korea's Ministry of Unification (MOU), and other trade databases. It shows shares of North Korea's total trade with the five interlocutors in the Six Party Talks—the United States, China, Japan, South Korea, and Russia—for 2000 through 2015, three years into the Kim Jong-un era.[15] These estimates should be viewed as at the high-end of the likely range for China and South Korea, especially since we include so-called noncommercial trade with South Korea. But in considering North Korea's trade with the rest of the world, the trends are clearly correct, as we show.

If we set aside the case of Russia discussed previously, the countries, or more accurately their governments, fall into two groups: those inclined to sanction the regime and those more willing to engage. The countries inclined to sanction North Korea either have negligible economic exchange with it (the United States) or have seen the significance of their economic ties shrink as a result of bilateral sanctions (Japan and South Korea under Lee

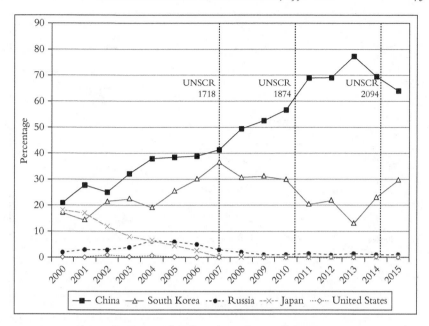

FIGURE 3.6   Share of DPRK total trade with Six Party Talks partners

SOURCE: Korea Trade-Investment Promotion Corporation data on North Korean foreign trade trends; Ministry of Unification statistics on inter-Korean relations, UN Comtrade database; and authors' calculations.
NOTE: Ten percent CIF/FOB conversion applied to values reported from partner countries; includes inter-Korean trade designated as "noncommercial" by the Ministry of Unification.

Myung-bak, 2008−2013, and extending into the Park Geun-hye administration, 2013−2018). Although the United States subsequently legislated new financial sanctions against North Korea, including the authority to impose secondary sanctions in 2016, there was little room among these "high-sanctions" countries to further curtail direct commercial trade. South Korea faced similar dilemmas. After the post-*Cheonan* sanctions, trade outside of the Kaesong Industrial Complex fell to zero and the Kaesong trade was shut down in 2016. The only way that South Korea could use trade was as an inducement in the form of a promise to *lift* sanctions.

Trade with the Rest of the World: The Failure to Diversify

What about trade with the rest of the world? Because trade in a state-socialist country is likely to follow the flag, Figure 3.7 tracks diplomatic ties between North Korea and the rest of the world since independence; it also tracks the parallel South Korean process, encapsulating in a single figure the intense competition for diplomatic recognition (Armstrong 2013). North Korea's tight

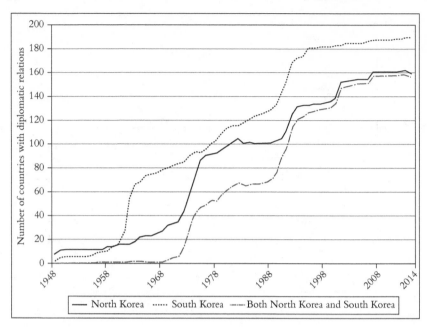

FIGURE 3.7   Diplomatic relations of North and South Korea, 1948–2014

SOURCE: Authors' calculations from Wertz, Oh, and Kim (2016).

dependence on the communist world can be seen in the surprisingly low number of countries—Russia, Mongolia, Poland, Yugoslavia, Romania, Hungary, Bulgaria, and Albania—that established diplomatic relations with it following independence in 1948. Subsequent expansion in part reflected decolonization and was more significant politically and symbolically than economically. The vast majority of new diplomatic ties in the 1960s and 1970s were in the developing world, with Africa heavily represented, and with a few European exceptions (mostly the Scandinavians).

After a pause in the 1980s, the burst of new ties in the early 1990s reflects in large part the collapse of the Soviet Union and the emergence of successor states. But the 2000s saw a re-engagement with the world following the "arduous march" of the famine years. North Korea mended fences with China following a period of some tension and hosted summits with South Korea (June 2000), Russia (August 2001), and Japan (September 2002). Many European countries recognized Pyongyang during this period, as did significant Middle Eastern oil producers (Kuwait, Bahrain, and the United Arab Emirates) and major emerging markets such as Brazil and Turkey.

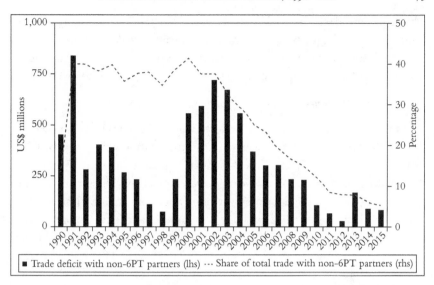

FIGURE 3.8   North Korea total trade with non–Six Party Talks countries, 1990–2015

SOURCE: Korea Trade-Investment Promotion Corporation data on North Korean foreign trade trends; Ministry of Unification statistics on inter-Korean relations; International Monetary Fund (2006); and authors' calculations.
NOTE: Ten percent CIF/FOB conversion applied to values reported from partner countries; includes inter-Korean trade designated as "noncommercial" by the Ministry of Unification.

Did these diplomatic efforts yield economic fruit? The answer is supplied by Figure 3.8. It is important to underline that a number of potentially important countries such as Iran are missing from this exercise. We show elsewhere in more detail how ties with the Middle East may be underestimated (Haggard and Noland 2011b). Moreover, the trade data do not capture other ways in which North Korea may secure support. Particularly interesting in this regard is North Korea's relationship with the Egyptian company Orascom Telecommunications. Orascom poured more than $200 million into the country after it was given a 25-year license to operate a nationwide cell phone network. Further investment halted as a result of disputes with the government over the repatriation of profits and capital (Noland 2009).[16] Merchandise trade data also does not capture more elusive services trade, such as labor exports.

As Figure 3.8 clearly shows, however, these diversification efforts were not matched by robust trade growth. The figure shows both trade and trade deficits; the latter can be treated as a rough proxy for the financing that North Korea receives from the rest of the world. On average over the 1990s, the non–Six Party Talks countries accounted for about 40 percent of North Korea's trade, although with declining trade deficits, and financing, during the famine and immediate postfamine period. From 2000, however, trade with the rest of the world fell steadily to virtual insignificance by 2012 before turning up slightly in 2013-2015 as the country once again came under pressure to diversify.

Twin Pillars: The Roles of China and South Korea and the Aid Question

Both Figure 3.6 and the evidence of declining trade and trade deficits with the rest of the world in Figure 3.8 underscore the central significance of China and South Korea to North Korea's foreign economic relations. Despite the high partner concentration of North Korea's trade, its vulnerability to sanctions did not necessarily increase over time. Such vulnerability hinges on the likelihood that one's trading partners will impose sanctions. China's share of North Korea's trade grew steadily throughout the nuclear crisis period before declining somewhat as a share of the total in 2014–2015. However, the figure does not capture a crucial development in 2016—the closure of Kaesong—which resulted in a dramatic upturn in the Chinese share as North-South trade fell to zero.

This trade growth underscores what might be called China's strategy of "deep engagement" with North Korea and its relative lack of interest in a wider-ranging sanctions regime, at least until new multilateral sanctions negotiated in 2016. We trace these initiatives in more detail in Chapter 7.

In the case of South Korea, the conservative Lee Myung-bak government ushered in a more conditional approach to engagement with the North. Following the sinking of the *Cheonan*, South Korean trade with the North outside of the Kaesong Industrial Complex contracted dramatically, generating recurrent South Korean concerns about China's "economic colonization" of the northern part of the peninsula. Kaesong remained significant in North Korea's total foreign exchange earnings, however, until it was closed in the first half of 2013 and again in 2016; as a result of the Kaesong closing, South Korea's share fell to virtually nothing in 2016.

A crucial issue in the engagement debate is whether increased economic ties on the part of these two countries might have had socializing or transformative effects. Important in this regard is the extent to which such interaction is on market-conforming terms or represents aid. Figure 3.9 provides a comparative estimate of aid flows from the two countries from 1998 through the end of the Kim Jong-il era.

Because China does not provide data on aid flows, the extent of Chinese aid is hard to gauge (Reilly 2014c; Yan 2016). Following the recognition of South Korea in 1992, China shifted its trade relations from "friendship prices" to a

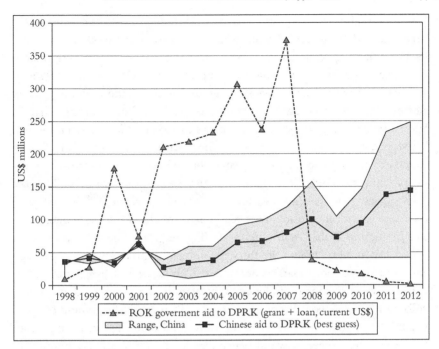

FIGURE 3.9   South Korean and Chinese government support, 1998–2012

SOURCE: Authors' calculations from Ministry of Unification statistics on inter-Korean relations; and Exim Bank ROK statistics.

more commercial foundation. This shift was rolled out formally in 2005 with the slogan "Government guidance with companies in the lead; market-based operations and mutual benefit" (Reilly 2014c, 1164). We detail in Chapter 7 how that political line persisted into the Kim Jong-un era.

Nonetheless, a combination of subsidized exports, humanitarian assistance, and politically timed gifts have persisted (Reilly 2014c). The gifts were probably substantial around the time of the transition from Kim Jong-il to Kim Jong-un (Cathcart and Madden 2012; Yan 2016). Infrastructure investment projects such as the paving of North Korean roads into Rason and construction of the export-processing zones Hwanggumpyong and Wihwa islands are also a form of aid, although these projects increasingly appear to be focused on upgrading infrastructure on the Chinese side of the border in line with Xi Jinping's Belt and Road initiative (Li 2016).

To draw comparisons with South Korea, we set a high estimate for Chinese support at 25 percent of all fuel and food shipments, although we suspect that this almost certainly overstates direct assistance. As can be seen, South

Korean aid substantially outstripped even this high estimate over most of the period. But there is some reason to doubt that even our modest best guess, let alone our high estimate, is correct. To test for whether Chinese trade is conducted on commercial terms, we compared Chinese export prices for food and fuel with world market prices.[17] Figure 3.10 shows the monthly price of rice exports since 2002 against two international benchmark prices: Thai A1 Special grade and Thai 25% grade. China's exports trended between the two between 2002 and 2008, when world food prices spiked. Data on Chinese exports to the DPRK then disappeared, but when they resumed the tracking of China's export prices against Thai A1 Special was very tight. The data even suggest that North Korea has been paying a premium.[18] We repeated the exercise with fuel, using three world benchmarks: West Texas Intermediate, Brent, and Dubai Arab Gulf crude (Figure 3.11). There has been some seasonality in oil trade, but the story is consonant with that reported for food and even shows more marked premiums. Chinese export prices track three world-market benchmarks in lockstep through the price spike and subsequent collapse of 2008–2009. From the start of 2011 until the beginning of 2014, when Chinese customs officials abruptly stopped reporting crude shipments, Chinese prices exceeded world benchmark prices by nontrivial amounts of between 20 and 30 percent.

It is important to underline the caveats. There is no consistent series of Chinese aid to North Korea. Our measures of the commercialization of trade in food and fuel could be masking internal subsidies from the government to exporters. Still, two conclusions emerge from this review. First, as a matter of policy China has increasingly sought to emphasize the commercial nature of its relationship with North Korea. Second, despite that emphasis and increasing pressure for more robust sanctions, China probably still provides humanitarian assistance, politically timed gifts, and infrastructure investment, although this assistance has not been adequate to stave off periodic distress, as we show in Chapter 4.

While we do not have reliable information on Chinese aid to North Korea, we have quite detailed data on the role that South Korean assistance plays in total trade with the North.[19] Figure 3.12 divides South Korean exports into three mutually exclusive categories: processing-on-commission trade and general trade, which we consider to be largely commercial; what the South Korean government calls "economic cooperation" trade; and noncommercial trade or aid. General trade—commercial trade not tied to processing-on-commission arrangements—is negligible. The most significant component of commercial trade, before falling off around 2011, was of the processing-on-commission

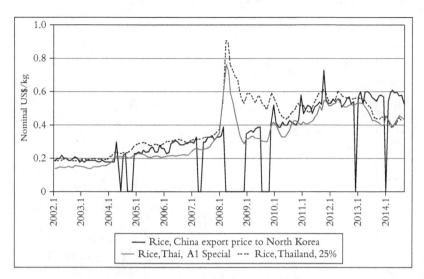

FIGURE 3.10 Benchmark world rice prices versus China export prices
to North Korea, 2002–2014

SOURCE: Authors' calculations from International Trade Council Trade Map statistics; and World Bank
GEM commodities data.

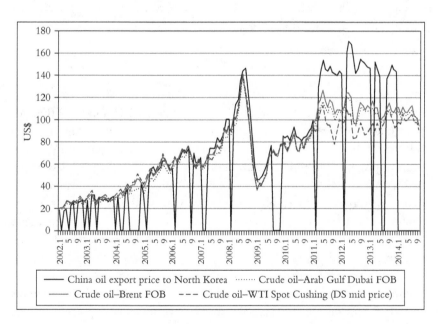

FIGURE 3.11 Benchmark world crude oil prices versus China export prices
to North Korea, 2002–2014

SOURCE: Statistics from International Trade Council Trade Map and Thomson Reuters DataStream.

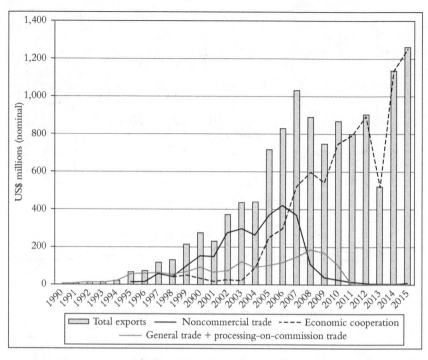

FIGURE 3.12   South Korea to North Korea total exports, 1990–2015

SOURCE: Ministry of Unification statistics on inter-Korean relations.

type, which excluded firms in the Kaesong Industrial Complex (KIC). Although nominally commercial, trade from the KIC has benefited from a myriad of subsidies, among them financial support to firms, political insurance, and the provision of infrastructure and power. As a result, it is classified as trade associated with "economic cooperation." Finally, purely noncommercial trade encompasses a succession of aid efforts, from the construction of the light-water reactor in connection with the Agreed Framework to shipments of heavy fuel oil during the Six Party Talks to the extensive food aid that we take up in more detail in Chapter 4.

What is striking is that at no point do general trade and processing-on-commission trade outstrip the sum of exports either related to economic cooperation or on noncommercial terms. Noncommercial exports were high during the Kim Dae-jung and particularly the Roh Moo-hyun years, but fell off under Lee Myung-bak. Through 2015, however, the decline in aid was more than offset by the dramatic increase in KIC-related trade.[20]

In sum, in the aftermath of the famine North Korea sought to diversify its foreign economic relations by normalizing diplomatic relations with a number of European and major middle-income developing countries. With the onset of the nuclear crisis, trade with countries inclined to impose sanctions fell (Japan and South Korea under Lee Myung-bak), creating strong incentives for the regime to seek out trading partners unlikely to impose sanctions for nonproliferation ends. This adjustment process was not costless, and North Korea paid for the loss of trade and remittances from Japan and the end of aid and commercial trade with South Korea. But these costs should not be exaggerated, as trade with China quickly substituted for the losses. Moreover, there is no doubt that some leakage occurred, as trade with both Japan and South Korea was partly rerouted through willing intermediaries in China. The well-known coordination problems that come with sanctions are not merely static but dynamic and endogenous to the shifting nature of sanctions and engagement coalitions.

A second major point to emerge from this analysis is the somewhat unexpected nature of trade with North Korea's two largest trading partners during the nuclear crisis. We cannot rule out Chinese aid, which continued throughout the crisis. But the exercises we present on prices suggest that Chinese aid should not be exaggerated, either. Trade with China appears largely commercial, which we confirm in our analysis of Chinese policy in Chapter 7. Trade with South Korea is characterized by a strong aid component during the Kim Dae-jung and Roh Moo-hyun years but with continued indirect state support via the Kaesong project until its ultimate closure in 2016. As we also discuss in more detail in Chapter 7, these findings have major implications for "transformative" engagement arguments since aid does not appear to have had the "spread" effects postulated and—whatever its humanitarian objectives— effectively served to support the regime.

Beyond the Merchandise Trade I: Illicit Activities

The data in the foregoing sections was based on reported merchandise trade. But North Korea has derived additional revenues from unobserved trade transactions, including both illicit, which we take up in this section, and legal, such as services exports, aid, and foreign investment that generate resources for the regime; these latter activities are discussed in the next section. We have grouped arms sales, drug trafficking, and counterfeiting as illicit, although at least some arms trade over the period arguably did not violate international law. In this section, we attempt an estimate of these activities through the end of the Kim Jong-il era in 2011.

At a loss to explain how North Korea managed to survive its isolation, a number of analysts have advanced the idea that the regime had come to rely heavily or even preponderantly on its illicit trade; according to Chestnut's well-documented work, the country had become a "Soprano state" (Chestnut 2005, 2007, 2014). The very existence of North Korea's weapons trade is a reminder of the obvious fact that not all external transactions are benign.

But how large is it? The various point estimates offered with respect to this trade are rarely constrained to fit within a balance-of-payments framework and thus are almost certainly exaggerated. It may appear obvious that arms sales and other illicit trade are not recorded and should simply be added to the balance of payments as exports, thus reducing the country's financing gap.[21] However, this assumption is erroneous; it is also possible and indeed probable that illicit trade is misreported in other commodity categories and therefore does not represent a dollar-for-dollar addition to North Korea's net exports.[22] But most analysts probably overstate their contribution (by assuming that they are entirely additional) rather than understate it (by making corrections for the likelihood that missiles are partly captured elsewhere in the trade data). Increased surveillance and interdiction probably curtailed the growth of missile sales. Nonetheless, illicit activity constitutes an important chapter in the country's economic history and is directly germane to ideas about the relationship between trade, engagement, and foreign policy behavior.

Military Hardware

In the 1980s, North Korea emerged as a significant player in the global arms market, supplying conventional arms based on Soviet designs, including short-range ballistic missiles, which we focus on here. According to the Arms Control and Disarmament Agency (1997), sales in the second half of the 1980s (1986–1990) averaged more than $500 million a year (in constant 1996 dollars) or just under 20 percent of total exports for that period. In the first half of the 1990s, however, sales fell as a result of the collapse of the Soviet Union and the loss of its technological support, the emergence of new suppliers, and a reduction in tensions among key customers (Pollack 2011). After a lull during the famine period, North Korea sought to revive missile sales to the Middle East, much to the consternation of both the Clinton and Bush administrations (Grimmett 2006; Pollack 2011). From 1997 to 2002, it also carried out a controversial set of exchanges with Pakistan that involved the barter of missiles and missile technology for uranium enrichment technology (Bhatia 2008; International Institute for Strategic Studies 2007; Corera 2006; Albright 2010).

The onset of the nuclear crisis in 2002 and the missile and nuclear tests of 2006, 2009, and 2013 brought this trade under much closer international scrutiny. The multilateral interdiction of a Cambodian-flagged vessel (the *So San*) carrying North Korean missiles to Yemen in November 2002 provided the impetus for President Bush's Proliferation Security Initiative (PSI) in 2003.[23] The PSI sought to provide a framework for international cooperation around interdiction of WMD-related trade (Wolf, Chow, and Jones 2008; Valencia 2010; Nikitin 2011).[24]

The first UN sanctions resolution, UNSCR 1695 (2006) focused narrowly on missiles and trade directly related to weapons of mass destruction. UNSCR 1718 (following the first nuclear test in October 2006) expanded proscribed imports and exports, authorized, but did not obligate, parties to stop and inspect shipments going to and from North Korea that were suspect of carrying prohibited items, and permitted targeted financial sanctions on individuals and companies involved with the DPRK's weapons programs. In 2009 UNSCR 1874 came close to making the PSI a formal multilateral effort.[25]

UN Security Council Resolution 2094 (March 2013, following the third nuclear test) included for the first time language urging member states to prohibit any financial flows that might be associated with weapons programs.[26] The new resolution also called on member states to deny ports or overflight rights to ships and airplanes believed to be involved in the military programs or in evasion of sanctions.

These measures all suffered from a "credible information" clause. That is, a government that did not want to enforce them could say that it lacked credible information or that the information provided to it did not meet the standard of "reasonable grounds." On the other hand, in UNSCR 2270 (2016) the measures gradually expanded from a narrow focus on WMD and missiles to the two-way traffic in other weapons systems, even including small arms. The UN resolutions came to encompass financial as well as trade sanctions and were matched by more invasive means of enforcement, particularly from the time of the second nuclear test in 2009.

Despite this heightened scrutiny, however, two caveats are worth noting. Although a number of North Korea's traditional customers peeled away, the interest of a small number of states in acquiring weapons did not abate. Iran, Syria, and their proxies in Hezbollah and Hamas headed this list (Bechtol 2009), but interdictions revealed efforts to sell to a number of other states: not only Egypt and Yemen, but also Myanmar. Moreover, the scrutiny given to direct weapons sales is harder to extend to weapons-related service contracts, technology transfer, and a variety of other cooperative activities that North

Korea undertook with Iran and Syria (Noland 2000, chap. 3; Bechtol 2009). The discovery and subsequent Israeli bombing of a reactor in the Syrian desert in 2007 was a stark reminder of this fact. Nevertheless, from an overall balance-of-payments perspective, we estimate that the role of arms sales and associated exports activities declined in the 1990s and probably never fully revived.

Drugs

Drugs constitute a second source of North Korea's illicit income. Exports appear to have been initially limited to drugs secured elsewhere, but in the mid-1990s North Korea began to produce drugs for export as well, beginning with opium and heroin but quickly diversifying into methamphetamines (Perl 2005, 7–10; Chestnut 2007, 2015; Zhang 2010; Yun and Kim 2010; Lankov and Kim 2013; Hastings 2014).[27] As with weapon sales, interdictions and particularly Chinese efforts to stem the trade probably slowed larger-scale shipments. Unlike weapon systems, however, small-scale production and proximity to China facilitated ongoing trafficking, helped by links with Chinese, Russian, and Japanese gangs (Hastings 2014).

Because the networks through which drugs are sold involve extraordinary markups as one moves down the distribution chain, estimates of the drug trade are easily inflated as analysts confuse street or retail prices with North Korean suppliers' wholesale prices.[28] David Asher (2005), who coordinated the North Korean Working Group at the Department of State, offered an estimate of $100–200 million a year from drug sales largely based at that time on estimated export of opiates. However, some simple calculations of estimated acreage under cultivation, likely output, and wholesale prices suggest that this estimate is exaggerated.[29] Satellite imagery has not supported claims of large-scale cultivation (Sovacool 2009), and seizures subsequently dropped to relatively low levels.[30]

The decline in seizures could reflect alternative means of bringing drugs into major export markets, including Japan, Russia, South Korea, and particularly China, where press reports of shipments of "ice" from North Korea increased sharply in the second half of the 2000s (Lankov and Kim 2013). However, the decline also reflects more effective surveillance and interdiction of North Korea's activities, including by China and Japan.[31]

Counterfeiting[32]

A final major form of illicit activity is counterfeiting. US government officials have suspected that North Korea is the origin of so-called supernotes, very high-quality counterfeits of one-hundred-dollar bills, which began to appear in 1989. Supernotes gained more attention after 2005 with a series of criminal cases and Treasury enforcement actions against Banco Delta Asia as a financial institution of "primary money laundering concern" (Chestnut 2007, chap. 4; Demick and Meyer 2005; Fifield 2006; Weisman 2006; Perl 2006; Nanto 2009); as we show in Chapter 6, this action played a central role in the breakdown of the Six Party Talks in late 2005 and their ultimate revival in early 2007.[33]

As with other illicit activities, estimating the value of counterfeit currency is difficult. As of 2010, US government officials estimated that $63 million of supernotes had been seized worldwide since 1989 and that the total amount of counterfeiting was very much larger than that, even in the hundreds of millions of dollars (US Department of the Treasury 2010). However like drug producers, supernote producers did not earn one hundred cents on the dollar; rather, the notes were typically marketed wholesale at a discount to their face value. Moreover, there remains substantial uncertainty about whether North Korea was the actual source of the supernotes. The Congressional Research Service (Nanto 2009) has estimated that North Korea earned $15–25 million a year from counterfeiting "over several years," but we take this estimate as generous. Recent press reports suggest that supernotes may have dried up altogether.[34]

Illicit Activities: Putting It All Together

As can be seen, there is extraordinary variation in the valuation of illicit trade. Many estimates make reference to prior periods, or peak levels of the given activity, and few make any adjustments for the possibility that foreign exchange earnings from the activity are truly additional to the balance of payments or hidden in other exports. Above all, estimates generally do not consider the likely effect of the closer scrutiny of North Korea's economic activity that has occurred since the onset of the nuclear crisis in October 2002 and particularly since the US Treasury's actions of 2005 and ever tightening formal sanctions in the wake of the missile and nuclear tests of 2006.

Figure 3.13 shows our estimates of all illicit revenues (inclusive of arms sales) as a share of merchandise exports from 1990 through the end of the Kim Jong-un era in 2011.[35] Admittedly these are highly speculative and as a consequence we include high estimates—incorporating other estimates than ours—as well as low estimates and a "best guess." As one can see, the illicit share of revenues has probably been drifting down for more than a decade as legitimate trade has expanded and as intensified interdiction efforts have crimped criminal activities. We estimate that at the end of the Kim Jong-il era in 2011, the illicit share of exports was in the range of 5–20 percent, with our best guess

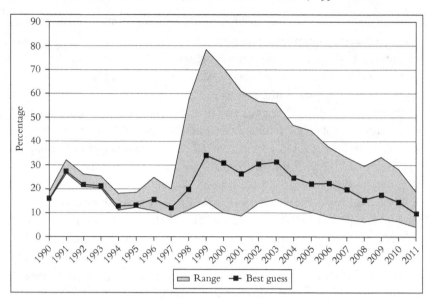

FIGURE 3.13   Arms and illicit exports as a share of commercial goods exports,
1990–2011

SOURCE: Authors' calculations.

at roughly 10 percent. It is possible, moreover, that not all of these earnings
flowed directly into state coffers.[36]

In sum, North Korea did have its Soprano state moment when illicit trade
loomed larger in its overall balance of payments. This history is revelatory of
the nature of international commercial networks that North Korea forged in
the past and could choose to rebuild in the future. The country appears to have
adjusted to the successful tightening of interdiction efforts aimed at its illicit
activities by expanding its legitimate trade, therefore reducing its vulnerability. It is unlikely that honing in on illicit trade, despite the merits of doing so,
will have significant material effect on the regime's behavior or its capacity to
generate foreign exchange. Yet the continued interdiction noted in Table 3.1
suggests that North Korea is still engaged in illicit trade and certainly in activities designed to circumvent sanctions.

Services Exports, Aid, and Foreign Direct Investment

Unobserved merchandise exports do not exhaust North Korea's current account transactions. The country has also diversified into a variety of services
activities, including the tightly supervised export of contract workers and a
limited amount of tourism. In addition, it has become an aid-seeking state,

and transfers to it have become one of the more significant points of controversy surrounding engagement with the regime, as we show in more detail in
Chapter 4.

North Korea also conducts cross-border financial transactions, although
of fairly limited magnitude. Given the country's virtually complete isolation
from international financial markets, much of the capital inflow likely takes the
form of foreign direct investment. For the most part confined to a few small
enclaves, particularly the export-processing zones and mining projects, the
scope of this investment has grown dramatically in recent years, with China
playing the dominant role.

Remittances, Labor Exports, and Services Transactions:
New Forms of Commercialization

Revenues generated by North Koreans abroad come primarily through channels of remittances and the organized export of labor.[37] These are distinct both
in balance-of-payments accounting terms and in their very different political
economies. We also consider the checkered history of North Korean tourism.

Private voluntary remittances generated by the North Korean diaspora are
similar to remittance flows in many other countries. Their magnitude, particularly from the Korean community in Japan, was once the subject of substantial controversy (Eberstadt 1996; Lind 1997; Noland 2000, 130–133; Hughes
2005). As with illicit activities, however, a string of events combined to reduce
Japanese remittances quite dramatically by 2004–2006. These included the
gradual shift to a virtual embargo on the country described previously.[38]

Japan is not the only source of remittances, however. North Koreans in
China, estimated to be as few as twenty thousand and as many as four hundred
thousand (the South Korean government estimates one hundred thousand)
send money back to North Korea (Chang, Haggard, and Noland 2006). The
amounts transferred are probably small and may well be declining as increased
policing discourages cross-border transit. There is also a Korean-Chinese
community in the Chinese border provinces that provides some support to
extended family members on the North Korean side of the border. This non-
refugee channel is probably more important in financial terms.

South Korea is another source. A 2010 survey conducted by the Organization
for One Korea, which supports North Korean defectors in the South, found
that nearly 80 percent of those surveyed had sent money to relatives in the
North, with average remittances ranging between 1.5 and 2 million won a year
($1,350–1,800).[39] Another press report cited an unnamed South Korean govern-
ment official claiming that remittances had reached $10 million a year, but this

amount must be discounted by commissions of up to 30 percent that end up in the hands of Chinese brokers.[40] The share going to the state, whether through official taxes, predation, or both, is almost certainly higher—as few as one out of every two won sent may reach its intended recipient.[41] Still, from a balance-of-payments perspective, all such remittances should be counted as income.

North Korea operates a variety of organized labor export programs. In contrast to remittances, where at least some share of the revenue goes to recipients chosen by the sender, the North Korean state receives the overwhelming share of the revenue from labor exports.[42] Recent estimates, although they extend beyond the time frame of our analysis, have been in the range of 50,000 to 81,000 workers (Shin 2014; Weissman 2014; Lee 2015), but even this range may be too low. In 2013, before the purge of Jang Song-thaek, China and North Korea were expanding legal work visas, with some reports putting the number as high as 120,000.[43] As with illicit activities, estimates of the value of these workers have frequently been exaggerated, even wildly so.[44] If one assumes that these workers cannot earn more than the average income in the host countries, the estimated revenues are in the hundreds of millions of dollars and certainly less than a half billion.

A brief word should be said about tourism because it figures quite prominently in the politics of North-South relations. The Mt. Kumgang tourist project had its origins in two agreements—one in October 1998 and one in August 2000 immediately following the summit of that year—between the Hyundai Group and the North Korean government. These agreements called for Hyundai to make $942 million in payments to North Korea over seventy-five months for exclusive rights to develop the Mt. Kumgang area and seven other projects, including the industrial park that eventually became the Kaesong Industrial Complex. At its peak, the Mt. Kumgang project provided North Korea with $72 million annually in rent plus an additional fee per visitor that ran $9–14 million a year.[45] These fees had fallen even prior to the July 2008 killing of a tourist by North Korean guards, which essentially shut down earnings from the project altogether.[46]

In addition to large-scale projects aimed at South Korean tourists, the Kim Jong-il and Kim Jong-un eras saw an effort to expand tourism from other sources. One of the country's many foreign tour operators estimates that about 2,000 Western tourists visit every year, but notes that as many as twenty thousand to thirty thousand may visit from China and the Japanese-Korean community.[47] An industry source privately indicated to us that revenues from Western tourists are approximately $250 per day but those from Chinese tourists are likely considerably lower.

Aid

North Korea first opened itself to humanitarian assistance from outside its network of communist allies during the famine of the mid-1990s. Aid seeking subsequently became a significant aspect of the country's foreign economic relations and, indeed, of its grand strategy as well. The nuclear negotiations that followed the onset of the second nuclear crisis in 2002.—just like those surrounding the resolution of the first crisis in 1994[48]—revolved in no small measure around the economic inducements the international community was willing to make in return for concessions on the nuclear issue.

As we already suggested, much of this aid was supplied by South Korea and China, sometimes in rather opaque ways, and was generally outside of organized multilateral efforts. For the rest of the world, however, the overwhelming majority of aid, reported in Table 3.2, has been in the form of in-kind transfers of food and other humanitarian items. Aid cannot be used to finance the trade deficit directly, but money is ultimately fungible. As we have documented elsewhere (Haggard and Noland 2007a) commercial imports of food

TABLE 3.2

Total humanitarian assistance by donor organization (US$ millions),
2000–2014

Year	Inside appeal Multilateral (through UN)	Outside appeal Bilateral	UN agencies	NGOs (including Red Cross)	Total
2000	153.1	58.6	0.1	12.5	224.2
2001	248.0	61.4	0.8	67.4	377.6
2002	220.0	79.2	3.0	58.6	360.8
2003	133.1	5.5	1.6	42.6	182.9
2004	151.5	123.6	2.2	24.5	301.8
2005	—	43.5	0.2	2.5	46.2
2006	—	39.6	0.0	0.4	40.0
2007	13.1	60.2	8.5	21.3	103.1
2008	—	53.3	3.4	—	56.7
2009	—	42.3	19.0	—	61.3
2010	—	11.1	13.4	—	24.5
2011	73.0	14.1	—	2.1	89.2
2012	103.9	11.7	1.3	0.9	117.8
2013	51.6	11.2	—	—	62.8
2014	23.0	7.3	—	—	30.3

SOURCE: UN-OCHA Financial Tracking Service, WFP (2006b).

dropped as aid increased following the famine. In this way, the government was able to conserve foreign exchange previously spent on food. Despite claims that humanitarian aid should not be linked to politics, however, it has clearly fallen since the onset of the nuclear crisis in 2003 and become much more erratic. We explore this issue with respect to food aid in Chapter 4.

Foreign Direct Investment

North Korea has been effectively excluded from international capital markets since defaulting on bank loans in the late 1970s; it was the only communist country to do so. Its ability to borrow internationally is limited to a relatively low volume of short-term trade credits and transactions through informal credit markets along the border with China. The major sources of capital inflow appear to be previously outlined aid and other official transfers. However, when we account for these sources of income to the extent possible, it is clear that for many years a significant funding gap has remained. We infer that inflows of foreign direct investment (FDI) have almost certainly become more important in the overall balance-of-payments picture.

The quality of data on FDI flows into and out of North Korea is quite poor. The standard source is UNCTAD's annual *World Investment Report* (Figure 3.14). These data probably miss some investment via China and Orascom's

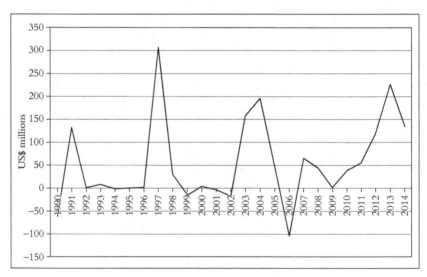

FIGURE 3.14   Foreign direct investment in North Korea (flows, US$ millions), 1990—2014

SOURCE: UN Conference on Trade and Development statistics.

investment described above, and should therefore probably be considered as defining a floor on actual inflows.

The data broadly confirm our review of North Korea's policy toward foreign investment in Chapter 2. Investment under Kim Jong-il before the nuclear crisis was highly erratic. In most years, it was effectively zero or even negative as frustrated investors disinvested and withdrew. After the onset of the nuclear crisis, investment was erratic as well, before starting to trend up in the late 2000s. Chinese official sources that we have analyzed in more detail elsewhere also show an increase in FDI after the nuclear tests of 2009, much of it going into the mining sector.[49]

Outside of mining and some other extractive sectors, South Korea, and increasingly China, appear to be creating enclaves where the more effective business-enabling institutions of one or the other are substituted for North Korea's weak institutional framework. Kaesong and Rason are the main examples, although the former was provisionally closed in 2016.

If, as we suspect, the UNCTAD yearly reports underestimate actual inflows into North Korea, and if outflows are modest, we have underestimated the credit side of the current account balance. The implications of this underestimation, taken up in the next section, are that North Korea has been running a larger-than-estimated current account surplus and/or has been running a surplus in additional years. It also means that the "errors and omissions" residual may be larger than estimated, implying an even bigger "missing spending" result than we have calculated.

Adding It All Up: North Korea's Balance of Payments Under Kim Jong-il

Previous sections considered the components of the balance of payments in isolation. But these estimates are not constrained by the underlying identity in balance-of-payments accounting: the current account deficit (or surplus) is the counterpart of a capital account surplus (or deficit). Deficits must be financed and surpluses are matched by corresponding capital outflows. In this section, we report on our efforts to "add it all up": to put these estimates together and meet the crucial accounting condition that the capital account and the current account should, in theory at least, perfectly offset each other.[50]

Figure 3.15 shows data on total current account credits and debits inclusive of unconventional sources of revenue. We report three series on each side of the ledger. The first is our baseline, or "best guess," which includes observed trade, transfers, and service flows, as well our judgments about the likely magnitude of nonreported trade, including missiles and illicit transactions (for a full

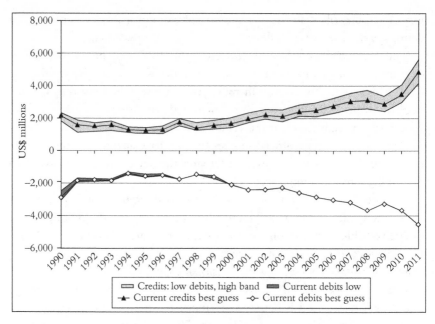

FIGURE 3.15   Total current account credits and debits, 1990–2011

SOURCE: Authors' calculations.

discussion of sources and the basis of our estimates, see Haggard and Noland 2007b). We also provide both high and low estimates, which we generate by applying the extreme estimates in the literature that we have reviewed.

Our estimate of North Korean credits on the current account, which includes exports, broadly follows the pattern visible in the official data reported in Figure 3.1, which is based on mirror statistics. Trade collapsed in the early 1990s, bottomed out in 1998, and began to revive thereafter. Uncertainty about the magnitude of these revenues increases in light of the famine because, in our view, nonconventional activities intensified in the mid- to late 1990s. Nonetheless, our estimates begin to diverge more sharply from the high estimates during that period because of our belief that illicit activities faced increasing constraints. Our best guess for 2011 current account credits, $4.8 billion, is roughly midway between our low estimate, $4.2 billion, and our high estimate, $5.6 billion. The uncertainty surrounding debits on the current account, which mostly comprises imports, is considerably narrower in part because there is no precise equivalent of illicit imports (although North Korea may want to conceal some weapons-related imports, and exports across the Chinese border may not be perfectly captured by Chinese customs). Overall debits rose to $4.5 billion in 2011.

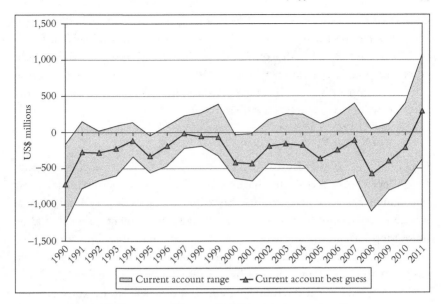

FIGURE 3.16   North Korean current account balance, 1990–2011

SOURCE: Authors' calculations.

Figure 3.16 combines the estimates of the current account balance derived from our analysis of exports, imports, income, and current transfers. In a moment we will return to the statistical discrepancy. The extreme bounds of the current account balance are calculated by combining the maximum (minimum) estimate of credits to the current account and services with the minimum (maximum) estimate of debits to the current account.

Uncertainty about the size of the current account deficit has increased in the last decade because of increased uncertainty, as just noted, about export revenues. Nonetheless, our best guess is that North Korea ran a current account deficit until 2011, with the cumulative deficit summing to $5.3 billion, before shifting to a modest surplus.[51] If FDI inflows have been underestimated, it may be that a surplus emerged in earlier years.

This analysis helps explain the apparent ability of North Korea to finance its current account deficits during this period. Following the onset of the second nuclear crisis in 2002, the current account deficit narrowed somewhat. However, it remained substantially larger than it was in the mid-1990s and even widened in 2008, before the 2009 provocations. The implied increase in the availability of external financing initially came in part from North Korea's transactions with what we have called "the rest of the world": the countries outside of the Six Party Talks. However, as we saw in Figure 3.8 these deficits contracted over time, reflecting a declining capacity to borrow as the nuclear crisis drove trade finance away. Rather, North Korea was initially sustained by bilateral aid from South Korea until the inauguration of Lee Myung-bak. After that point, we suspect, Chinese FDI and new activities we take up in our overall conclusions in Chapter 8 played an increasing role in financing the North Korean current account deficit.

Conclusion: Into the Kim Jong-un Era

Our review of North Korea's foreign economic relations during the Kim Jong-il era clearly reveals the dynamic nature of economic diplomacy: how the country has adapted to external shocks, including multilateral and bilateral sanctions, by seeking out new sources of trade, investment, and aid, and by innovating activities when old sources of revenue, including illicit ones, were sanctioned. These dynamics, as well as the design of the sanctions regime, help explain why multilateral sanctions have had such a marginal effect.

The first, and by far the most substantial, shock that North Korea faced in the post–Cold War period was the collapse of the Soviet Union. Since that time, despite good intentions, Russia has never played a significant economic role with respect to North Korea, hobbled as it has been by lack of complementarities and its own financial distress.

Even before the missile and nuclear tests of 2006, Japan had drifted toward a de facto sanctions policy, with both trade and remittances falling sharply (Hughes 2006). These trends became even more pronounced in the second half of 2006, and particularly following the 2009 missile and nuclear tests as Japan opted for a near complete embargo.

North Korean diplomacy expended great effort in establishing diplomatic, trade and investment relations with Europe and emerging markets in the developing world in the mid-1990s and later, achieving some success. But these relations stalled in the early 2000s even before the onset of the crisis in October 2002, and they stagnated thereafter. The European Union in particular strongly backed sanctions against North Korea in the wake of the 2006 missile and nuclear tests. The rounds of tests in 2009, 2013, and 2016 have simply reinforced these trends.

The United States' trade and investment ties with North Korea were always minimal. The United States was a large aid donor in the aftermath of the famine, but its humanitarian assistance trended down after 2002. The capacity of the United States to impose sanctions thus appears limited, although its actions against Banco Delta Asia (BDA) in September 2005 might have deterred trade and investment from third countries and complicated North Korea's external financial transactions.

However, US actions were offset by developments with respect to South Korea and China, leading us to ask if these props will continue to sustain the Kim Jong-un regime going forward. The more volatile of the two trading partners has been South Korea. At one time accounting for nearly 40 percent of North Korea's trade at the end of the Roh Moo-hyun era, inter-Korean trade has proven vulnerable to the North's lack of reciprocity, changing political dynamics in the South, and a succession of North Korean provocations.

The Park Geun-hye government came into office in 2013 showing a willingness to engage. But by 2016, its initiatives had been rebuffed, post-*Cheonan* sanctions were still in force, and Kaesong, the surviving symbol of North-South détente, had been closed altogether following the fourth nuclear test in 2016. Even under the most auspicious circumstances, it is unlikely that South Korea will be a significant source of trade, investment, and aid for North Korea in the absence of a fundamental turn in its grand strategy, and it is certainly unlikely to return to the open-ended engagement of the Roh Moo-hyun years.

This state of affairs has left North Korea more dependent on China than ever, and the regime's vulnerability is not simply political. The slowdown in China and the weakening of global commodities prices are beginning to weigh on merchandise exports (Hendrix and Noland 2014).[52] Nonetheless, political calculations in Beijing will determine whether the coordination problems we have highlighted persist. In the immediate aftermath of Kim Jong-il's death, China moved with alacrity to support the succession of Kim Jong-un (Cathcart and Madden 2012). As we detail in Chapter 7, its patience waned in the wake of the February 2013 nuclear test, when it supported further restrictions on North Korea in UNSCR 2094. As we discuss in our conclusions in Chapter 8, new sanctions imposed in the wake of nuclear and missile tests in January and February 2016 had the potential, if fully exploited, to force the North Korean regime to make fundamental political choices. Yet there were also countervailing signs of Chinese reticence to fully exploit its leverage as well as increasing evidence that North Korean state trading companies had developed ties with powerful Chinese brokers that have limited the effects of Chinese sanctions (Park and Walsh 2016; Center for Advanced Defense Analysis 2016).

Although focused primarily on outlining the economic terrain that has generated coordination problems among the five parties—North Korea, South Korea, Japan, China, and Russia—the findings of this chapter have important implications for arguments about the transformative effects of engagement.

Even under the conservative governments of Lee Myung-bak and Park Geun-hye, South Korea's economic ties to North Korea continued their relatively high level of state involvement, either directly (in the relatively high share of aid and financial transfers in total bilateral transactions) or indirectly (through subsidies to, or guarantees on, nominally commercial transactions). As trade dwindled to the export-processing zone in Kaesong, it became harder and harder to claim that the zone could become the locus of a wider economic and social, let alone political, transformation.

China's economic relations with North Korea, in contrast, are growing increasingly commercial. Even large projects involving complementary infra-structure investments by larger Chinese firms do not appear to be subsidized by Beijing and are thus carried out with an eye to profitability. As we argue in Chapter 8, it is at least possible that such ties may, if sustained, gradually pull North Korea into a more reformist course.

We noted previously that the composition of North Korea's trade also speaks directly to arguments about transformation. First, we looked at the long history of illicit and weapons-related trade—hardly a form of engagement with the world economy likely to generate transformation. As the regime's il-licit activities waned, there was a shift toward extractive exports, which remain largely under state control. As we show in Chapter 5, the failure to develop formal business-enabling institutions, or even robust second-best informal institutions, mitigates against more complex forms of exchange. It similarly has mitigated, at least to date, against the emergence of groups in North Ko-rea whose interest in maintaining external economic ties would temper the regime's bellicosity; on the contrary, North Korean firms are tasked with evad-ing sanctions precisely to finance the regime's nuclear ambitions. The so-called *byungjin* line discussed in Chapter 2 reflects the apparent belief that economic development and maintenance of the country's nuclear capacity can go hand in hand, calling into question the effectiveness of both sanctions and engagement.

Appendix

Data on bilateral trade between China and North Korea illustrates an upward trend during the nuclear standoff starting in 2002, albeit with strong seasonality. Trade volumes dropped off in the winter probably because of economic activity slowdowns and/or the impassibil-ity of unpaved roads on the North Korean side of the border. However, simple statistical models can be used to detect the impact of sanctions and the more general increase in politi-cal risk that might not be apparent. In this appendix, we report the results of such models of monthly exports and imports from January 2000 to February 2012, the end of the Kim Jong-il era, incorporating only a time trend, seasonal dummies, and dummy variables for sanctions resolution periods (Table A.1).

There are positive time trends in all of the regressions and some evidence of the seasonality noted previously, with the monthly data appearing to show a significant decline in activity in the winter months. Given the simplicity of these models, we must approach them with caution[53]; even so, the regressions provide no evidence that either the 2006 or 2009 sanctions had a depressing effect on trade. Regressions A1.4 and A1.6 show no effect of the 2006 sanctions on Chinese imports from North Korea. On the contrary, with the exception of model A1.4, which includes a dummy only for the 2006 sanctions, they actually show an *increase* in trade following the imposition of sanctions, with the technical reservation just noted.[54]

Because of data limitations, the regressions on monthly trade data are very spare, including only a time trend, controls for seasonality, and sanctions dummies. A more complete characterization would take the level of economic activity and price effects into account. Doing this for North Korean exports poses some serious analytic and data constraints,[55] but North Korea can be considered a "small country" with respect to its imports, which are so small relative to the exports of either of its principal partners (less than 0.25 percent of total exports in both cases) that they represent a "price taker" facing a perfectly elastic supply of exports and a parametrically given price. This justifies single-equation reduced-form estimation.[56] Moreover, the fact that the UN sanctions were largely on exports to North Korea, not imports from it, provides further justification for focusing on this side of the trade equation.

Table A.2 reports regressions incorporating these two additional variables, estimated on a quarterly basis because some of the data were only at that frequency. The North Korean economic activity term is derived by quarterly interpolations of Bank of Korea annual GDP growth estimates.[57] Getting at prices is more complicated. For North Korea, the relative price of imports is a function of foreign prices converted to North Korean won via an exchange rate, $P*E/P$. The problem is that we cannot observe P, North Korean prices, directly; we can observe only E, the exchange rate. We use the log inverse black-market exchange rate in the hope that exchange rate movements dominate relative price changes. We expect appreciation to be associated with a larger volume of imports and depreciation to be the reverse.

Even with this more realistic specification, sanctions do not depress Chinese exports to North Korea; instead, we again obtain the perverse result (in regressions A2.1 and A2.3) that the 2006 sanctions appear to have increased trade! At best, the imposition of sanctions did not increase the risk premium to the extent that it led to a broader decline in trade, and by implication this attempt at "smart sanctions" did not appear to have broader spillover effects that might have harmed the general population.

The estimated income elasticities are extremely large, with changes in economic activity having large effects on imports. There are two possible interpretations, both with implications for sanction strategies. The first is that the behavior of North Korean households and importing firms was changing during the sample period and that exposure to new products from China in effect shifted demand away from domestic production toward imports. A second, related possibility is that the development of new institutional channels of trade greatly reduced transaction costs; these channels are captured in the activity term. In either case, however, the regressions support what is obvious from the descriptive statistics: during the sanctions period, North Korea's economic integration with China has deepened significantly.

As a kind of robustness check on the findings in Table A.2, we conducted the same exercise using data on North-South trade. As can be seen in Figure A.2, trade was trending up prior to the sanctions, although the inter-Korean data show somewhat more volatility related to security and political developments on the peninsula. The impact of UN sanctions is not obvious, but there appears to be a trend break associated with unilateral sanctions measures following the 2010 sinking of the *Cheonan* which is confirmed by econometric estimates.

Figure A.2's simple visual interpretation is confirmed by the regressions on quarterly data 2001:1–2011:4 reported in Table A.3. In addition to showing income and price effects, the results are consistent with our observation of a more politicized North-South relationship.[58] Both the 2009 multilateral sanctions and the 2010 unilateral sanctions had a depressing effect on trade. These coefficients may be capturing the wider effects of Lee Myung-bak's new approach to the North, but that interpretation is not mutually inconsistent. The fact that we do see sanctions having a dampening effect in this case gives us greater confidence in the models' ability to detect such effects if they exist in the Chinese data. This should increase confidence in the nonfindings with respect to the effects of sanctions on North Korea's bilateral trade with China.

Data and Data Sources

Sample periods:	ROK	2001 Q1–2011 Q4
		2001 Jan–2012 Feb
	PRC	2000 Q1–2011 Q4
		2000 Jan–2012 Feb
Trade:	ROK	Ministry of Unification, Korea Investment Trade Agency (KITA)
	PRC	Ministry of Commerce of the People's Republic of China
		International Monetary Fund (IMF), *Direction of Trade Statistics* (*DOTS*)
Income:	DPRK	Bank of Korea Economic Statistics System (ECOS)
Exchange rate:		*Good Friends*, "North Korea Today" (various issues); *NK Net, NK In & Out* (various issues); *DailyNK* (various issues); *Open Radio for North Korea* (various editions); Institute for Far Eastern Studies–Kyungnam University, *NK Brief* (various issues); IMF, *International Financial Statistics* (*IFS*)
Nuclear Sanctions:		UN Resolution 1718, October 14, 2006, http://www.un.org/News/Press/docs/2006/sc8853.doc.htm
		UN Resolution 1874, issued June 12, 2009, http://www.un.org/News/Press/docs/2009/sc9679.doc.htm,
		South Korea Unilateral Sanctions, issued May 24, 2010, http://www.cfr.org/north-korea/south-korean-president-lees-national-address-may-2010/p22199

Data Preparation

Trade data: Trade with North Korea is recorded from the perspective of North Korea's trading partners, in this case either China or South Korea. The data were originally recorded in monthly increments and were summed over quarters to yield quarterly numbers. The natural log of these quarterly totals was used as the dependent variable in the trade equations.

TABLE A.I

China-North Korea monthly trade (time trend, seasonal dummy, and nuclear sanctions variables included)

	Log Chinese exports to North Korea			Log Chinese imports from North Korea		
	(1)	(2)	(3)	(4)	(5)	(6)
Nuclear sanction (2006) (Dummy variable)	0.613*** (0.078)		0.450*** (0.079)	0.153 (0.115)		-0.046 (0.120)
Nuclear sanction (2009) (Dummy variable)		0.579*** (0.080)	0.389*** (0.080)		0.455*** (0.109)	0.475*** (0.121)
Logged time trend	0.382*** (0.042)	0.481*** (0.036)	0.357*** (0.039)	1.032*** (0.062)	0.988*** (0.049)	1.001*** (0.060)
Month 1	-0.292** (0.141)	-0.223 (0.144)	-0.285** (0.130)	-0.523** (0.207)	-0.520*** (0.195)	-0.514*** (0.196)
Month 2	-0.638*** (0.140)	-0.576*** (0.144)	-0.629*** (0.129)	-0.634*** (0.207)	-0.628*** (0.195)	-0.623*** (0.196)
Month 3	-0.090 (0.143)	-0.015 (0.146)	-0.064 (0.132)	-0.360* (0.210)	-0.334* (0.199)	-0.329 (0.200)
Month 4	-0.019 (0.143)	0.052 (0.146)	0.008 (0.132)	-0.210 (0.210)	-0.182 (0.198)	-0.177 (0.199)
Month 5	-0.009 (0.143)	0.057 (0.146)	0.018 (0.132)	-0.374* (0.210)	-0.344* (0.198)	-0.340* (0.199)
Month 6	-0.019 (0.142)	0.044 (0.146)	0.009 (0.131)	-0.204 (0.210)	-0.172 (0.198)	-0.168 (0.199)
Month 7	-0.024 (0.142)	-0.011 (0.146)	-0.027 (0.131)	-0.162 (0.210)	-0.167 (0.198)	-0.165 (0.199)
Month 8	-0.073 (0.145)	-0.072 (0.149)	-0.074 (0.134)	-0.052 (0.214)	-0.053 (0.202)	-0.053 (0.203)

(continued)

TABLE A.1 (*continued*)

Log Chinese exports to North Korea	(1)	(2)	(3)
Month 10	-0.070	-0.065	-0.071
	(0.142)	(0.146)	(0.131)
Month 11	-0.053	0.000	-0.040
	(0.142)	(0.146)	(0.131)
Month 12	0.195	0.246*	0.209
	(0.142)	(0.146)	(0.131)
Constant	9.679***	9.377***	9.754***
	(0.189)	(0.180)	(0.175)
N	144	144	144
R-squared	0.797	0.786	0.828
F	39.17	36.63	44.50
p	0.000	0.000	0.000
Durbin–Watson d-statistic	1.166	1.114	1.392
Durbin's alternative test for autocorrelation, Prob > chi2	0.000	0.000	0.001
Breusch-Godfrey LM test for autocorrelation, Prob > chi2	0.000	0.000	0.001

Log Chinese imports from North Korea	(4)	(5)	(6)
Month 10	-0.103	-0.104	-0.104
	(0.209)	(0.198)	(0.199)
Month 11	-0.115	-0.103	-0.099
	(0.210)	(0.198)	(0.199)
Month 12	0.001	0.014	0.018
	(0.210)	(0.198)	(0.199)
Constant	6.496***	6.626***	6.587***
	(0.278)	(0.244)	(0.265)
N	144	144	144
R-squared	0.827	0.846	0.846
F	47.95	54.84	50.60
p	0.000	0.000	0.000
Durbin–Watson d-statistic	0.505	0.568	0.570
Durbin's alternative test for autocorrelation, Prob > chi2	0.000	0.000	0.000
Breusch-Godfrey LM test for autocorrelation, Prob > chi2	0.000	0.000	0.000

NOTE: Standard errors in parentheses; Month 9 was omitted.

*** $p < 0.01$, ** $p < 0.05$, * $p < 0.1$.

TABLE A.2

Determinants of China-North Korea trade (GNI, exchange rate, seasonal dummy, and nuclear sanctions variables included)

Log Chinese exports to North Korea	(1)	(2)	(3)
Nuclear Sanction (2006)	0.229**		0.237**
(dummy variable)	(0.097)		(0.097)
Nuclear Sanction (2009)		−0.113	−0.136
(dummy variable)		(0.129)	(0.122)
Log NK GNI Index	3.275***	3.973***	3.173***
	(0.597)	(0.535)	(0.602)
Log Inverse Exchange Rate Index (export price proxy)	−0.006	−0.013	−0.031
	(0.035)	(0.043)	(0.041)
Quarter 1	−0.504***	−0.531***	−0.508***
	(0.081)	(0.085)	(0.081)
Quarter 2	−0.135	−0.161*	−0.140*
	(0.081)	(0.085)	(0.081)
Quarter 3	−0.123	−0.141	−0.119
	(0.081)	(0.085)	(0.080)
Constant	−3.390	−6.699***	−3.047
	(2.657)	(2.339)	(2.666)
N	48	48	48
R-squared	0.927	0.919	0.930
F	87.25	77.57	75.43
p	0.000	0.000	0.000
Durbin-Watson d-statistic	1.262	1.125	1.360
Durbin's alternative test for autocorrelation, Prob > chi2	0.0172	0.0026	0.0444
Breusch-Godfrey LM test for autocorrelation, Prob > chi2	0.0146	0.0029	0.0337

NOTE: Standard errors in parentheses; Quarter 4 was omitted.
*** $p < 0.01$, ** $p < 0.05$, * $p < 0.1$.

Income data: Annual observations from the Bank of Korea on North Korea's real GDP were interpolated to generate quarterly data. Following normal procedures, once quarterly real GDP was calculated, an index was created in which the first observation was set equal to 100 and the natural log was used in the trade equations.

Exchange rate data: Exchange rate data came from various sources and were originally priced in either US dollars (US$) or renminbi (RMB). We found in the past that implied US$–RMB exchange rates, in terms of relative won prices, tended to be very close to actual dollar–RMB rates. We were therefore willing to use the NK won–US$ exchange rate data to determine both RMB (where NK won–RMB data were not available) and NK won–SK won exchange rates. The NK won was always in the numerator for our samples, and the exchange rate was indexed to 100 for the first observation of each sample. For use as an

TABLE A.3

Determinants of South Korea–North Korea trade (GNI, exchange rate, seasonal dummy, and nuclear sanctions variables included)

Log South Korean exports to North Korea	(1)	(2)	(3)	(4)
Nuclear sanction (2006)	0.186			0.130
(Dummy variable)	(0.227)			(0.190)
Nuclear sanction (2009)		−0.623**		−0.384
(Dummy variable)		(0.244)		(0.231)
South Korea unilateral sanctions (2010)			−1.064***	−0.899***
(Dummy variable)			(0.272)	(0.283)
Log North Korea GNI index	1.616	2.740**	1.154	0.993
	(1.538)	(1.113)	(1.059)	(1.328)
Log inverse exchange rate index (export price proxy)	−0.035	−0.093	−0.223**	−0.252***
	(0.081)	(0.078)	(0.084)	(0.085)
Quarter 1	−0.420**	−0.479***	−0.485***	−0.486***
	(0.185)	(0.171)	(0.156)	(0.156)
Quarter 2	0.041	−0.020	−0.032	−0.034
	(0.185)	(0.171)	(0.156)	(0.155)
Quarter 3	0.118	0.108	0.124	0.140
	(0.184)	(0.170)	(0.155)	(0.154)
Constant	3.693	−1.983	4.792	5.362
	(6.906)	(4.964)	(4.633)	(5.946)
N	44	44	44	44
R-squared	0.547	0.608	0.674	0.701
F	7.45	9.57	12.75	10.28
p	0.000	0.000	0.000	0.000
Durbin-Watson d-statistic	1.119	1.356	1.674	1.897
Durbin's alternative test for autocorrelation, Prob > chi2	0.0037	0.0399	0.3100	0.7671
Breusch-Godfrey LM test for autocorrelation, Prob > chi2	0.0038	0.0316	0.2685	0.7365

NOTE: Standard errors in parentheses; Quarter 4 omitted.

*** $p < 0.01$, ** $p < 0.05$, * $p < 0.1$.

explanatory variable, in the absence of a relative price term, we took the natural log of this index used in the trade equation.

Nuclear sanctions: UN Resolution 1718 (2006) went into effect in October 2006. This dummy variable was equal to zero from the beginning of the sample through the third quarter of 2006 and equal to one from the fourth quarter of 2006 through the end of the sample period. The monthly data set sets the binary equal following October 2006. UNSC

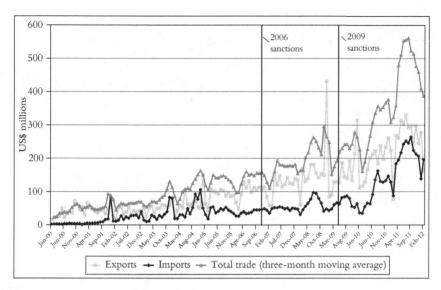

FIGURE A.1   China–North Korea trade, 2000–2012

SOURCE: PRC Ministry of Commerce data; and IMF Direction of Trade statistics.

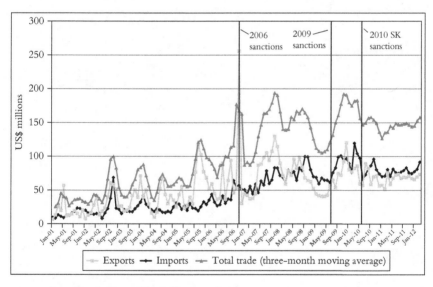

FIGURE A.2   South Korea–North Korea trade, 2001–2012

SOURCE: Korea International Trade Administration data.

Resolution 1874 went into effect in June 2009. This dummy variable was equal to zero from the beginning of the sample through the second quarter of 2009 and equal to one from the third quarter of 2009 through the end of the sample. The monthly data set sets the binary variable equal to one following June 2009. The South Korean unilateral sanctions were announced in late May 2010. This dummy variable was equal to zero from the beginning of the sample through the second quarter of 2010 and equal to one from the third quarter of 2010 through the end of the sample period.

4

Humanitarian Dilemmas
The Political Economy of Food

We saw in the last chapter that, despite the onset of the nuclear crisis, the North Korean government was able to tap external resources that equaled or exceeded those available to the country at any time since the famine; indeed, trade, particularly with China, grew apace. Regardless of this de facto economic opening, however, the regime was unable to avoid recurrent food shortages during the nuclear crisis period. These shortages created significant policy and moral dilemmas for donor governments and NGOs. As we outlined in our introduction in Chapter 1, the use of sanctions raises well-known humanitarian concerns. Experience in the 1990s in Haiti, in the former Yugoslavia, and in Iraq demonstrated these risks and target governments' use of sanctions and alleged humanitarian aid to effect their own diplomatic or propaganda ends.[1]

Yet assistance raises its own policy dilemmas, including the potential to undercut the effect of sanctions. When used as a tool of diplomacy, inducements resting on humanitarian assistance also raise their own moral hazard problems. Does assistance simply encourage bad behavior, reward the regime, or even contribute to its longevity? And if it does, is such aid vulnerable to political backlashes? Reluctance to extend aid of any type to an adversary, particularly an isolated one, runs the risk of underestimating the humanitarian fallout from failing to act.

The North Korean case illustrates these dilemmas in spades. The international community responded relatively generously to the famine, and for a number of years after North Korea managed to maintain substantial levels of assistance. In a near-classic example of the coordination problems outlined in Chapter 1, donor disenchantment was offset by North Korea's successful aid seeking from others, particularly South Korea during the Kim Dae-jung (1998–2003) and Roh Moo-hyun (2003–2008) years and possibly from China thereafter.

North Korea's foreign policy behavior ultimately had negative effects on both the level and volatility of aid flows and, as a result, on human welfare in the country. The reasons were related to moral hazard problems. From the very beginning of the aid effort in the mid-1990s, North Korean authorities made it clear that they were unwilling to acquiesce to standard norms governing humanitarian assistance: donor access to target populations; transparency of aid operations; nondiscrimination in distribution; and a focus on the most vulnerable groups (Flake and Snyder 2003; Smith 2005; Haggard and Noland 2007a). Unaccountable to its population, the regime was slow to acknowledge need and each program required extensive, and frustrating, negotiation over terms of access that were ultimately under the authority of the Ministry of Foreign Affairs. Because they guaranteed the integrity of the aid program and limited diversion, monitoring and assessment arrangements played a central role in these negotiations; thus, they were crucial to maintaining political support for assistance. Rather than treating these arrangements as a common interest between donor and recipient, North Korea modulated the level of transparency to the aid effort, compounding informational problems for outsiders and eroding trust in the integrity of programs.

It appears that the country's foreign policy behavior mattered to donor support as well. North Korea's self-imposed isolation during the first nuclear crisis of 1993–1994 was a contributing factor to the "arduous march" of the famine years (Natsios 2001; Haggard and Noland 2007a). During the famine and its aftermath, as we saw in Chapter 3, the country began to diversify its foreign economic relations, including the pool of donors from which it could draw. However, the onset of the nuclear crisis, the missile and nuclear tests of 2006 and 2009, the military provocations of 2010, and the recurrence of tests in 2012–2013 repeatedly complicated the regime's ability to tap external sources of supply.

These political constraints on aid were most evident with respect to South Korea, which initiated a permanent reduction in aid following the election of Lee Myung-bak in 2007 that persisted into the Park Geun-hye era. However, the abrupt turn in South Korean aid policy was only the most extreme example of heightened attention to moral hazard problems paid by the major donors. To varying degrees, multilateral organizations, governments, and NGOs all faced increasing political criticism of assistance. In arguments that parallel quite precisely those for sanctions, some critics even argued that the pain inflicted on civilians by withholding needed assistance could be positive if it forced the regime to accommodate or generated protest from below (see, for example, Hill 2011). As a result, the ability of the North Korean government to substitute multilateral or other bilateral sources of aid for South Korean support diminished over time, undercutting the crucial safety net function of international humanitarian assistance and contributing to distress during the nuclear crisis period.

We consider these dilemmas in two steps. In the first section, we provide a brief overview of the food economy and the recurrence of shortages. In the second, we turn to the political economy of food aid, which oscillated sharply between periods when aid was extended on both political and humanitarian grounds and periods when it was held in abeyance. We consider both the political economy of multilateral assistance and the politics of food aid in the United States, South Korea, and China. In all cases, the regime's nuclear priorities and/or acute bargaining problems around the monitoring of assistance resulted in delays in reaching needed agreements, shortfalls in the delivery of assistance, and acute humanitarian distress.

The Perils of "Self-Reliance"

Given North Korea's high ratio of population to arable land and its inauspicious growing conditions, the pursuit of self-sufficiency in agriculture has always been fundamentally misguided. Weather-related shocks have played a recurrent role in its food problems, to be sure, most notably floods in 1995 and 1996 during the famine period and more recently bad floods in 2006, 2007, and 2012 and drought conditions in 2012 and 2014–2015. Rising world market prices were also a plausible contributing factor in the recurrent crises of the early 2000s, affecting both the ability to import on commercial terms and to access aid.

Still, weather is consistently adverse and volatile in North Korea, and therefore the rational strategy for the country is to *reduce* dependence on domestic sources of supply, not increase it. The ultimate solution to the country's chronic food problems lies not solely in reform of the agricultural sector but in reform, revitalization, and reorientation of the industrial economy as well. These reforms include opening to trade and foreign direct investment that would permit a more export-oriented growth strategy to enable the country to earn the foreign exchange needed to import bulk grains on a commercially sustainable basis and reduce the country's reliance on aid. Facing similar constraints, South Korea, Japan, and even China adopted this strategy as their economies took off.

Despite the de facto opening noted in Chapter 3, we begin with a brief overview of how this opening was inadequate to forestall chronic food problems. We review evidence derived from examinations of grain quantities/ prices and nutritional surveys; the latter are particularly important in showing sharp differences in North Koreans' access to food.

Grain Balances

The logic of a quantity balance is simple: the gap between domestic needs and production is the uncovered food balance that must be met through imports, which can come in the form of either commercial purchases or aid. The figures most commonly cited in public discussions are those produced by the Food and Agriculture Organization (FAO), but components on both the supply and demand sides of the balance sheet are subject to significant uncertainty,[2] with data on production prone to politicization. To generate external support for aid, the regime exaggerates shortfalls, which the FAO is under some diplomatic pressure to accept. Shortfalls in official harvest data may simply reflect weak infrastructure for storage and transport and postharvest losses, or they may reflect the fact that the state is having a harder time obtaining grain. The confiscatory measures we reported in Chapter 2 certainly buttress this interpretation.

In addition to factors influencing domestic supply, the extent of Chinese aid is uncertain. In Chapter 3, we suggested why we thought that aid might be exaggerated. Trends in prices do not appear to indicate subsidies, but the lack of transparency makes it difficult to know whether North Korea has access to Chinese grain on concessional or only on commercial terms. We return to this issue in more detail later.

The demand side is not much better. There is uncertainty about the size and demographic composition of the North Korean population and, per Smith (1998) about the validity of the FAO's estimate of the role of grains in its diet and the magnitude of grain diverted for use as livestock feed.

In response to these considerations, we present two grain balance series through the 2013–2014 harvest cycle (Figure 4.1). The first is the official FAO–World Food Program (WFP) figure. The second uses US government grain production estimates and adjusts the demand estimate for possible overestimation of the role of grains in the North Korean diet. The zero-balance

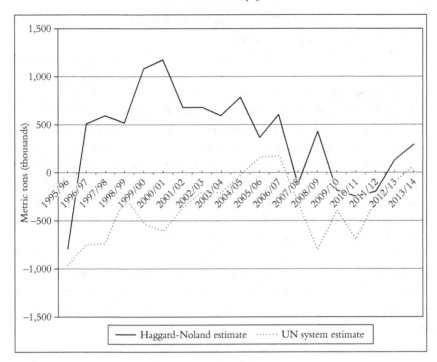

FIGURE 4.1   Minimum cereals requirement surplus/deficit, 1995/1996–2013/2014

SOURCE: Food and Agriculture Organization/World Food Program reports; US Department of Agriculture Foreign Agricultural Service *Production, Supply, and Distribution Online* database.

point is defined in terms of minimum human needs, although it should be recognized that total consumption at this highly compressed level would not avoid hunger and even starvation; food would have to be distributed with utmost precision across the entire population.[3]

United Nations figures imply that, after the 1995–1996 harvest cycle, North Korea was in a chronic food deficit. This is clearly implausible. No credible observer believes that North Korea was in continual famine over this entire period. According to our preferred estimate of grain needs, the peak of the mid-1990s famine is reflected in the very large uncovered deficit in the first two years of the series. The country achieved a surplus in the late 1990s as it pulled out of the famine, and through the period of reform available supply exceeded minimum grain requirements. After the onset of the nuclear crisis, the surplus narrowed and ultimately disappeared in the early 2010s. More recently, overall food balances have improved, perhaps reflecting some marginal effect of pilot reforms. However, a more expansive notion of consumption than minimum human needs would generate more dire results, and in 2014–2015 the balance probably worsened marginally once again, with FAO–WFP estimating a modest uncovered deficit of 107,000 tons.[4]

As Figure 4.1 demonstrates, North Korea is not comfortably self-sufficient in grain production. Imports, commercial and concessional, are therefore essential in meeting human needs on a sustained basis. Again, there are significant uncertainties, but it is possible to track most commercial imports and most aid, or at least the share passing through the WFP and South Korea. It is difficult, if not impossible, to decompose imports from China into commercial and aid components, but as we suggested in Chapter 3 the concessional component is probably limited. In this analysis, we use the figures found in the WFP's International Food Aid Information System (INTERFAIS). Figure 4.2 shows the aggregate amount of grain entering the country broken down into commercial import and aid components.

During the 1990s, North Korea was able to use aid as implicit balance-of-payments support, offsetting commercial imports.[5] As shown in Figure 4.2, commercial imports fell as aid flowed in. It is important to underscore that this development was not simply a matter of aggregate imports collapsing,

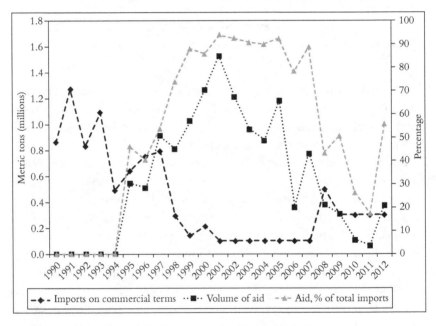

FIGURE 4.2   North Korean food imports and aid, 1990–2012

SOURCE: For imports, Food and Agriculture Organization/World Food Program reports; for aid, World Food Program INTERFAIS database.

given that starting in 1998 overall imports began to recover but food imports remained flat. Rather, this appeared to reflect the regime's strategy to cut commercial imports as aid rose despite ongoing shortages. It is particularly striking that this period of high dependence on aid and low commercial imports overlaps almost exactly with the Roh Moo-hyun administration, during which food and fertilizer aid underpinned efforts at political engagement.

Following the nuclear test of 2006, donors tired of provocations and the lack of commitment to reform. Aid declined, forcing a greater reliance on commercial imports during the second half of the 2000s and into the 2010s. Unfortunately, this increased reliance coincided with a period of rising global grain prices. In the context of a development strategy characterized by chronic balance-of-payments constraints (Chapter 3) and a regime with limited commitment to, or accountability for, basic human needs (Chapter 2), recurrent humanitarian problems were to be expected and in fact materialized.

Evidence from Prices

Just as the poorest members of society are most vulnerable when shortages appear, so too are the poorest countries most vulnerable when global markets are under stress. Beginning in 2005, world grain prices began rising, spiking in 2007–2008 and again in 2011 and 2012. A number of developments drove these outcomes,[6] but none are likely to be reversed, at least in the short run and North Korea will likely face continuing pressure on food availability emanating from the global market.

These price trends have had three disadvantageous effects:

- Rising prices have made it more difficult for North Korea to import grain on commercial terms, in part because of the proliferation of export controls put in place by major suppliers, including China.
- Adverse price trends have made it more difficult for multilateral and bilateral aid agencies to access grain and to meet their commitments.
- Price inflation has had a direct effect on North Korean households, which over time have become more dependent on markets for food because of ongoing problems in the public distribution system (PDS), the state-run rationing system on which roughly two-thirds of the population theoretically depends.

North Korean authorities do not provide information on market prices; on the contrary, they have acted to squelch the outflow of such information. Nonetheless, the growth of trade across the Chinese border, the operation of NGOs, and the spread of technologies such as illicit cell phones in the border areas have allowed outside researchers to assemble price data.[7] These data, fragmentary and imperfectly observed, indicate that in the years following the currency reform of November 2009, rice and corn prices rose at a rate well in excess of 100 percent annually until finally starting to moderate in 2013.

One explanation for these price movements is that North Korean markets are surprisingly integrated with trends in global market prices. As Figure 2.3 showed, rice prices are highly correlated with the black-market exchange rate. The co-movement of the black market exchange rate and grain prices is consistent with a small, open economy in which prices are roughly constant in hard currency terms but skyrocketing in terms of the rapidly depreciating domestic currency. This is an important finding, indicating that the North Korean market is increasingly integrated with the global market.[8]

Direct Observation

The North Korean government systematically impedes foreign observers' access, rendering any efforts to collect systematic data on conditions suspect. Nonetheless, we have access to assessments carried out by the WFP and/or UNICEF from 1998 to 2009 as well as a UNICEF Multiple Indicator Cluster Survey from 2012, all of which indicate ongoing distress.[9] Table 4.1 reports 2009 stunting and underweight numbers by province along with figures for 1997, 2002, and 2004 from earlier surveys. The change in global acute malnutrition between 2004 and 2009 is also reported.[10] The overall trends provide evidence of continuing distress in the second half of the 2000s. Countrywide rates for stunting (low height for age) declined by less than 7 percent between the 2002 and 2009 surveys. National rates for underweight (low weight for age) fell by just over 1 percent. Rather than declining, malnutrition was only leveling off at the time of the 2009 survey. Much of this can be attributed to lack of improvement in the Northeast, but Pyongyang itself was hardly spared: according to the UNICEF survey, 22 percent of children in the capital were stunted at the end of the period and 14 percent were under weight.

Unfortunately, conditions worsened after 2009, confirming the tightening of grain balances reported previously and, not coincidentally, overlapping with an intensification of conflict on the peninsula that further isolated the country. Despite an emergency operation launched by the WFP in April 2011, large swaths of the population experienced prolonged food deprivation from May through September 2011.[11] With the usual caveats about potential biases in surveys conducted in North Korea, the 2012 UNICEF exercise painted a dismal picture. Focusing on the height-for-age measure, a long-term indicator relatively unaffected by seasonal nutritional swings, nearly 10 percent of this

TABLE 4.1
Nutritional status by region (percentage)

	North Hamgyong	North Hwanghae	North Pyongan	Pyongyang	Ryanggang	South Hamgyong	South Hwanghae	South Pyongan	Overall
1997									
Stunting	n/a	47.5	n/a	n/a	n/a	35.9	26.0	53.1	38.2
Underweight	n/a	n/a	n/a	n/a	n/a	n/a	n/a	n/a	n/a
2002									
Stunting	42.8	39.4	42.4	27.0	46.7	45.5	38.6	42.2	39.2
Underweight	20.3	20.7	17.8	14.8	26.5	24.2	20.2	18.7	20.2
2004									
Stunting	40.0	41.0	41.2	25.9	45.6	46.7	36.7	29.7	37.0
Underweight	26.6	24.8	21.6	18.8	30.8	29.3	23.4	19.6	23.4
2009									
Stunting									
Global	38.0	30.8	30.4	22.5	44.9	38.5	29.2	30.5	32.4
Moderate	27.6	22.1	21.9	18.2	29.1	27.1	22.0	25.1	24.0
Severe	10.4	8.7	8.5	4.3	15.8	11.4	7.2	5.4	8.4
Underweight									
Global	21.0	18.0	18.0	14.4	25.4	21.5	17.4	17.7	18.8
Moderate	16.2	14.4	14.1	11.6	20.0	16.9	14.1	14.4	14.9
Severe	4.8	3.6	3.9	2.8	5.4	4.6	3.3	3.3	3.9

(continued)

TABLE 4.1 (*continued*)

	North Hamgyong	North Hwanghae	North Pyongan	Pyongyang	Ryanggang	South Hamgyong	South Hwanghae	South Pyongan	Overall
2012									
Stunting									
Global	28.7	28.7	29.4	19.6	39.6	32.9	25.6	25.8	27.9
Moderate	20.5	20.6	21.3	15.6	27.5	23.5	18.9	21.2	20.7
Severe	8.2	8.1	8.1	4.0	12.1	9.4	6.7	4.6	7.2
Underweight									
Global	16.4	14.6	17.1	10.0	20.0	18.6	14.6	13.0	15.2
Moderate	14.0	12.0	13.3	8.8	14.5	13.9	11.4	11.5	12.4
Severe	2.4	2.6	3.8	1.3	5.5	4.6	3.2	1.4	2.9
Change since 2009 (global)									
Stunting	−9.3	−2.1	−1.0	−2.9	−5.3	−5.6	−3.6	−4.7	−4.5
Underweight	−4.6	−3.4	−0.9	−4.4	−5.4	−2.9	−2.8	−4.7	−3.6

SOURCE: 1997: Katona-Apte and Mokdad (1998); 2002: Central Bureau of Statistics (2002); 2004: Central Bureau of Statistics (2005); 2009: UNICEF (2010); 2012: UNICEF (2012).

generation appears to be severely stunted. Although the overall average for the sample is only 7.2 percent, the incidence of stunting accumulates through the successive age cohorts until reaching a peak of roughly 10 percent at age two. At this age, stunting is irreversible and confers a lifelong set of physical and mental challenges that are passed down through generations.[12]

The Perils of Self-Reliance: A Reprise

Evidence from grain balances, prices, and direct observation confirm a gradual deterioration in the food situation in North Korea from the middle of the 2000s forward, moderating only somewhat in 2012–2015. The causes of this deterioration are multiple, ranging from structural issues in the agricultural sector to weather shocks. However, the evidence suggests that policy choices and broader political circumstances were in play. The government failed to prioritize commercial imports of food, and the bungled currency reform of 2009 had dire consequences for food prices. These developments also followed closely on the heels of the collapse of the Six Party Talks and a resumption of tensions on the peninsula that had implications for the aid regime as well.

Humanitarian Dilemmas: The Political Economy of Food

Claims of self-sufficiency notwithstanding, North Korea has long been dependent on aid. However, this dependence replaced one potential source of vulnerability, heavy reliance on domestic sources of supply, with another, reliance on the kindness of strangers. From the onset of the famine-related assistance of the mid-1990s through the early 2000s, aid accounted for a rising share of total supply (Figure 4.2). Despite conflicts with individual donors, most notably Japan, North Korea was able to exploit coordination problems to sustain relatively high aggregate aid flows. The rise of the Sunshine Policy in South Korea was particularly important in this regard. As we saw, the regime even exploited the increase in aid to curtail imports rather than augment aid with commercial sources of supply to more fully achieve food security.

Aid became more erratic in the 2000s and overall levels began to decline (Figure 4.2). Had this been the result of a sustained agricultural recovery and improving nutrition, it would have been a welcome development. Almost exactly the opposite was the case, as we have seen: overall food balances were worsening over time.

Political conflicts between donors and North Korea played a prominent role in the volatility of aid and at two levels. First, food aid was increasingly politicized, related to progress in the Six Party Talks and in subsequent bilateral negotiations once the talks broke down in 2008. During some periods, including

2005, 2008, and 2012, progress in the talks was associated, as both cause and effect, with increases in promised assistance. At other moments, however, including the aftermath of the 2006 tests, with respect to South Korea from 2008, and more generally in the 2009–2016 period, the country's overall foreign policy stance undercut the willingness of donors to extend humanitarian assistance. In 2009 and 2012, the regime even walked away from large food aid packages as political relations with the United States deteriorated, despite ongoing evidence of distress.

Second, the course of aid was adversely affected by conflicts with donors over the design of humanitarian programs. As in the past, the North Korean regime was slow in acknowledging its need for food assistance, failed to provide adequate or accurate information to potential donors, and was unwilling to guarantee the integrity of its aid programs. Aid was periodically roiled by evidence of diversion to both the military and the market.[13] Moreover, North Korea always treated negotiations over food as a strict quid pro quo. When aid increased, so did access for aid workers; when aid decreased, for any reason whatsoever, North Korean access was reduced. Such manipulation only magnified doubts about the aid program, generating opposition to continued assistance among major donors.[14]

We begin by looking at the coordinated multilateral aid effort through the WFP. We then consider the policies of the United States, South Korea, and China.

The WFP

The WFP is the multilateral organization with primary responsibility for humanitarian food assistance.[15] It does not directly control stocks of food, however, but serves a coordinating function by negotiating agreements with recipients, issuing appeals and coordinating subsequent contributions from donors, and overseeing logistics monitoring of delivery and assessment. Without political support from key donors, it would be impossible for the WFP to operate.

For our purposes, the WFP can be turned to methodological advantage. Shortfalls in meeting WFP appeals may in part reflect divergent assessments of need by major donors and constraints on aid budgets; we do not altogether rule out these factors. But the WFP typically does not launch an appeal unless there is defensible evidence of need and at least some hope of gaining political support for it. As a result, the extent to which appeals are realized reflects the revealed willingness of donors to assist North Korea.

Table 4.2 summarizes the history of WFP's North Korea programs. Recall from Figure 4.1 that at virtually no time during this period—with the

TABLE 4.2

Results of UN consolidated appeals process (US$ millions), 1995−2015

Appeal	Target	WFP % of total target	Actual	WFP % of total income	% fulfilled
1995	n/a	—	n/a	—	n/a
WFP	8.9	n/a	6.7	n/a	75.3
1996	43.6	—	34.4	—	78.8
WFP	26.8	61.5	26.2	76.2	97.8
1997	184.4	—	158.4	—	85.9
WFP	144.1	78.1	134.3	84.8	93.2
1998	383.2	—	215.9	—	56.3
WFP	345.8	90.2	202.7	93.9	58.6
1999	292.1	—	189.9	—	65.0
WFP	141.6	48.5	177.9	93.7	125.6
2000	313.8	—	153.1	—	48.8
WFP	222.5	70.9	145.6	95.1	65.4
2001	384.0	—	248.0	—	64.6
WFP	315.9	82.3	240.1	96.8	76.0
2002	246.8	—	220.0	—	89.1
WFP	216.7	87.8	206.1	93.7	95.1[a]
2003	229.4	—	133.1	—	58.0
WFP	202.7	88.4	117.8	88.5	58.1
2004	208.8	—	151.6	—	72.6
WFP	172.3	82.5	118.9	78.4	69.0
2005	n/a	n/a	n/a	n/a	n/a
WFP	n/a	n/a	n/a	n/a	n/a
2006	n/a	n/a	n/a	n/a	n/a
WFP	n/a	n/a	n/a	n/a	n/a
2007	14.5	—	13.1	—	90.3
WFP	5.1	34.9	5.0	38.4	99.4
2008	n/a	n/a	n/a	n/a	n/a
WFP	n/a	n/a	n/a	n/a	n/a
2009	n/a	n/a	n/a	n/a	n/a
WFP	n/a	n/a	n/a	n/a	n/a
2010	n/a	n/a	n/a	n/a	n/a
WFP	n/a	n/a	n/a	n/a	n/a
2011	218.7	—	82.0	—	37.5
WFP	174.7	79.9	65.0	79.2	37.2
2012	n/a	n/a	n/a	n/a	n/a
WFP	n/a	n/a	n/a	n/a	n/a
2013	150.1	—	72.3	—	48.2
WFP	96.0	64.0	47.4	65.6	49.4

(continued)

TABLE 4.2 (*continued*)

Appeal	Target	WFP % of total target	Actual	WFP % of total income	% fulfilled
2014	115.3	—	48.3	—	41.9
WFP	67.4	58.5	30.2	62.5	44.8
2015	110.9	—	18.9	—	17.0
WFP	69.4	62.6	13.4	70.9	19.3
Total 1996–2015	**2,895.7**	—	**1,599.5**	—	—
WFP					
1996–2015	**2,201.0**	**76.0**	**1,530.6**	**95.7**	—

source: UN-OCHA Financial Tracking Service; FAO/WFP *Crop and Food Security Assessments,* various issues.

note: n/a = no data.

ᵃReported achievement rate reflects amount received during the appeal relative to the target and excludes $99.3 million carried over.

exception of the 2005–2006, 2006–2007, and 2013–2014 crop cycles—did UN assessments suggest the absence of humanitarian need, and even then the margin of safety was razor thin. Until the very end of the period, food balances were steadily deteriorating, but we see an increasingly erratic trend in aid commitments. Particularly after 2008, when the Six Party Talks broke down, the ability of the WFP to secure funding commitments fell off sharply. A brief overview of these programs suggests that North Korean policy choices and the resulting political constraints on donors combined to generate this result.

After the flood of assistance in the immediate aftermath of the famine, North Korean authorities began to curtail monitoring visits in 2004. In the summer of 2005, they announced that they would not participate in the UN's annual consolidated appeal, requested the dissolution of the UN Office for the Coordination of Humanitarian Affairs (OCHA) in Pyongyang, and threatened to expel NGOs that did not bring in sufficient volumes of aid. These developments were partly the result of improved agricultural conditions and access to external sources of supply but, as we argued in Chapter 2, they also had to do with a more wide-ranging reversal of reform.

In the fall of 2005, North Korea experienced its best harvest in a decade and South Korea ramped up its aid efforts, weakening the bargaining power of the WFP and its ability to monitor and assess assistance. The WFP suspended its operations in North Korea at the end of 2005 and then initiated a greatly scaled-down program in February 2006.[16] From the outset of this program, however, board members expressed reservations about monitoring arrangements (WFP 2006).[17] Moreover, outside agencies openly voiced concerns that the regime was not doing its part to prioritize commercial food imports, in effect seeking foreign exchange support indirectly through its appeals for assistance (Food and Agriculture Organization 2008). As can be seen from Table 4.2, even scaled-back targets were not met.

Not coincidentally, these difficulties in securing support overlapped with a period of heightened tension over US financial sanctions (September 2005), missile and nuclear tests (July and October 2006), and a break in the Six Party Talks that would last for just over a year (November 2005–December 2006). The United States had committed itself to securing much more robust monitoring arrangements prior to extending any further assistance. By April 2008—just prior to the announcement of a new US food aid package—the 2006 program was still only half-funded and about 30 percent of that funding came from an injection of South Korean assistance that followed the break-through in the nuclear talks (World Food Program 2008).

Progress in the nuclear talks in early 2007 provided the political foundation for a resumption of aid.[18] In 2008 the FAO (2008) and other observers (Haggard, Noland, and Weeks 2008) were once again issuing warnings about the food situation in the DPRK, with evidence that conditions were worse than they had been at any time since the great famine of the mid-1990s. In May the DPRK and the United States announced an agreement in principle that allowed for the distribution of up to 500,000 tons of food assistance[19] Although not formally a quid pro quo, it was clear that the humanitarian opening ran parallel to the halting progress on the nuclear implementation agreements that had been reached in February and October 2007 (see Chapter 6).

The political breakthrough also provided the context for FAO-WFP and NGO assessment missions in June 2008 (Anderson and Majorawitz 2008; Food and Agriculture Organization 2008). These assessments confirmed outside suspicions about the state of North Korea's food economy: yawning aggregate food deficits (Figure 4.1); progressive reductions in PDS rations; a decline in dietary diversity; and coping strategies that signaled prefamine conditions, such as an increased proportion of respondents collecting wild foods. Moreover, although the North Koreans blocked the assessment teams' access to markets, the WFP was openly monitoring outside information on prices, which also provided ample signs of distress (Food and Agriculture Organization 2008).

The food assessments of 2008 became the formal basis for a new WFP program, initiated in September 2008,[20] the core of which were new monitoring and assessment protocols.[21] Table 4.3 outlines the terms of the 2008 agreement, the decline in access that followed the collapse of the program in 2009, and the initial letter of understanding that was negotiated in 2011, when North Korea once again made an open appeal for assistance. These negotiations demonstrate

TABLE 4.3

WFP-DPRK Letters of Understanding, 2008 and 2011

Issue	June 2008 LOU	New operating conditions effective June 2009	April 2011 LOU	Comment
Geographic coverage	8 provinces, 131 counties (expanded from 50 counties of the previous agreement)	6 provinces, 57 counties; Ryanggang, South Pyongan, and Pyongyang excluded	8 provinces, 107 counties	DPRK did not grant WFP access in all counties because of "no access, no food" norm
International staff numbers	Up to 59 international staff, with numbers linked to food shipments	Strict quid pro quo: 1 international staff person per 10,000 tons of food commodities; staffing bottoms out at 10	Up to 59, with 60% involved in monitoring activities	Largely status quo ante
Korean speakers	Agreement to recruit international Korean speakers for the first time, with maximum of 8 starting in August 2008	International Korean speakers cut; last one departs June 2009	Provision for Korean speakers, but exact terms not released	Status quo ante
Suboffices	5 field offices (Hyesan, Chongjin, Hamhung, Wonsan, Haeju) to complement WFP country office in Pyongyang	Only Chongjin and Wonsan allowed outside Pyongyang, but Hyesan and Hamhung closed because of lack of funding	Allows for 6 field offices; exact locations not released	WFP claims best access outside Pyongyang since 1996

Assessments	Crop and Food Supply Assessment in October 2008; joint WFP/UNICEF Nutritional Assessment postponed	No arrangements for assessments, but UNICEF carries out Multiple Indicators Cluster Survey in October 2009	Crop and Food Supply Assessment scheduled for September/October 2011; nutritional assessment in 2011; anthropometric measurements (middle upper arm circumference) allowed; access to markets for monitoring and tracking prices and determining commodity composition	Significant changes but dependent on North Korea actually allowing nutritional assessments and market visits to take place
Access/monitoring	Field visits with 24 hours notice; random access in designated area to beneficiary institutions, factories, households, etc.	1-week advance travel plan; no formal changes on randomness but 1-week advance travel plan reduces it	Field visits with 24 hours notice, but which institutions to visit decided on arrival at location	Randomness is crucial to effective monitoring; subtle improvement
Distributions	Global Implementation Plan (GIP) lists all institutions/outlets; monthly distribution plans issued by WFP to government	No formal change but obvious adjustments in the face of declining aid flows	Similar to 2008 agreement	
Supply chain management	Dedicated warehousing for WFP commodities; local food production (LFP) in 13 factories	No changes in dedicated warehousing; government wanted to run LFP factories but outcome not clear with declining coverage	WFP can access any facility where food stored; new elements include access at any time to warehouses at entry points (ports, rail heads); use of computerized commodity tracking and greater timeliness of documentation	Given credible reports of large-scale diversion at the time food delivered during great famine, a significant improvement

SOURCE: Haggard and Noland (2011c).

the difficulty faced by humanitarian agencies in gaining access to North Korea and in guaranteeing the integrity of their programs.

North Korean authorities had vociferous objections to the 2008 program from the outset and refused to fully adhere to its terms. Although accounts differ, WFP management explicitly or implicitly signaled that strict adherence to the protocols was not necessary, in part because of the fear, and implicit threat, that strict adherence would result in reduced access.[22] As donors failed to make good on contributions, distributions dropped to 30 percent of those originally planned in November 2008 and to 12 percent by January 2009. Negotiations in December to resolve outstanding differences failed, just as discussions of the nuclear program were also collapsing. In March 2009, North Korea terminated the NGO component of the food program and in June introduced new operating conditions that further limited access. At the time of this announcement, the WFP reported that the existing program, which had not been formally canceled, was less than 15 percent funded.

The cycle of delay in identifying need, undersubscription in funding, and program revision played out again over the course of the 2009–2010 through 2015–2016 crop cycles. After the collapse of the nuclear talks, the international community once again detected signs of distress related not only to weather (rains and flooding in both periods, a particularly severe winter in 2010–2011) but also to policy shocks, most notably the currency conversion of November 2009. In June 2010, a Protracted Relief and Recovery Operation sought to address the targeting and monitoring problem by focusing on nutritional support for women and children (WFP 2010). Yet by early 2011 this program, too, was less than 20 percent funded and had to be drastically revised in response to a new emergency appeal by the North Korean government in January.[23] No fewer than four food security assessments in the first half of 2011, by the UN, the United States, US NGOs, and the European Union, painted a common picture of severe distress, with a particularly sharp falloff in PDS rations early in the crop cycle. A controversial program of grain exactions for the military also suggested the depth of shortages.[24]

The WFP launched its appeal for a new emergency program in April 2011, but commitments to it were slow in coming (WFP 2012a, 2012b), as were commitments to its successors. It is hard to avoid the conclusion that the tensions around the satellite launches and nuclear tests in the winter of 2012–2013 played a role. By January 2013, breaks in the pipeline had emerged and the WFP was forced to triage (WFP 2013b). As political tensions continued, only Russia and Switzerland supported the program in the spring of 2013; the remainder was made up by internal funding from the multilaterals themselves. Yet another program negotiated in mid-2013 faced the same fate. Extended twice (at the time of writing, scheduled to run through June 2016), the program has received less than half of its programmed funding and the WFP has been forced to scale back operations accordingly. Except for a small handful of countries—Switzerland, Russia, South Korea, and Australia—support for WFP programming in North Korea has virtually evaporated.[25]

Without descending to the donor-country level, which we do in the following sections, we cannot demonstrate definitively that the difficulties that the WFP faced in funding were due to the ongoing nuclear confrontation and North Korean failures to assure donors of the integrity of food aid. But several crucial shifts in its programming appear to be linked to strategies of the major donors and coordination problems among them, most notably the United States and South Korea.

Declining US commitment to multilateral assistance from the beginning of the George W. Bush administration corresponded with a period during which North Korea believed that it did not need multilateral or NGO assistance. An important factor in this calculus was clearly the willingness of the Roh Moo-hyun government to provide massive aid on an ongoing basis, with the important exception of a brief reaction to the missile tests in 2006; as Figure 4.2 shows, commercial imports contracted to virtually nothing during this period.

The tentative progress on disabling the Yongbyon nuclear facility over the course of 2007–2008 and new monitoring protocols once again opened the door to multilateral and bilateral assistance. Yet progress on the nuclear front quickly stalled, and with Kim Jong-il's stroke in August 2008 North Korean policy entered a new phase. The missile and nuclear tests of April and May 2009, the sinking of the *Cheonan* and the shelling of Yeonpyeong Island in March and November of 2010, and the satellite launches and third nuclear test of 2012–2013 all served to heighten tensions between North Korea and potential donors and create more pointed political opposition to food aid. Moreover, these connections were well understood by the humanitarian community (UN Development Program 2009).[26] We can observe these political dynamics more closely by considering the approaches of the United States, South Korea, and China.

US Policy

It is ironic that, despite the enmity between the United States and North Korea, the former has been by far the latter's largest donor. Table 4.4 outlines the US

TABLE 4.4

US food assistance to North Korea, 1995–2013

Calendar or fiscal year (FY)	Commodity value (US$ millions)	Metric tons
1995	0.0	0
1996	8.3	19,500
1997	52.4	177,000
1998	72.9	200,000
1999	222.1	695,194
2000	74.3	265,000
2001	58.1	350,000
2002	50.4	207,000
2003	25.5	40,200
2004	36.3	110,000
2005	5.7	25,000
2006	0.0	0
2007	0.0	0
2008	93.7	148,270
2009	5.6	21,000
2010	2.9[a]	0
2011	0.0	0
2012	0.0	0
2013	0.0	0
Total	**708.2**	**2,258,164**

SOURCE: Manyin and Nikitin (2014).

[a]$2.9 million in FY2010 represents a budgetary adjustment for contributions provided in FY2008.

contribution from the onset of famine-related assistance in 1995 through the end of the first Obama administration in 2013; no aid was provided in 2011 as the Leap Day Deal was being negotiated and none after the agreement fell apart in 2012. Nearly half of total aid was the result of US commitments under the Agreed Framework of 1994 through the Korean Peninsula Energy Development Organization (KEDO) and the subsequent Six Party Talks process.[27] The bulk of US aid, however, more than $700 million, took the form of food assistance that was mostly channeled through the WFP.

Table 4.5 traces the diplomatic context of various US aid initiatives over the period. Humanitarian motives played a central role in mobilizing US assistance in the wake of the great famine, but from the outset aid was closely tied with the efforts of the Clinton administration to engage North Korea, particularly during the "high engagement" period of 1998–1999. The administration

TABLE 4.5

Food for talks, 1996–present

Date	Value	Form	Channel	Diplomatic objective
February 1996	$2 million	Food	WFP	Encourage North Korean adherence to Agreed Framework during period of increasing tension between two Koreas
June 1996	$6.2 million	Food	WFP	Encourage North Korean flexibility toward secret proposal for four-way talks between United States, North Korea, South Korea, and China
February 1997	$10 million	Food	WFP	Quid pro quo for North Korean agreement to participate in joint US-South Korea briefing on Four Party Talks proposal
April 1997	$15 million	50,000 MT food	WFP	Quid pro quo for North Korean agreement to participate in missile proliferation negotiations
July 1997	$27 million	100,000 MT food	WFP	Quid pro quo for North Korean agreement to participate in Four Party Talks
October 1997	$5 million	Grant	UNICEF	Quid pro quo for North Korean acceptance of 10 additional food relief monitors
February 1998	n/a	200,000 MT food	WFP	Quid pro quo for North Korean agreement to participate in ad hoc committee meeting associated with Four Party Talks
September 1998	n/a	300,000 MT food	WFP	Quid pro quo for North Korean agreement to resume missile talks, attend 3rd plenary session of Four Party Talks, enter negotiations over second suspected nuclear site, and resume talks aimed at removing North Korea from list of states sponsoring terrorism
April–May 1999	n/a	600,000 MT food, 1,000 tons potato seed	WFP	Quid pro quo for agreement on access to North Korea's underground construction site and participation in Four Party and missile talks; 400,000 MT of this commitment announced one day before US mission to Pyongyang
September 1999	n/a	Sanctions eased	n/a	Quid pro quo; agreement in principle on missiles

(continued)

TABLE 4.5 (*continued*)

Date	Value	Form	Channel	Diplomatic objective
September–October 2000	Unspecified	n/a	n/a	Prospective quid pro quo. North Korea agrees to drop demand for cash compensation for ending missile program, but seeks equivalent in in-kind aid including food. In subsequent talks, U.S. promises unspecified aid but talks do not reach conclusion.
June 2002	Unspecified	n/a	n/a	Prospective quid pro quo; administration announces "baseline" approach; additional aid over 155,000 metric tons conditional on improvements in access and monitoring
January 2003	Unspecified	n/a	n/a	Prospective quid pro quo; administration offers "bold approach" including food aid in return for North Korea dismantling its weapons program
June 2004	Unspecified	n/a	n/a	Prospective quid pro quo; in context of Six Party Talks, administration offers package of measures, including unspecified assistance in return for "complete, verifiable, irreversible dismantlement" of North Korea's nuclear program
July–August 2005	Unspecified	n/a	n/a	Prospective quid pro quo; administration continues commitments of 50,000 MT per year in 2003, 2004, and 2005, but claims they are unrelated to talks; in 2005, reiterates its commitment to unspecified assistance in return for resolution of nuclear issue; supports South Korean promise to supply energy
August 2011	$900,000	n/a	n/a	Prospective quid pro quo; announcement of $900,000 in flood aid coincides directly with announcement of resumption of talks over proceeding with excavation of remains of American soldiers killed during Korean War
February 2012	240,000 MT	n/a	n/a	Apparent quid pro quo because food aid agreement announced simultaneously with partial freeze on nuclear and missile programs; aid program reversed with North Korean decision to launch satellite

SOURCE: Adapted and updated from Noland (2000, table 5.3).

extended food as a lubricant for talks, generating opposition from both the NGO community and Republican critics (Aaltola 1999; Manyin and Jun 2003; Schloms 2004; Haggard and Noland 2007a). In the face of these domestic political constraints, it shifted to a more conditional approach in which substantive progress in negotiations and improved access and monitoring were given greater weight (Hathaway and Tama 2004).

The Bush administration pulled back from this engagement strategy and sought to make the provision of aid more sharply conditional on improved access and monitoring agreements. In June 2002, the US Agency for International Development (USAID) outlined a new approach under which the United States would provide food aid at a "baseline" 155,000 metric tons with additional amounts conditional on improved access. Following the onset of the nuclear crisis, the Bush administration continued to make commitments but at a much more modest level.[28]

In the fall of 2004, just as the WFP and North Korean authorities were entering their standoff over monitoring, Congress passed and President Bush signed the North Korean Human Rights Act. The legislation sought to institutionalize the administration's more conditional approach to humanitarian assistance by requiring USAID to report any changes in transparency, monitoring, and access of food aid and other humanitarian activities. It also included "sense of Congress" language that any "significant increases" in humanitarian assistance be conditioned on "substantial improvements" in transparency, monitoring, and access. Although the administration announced another contribution of 50,000 tons in June 2005, the same level that had been offered in 2003 and 2004, it suspended further aid commitments later in the year pending the outcome of negotiations between the WFP and North Korea over continuing operations.

Overall US strategy began to shift during the second Bush administration toward more active engagement (Chapter 6). The administration tabled a number of possible inducements, although again conditional on North Korea being more forthcoming in the nuclear negotiations.[29] Progress was interrupted by conflicts with the regime over financial sanctions and the missile and nuclear tests of 2006, and it was not until January 2007 that these issues were resolved and not until August 2007, under the political cover of the floods, that the administration offered small amounts of humanitarian assistance. Following the floods, the administration signaled that it was "prepared to engage with North Korean officials on arrangements for a significant food aid package" contingent on "appropriate monitoring procedures."[30] An intra-agency delegation visited Pyongyang in December, and the two countries signed the letter of understanding, described previously, in June 2008 (see Table 4.3).

To what extent was progress and regress on the nuclear question linked to the rise and fall of food aid during the Bush administration? Explicitly, at no point, and the Bush administration continued to deliver at least some aid after the Six Party Talks had collapsed. However, the negotiations over food aid that began in late 2007 overlapped with the intense diplomacy around the implementation of disablement agreements reached in February and October 2007. These agreements did include explicit quid pro quos—albeit on fuel oil, not food—and it is probable that North Korea saw the nuclear issues and aid as linked even if the United States sought to keep them separate.

The missile and nuclear tests of 2009 and the military provocations around the Northern Limit Line, a disputed maritime border between North and South Korea, in 2010 made it politically difficult to provide assistance, despite ample evidence of distress. Critics of food aid gained traction on both political and humanitarian grounds.[31] Continuing budget resolutions passed in 2010 and 2011 stipulated that no aid should be extended unless specifically legislated. In June 2011, Representative Ed Royce (R-California) offered an amendment, which passed on a voice vote, that prevented any aid going to North Korea. Justification relied not only on monitoring arguments but on moral hazard grounds as well: providing food aid "delays the day when real, structural reform will come to North Korea."

Despite these domestic constraints, the Obama administration gambled on the offer of an extensive food aid program totaling 240,000 tons, which was officially announced on February 29, 2012. This was the so-called Leap Day Deal. Although based on well-documented need, the program was finalized in the context of negotiation of a major agreement on nuclear issues, including a moratorium on long-range missile launches, nuclear tests, and nuclear activities at Yongbyon. The DPRK also agreed to the return of IAEA inspectors. Despite denials of a quid pro quo, the language of North Korea's parallel announcement strongly suggested that Pyongyang saw a linkage. The new leadership nonetheless decided to go ahead with a planned "satellite" launch, despite being warned that doing so would scuttle the aid package. The United States called off the deal, underlining both the extent to which the freeze and food aid were in fact linked and that the regime's military priorities trumped humanitarian concerns.

South Korea

South Korea's strategy of engagement with North Korea had important antecedents in Roh Tae-woo's *Nordpolitik*, and the Kim Young-sam government made a large, one-off humanitarian contribution in 1995.[32] But as we saw in Chapter 3 (Figure 3.9) and detail in Chapter 6, the pattern of humanitarian assistance from South to North closely followed the rise and fall of the so-called Sunshine Policy under Kim Dae-jung (1998–2003) and Roh Moo-hyun (2003–2008). During both administrations, food and fertilizer aid clearly sought to address humanitarian concerns but it was also rooted in a highly diffuse conception of reciprocity designed to gradually transform North-South relations in a more cooperative direction. Despite one important episode of linkage—when aid was cut in the summer of 2006 in the wake of missile tests—the two liberal South Korean administrations did not directly link aid to military or political quid pro quos or even make it conditional on compliance with humanitarian norms.

Partisan consensus on North Korean policy in South Korea was even thinner than in the United States, however. As a result, the election of a conservative president in December 2007 resulted in a hard policy swing. Conditionality and explicit linkage came to infuse all aspects of South Korea's policy toward the North, including humanitarian assistance. As Figure 3.9 showed, large-scale assistance fell off sharply from 2008 and by no means recovered under the administration of Park Geun-hye (2013–2018) at the time of this writing.

Several overall features of food aid during the engagement period are worth noting because they have implications for the coordination problems facing the five parties. The first is that, while the government made modest contributions through the WFP, the overwhelming majority of food aid passed through bilateral channels in the form of concessional loans for both food and fertilizer. Since this aid did not pass through the WFP—and indeed was not technically aid at all but loans—it was not subject to any of the WFP's protocols with respect to targeting, access, monitoring, or assessment. In July 2004, North Korea finally agreed to establish a monitoring regime for South Korean food assistance, but it was substantially weaker than the WFP regime and made no pretense of population targeting. Food aid essentially went directly to the regime, with the bulk of it probably going into the PDS.

The second feature of South Korean aid was that approximately one-third passed through qualified NGO channels over the entire period.[33] In contrast to the larger US and European NGOs, these support groups were smaller, Korea-specific organizations, some supported by local governments in the South, that were generally more intent on establishing working relationships with their counterpart organizations than in hewing to humanitarian norms (Flake and Snyder 2003)

The Kim Dae-jung strategy with respect to food aid was articulated in 1999 and from the outset included both food aid and fertilizer, seeds, and pesticides.

As the administration stepped up its multifaceted push to orchestrate a summit meeting between Kim Dae-jung and Kim Jong-il in the spring of 2000, bilateral food and fertilizer aid increased dramatically, and there can be little doubt that these efforts were related to a broader "food for talks" strategy. South Korea provided 200,000 tons of fertilizer aid to the North in 1999, 300,000 tons in 2000, 200,000 tons in 2001, and 300,000 tons in 2002, which was the final year of the Kim Dae-jung administration.

The election of Roh Moo-hyun occurred just as the second nuclear crisis was breaking in late 2002, and the new president's commitment to the Sunshine Policy quickly became an issue of contention with the Bush administration (Chapter 6). On coming to office, the Roh administration made a contribution (100,000 tons of maize) through the WFP, but aid policy reverted to the bilateral format that had developed after the 2000 summit. The bilateral Inter-Korean Economic Cooperation Promotion Committee became the venue for discussion of aid commitments. In May 2003, while the nuclear standoff with the United States was continuing, the North Koreans requested 200,000 tons of fertilizer, which the South Koreans delivered, and a total of 500,000 tons of grain, approximately 400,000 tons of which South Korea ultimately supplied for the year; this was an amount equal to nearly half of the country's uncovered food deficit. Requests to maintain these levels of support were subsequently made in the June 2004 meetings of Inter-Korean Economic Cooperation Promotion Committee and approved by the South Korean side.

After this meeting, bilateral relations froze and would not thaw until nearly a year later when a high-level South Korean envoy met directly with Kim Jong-il in May 2005. The Sunshine approach was particularly tested by the February 10, 2005, announcement that North Korea was suspending its participation in the Six Party Talks and that it had nuclear weapons. Only a month before this announcement, the North Korean government had made its largest aid request to the South Korean government ever: 500,000 tons of fertilizer. The government was divided over how to respond to the February 10 statement and the aid request, and was pressured by the United States not to grant it. Nonetheless, the administration stuck to the strategy of separating humanitarian engagement from politics and extended even more assistance as a component of its strategy of bringing North Korea back to the talks that had led to the important September 2005 Joint Statement.

Following the bumper harvest of fall 2005, North Korea initially limited its aid requests to South Korea to fertilizer (450,000 tons). By April, however, the PDS was once again under stress and the DPRK came back to the South with a request for 500,000 tons of food and a resumption of fertilizer shipments.[34] In an important *volte face* from previous policy, South Korean foreign minister Ban Ki-moon warned in July that the Roh government would suspend further humanitarian assistance if North Korea proceeded to conduct missile flight tests. With the exception of a one-off aid package following the floods in August, the administration carried through on that threat and even interrupted emergency flood program deliveries following the nuclear test in October.[35]

Within a month of reaching the first implementation agreement in February 2007, North-South interministerial meetings began, and the Roh administration once again offered commitments equal to those discussed in the past.[36] Serious flooding in August generated new emergency commitments, and in the run-up to the inter-Korean summit meeting in October the Roh administration outlined a wide array of economic inducements.

These commitments did not bind the incoming government, however. Lee Myung-bak had run on a platform of reciprocity: both aid and other forms of economic cooperation would be conditional. His wide-ranging "Vision 3000" program offered a plethora of incentives to the North, but all were prospective, contingent on progress with respect to commitments under the February and October 2007 Six Party agreements and progress on North-South relations.

After Lee's inauguration, there was uncertainty about whether this concept of reciprocity extended to humanitarian assistance. Not until late March 2008, over a month into his presidency and with rapidly mounting signs of distress, did he clarify that he would extend humanitarian assistance regardless of progress in the nuclear talks. However, the humanitarian offer came with its own set of conditions, including that the North make a formal request for aid that would reactivate the diplomatic channels that had been severed by the North following his inauguration. The North Korean regime vigorously rejected these conditions and decided to pursue a highly confrontational policy toward the South. In early April, despite clear signs of a deterioration in the food picture, Pyongyang announced that it would not seek aid from South Korea, turning almost immediately to China for assistance.

At various points during Lee Myung-bak's tenure, his administration sought to outline principles for humanitarian assistance, but it largely codified the policy that emerged in its early months. First, the administration's protests to the contrary, the conclusion is hard to avoid that humanitarian assistance was contingent on progress on the nuclear issue and particularly on North-South relations.[37] Second, humanitarian assistance was both defined more narrowly—for example, in response to the floods of 2010—and linked to a wider agenda of humanitarian issues.[38]

The humanitarian agenda was consistently defined to include family reunions, POWs, abductees, and even human rights. Although the Lee administration did not expect North Korea to respond to prospective inducements
with respect to the nuclear issue and high politics, it continually suggested that
humanitarian assistance required reciprocity on humanitarian issues of interest to the South. The first initiative, noted previously, sought a resumption of
family exchanges in return.

Finally, the Lee administration not only sought to minimize South Korea's public aid commitments but acted to curtail growing NGO activity as
well. This activity included aid funded by the Inter-Korean Cooperation Fund
(IKCF), which then collapsed to virtual insignificance. Even during periods of
extreme distress, such as the spring of 2011, permission to provide assistance
was parceled out only to a limited number of NGOs conditional on adequate
distribution and monitoring plans.

The election of Park Geun-hye marked another shift in the approach to
humanitarian assistance in an attempt to straddle the engagement and Lee
Myung-bak approaches. The core concept of *Trustpolitik* was incrementalism:
offering small but reciprocated steps, of which limited humanitarian support
would be one instrument. Through 2016, however, Park's *Trustpolitik* approach
remained hostage to tensions generated by the satellite launch of December
2012, the third nuclear test of February 2013, sanctions inherited from the Lee
Myung-bak government, and her own commitment to unification on South
Korean terms, most notably stated in her Dresden speech of March 2014. The
aid actually provided was a modest departure from that of the Lee administration, but it was inadequate to provide a focal point for sustained North-South
talks, let alone rapprochement. Despite the attempt to outline a conceptually
different approach, and several modest aid initiatives over the course of 2014
and 2015, the Park administration's overall efforts ended up resembling Lee
Myung-bak's in its policy of tightly coupled quid pro quos and sharply defined
humanitarian need.[39]

China

China's trade in food with North Korea has historically involved components
that are both difficult to separate and virtually impossible to measure with any
confidence. These include large-scale trade, mostly from state-licensed entities, several of which are located in the Northeast of the country, as well as a
border trade that involves small traders, families, and North Koreans moving
across the border. As we saw in Chapter 3, in aggregate this trade appears
to be carried out largely on commercial terms, but it is possible that larger

firms receive subsidies from the central government. It is widely suspected that there is a "gift economy" of discretionary commitments associated with high-level diplomatic meetings (Reilly 2014b), and provincial governments in the Northeast have also given aid (Yan 2016). Foreign NGOs run their food operations through China as well, although the number doing so rises and falls with North Korea's openness to such operations and at least some of this trade is captured in multilateral aid data (Yan 2016).

Given that the Chinese treat their aid to North Korea as a state secret, public statements and reports on it are wildly contradictory: some suggest only limited assistance; others claim a long history of regular food aid.[40] However, we can ask two questions: whether the timing of Chinese aid shipments suggests a willingness to act as a supplier of last resort during periods of shortages; and whether the price data suggest subsidy, keeping in mind the caveat about possible hidden subsidies noted previously. To answer these questions, we combine a consideration of total reported shipments from the onset of the nuclear crisis through the first year of Kim Jong-un's rule (Figure 4.3), and reconsider

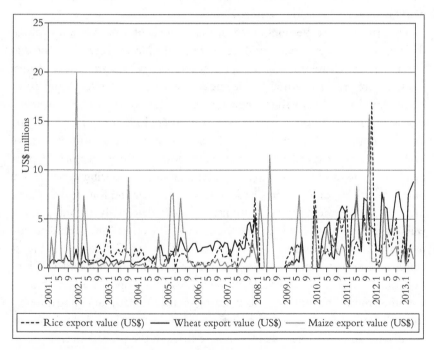

FIGURE 4.3   Chinese grain exports to North Korea (value)

SOURCE: Korea International Trade Association K-Statistics database.

our findings on prices from Chapter 3 (see Figure 3.10). Recall that from the 2006–2007 crop cycle through 2011–2012, North Korean total food balances show a steady deterioration, with the exception of 2008–2009, before marginally improving (Figure 4.1).

The quantity of Chinese exports is characterized by a number of spikes, typically driven by increases in corn shipments: in 2005, during the major run-up in world prices in 2007–2008 (although reporting was interrupted), and again in late 2010 and late 2012, also a period witnessing notable increases in global prices. There is therefore at least suggestive evidence that China may have been responding to the distress in those periods and that it was providing aid in support of the succession. However, when we consider the price data from Chapter 3, we do not see evidence of increased support. On the contrary, missing data preclude a firm judgment of whether there was a subsidy component to shipments during the price spikes in 2008, but there is suggestive evidence that there was one for rice: when reporting resumed in 2009, Chinese rice export prices appeared well below world benchmarks. However, in exercises on prices parallel to that on rice (Chapter 2), we found this was not true for corn or wheat, and if anything Chinese export prices actually *exceeded* world market prices in the early 2010s.

The data need to be considered in the context of what we know about the course of Chinese policy, with respect both to North Korea—detailed in our discussion of diplomacy in Chapters 6 and 7—and to agricultural exports (USDA Foreign Agricultural Service 2012; International Crisis Group 2006; Glaser, Snyder, and Park 2008; Snyder 2009).[41] The export of both wheat and rice is controlled by the licensing of a very limited number of state-trading organizations, only two in the case of rice, as well as discretionary use of VAT rebates and export quotas. Following closely on the Treasury Department's designation of Banco Delta Asia as a money-laundering concern, Hu Jintao visited North Korea in October 2006. This meeting followed the signing of a new economic cooperation agreement that likely included aid as well as agreements facilitating transport links and other joint infrastructure projects, Chinese investment, and joint oil exploration.[42] The agreement established a formal consultative mechanism in the form of the DPRK-China Economic, Trade and Scientific and Technological Cooperation Committee, with the "mutual benefit" approach resting on three pillars, including not only strengthened government-to-government relations but expanded reliance on the market and a leading role for Chinese firms in the process (Snyder 2009, 126–127; Reilly 2014a, 2014b, 2014c).

The effort to make aid an inducement to progress in the Six Party Talks was strained by the missile and nuclear tests of 2006 (Chapter 6). China even voted for the UN Security Council sanctions on North Korea, although these sanctions did not include commercial trade or humanitarian assistance. Moreover, North Korean practices on the ground continually challenged the "mutual benefit" concept. In an infamous 2007 episode, China halted railroad shipments to North Korea in response to North Korean theft of Chinese rail wagons.[43]

In 2008, the food trade began growing more complicated because of a broader set of policy concerns in China. As world prices began to rise in 2007–2008, worry over inflation led Chinese authorities to impose a succession of food export controls.[44] Informal reports suggest that the Chinese did step in to provide emergency assistance during the spring of 2008, and that high-level diplomatic initiatives by the North Koreans, including from Kim Jong-il himself, sought to ingratiate the regime to Beijing as the crisis broke (Snyder 2008).[45] However, we cannot rule out the fact that the "assistance" provided by China during the crisis was largely in the form of ensuring adequate supplies, not large-scale aid or subsidies. This fact comports with the conceptual framework laid down by the Chinese following the important visit of Wen Jiabao to Pyongyang in October 2009, which initiated an intense period of diplomatic exchanges at the highest level, including three visits by Kim Jong-il to China (Chapter 7).

Despite the announcement of a number of joint projects, the approach articulated by the Chinese followed the Hu Jintao line of cooperation: "government-guided, enterprise-based, market oriented, mutually beneficial." Outside a one-off infusion of aid following the death of Kim Jong-il to ensure a smooth transition, there is no indication that this framework has changed in the Kim Jong-un era. If anything, the execution of Jang Song-thaek—suspected of managing what Li (2016) calls a number of "cooperation platforms" between the two countries—appears to have had a material effect. In 2015 food shipments fell sharply, although in a context of mildly improved domestic supply of grains.

With substantial uncertainties noted, several points emerge from this overview of China's food trade with North Korea. China has almost certainly used material inducements, including food aid, to advance its diplomatic objectives, including in the Six Party Talks. But there is a tendency for Korea watchers to overemphasize foreign policy concerns in the bilateral aid relationship and overlook its commercial dimension. First, we can see a long-term effort, dating to the early 1990s, to gradually shift Chinese-DPRK relations onto a more commercial footing. This is most obvious in the 1992 decision to price exports and imports in convertible currency and in the renewed push for a "mutual benefit" approach to bilateral relations under Hu Jintao.

Second, we have uncovered an overlooked feature of the aid relationship: the extent to which it is driven by China's domestic preoccupations with harvests, prices, and self-sufficiency. Elsewhere we documented how a sharp decline in agricultural exports from China in 1994, as China gave priority to its own domestic needs, was an important proximate cause of the North Korean famine (Haggard and Noland 2007a, 154–160). More recently we saw that while China has certainly continued to export grains to North Korea since the global food price increases of 2008 and deteriorating food balances in the DPRK, those exports have clearly not been adequate to forestall recurrent distress.

Conclusion

A consistent challenge posed by both sanctions and engagement strategies is humanitarian. Strategically withholding humanitarian aid contributes to distress, but open-ended aid invites moral hazard. We have shown that North Korea's foreign policy behavior had ultimately negative effects on the level and volatility of aid flows and, as a result, on human welfare.[46] There were two reasons for this. First, the country's adversarial stance toward donors, its consistent violation of humanitarian norms, and its unwillingness to undertake needed agricultural reforms made it politically difficult for donors to sustain large-scale aid programs. This appears to be the case with respect to China as well.

It is also clear, however, that the country's foreign policy behavior mattered. Notwithstanding humanitarian norms, food aid was periodically used as a bargaining chip in nuclear negotiations. The downside of this linkage was that the collapse of talks or provocative behavior was followed by aid reversals, which suggest some fundamental limits on the use of inducements. The ethical case is strong that outside donors should not tie humanitarian assistance to political objectives. Nevertheless, in a number of episodes, some of stunning magnitude, the North Korean regime preferred to walk away from food aid rather than make even marginal concessions in its foreign policy. It is clear, moreover, that the regime was unwilling to import adequate supplies on commercial terms to forestall recurrent distress, particularly during the 2006–2012 period (Figure 4.1). Sanctions can be and have been crafted to permit continuity in humanitarian operations, but outside donors cannot force the regime to prioritize the feeding of its population. North Korea's foreign policy is ultimately responsible for the fact that the country receives less aid than it could be receiving and that it is unable, or unwilling, to finance adequate commercial imports to meet human need.

5

The Microeconomics of Engagement

As we stated in our introduction in Chapter 1, advocates of engagement have long argued that increased cross-border exchange can moderate a target state's foreign policy. Such moderation arises either from quid pro quos (which we consider in Chapters 6 and 7) or through broader transformative effects on the economy, politics, and eventually, the foreign policy of the target state. Increased economic integration either gives new groups in the target a direct material stake in external economic relations or strengthens groups within the polity that already have such stakes. These stakeholders not only constrain or encourage the target regime to undertake further economic reform and develop supportive market-conforming institutions,[1] but ultimately act as a political constraint on the regime's wider foreign policy choices as well. Over time, international ties may have socializing and learning effects; individuals, firms, officials, and even high-ranking politicians come to reassess their strategies in light of new information provided through increasing political and economic integration.

Yet the conditions required for this benign circle to operate may be more restrictive than proponents of engagement suggest. The precise mechanisms through which this sequence of economic-cum-political changes occurs are seldom if ever spelled out, let alone analyzed empirically.[2] Target governments may have little interest in the development of markets outside their control or in the development of either informal or formal market-supporting institutions that would strengthen the hand of private actors. Such developments might threaten the state's capacity to maintain control—including control of information—and to extract rents through corruption. Indeed, authoritarian targets are likely to structure economic exchanges precisely so that they maximize such control and limit the risks associated with the emergence of markets and informal and formal institutions. As we have seen, the North Korean regime has been constrained to tolerate what we call marketization from below, but it has only sporadically endorsed it officially through policy reforms.

These claims and counterclaims are amenable to test, although there are few if any efforts that we know of to subject them to scrutiny. The first question is straightforward and empirical: whether foreign transactions are effectively captured by the state- or military-controlled enterprises in the target state. We provide evidence that, at least for those of significance, the answer is yes. Rather than build reforms on the process of marketization from below, North Korean authorities have responded to the market with recurrent efforts to control decentralized cross-border trade. They have also centralized the investment approval process and channeled economic integration with China and South Korea through entities under direct central political control. Indeed, the existence of sanctions may act as an enabler in this regard: there is an ample theoretical and empirical literature showing that sanctions have the effect of creating rents that leaders in the target country can exploit, thus offsetting their adverse effects on core constituencies (Kaempfer, Lowenberg and Mertens 2004; Andreas 2005).

A second question is whether cross-border trade has spilled over into the evolution of market-enabling institutions that favor private exchange. It is well established that institutional quality has a significant impact on cross-border trade and investment (Wei 2000; Levchenko 2007, 2011; Anderson and Marcoullier 2002; Moenius and Berkowitz 2011; Feenstra, Hong, Ma, and Spencer et al. 2012). Particularly important to such exchanges are the extension of credit and the institutions that support it. The policy environment and formal institutions, including dispute settlement mechanisms, obviously matter to the enforcement of such contracts. The development of market-supporting institutions, even if informal, may in this way also constitute a measure of whether engagement strategies work.

It goes without saying that North Korea's institutional environment is extraordinarily weak. The 2015 Transparency International survey on corruption placed North Korea dead last, tied with Somalia in 167th place (Transparency International 2015). But we provide additional evidence from the perspective of firms that market-supporting institutions were not emerging even when the nuclear negotiations were going well in 2007. The actors in question reported that the nature and volatility of the regulatory environment constituted a barrier to trade and investment and that corruption was high. This finding is in line with our overview of policy in Chapter 2.

As a second best, informal institutions can complement formal institutions or even substitute for them altogether where they are lacking. A growing body of literature, much of it derived from the experiences of other transitional economies, has looked at alternative means through which exchange might be supported in the absence of institutions. These mechanisms include collective action by merchants themselves or other forms of personal networks rooted in kinship or family that generate trust (Milgrom, North, and Weingast 1990; Greif 1993; Greif, Milgrom, and Weingast 1994; Clay 1997a, 1997b; Johnson, McMillan, and Woodruff 1999, 2002; McMillan and Woodruff 1999a, 1999b). As we show, these mechanisms appear weak as well, and trust, as measured by indicators such as the willingness to extend credit, is low. Rather, we find a bifurcated economic exchange structure, anchored at one end by dyads of large state-owned enterprises that are protected by higher-level political exchanges and at the other end by smaller firms that try to fly underneath the regulatory radar.

It is important to underscore that our skeptical conclusions are subject to revision. Since our surveys were conducted, de facto marketization has continued apace and we take up its possible effects in our conclusions in Chapter 8. Moreover, we must entertain the possibility that, despite formal patterns of ownership, state-controlled entities and a hybrid state-private capitalist class might be emerging and could come to constrain the regime's foreign policy behavior over time. As Solingen (1998, 2012a) argues, however, statist political coalitions are perfectly aware of the potentially corrosive effects of market-oriented engagement and, for that precise reason, seek to control it. As we show in Chapters 6 and 7, there are no signs of moderation in North Korea's foreign policy; rather, as we also showed in Chapter 2, the regime appears perfectly willing to sacrifice expanded commercial relations outside of China for the pursuit of its nuclear weapons program.

To examine both the nature of cross-border exchange and the formal and informal institutions that underpin it, we draw on two unprecedented surveys of firms based in China and South Korea engaged in trade and investment with North Korea (see the chapter appendix for full survey descriptions). The China survey was conducted in late 2007, near the apex of the Six Party Talks, and involved two hundred and fifty firms or enterprises. The South Korea survey was conducted in November 2009 and March 2010 and involved two hundred firms[3]; its timing was also auspicious—just before the fallout from the sinking of the *Cheonan* in March 2010.

We begin in the first two sections by detailing the survey participants and their mode of entry into North Korea: the characteristics of the Chinese and South and North Korean firms engaged in cross-border trade and investment. Not surprisingly, state entities figured prominently on the North Korean side of these cross-border exchanges. The designation of firms as state-owned enterprises (SOEs) cannot be taken at face value, and it is increasingly possible that a gradual de facto privatization of trade may have been occurring. At least as measured by ownership, however, the North Korean regime seems to have been intent on trying to maintain control over foreign exchange–generating activities in particular.

An important finding on entry pertains to the role that government support plays in these exchanges and the extent to which engagement has taken a commercial form. In the case of China, there were basically two types of Chinese enterprise doing business in North Korea at the time of the survey: large state-owned enterprises with long-standing relationships with their North Korean counterparts and small, essentially private businesses that restricted themselves primarily to trading activities. Neither type reported receiving much support from the Chinese government.

South Korea, in contrast, attempted to circumvent the North Korean system by adopting an enclave model, particularly represented by the KIC. We find that public policies played a much more central role in inducing South Korean firms to enter North Korea. In effect, the state had partly socialized the risk of commercial exchanges with the North, a finding that comports with our analysis in Chapter 3 of the noncommercial nature of much North-South trade. This calls into question the extent to which such exchanges have transformative or socializing effects.

We then turn to subjective assessments of the business environment. Most respondents indicated that they regarded the trend toward liberalization as irreversible, possibly an effect of the timing of the surveys.[4] Nonetheless, Chinese appraisals of the actual North Korean business environment were generally negative. A large majority of the respondents complained not only about infrastructure but about the regulatory environment, the risk of arbitrary changes in rules, the lack of reliable dispute adjudication, and outright expropriation. Nearly the same share of South Korean firms saw the lack of infrastructure and the risk of asset appropriation as problems for business but, because of the controlled institutional environment, were less inclined than their Chinese counterparts to complain about labor quality or the regulatory environment.

We then turn to the question of dispute settlement, corruption, and market-supporting institutions. It is unsurprising that formal mechanisms for settling disputes were seen as limited; firms operating in North Korea were on their own. Bribery and corruption were also pervasive features of the business environment and might be seen as a rational response to the lack of property rights protection. If bribery results in credible protection, it is one political mechanism for ensuring trade and investment. However, there is some evidence that firms faced a greater likelihood of economic predation as they grew in size. As a result, Chinese enterprises and Korean firms outside of Kaesong limited their exposure by generally choosing trading over investing, conducting transactions in China (in the case of Chinese firms), holding their North Korean counterparts to tight settlement terms, and demanding payment primarily in US dollars or Chinese yuan.

Finally, we consider the evolution of informal institutions and trust. Although there is some evidence of such mechanisms, trust was found to be extraordinarily low as measured by standard proxies such as the willingness to extend credit. The rapid growth in trade and investment up through the time of the survey appears to have rested on a distinctly bimodal set of relationships in the Chinese case: short-term and smaller-scale exchanges that resembled a spot market and SOE-to-SOE relationships embedded in higher-level political relationships and the voracious Chinese appetite for minerals and coal.

The surveys' findings have wider theoretical and methodological implications for the debate about sanctions and engagement. In the absence of formal institutions and policy reforms, cross-border integration with hard targets such as North Korea may be self-limiting rather than self-reinforcing. Even with China at the time of the survey, the absence of institutions deterred integration, deterred investment relative to trade, limited the extent of purely private exchange, and inhibited the development of informal networks and relational contracting. These results are consistent with our finding in Chapter 3 that North Korea's trade and investment were increasingly concentrated on China and, until the final closure of Kaesong in 2016, South Korea. Trade and investment with these two countries probably grew as a result of other enforcement mechanisms and complementary public and private investments that substituted for the weakness of North Korean institutions. In the absence of further reforms—and a moderation of the country's foreign policy behavior—these institutions may not be available for other potential partners.

Who Were the Participants?

Ironically, Chinese enterprises had much more direct exposure to the North Korean policy environment than their South Korean counterparts, some of which operated in the Kaesong Industrial Complex. These differences in institutional setting were reflected not only in the perceptions of the firms surveyed but in the very composition of the sample.

The Chinese Firms

Chinese firms doing business in North Korea were engaged in import/export, investment, and the various permutations and combinations of these activities.[5] Pure exporters made up the largest group, with most of them relatively small private enterprises (Figure 5.1). If the processes of marketization implicit in the engagement model were to hold, they would most likely occur among this group of enterprises.

With respect to ownership, 58 percent of the firms doing business in North Korea were private enterprises, and another 14 percent were sole proprietorships; only 3 percent were foreign firms operating in China. There was a distinct minority of a dozen large SOEs, some of which had been doing business with North Korea for more than a quarter-century, but over 80 percent of respondents entered in the ten years prior to the survey.[6]

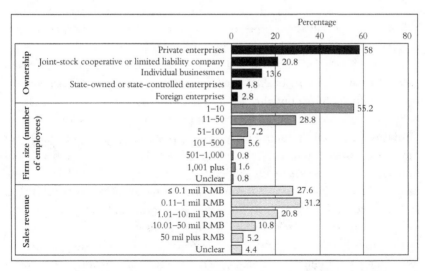

FIGURE 5.1 Characteristics of Chinese firms engaged in business with the DPRK

SOURCE: Haggard and Noland (2012b).

More than half of the Chinese enterprises doing business in North Korea were involved principally in trading; another 5 percent identified themselves as diversified with trading operations. The traders were asked about the most important product that they exchanged with their largest customer or supplier, and the findings comport broadly with what we know about bilateral trade at the time of the survey from aggregate trade data.[7] Beyond trading, activities represented included construction (16 percent), services (10 percent), and agriculture (6 percent); larger mining firms were also represented but at this stage in the bilateral relationship accounted for a smaller share of the sample.

Among investors, the most frequently cited motivations for trade with North Korea were to expand business in the domestic market (29 percent), to sell there (21 percent), or to exploit natural resources (27 percent). Only 23 percent were locating in North Korea as an export platform, either back to China (13 percent) or to third markets (10 percent). We interpret these results as reflecting in part weak infrastructure and in part prevailing policies and incentives that limited opportunities for export-oriented investment. The regime's attempt to build more export-processing zones was still five years away. However, as we argued in Chapter 2, we cannot rule out the effects of political risk on investor perceptions, including through sanctions.

While our understanding of Chinese participants is relatively complete, our understanding of their North Korea counterparts is much weaker. Figure 5.2 shows Chinese firms' responses to a question about the legal status of their primary North Korean counterparty, broken down by importers, exporters, and investors. In all three types of cross-border exchange, the majority of respondents reported that their main counterparties were SOEs. Nonetheless, important distinctions emerged across types of exchange. Importers, and particularly investors, reported a much greater dependence on official entities: overwhelmingly SOEs but also government bureaus and the military. Eleven of the twelve Chinese SOEs in the sample reported that a North Korean SOE was their primary counterparty. Pure exporters reported a wider array of North Korean counterparties, including Chinese brokers, private firms, and individual entrepreneurs; again, evidence for the engagement model was more likely to be found among this group, although official entities—SOEs, urban and rural collective enterprises, government bureaus, and the military—still dominated as counterparties for this group of firms as well.

Findings about the identity of counterparties suggest some important limits on the spread effects of cross-border marketization. However, caution is warranted because the SOE category encompassed entities and economic behaviors of at least three different types, some of which reflected the process

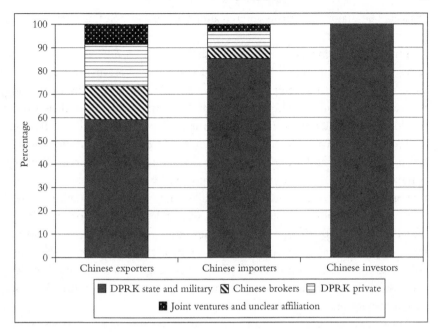

FIGURE 5.2   Ownership of North Korean counterparties by Chinese respondent type

SOURCE: Haggard and Noland (2012b).

of marketization from below. The first were SOEs engaged in their traditional, legally sanctioned lines of business, presumably subject to extensive
direct political control. The second were SOEs whose managers exploited
the company's legal status and resources to initiate nontraditional and in some
cases completely unrelated (and even illicit) lines of business. Third, because
entrepreneurs affiliated with SOEs for political protection (Kim 2007), the
SOE may in fact have been a shell for an effective joint venture partnership.
Thus, while the majority of counterparties were identified as SOEs, de facto
privatization of exchange was probably occurring under the mantle of the
state, including through corruption. We return to this in more detail in our
conclusions in Chapter 8.

The South Korean Firms

South Korean involvement in the North was a direct outcome of the gradual
political relaxation of relations that followed democratization in the South.
The earliest that any respondent indicated entering the North Korean market was 1986, but the political breakthrough of the 2000 summit was clearly

critical. The majority of firms entered after 2004, corresponding to the initiation of activities at KIC.[8]

South Korean engagement with North Korea had a different profile and raises somewhat different issues. Most of the South Korean firms surveyed were small (less than 10 employees), and relatively young (established within ten years of the survey), although a handful of large firms (more than 1,000 employees) and established firms (more than 50 years old) were surveyed as well.[9] The South Korean firms doing business in North Korea had surprisingly diverse operations and were by no means limited to the KIC. South Korean firms were also engaged in importing, exporting, and investment through either arm's-length transactions or POC trade. In contrast to the Chinese case, however, nearly all of them (92 percent) were involved in importing, either directly from North Korean counterparties (59 percent) or via some kind of processing relationship (33 percent). Fewer than half (45 percent) were involved in exporting, with the bulk of the exporting firms operating through processing relationships (33 percent); only 12 percent sold to North Korean counterparties outside of POC relationships.

Thirty-two firms (16 percent of the sample) had invested in North Korea. Much of this investment occurred at Kaesong and so was in stark contrast to Chinese investment, which was largely forced into joint ventures. Not surprisingly, when asked about their motivation for investment, most respondents said that they established operations aimed at selling to the South Korean market. This occurred through POC trade or export-oriented foreign direct investment.[10] Most of these investing firms reported stand-alone investments without North Korean partners (72 percent). Also not surprising is that POC firms were more concentrated in manufacturing (89 percent), and the KIC firms were engaged exclusively in this sector.[11] This pattern contrasts with that in the China survey, where pure trading activities were more prevalent.

On the export side, trade was concentrated in textiles and clothing, particularly among firms engaged in processing activities, including at the KIC (Table 5.1). On the import side, food and fisheries products were most important, followed by textiles and apparel, the latter reflecting the return side of POC relationships as well as assembly activities at the KIC.

As in the China survey, we have less information on the primary counterparties of the South Korean firms having done business in North Korea, but location provides some clues. A plurality of respondents reported their main location in North Korea as Pyongyang (29 percent) followed by the KIC (26 percent)—where there were no North Korean counterparties—and

TABLE 5.1

Product categories of South Korean firms operating in North Korea

Category	Full sample		Non-KIC		KIC	
	Exporters (%)	Importers (%)	Exporters (%)	Importers (%)	Exporters (%)	Importers (%)
Chemicals and chemical products	4	1	3	1	7	0
Clothing/textiles	56	35	54	34	61	42
Consumer goods and components thereof	9	7	8	2	11	30
Food and fishery products	6	42	7	50	4	6
Industrial/transportation equipment and inter-mediates	16	4	18	3	11	12
Minerals and forestry products	4	4	3	5	7	3
Wood products and paper	4	1	7	1	0	0
Miscellaneous goods	0	5	0	5	0	6
Category	Nonprocessors		Processors		Investors	
	Exporters (%)	Importers (%)	Exporters (%)	Importers (%)	Exporters (%)	Importers (%)
Chemicals and chemical products	4	0	5	2	8	0
Clothing/textiles	13	20	71	62	56	44
Consumer goods and components thereof	13	3	8	15	4	22
Food and fishery products	9	63	5	6	8	15
Industrial/transportation equipment and inter-mediates	43	3	6	8	12	11
Minerals and forestry products	4	6	5	2	8	4
Wood products and paper	13	0	2	2	4	0
Miscellaneous goods	0	6	0	5	0	4

SOURCE: Haggard and Noland (2012a).

North Hamgyong (20 percent), with other locations less frequently cited. More than 80 percent reported involvement with only a single North Korean counterparty.[12] Moreover, nearly half of both exporters and importers reported that a majority of their revenues were accounted for by North Korean transactions (Figure 5.3). This subsample of firms was clearly dominated

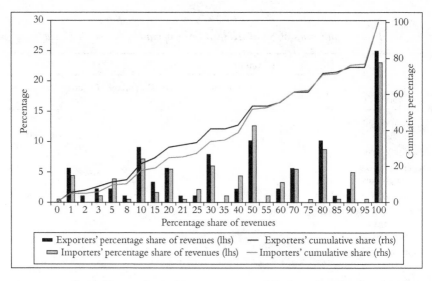

FIGURE 5.3   South Korean share of revenues accounted for by transactions
with North Korea

SOURCE: Haggard and Noland (2012a).

by small firms largely dedicated to doing business with North Korea. Such
dependence appears to have been particularly notable for firms engaged in
processing activities.

One of the critical differences between the two samples is the much more
prominent role of non–North Korean counterparties in the South Korea survey (Figure 5.4). Pure importers and exporters reported that a majority of their
counterparties were North Korean entities, mostly state-owned enterprises
(SOEs), followed by governmental units. Those connected with the other modalities reported more diverse counterparties, but firms operating in the KIC
are particularly distinct for having had no involvement with North Korean
SOEs; rather, they did business to a much greater extent with South Korean or
third-party firms, a factor that no doubt also influenced the risk environment.

Entry and Modality

Choices about entering North Korea and the types of activity in which to
engage are revealing of perceptions of political and policy risk and the nature
of the operating environment. Our control group of firms not engaged with
North Korea allows us to distinguish enterprises that entered the market from
those that did not. Our survey also allows us to examine why firms chose
to export and import only or to invest or engage in some more complex

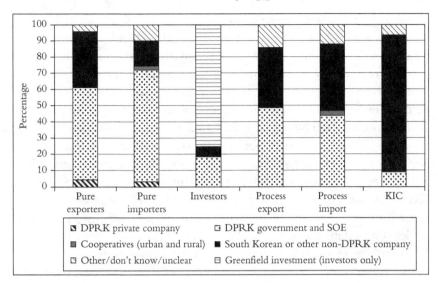

FIGURE 5.4 Ownership of North Korean counterparties, South Korean respondents

SOURCE: Haggard and Noland (2012a).

combination of business activities. We expect property rights, contracting, and the regulatory environment to have mattered more to investing firms.

Obviously, given the differing institutional setups and degrees of state involvement, the determinants of entry and choice of modality differed considerably across both the China and the South Korea surveys. We start with China.

The Chinese Firms

Econometric estimates reported in Haggard, Lee, and Noland (2012) indicate that ownership type and size matter with respect to propensity to initiate business with North Korea. Private ownership is positively associated with entry, and size as measured by number of employees is negatively associated with entry. Chinese firms choosing to engage in business with North Korea are smaller and more likely to be private than their counterparts.[13]

We wanted to know how ex ante appraisals of the North Korean business environment affect the likelihood of entry, but we faced a specification problem in teasing this out of our survey data. The 260 enterprises with current or past experience in North Korea gave appraisals that were informed by experience ex post. This situation creates a statistically insolvable problem with respect to determining the direction of causality. Nevertheless, one particular null finding deserves mention: the belief that bribery was necessary to do business with North Korea was uncorrelated with entry. Approximately 70 percent of both Chinese firms that entered and did not enter North Korea believed that bribery was required to operate in the country, but this information did not constitute a deterrent. Indeed, expectations of the need to bribe were even positive and significant in some of the regressions reported by Haggard, Lee, and Noland (2012). For the reasons of simultaneity outlined previously, these results should not be given a causal interpretation; bribery did not lead to more investment. Nonetheless, the results suggest that firms with a more extensive understanding of the North Korean economy understood perfectly well the ubiquity of corruption. As we will see subsequently, however, there is evidence that the survey respondents' ex ante assessments may have underestimated the actual extent of corruption in North Korea.

Investment in a setting such as North Korea involves substantial risk. We found that in contrast to general determinants of entry, size did influence the propensity to invest, perhaps because of the political weight and connections larger firms could bring to bear to protect their stakes.

But we also wanted to know whether the perceived ability to resolve disputes through different channels influenced the decision to invest. We considered four broad paths of dispute resolution: informal North Korean resolution through direct appeals to North Korean officials; formal North Korean resolution through the courts; official Chinese resolution, including through both the courts and political appeals; and informal resolution through Chinese third-party networks such as industry associations. The expectation that one could appeal to North Korean officials for dispute resolution was positively associated with investing; firms that felt they could resolve a dispute through appeal or connection to officials were more likely to invest. Interestingly, however, neither formal institutions in North Korea nor formal or informal Chinese institutions mattered. Although China-North Korea trade was often treated as highly political, the firms that invested appear to have recognized that they were on their own. They recognized the need to engage in bribery, appear to have accepted corruption as part of the operating environment, and relied not on formal dispute settlement mechanisms but rather on their connections with North Korean officials.

The South Korean Firms

Status as a small- or medium-sized enterprise (SME) was positively related to the entry of South Korean firms into North Korean markets (Haggard and Noland 2012a). More weakly, firms listing trade as their primary activity were also more likely to enter; those citing manufacturing as a principal activity were less likely. The most interesting comparative finding between the two surveys, however, centered on the role of public policy: that access to public support, including in the form of lending, was a significant determinant of entry for South Korean firms.[14]

A closer examination of this finding reveals that 70 percent of firms reported receiving no direct support (Table 5.2), capturing the many smaller enterprises working outside of Kaesong.[15] But when the responses were disaggregated, we found that a majority of firms operating in the KIC reported receiving some kind of policy support. As we noted in Chapter 3, the Kaesong trade as well as some joint cooperation projects initiated under the Roh Moo-hyun government operated in a distinctly gray area between commercial and noncommercial trade.

Conditional on entry, we similarly asked whether firms engaged in arm's-length trade and investment, POC trade, or production in the KIC. These distinctions are interesting because they can be thought of as embodying a categorical choice ordered by decreasing exposure to North Korean policy and infrastructure (i.e., arm's length being the most exposed followed by POC, followed by the KIC) (Table 5.3).[16] The findings confirm the point: the availability of commercial bank finance, finance via state-affiliated institutions, and access to special financing opportunities were all associated with a reduced likelihood of choosing arm's-length transacting and a greater likelihood of locating in the KIC. Econometrically, it is unclear whether this was a matter of these financing opportunities pushing firms away from arm's-length transacting and toward the KIC, or whether business activity less exposed to North Korean policy (and infrastructure) attracted financing. However, it is certainly

TABLE 5.2

South Korean government support for South Korean firms operating in North Korea

Support received	Total (%)	Non-KIC (%)	KIC (%)	Quitters (%)
Special tariff reduction/preferential trade treatment	23	21	33	6
Special financing convenience	8	2	33	0
Export/import insurance	4	1	18	0
Investment guarantee	3	0	15	0
No government support	70	76	39	94

SOURCE: Haggard and Noland (2012a).

TABLE 5.3

South Korean respondent introduction networks

Introduction networks by importer/exporter	Exporters		Importers	
	Non–North Korean counterparty (%)	North Korean counterparty (%)	Non–North Korean counterparty (%)	North Korean counterparty (%)
Direct contact/knew management	0	4	4	2
DPRK public and private	6	13	2	6
ROK government	41	5	40	4
Other ROK businesses	50	47	38	43
China public and private	6	24	15	38
Other	3	13	4	10

	KIC Only			
	Exporters		Importers	
Introduction networks (for KIC only)	Non–North Korean counterparty (%)	North Korean counterparty (%)	Non–North Korean counterparty (%)	North Korean counterparty (%)
Direct contact/knew management	0	0	3	0
DPRK public and private	4	0	0	0
ROK government	57	0	55	0
Other ROK businesses	39	80	34	75
China public and private	0	0	0	0
Other	0	20	7	25

	Investors Only			
	Exporters		Importers	
Introduction networks (for investors only)	Non–North Korean counterparty (%)	North Korean counterparty (%)	Non–North Korean counterparty (%)	North Korean counterparty (%)
Direct contact/knew management	0	0	0	0
DPRK public and private	6	0	0	0
ROK government	61	0	65	0
Other ROK businesses	33	57	25	43
China public and private	0	29	0	29
Other	6	14	10	29

SOURCE: Haggard and Noland (2012a).

plausible that the manufacturing firms that entered North Korea required state support to invest, and that the KIC provided both assurances to creditors and a more secure institutional environment.

It is again important to underline the contrast between the two samples in this regard. Few Chinese businesses (and surprisingly none of the SOEs) reported any support from the Chinese government for their activities, which comports with Chinese government policy toward North Korea noted in Chapter 3 and elaborated in more detail in Chapter 7. Seven percent of the respondents indicated that they received special tariff reductions or exemptions, presumably under Chinese provisions for preferences for local firms engaged in small-magnitude "border trade." A handful of firms reported receiving trade insurance, investment guarantees, or preferential finance, but government support, narrowly construed, does not appear to play a significant role in China's trade with North Korea. The Chinese policy of promoting commercial relations, as opposed to aid or commercial activities is noticeable in the firm-level data.

Subjective Assessments of the North Korean Business Environment

Generally, Chinese and South Korean firms negatively assess the business environment in North Korea, with the Chinese holding somewhat more negative views (Figure 5.5).[17] The pattern of responses across the Chinese and South Korean firms are correlated. Large majorities identified inadequate infrastructure (79 percent in the Chinese survey; 78 percent in the South Korea survey) and the ban on cell phones at the time of the survey (86 percent in the Chinese survey; 62 percent in the South Korea survey) as constraints.[18] However, the policy environment was also identified as a major hindrance to business. Other major obstacles reported were changing regulations (79 percent in the China survey; 66 percent in the South Korea survey), the nature of regulations (70 percent in the China survey; 50 percent in the South Korea survey), and threat of expropriation (62 percent in the China survey; 63 percent in the South Korea survey).[19]

An apparent surprise emerges when the responses from the South Korean survey are disaggregated between those inside and those outside the KIC (Figure 5.6). Relative to firms operating outside the zone, KIC firms gave *more* negative appraisals of the regulatory environment, risks created by capricious regulation, and the possibility of expropriation. Why did firms in the KIC— at least partly sheltered from North Korean institutions—have a more negative view, particularly given that their responses were informed by experience and

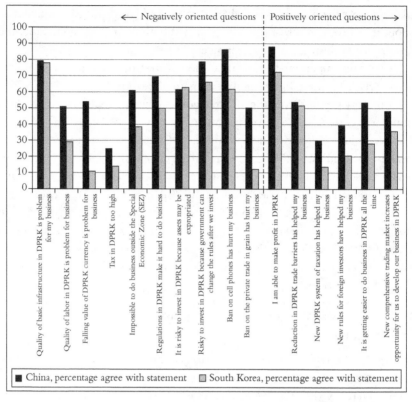

FIGURE 5.5   China–South Korea perceptions on doing business in North Korea

SOURCE: Haggard and Noland (2012b).

expectations prior to entry? A plausible interpretation is that the KIC firms chose to use this modality precisely because their relatively negative appraisals of conditions outside the zone.[20]

We can see similar differences in perceptions by comparing the attitudes of Chinese firms doing business in North Korea with those not doing business there, using simple t-tests. Perceptions on some issues were not significantly different between the two sets of firms; companies of both nationalities gave similarly negative assessments along these dimensions—for example, quality of infrastructure and barriers posed by weak telecommunications. However, there were statistically significant differences in the views of North Korea's institutional environment. Chinese firms not doing business with North Korea were more likely to see high taxes and the regulatory environment (at the 1 percent level) and the perceived difficulty of doing any business outside the

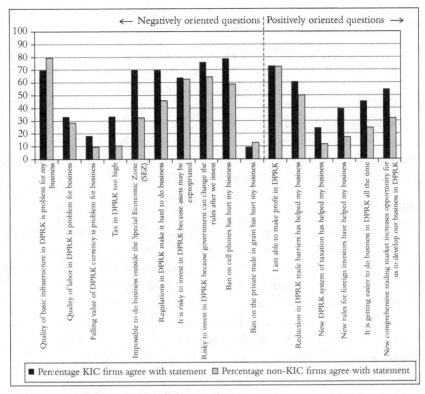

FIGURE 5.6   South Korean perceptions of DPRK business environment, KIC versus non-KIC firms

SOURCE: Haggard and Noland (2012a).

special economic zones (at 5 percent level) as barriers. Perceptions of a problematic business environment likely deterred entry.

But cognizance of risks was by no means limited to firms that chose to stay out. Chinese trading firms doing business in North Korea were more likely to agree (at the 5 percent level) with the statement that it is too risky to invest because of potential expropriation, suggesting that such fears pushed firms away from investment and toward trading modalities. This finding confirms that the overall investment climate—and even the fear of outright expropriation of assets—deters longer-run investment relations. Likewise, compared to those not doing business, investors complained even more frequently (at the 5 percent level) than traders about high taxes (at the 10 percent level), which can be interpreted broadly as a proxy for government-related costs of doing business.

Dispute Resolution and Corruption

Respondents' answers to questions about the legal and regulatory environment suggest that cross-border integration takes place in a setting characterized by an unfavorable and capricious policy environment and the absence of conventional property rights protections (Chapter 2). Corruption is simultaneously a deterrent to entry and an informal mechanism through which firms seek protection from the weak policy environment. In this section, we extend this finding to the weakness of dispute settlement mechanisms and the likely role played by corruption in protecting firm interests.

Dispute Settlement

A critical feature of any cross-border institutional environment is the capacity of investors and traders to resolve disputes. Formal institutions of dispute settlement, typically courts or other means of formal arbitration, are often seen as the very cornerstone of a market economy even if they are supplemented with informal mechanisms. Courts have been found to improve the functioning of relational contracts and to contribute to expanded trade and investment. Indeed, such institutions appear to be most important at the start of a trading relationship and in economies in transition (Johnson, McMillan, and Woodruff 1999, 2002).

How do actors assess the opportunities for dispute settlement? The China survey reveals that disputes were not uncommon. Twenty-one percent of these relationships had generated disputes but with differences depending on the nature of the business relationship. Fully 41 percent of investors reported disputes, an indication of the extent of holdup risk. Only 4 percent of pure exporters did. Weak dispute settlement appears to push firms back to less risky, "cash and carry" transactions.

When asked how they would resolve a dispute, the pattern of responses across Chinese exporters, importers, and investors differed in predictable but interesting ways; we focus here on the differences between exporters and investors. More than one-quarter of exporters indicated that there were no third parties from which they could seek help. To the extent that they did believe there was recourse, it was entirely on the Chinese side of the border: 20 percent indicated that they would seek help from Chinese government officials, 19 percent would look to other Chinese companies or business associations, and 17 percent would use the Chinese court system.[21] Although the number of pure exporters reporting disputes was small (only 5 of 113), their pessimism was warranted; none of the five reported that they were satisfied with the dispute resolution process.

For investors, more than 35 percent would try to settle matters privately, 31 percent would appeal to North Korean local officials, and 22 percent would appeal to Chinese officials, presumably reflecting the far greater importance of North Korean officials in settling investment disputes that involved the foreign investor's physical presence in North Korea. It is also notable that the number reporting that they would appeal to local officials (31 percent) exceeded that of provincial officials (16 percent) and central government officials (12 percent). This pattern is consistent with the fact that investors may see local officials as more forthcoming.

Whatever the investors thought ex ante, their disaffection after the fact was high: 77 percent reporting disputes also reported that they were not satisfied with the way their dispute was settled. Recall that the number of investors reporting disputes was also much higher than the number of firms involved in export only. When asked how they would settle disputes in the future, respondents suggested that local and provincial officials might be more willing to protect property rights than their higher-ups would be.[22]

Taken together, these results suggest that "marketization from below" may have at least one political correlate supportive of the transformation model. As local officials seek to attract trade and investment, firms may see local officials as more forthcoming. This is particularly true as the central government remains cautious about loosening controls. However, as we noted in Chapters 2 and 3, this positive development may be partly offset by central government efforts precisely to recentralize decision making vis-à-vis foreign investors.

In contrast to their Chinese counterparts, the South Korean firms reported relatively few disputes. The survey permitted respondents engaged in multiple types of business to characterize each of their principal business relationships separately—for example, a single firm could report on relations with its main import, export, and investment partner. Overall, 6 percent of investors, 7 percent of exporters, and 11 percent of importers reported disputes with their primary counterparties—far below the percentages reported in the China survey.[23]

However, this relatively sanguine picture changes if the respondents are disaggregated by modality and counterparty. Disputes were less frequent for firms involved in POC and KIC activities or for those transacting with non-North Korean counterparties.[24] Still, 25 percent of exporters and 20 percent of importers doing arm's-length transactions with North Korean counterparties reported disputes, comparable to the figures obtained in the China survey. In short, disputes were less common for firms less exposed to the North Korean economy. On one point, however, the Chinese and South Korean firms converge: of those Korean firms experiencing disputes, only a minority reported satisfaction with the resolution.[25] Interestingly, while the incidence of disputes was lower for POC and KIC firms than for firms engaged in arm's-length transactions, these firms did not report higher satisfaction with the resolution of their disputes.

What recourse did South Korean firms believe they had? Among the sub-sample of firms that had experienced disputes, nearly all indicated either that they settled matters privately or that they had no access to third-party inter-vention. In the China survey, firms expressed a much greater willingness to use contacts in North Korean local and provincial governments to resolve disputes; indeed, they indicated that disputes were less likely to be resolved successfully if they were escalated from local to provincial to central government con-nections. In contrast, the only third-party dispute settlement mechanism that received any support in the South Korean sample was appeal to the North Korean central government and that was mentioned by only 7 percent of re-spondents who had had disputes.

This finding has important implications for arguments about engagement. South Korean firms are under much closer political scrutiny by the North Ko-rean authorities than their Chinese counterparts, and as a consequence they are less able than Chinese enterprises to work out disputes at lower political levels. Additionally, most of the South Korean firms, even those in the KIC, reported that they were required to obtain permission or approval from some level of the North Korean government (generally the central government) to do business in North Korea. At least as political relations between the North and South were structured at the time of the survey, firm-level data show a strong North Korean intent to control the relationship with South Korean entities. After that time, trade and investment relations collapsed as a result of sanctions and the first closure of the KIC in 2013 (it was closed indefinitely in 2016).

Corruption

A standard result in economics is that the nature and extent of regulation can create rents and hence opportunities for bribery and corruption. Before turn-ing to our findings on corruption, it is worthwhile to consider the regulatory controls on foreign business that give rise to the need to bribe in the first place, filling in our general account of the business environment in Chapter 2 with detail gleaned from the surveys.

Most Chinese firms in our survey were required to obtain permission or approval from some level of the North Korean government to do business in North Korea, although there were differences across firm types. All of the

Chinese SOEs reported having obtained permission before starting a business. Only 9 percent of investors, or six firms, reported that they had no need of government approval. However, 29 percent of private businesses reported that they did not obtain any permission or approval. Twenty-nine percent of traders and 47 percent of those engaged only in exports to North Korea reported that they had no need of government approval. Clearly, small private businesses engaged largely in trade sought to fly below the radar, but once in they were also more likely to fear predation.

Given the institutional setting, it is not surprising that a majority of the firms in our China survey reported a need to bribe to do business (55 percent). These findings are consistent with evidence from refugee surveys, including testimonies of former state and party officials, of high—and possibly rising—levels of corruption in North Korea (Haggard and Noland 2010b; Kim 2010).

Which firms are most at risk of being preyed on for bribes? Despite the fact that small firms are more likely to enter, and despite the fact that they engage in activities that reduce risk, such as focusing solely on exports and avoiding contact with officials, they are nonetheless more likely to find the regulatory environment a problem. In contrast, large SOEs appear relatively untroubled, which may reflect size or the ability of such firms to draw on their political connections in order to operate. However, investors are significantly more likely to report a need to bribe (73 percent) than traders (54 percent) or those engaged in exporting only (44 percent). Despite the fact that smaller firms have more adverse views of the business environment and are more likely to fear expropriation, larger firms perceive a greater need to bribe (Haggard and Noland 2012c). Given weak property rights, larger firms and those involved in more complex investment relationships are clearly more vulnerable to the holdup problems associated with a weak institutional environment.

We also asked about actual bribe costs, and the differences between investors and traders are once again clear. Nineteen percent of firms reported spending more than 10 percent of revenues on bribes, but more than half of investors (53 percent) reported doing so.

The views of Chinese and South Korean firms diverge strongly on the extent of corruption. A majority of South Korean respondents strongly disagreed with the claim that bribery was necessary to conduct business—a view widely shared across firms engaged in arm's-length transactions, POC trade, and KIC activities. To our surprise, institutional setting did not appear to matter in this regard. Not surprisingly, investors, who were more exposed to regulatory and direct expropriation risk, had slightly less sanguine views on this topic, but even this group regarded the phenomenon as much less of an issue than did either the Chinese enterprises or the North Korea refugees previously surveyed. This apparent lack of vulnerability could be related to a combination of better language and cultural skills that allowed firms to more effectively avoid disputes in the first place and fend off predation more adroitly than their Chinese counterparts could. However, the pattern of responses could also reflect a reluctance on the part of the respondents to address this topic truthfully given the sensitivity of the corruption issue in the South.

Risk, Financial Settlement Terms, and Trust

A final indicator of the trade and investment networks at the time of the survey can be found in indicators of interfirm trust. Earlier research on transitional economies in Europe and Asia found the extension of credit and financial settlement terms to provide more broad insight into the credibility of the operating environment, the nature and extent of risk, and the evolution of trust (Johnson, McMillan, and Woodruff 1999, 2002; McMillan and Woodruff 1999a, 1999b).

With respect to settlement currencies, none of the respondents in either survey reported doing any business in North Korean won. While this might reflect simple exchange rate risks, a long history of currency revaluations—culminating in the conversion of November 2009—suggests that the risk was also political. Most Chinese exporters to North Korea reported using Chinese yuan as the settlement currency (55 percent), possibly reflecting the small traders' preference to be paid in local currency, followed by US dollars (34 percent), and then barter (8 percent). Imports, in contrast, were settled primarily in US dollars (52 percent), followed by Chinese yuan (29 percent), and then barter (15 percent).[26] Similarly, most South Korean respondents indicated that most transactions were done in US dollars, with barter and the euro distant second and third, respectively.

More important than the settlement currency per se is that settlement terms were typically very tight, reflecting lack of trust and credit. As one would expect, there was a positive relationship between the length of the relationship between firms and their clients and settlement terms. Nonetheless, in the China survey less than 5 percent of traders reported extending credit to their suppliers. Of these, 60 percent were SOEs—an enormously disproportionate presence relative to the occurrence of SOEs in the sample (5 percent). Outside of these inter-SOE interactions and some relationships of longer standing, economic transactions were cash-and-carry. Most trade was settled at time of delivery; the next most frequently occurring moment of payment was at time of order placement. Less than 10 percent of import and 5 percent of export transactions occurred more than 30 days after delivery. Particularly given dissatisfaction with dispute settlement and the broader institutional environment, it is not difficult to understand why credit was limited.

The South Korea survey also reveals an almost complete absence of lending between counterparties: Only a single South Korean importer out of 136 reported extending loans to its North Korean counterparty.[27] However, relaxed settlement terms can be interpreted as an indirect form of financial support. While the overall numbers suggest that counterparties were permitted lax payment terms, it is clear that North Korean counterparties—as distinct from South Korean or third-country counterparties—were discriminated against in this regard (Tables 5.4 and 5.5). Moreover, the provision of loose settlement terms was greatest with KIC transactions, followed by POC transactions and then arm's-length transactions. Here institutional setting clearly matters. Two-thirds of pure exporters demanded payment from their North Korean customers when the order was placed or at time of delivery. In contrast, none of the South Korean firms reporting imports via KIC paid less than 30 days after delivery.

Elsewhere (Haggard and Noland 2012b) we reported multivariate analyses of the determinants of trust as proxied by the financial terms on which exchange occurs. There is evidence that firm characteristics and the nature of interfirm relationships are related to trust. In the China survey, the most highly correlated variable with trade credit was the respondent's status as a Chinese SOE. This is a striking result insofar as the primary counterparty of every Chinese SOE in the sample save one was a North Korean SOE. In essence, trust as measured by both extension of credit and settlement terms was most robust in inter-SOE interactions: Chinese SOEs extended credit to their North Korean counterparts or allowed them to run up arrears. At least as measured by the extension of credit, trust did not emerge in the market but was most evident in economic relations embedded in the higher-order political relationship between the two countries.

The South Korean survey provides another perspective on these issues given the variety of institutional settings and the much higher incidence of non-North Korean counterparties. Clearly, North Korean counterparties were considered risky (or simply as having little negotiating leverage). South Korean exporters received significantly more relaxed payment terms than did North Korean exporters, and transactions that involved a North Korean counterparty (some involved South Korean or third-country counterparties operating in North Korea) involved more demanding terms than those that did not (Haggard and Noland 2012a).

TABLE 5.4
Exporter settlement terms for South Korean respondents

Most common method of payment	All exporters All counterparties (%)	Pure exporters Non–North Korean counterparty (%)	Pure exporters North Korean counterparty (%)	Process exporters Non–North Korean counterparty (%)	Process exporters North Korean counterparty (%)	KIC Non–North Korean counterparty (%)	KIC North Korean counterparty (%)
Time of order placement	11	0	33	0	10	0	0
Time of delivery	23	38	33	0	26	0	0
1–30 days	27	25	27	19	32	7	0
After 30 days	39	38	7	81	32	93	100
Total	**100**	**100**	**100**	**100**	**100**	**100**	**100**

SOURCE: Haggard and Noland (2012a).

TABLE 5.5

Importer settlement terms for South Korean respondents

Most common method of payment	All importers	Pure importers		Process importers		KIC	
	All counterparties (%)	Non–North Korean counterparty (%)	North Korean counterparty (%)	Non–North Korean counterparty (%)	North Korean counterparty (%)	Non–North Korean counterparty (%)	North Korean counterparty (%)
Time of order placement	18	10	29	0	5	0	0
Time of delivery	36	30	48	0	29	0	0
1–30 days	31	50	23	36	40	42	0
After 30 days	15	10	1	64	26	58	100
Total	100	100	100	100	100	100	100

SOURCE: Haggard and Noland (2012a).

We were particularly interested in the effects of the institutions and public policies of the South Korean government, and we found that activity in the KIC was associated with looser settlement terms than the other two modalities, even controlling for the absence of North Korean counterparties in the KIC relative to those modalities. Transactions with firms that had access to South Korean government support were also looser, although the precise causality is not clear.[28] Correlation between payment terms and South Korean public policy and the lack of correlation with indicators of the institutional environment, such as introduction networks, duration of relationship, and bribery strongly suggests that the South Korean government has socialized risk.

Conclusion

This chapter used two firm-level surveys, one conducted in China and the other in South Korea, to explore whether the nature of observed cross-border exchange supports the transformative case for engagement. The evidence is mixed at best. Much of the North Korea-China economic relationship rests on a self-interested commercial logic. The Chinese firms engaging in cross-border trade are largely private, do not appear to have substantial support from the Chinese government, and have a limited belief in the ability of their government to protect them in the face of disputes.

At the time of the survey, however, the counterparties of both the China and the South Korea firms surveyed were largely the core institutions of the North Korean state, either directly as revealed by the China survey or indirectly at the KIC, the centerpiece of North-South engagement. This was particularly true for enterprises that had established an investment presence: either they were in joint ventures with government, party, military entities, or SOEs, or they were in the KIC, a zone ultimately subject to North Korean sovereignty as Pyongyang showed when it closed it in 2013. Chinese traders did not interact with a wider array of North Korean counterparties, including private firms, and such wholesale trade no doubt fed retail "marketization from below," supporting the engagement-as-transformation approach. However, most transactions that generated foreign exchange for the regime—namely, North Korean exporters and joint ventures with Chinese firms—were dominated by state entities. At least as measured by ownership of North Korean counterparts, cross-border trade remained largely in state hands.

Despite the fact that Chinese and South Korean firms reported the ability to make a profit, they offered a uniformly negative appraisal of the North Korean operating environment, including with respect to economic regulation. In response they adopted various market and political strategies to reduce risk.

In the case of private Chinese enterprises, such hedging strategies included limiting their activity to trading, particularly exporting. These strategies were particularly prevalent among small and small private enterprises and firms that did not believe that they could call on political connections in North Korea. Transactions were undertaken in ways that limited risk but also limited trust, including not only settlement in hard currencies but very stringent payment terms and limited credit. In effect, they conducted "cash-and-carry" businesses. All of these strategies prevented cross-border integration from becoming what it might have been.

Large natural resource investments have different strategies for protecting themselves. However, our findings raise the issue of whether North Korea's export specialization in natural resource exports, also noted in Chapter 3, is less a manifestation of underlying comparative advantage than a signal of institutional weakness impeding the emergence of more complex forms of production. In these sectors, control by the state and the rentier nature of investments is particularly marked, and with potentially adverse rather than beneficial effects for policy, as a large literature has shown (Ross 2013; Hendrix and Noland 2015).

In the absence of formal institutions, Chinese firms devise political strategies for reducing the risks of predation. There is some evidence that they protect themselves via informal networks capable of imposing reputational penalties on North Korean actors. But they mainly rely on personal connections in North Korea, including through pervasive corruption and bribery of public officials. Obviously, these strategies are decidedly second best; there are clearly gains to be had from stronger North Korean institutions. This is particularly the case when we consider the fact that predation is correlated with size, which can add a self-limiting aspect to the expansion of cross-border integration. Firms appear to limit the scale of involvement in order to fly beneath the radar of a predatory state.

In sum, the survey evidence provided here buttresses the analysis of aggregate data in Chapter 3. Despite the rapid growth of trade and investment with China, the weakness of the institutional environment deters North Korean integration with the world economy, prevents more complex investments relative to trade and natural resource ventures, probably limits the extent of purely private exchange, and inhibits the development of informal networks and relational contracting. The surveys certainly demonstrate that some process of marketization is occurring. But they cast doubt on the expectation that engagement between China and North Korea, at least during the period covered here, fostered the internal changes in North Korea that would lead either to further economic reform or to a moderation of the country's external behavior. On the contrary, at the time of the surveys the country appeared caught in a partial-reform equilibrium.

Since these surveys were conducted, there have been changes in North Korea's foreign economic relations, but they do not necessarily overturn our findings. After the currency reform, North Korea initially moved to further strengthen the state role, centralizing the investment approval process and channeling cross-border economic integration through entities under even more direct central political oversight. In 2010, the regime established a State Development Bank. Late the following year, it announced a "10-Year State Strategy Plan for Economic Development" and designated a specialized body to oversee FDI under it. The Taepung Group was established at the same time as a holding company for joint ventures and other initiatives outside the central plan. Headed by a Korean-Chinese businessman with ties to the North Korean military, its board consisted of regime heavyweights. However, its creation generated uncertainty about the investment approval process, since the mandate of the group appeared to conflict with the authority of the Joint Venture and Investment Commission (JVIC), which is akin to a conventional investment promotion agency operating under the cabinet. The two organizations were merged in February 2012 (IFES 2012), apparently in part at Chinese instigation, to deal with the problem of cascading corruption. As we noted in Chapter 2, however, this move did not appear to have substantial effect on investment given the foreign policy constraints the regime had created for itself following the breakdown of the Six Party Talks in 2008.

Additional uncertainties for Chinese firms came about with the December 2013 purge and the execution of regime heavyweight Jang Song-thaek, who had played a central role in investment institutions and had served as the chief interlocutor in North Korea's economic relations with China. Given the absence of well-functioning institutions and the reliance on political connections to resolve disputes that we have documented, Jang's ouster was surely disruptive to economic relations in the short run, particularly with respect to investment (Li 2016).

How to solve these problems? At the time of this writing, there has been growing evidence on both the Chinese and North Korean sides of the border of an interest in the "enclave" solution to the problems identified here and even for state-trading companies to move their operations into China altogether (Park and Walsh 2016; Center for Advanced Defense Analysis 2016). The Chinese surfaced the dirt road linking Hunchun with Rason which had languished for years, the Russians refurbished the rail link and promised further investment in Russian-linked infrastructure, and transmission lines now bring in electricity from China (Abrahamian 2012). North Korea will make pure rents off the port of Rason, particularly in the transit trade with Russia. Moreover, North Korean law now gives extraordinary power and discretion to the Rason City People's Committee relative to the previous rules. Such localization of decision making may encourage greater pragmatism.

A test of the possibility that North Korea's special economic zone (SEZ) strategy will spread can be found in the China-focused initiatives centered on the Hwanggumpyong and Wihwa islands zones, a strategy that has proven unsuccessful to date. China initially rejected North Korean statutes on the zones, complaining about problems with taxation, accounting, investment security, management autonomy, and profit remittance. These complaints were lodged despite the fact that the terms under discussion for Chinese activities in the zones—the right to use Chinese currency and cell phones, the establishment of independent banks, internet access, and the right to lend and sublease land—compared favorably to both the KIC and Rason. The Hwanggumpyong and Wihwa islands regulations were far more detailed, more clearly delineating the responsibility of the zone's management committee, the provincial People's Committee, and the central government, as well as affording foreign investors greater investor rights. Yet as of mid-2016, the two island zones remained stalled and none of the new zones announced in 2014 had attracted outside investment. Kaesong itself was finally closed in the wake of the fourth nuclear test, which demonstrated clearly the priority that the regime assigned to its nuclear program over policies of reform and opening. In any case, the expansion of such enclaves appeared to be driven by the opportunity to increase foreign exchange earnings channeled directly into government coffers.

In our conclusions in Chapter 8, we consider the possibility of a more fundamental reform of North Korea's foreign economic policy and what its implications may be for strategies of engagement. For the period covered by this study, however, the pursuit of enclave strategies by both of North Korea's major trade partners can be regarded not as a signal of the success of engagement but rather an admission of failure: a sign of the fundamentally control-oriented approach of the North Korean regime toward trade and investment.

Appendix

This appendix describes the two firm-level surveys reported in this chapter.

The China Survey

A pilot survey was conducted in September 2007 using a survey instrument designed by the authors, with actual interviews conducted by the Horizon Research Consultancy Group.

Horizon was responsible for securing any local permits and ensuring that the survey was conducted according to the European Society for Opinion and Market Research (ESOMAR) rules (http://actrav.itcilo.org/actrav-english/telearn/global/ilo/guide/iccmar.htm). The final survey was conducted during October and November 2007, predominantly through face-to-face interviews although some were conducted by telephone. The interview success rate was around 7 percent. Among the reasons that interviews could not be conducted were refusal to participate prior to or during the interview, inability to establish contact, and the unavailability of an enterprise representative eligible to respond according to the survey instrument (chairman, manager, etc.). The data, particularly firm addresses, were subject to postsurvey verification by random spot-checking.

Given that there are no known or available registries of all Chinese firms doing business with North Korea, the sample was of necessity one of convenience. It was developed using North Korean, Chinese, and Western press accounts, authors' interviews in Northeast China in the summer of 2007, and information gathered by the Horizon Group during the pilot and in interviews with other firms. The sample was drawn from enterprises operating in two border provinces, Jilin and Liaoning, because of the practical impossibility of implementing the survey on a nationwide basis, particularly with respect to the control group of firms not doing business in North Korea.

The survey design involved 300 firms, with 250 doing business in North Korea and 50 not doing business there; in the end, we had 53 responses from the latter. We defined firms doing business with North Korea to include those involved in trading (import, export, or both) or investment, or those that maintained representative offices in North Korea. Firms not doing business included 10 that had done business and quit ("the quitters") and 43 that had never done business ("the never-weres").

The survey began with a pilot of 30 firms from Jilin and Liaoning provinces (20 doing business and 10 not doing business in North Korea). Although it was understood that this was a sample of convenience, enterprises reflecting a broad distribution of size, sector, and provincial location were targeted. Following the successful completion of the pilot—which did not require fundamental modification of the survey—we were able to transit directly to the full survey and all of the pilot firms were included in the final 300. Once the sample of 250 enterprises operating in North Korea was completed, the control group was selected by random sampling of business registries for Jilin and Liaoning provinces.

The South Korea Survey

A pilot survey was conducted in November 2009 using a survey instrument designed by the authors, with the actual interviews conducted by Millward Brown Media Research. Millward Brown was responsible for securing any local permits and ensuring that the survey was conducted according to the European Society for Opinion and Marketing Research (ESOMAR) rules (http://actrav.itcilo.org/actrav-english/telearn/global/ilo/guide/iccmar.htm). The final survey was conducted during November 2009 and March 2010, predominantly through telephone interviews, although some were conducted face to face. Among the reasons that interviews could not be conducted were refusal to participate prior to or during the interview, inability to establish contact, and the unavailability of an enterprise representative eligible to respond according to the survey instrument (chairman, manager, etc.). The data, particularly firm addresses, were subject to postsurvey verification by random spot-checking.

Given that there are no known or available registries of all firms doing business with North Korea, the sample was of necessity one of convenience. It was developed using North Korean, South Korean, and Western press accounts, as well as information gathered by Millward Brown during the pilot survey and in interviews with other firms. The sample was drawn from enterprises operating throughout South Korea, including the control group of firms not doing business in North Korea.

The survey design involved 250 firms, with 200 doing business and 50 not doing business in North Korea; in the end, we had 50 responses from firms not doing business and 199 firms doing business in North Korea. We defined the latter to include those involved in trading (import, export, or both), investment, processing-on-commission activities, or those that maintained representative offices in North Korea, as well as the 18 firms that had done business and quit. The control group consisted of 50 firms that had never done business with North Korea.

The survey began with a pilot of 50 firms from throughout South Korea. Although it was understood that this was a sample of convenience, enterprises reflecting a broad distribution of size, sector, and provincial location were targeted. Following the successful completion of the pilot, which did not require fundamental modification of the survey, we were able to transit directly to the full survey, and all of the pilot firms were included in the final 249. Once the sample of 199 enterprises operating in North Korea was completed, our aim was to select 50 without business relationships with North Korea but with qualities similar to those of the firms in our treatment group, those doing business with North Korea (198, excluding 1 foreign-owned firm). Not all quality variables were available for comparison—we first teased out the firms engaged in manufacturing since the majority of our treatment group was in that sector. The variables of the two groups were then adjusted so that their categorizations were comparable. The variables (regions, firm ownership, and firm size) were dummified, and we applied coarsened exact matching (CEM) in the STATA statistical software package to identify 199 matching firms. We provided a list of 199 firms as lower response rates were expected, and of those 50 were ultimately selected for our control group.

Negotiating on Nuclear Weapons I
The Rise and Fall of the Six Party Talks, 2001–2008

As we argued in our introduction in Chapter 1, the effectiveness of sanctions and inducements in securing policy changes are conditional both on features of the target and on the wider strategic setting. North Korea's status as a "hard target" is relatively constant, but we can nonetheless trace the ways in which the authoritarian and statist nature of the country's political economy affected responses to both sanctions and inducements.

We pay particular attention to problems of coordination and bargaining. In Chapter 3, we outlined the broad contours of North Korea's foreign economic relations, noting how the country's trade and investment relations shifted with the imposition of sanctions and the gradual reopening to China after 2000. In this chapter and the next, we move from these broad economic parameters to how sanctions and economic inducements were used during the negotiations over North Korea's weapons programs, both within and outside of the Six Party Talks after the talks collapsed in 2008.

We break the analysis into two distinct phases. The two administrations of George W. Bush correspond to the rise and fall of the Six Party Talks process, initiated in 2003 following the onset of the second nuclear crisis and ultimately breaking down in the last year of the second Bush term in 2008; we address that history in this chapter. In the second period (2009–2016), formal negotiations were in abeyance but the six parties nonetheless engaged in an intricate set of strategic interactions in which sanctions and inducements continued to play a significant role. By coincidence, this period largely corresponds with the two administrations of Barack Obama, and we review it in Chapter 7.[1] During this second period, multilateral sanctions deepened in the wake of further missile tests and four additional nuclear tests in May 2009, February 2013, January and September 2016, but they had little effect on reopening negotiations.

Our approach takes a narrative format in which bargaining episodes involving sanctions and inducements are analyzed for their effects. The approach follows the work of Nincic (2005) and an extensive body of analysis on North Korea by Sigal (1998, 2002, 2005, 2009, 2010, 2016) as well as the wider literature on sanctions reviewed in Chapter 1.

Choosing which moves in the game to treat as the starting point is no easy task: what some view as a North Korean "provocation" others might view as a rational response to a prior US move. However, given the centrality of the US–North Korea relationship to the course of the negotiations, we focus particular attention on US strategy, considering how its efficacy has been affected by the responses of North Korea as well as the behavior of other parties in the talks.

The broad outlines of the negotiations are provided in Tables 6.1 and 7.1. We find little evidence that sanctions "worked" in the immediately instrumental sense of advancing the course of negotiations; to the contrary, they tended to generate escalatory responses from North Korea. So-called smart or targeted sanctions (Cortright and Lopez 2002) did not fare much better. Sanctions on weapons sales and particularly financial sanctions no doubt had effects on both commercial trade and foreign accounts under the leadership's control and may have had both signaling and purely defensive value. However, these material effects did not translate into the desired *political* response. To the extent that financial sanctions worked, they did so only when coupled with a willingness to negotiate and offer inducements that went beyond the promise of terminating them.

Aside from the underlying political issues raised in Chapter 2 about the nature of the regime, two further bargaining issues outlined in Chapter 1 help account for these suboptimal outcomes: coordination problems and problems of credibility and sequencing. The US strategy of putting pressure on North Korea was strongly affected by the behavior of China and South Korea, not only in the talks but in their broader bilateral relations with North Korea. The South Korean governments of Kim Dae-jung (1998–2003) and particularly Roh Moo-hyun (2003–2008) had little interest in pursuing a comprehensive sanctions strategy; neither did China throughout the entire period. To the contrary, the diplomacy of the progressive South Korean presidents tended to limit the scope of possible sanctions, including the multilateral sanctions put in place after 2006, or to undermine them indirectly by maintaining commercial economic ties and foreign aid.

TABLE 6.1

US economic statecraft 2001–2008: Six Party Talks phase

Timeline	Economic and other inducements	Sanctions and constraints	North Korean response
Precrisis, January 2001–October 2002	Continuation of food aid as well as oil shipments under Agreed Framework; internal discussion of extending prospective benefits, but in return for a widened agenda	Unwillingness to negotiate and strategy of "tailored containment"; assertion of right to preempt against proliferators and suspension of HFO shipments under Agreed Framework	Proposal to negotiate a wide-ranging settlement, June 2001
Onset of crisis to Six Party Talks, October 2002–August 2004	None	Initiation of Proliferation Security Initiative; strengthening of illicit activities initiatives	Restatement of willingness to negotiate followed by escalation including ejection of IAEA inspectors, withdrawal from NPT, reprocessing of spent fuel
First three rounds of Six Party Talks, August 2003–January 2005 (scheduled fourth round of talks do not take place)	First offer of inducements at 3rd round of talks, June 2004; offer of security guarantees, but economic inducements to follow North Korean compliance	Continuation of existing initiatives	Proposed exchange with economic inducements for declaratory commitments to precede irreversible North Korean actions; dismantlement only with provision of light-water reactors (LWRs)
To "road map" agreements, January 2005–October 2007	Statement of Principles offers broad economic quid pro quos but wholly prospective: lifting of sanctions, aid, normalization, and discussion "at appropriate time" of LWRs; South Korea provides electricity; Resolution of BDA case permits February and October 2007 agreements, offering tightly coupled economic inducements in form of oil shipments	Refinement of Illicit Activities Initiative, Banco Delta Asia (BDA), and other financial sanctions	Escalatory response to BDA action, including missile and nuclear tests in 2006; settlement of BDA issues followed by return to negotiations and February and October 2007 agreements
Implementation and collapse of talks October 2007–January 2009	Step-by-step approach with HFO shipments, food aid, and initial steps toward lifting of sanctions conditional on North Korean performance including with respect to verification	US chooses not to rescind North Korea's designation as state sponsor of terrorism as a result of conflict over verification	Mixed compliance; most disablement steps completed, but questionable declaration of nuclear activities and programs; regime initially accepts compromise with US on verification but escalates in response to US reversal on terrorism list and ultimately quits talks

The United States thus entered the Six Party Talks with surprisingly little economic leverage. Its long-standing and wide-ranging sanctions regime had already reduced trade with North Korea to a trickle. Oil shipments under the Agreed Framework and humanitarian aid were the only leverage directly under US control, and for reasons outlined in Chapter 4 the United States was initially reluctant to exploit the latter. Until it stumbled on new financial instruments in 2005, it could only put pressure on North Korea by convincing other parties to act, by threatening military options that were ultimately not credible, or by turning back to a diplomacy of inducements and quid pro quos.

However, it is a faulty inference to jump from sanctions' mixed record to the presumption that engagement fared any better. First, the extension of inducements faced a panoply of credibility and sequencing problems, both in negotiation and in implementation. Would inducements be extended in advance of North Korea fulfilling its stipulated obligations simultaneously, or only afterward? Given the mutual belief that important commitments had not been met in the past,[2] both sides sought to "front-load" the benefits of interest to them. As the North Koreans insisted throughout the negotiations, denucle-arization should proceed on the basis of "words for words" (or "commitments for commitments"), "actions for actions." North Korea had a revealed prefer-ence for immediate transfers such as the delivery of fuel oil, electricity, food, or even cash, as had occurred in the context of the 2000 North-South summit and again during 2007–2008. South Korean food and fertilizer aid under Roh Moo-hyun also provided clear, tangible, and fungible benefits.

Promises of future payoffs were less appealing, in part because of credibility problems and in part because of their ambiguous economic benefits to an au-thoritarian regime sitting atop a fraying state socialist economy. North Korean arguments were consistent that the lifting of sanctions was a crucial signal of US intent. However, the material effect of lifting sanctions depended both on complementary economic policies in North Korea and on the reaction of pri-vate actors, who might still be deterred from trade and investment as a result of the general uncertainty surrounding North Korea's economic policy.[3] From the perspective of North Korea, resources in the hand—the sorts of direct transfers visible under both the Agreed Framework and the 2007–2008 "road map" agreements—were preferable to promised benefits that might only ma-terialize if North Korea's own policies underwent fundamental change.

We find ample evidence in the empirical record that, for its part, the United States was concerned about the moral hazard problems of extending aid and being played for a sucker. The North Korean regime frequently sought in-ducements simply to talk, in exchange for declaratory statements of intent, or to take actions that were easily reversible, most notably a "freeze" of existing activities. It also sought discrete payments for highly disaggregated actions—the "salami" tactic—with the effect that important stages in the denuclearization process were effectively put off into the distant future. On some issues, including a full and accurate declaration of its nuclear activities and submission to robust verification, the regime seemed disinclined to make concessions altogether. In the interim, it retained and even expanded its nuclear capabilities. As a result of these difficulties, critics of the negotiations argued repeatedly that the United States and the other parties to the talks should extract meaningful concessions in advance of any inducements—or more tightly coupled with them. The talks ultimately broke down precisely over the failure to extract just such a concession with respect to verification.

Stalemate: 2001–2004

The deep divisions that existed in the first Bush administration over North Korea policy have now been thoroughly documented (Mazarr 2007; Pritchard 2007; Chinoy 2008; Cha 2012). On the one hand, there was a willingness, albeit grudging, to abide by formal commitments made by the Clinton administration. Inducements under the Agreed Framework—fuel oil shipments to North Korea and efforts through KEDO to complete the long-delayed construction of the promised light-water reactors (LWRs)—remained intact despite efforts within the administration to kill them (Bolton 2007, 99–129; Chinoy 2008, 75–77; see also Cheney 2011, 473–475). The United States also initially maintained its commitment to provide humanitarian assistance, and Secretary of State Colin Powell signaled his support for a continuation of the talks initiated by the Clinton administration.[4]

However, administration hawks bitterly opposed the Agreed Framework or any negotiations with Pyongyang, let alone additional inducements. The president himself expressed doubts about the utility of engagement. This occurred most notably in his repudiation of Powell's stated intention to pursue the Clinton negotiations on missiles, in the open clash with President Kim Dae-jung during his state visit in March 2001 over the utility of his Sunshine Policy, and in the infamous "Axis of Evil" comment in the 2002 State of the Union address. The difference in approach between the Clinton and Bush administrations is clearly visible in a speech by Colin Powell before the Asia Society in June 2002.[5] Although nominally endorsing the Sunshine Policy, Powell made progress in bilateral relations conditional on a number of prior actions by the North Koreans: on humanitarian issues, conventional force deployments, missiles, and the country's obligations under both the Agreed

Framework and the Nuclear Nonproliferation Treaty (NPT), including International Atomic Energy Agency (IAEA) inspections.

The approach to humanitarian aid also underwent a gradual transformation under the Bush administration as we saw in Chapter 4 (see also Haggard and Noland 2007a, chap. 5). Effectively linked to a broader engagement approach under President Clinton—what we have called "food for talks" (Table 4.5)—Bush showed an increasing tendency to see aid in more narrow terms, emphasizing the risks of moral hazard and seeking more effective monitoring and even progress on human rights.[6] Although nominally delinked from the breaking nuclear crisis, aid fell in both 2003 and 2004. In the fall of 2004, as the World Food Program (WFP) and North Korean authorities were entering a standoff over monitoring, Congress passed and President Bush signed the North Korean Human Rights Act, which required that nonhumanitarian assistance be contingent on North Korea making "substantial progress" on a number of specific human rights issues. The legislation also required the US Agency for International Development (USAID) to issue a report to Congress that included any changes in transparency, monitoring, and access of food aid and other humanitarian activities. Any "significant increases" in humanitarian assistance would be conditioned on "substantial improvements" in these areas.

Internal discussions in the United States did consider possible inducements: replacing the LWRs promised under the Agreed Framework with thermal and hydropower plants, aid for infrastructure, construction of schools and hospitals, and support for North Korea's admission to the World Bank and Asian Development Bank (Sigal 2005). But these were publicly outlined only in prospective terms; in Powell's formulation in the speech cited previously, "the United States is prepared to take important steps to help North Korea move its relations with the US toward normalcy." But as Powell's circuitous formulation suggests, the ball was seen to be in North Korea's court and US actions would come only *after* satisfactory steps were taken on the administration's agenda.

In addition to the shift in strategy with respect to North Korea policy itself, the attacks of 9/11 resulted in a much more aggressive posture toward proliferators more generally, including the assertion of a right of preemption.[7] Victor Cha (2012, 310–317) has outlined in some detail public statements made by the administration, including the president himself, to reassure North Korea that United States did not harbor hostile intent. When coupled with the Bush administration's initial unwillingness to reiterate the Clinton administration's statement of peaceful intent, however, along with public speeches by members of the administration outlining North Korean derogations on its obligations under the Agreed Framework,[8] it was plausible for Pyongyang, and the North Korean military, to conclude that North Korea required a strengthened deterrent. The invasion of Iraq, which occurred precisely as the crisis was breaking, no doubt only deepened these concerns.

Did the Bush administration's hardened stance—the drift away from inducements and the imposition of more constraints, including economic ones—have effect? The short answer is no. The North Koreans responded negatively to the Bush initiatives. Pyongyang sought to focus any discussion around full implementation of the Agreed Framework, including completion of the LWRs and compensation for lost electricity. Nonetheless, Pyongyang did signal a willingness to negotiate a broader agreement.[9] These overtures were ignored.

From the Onset of the Crisis to the Six Party Talks:
October 2002–August 2003

It was not until the ASEAN Regional Forum meeting in July 2002, a year and a half into office, that Secretary Powell communicated US willingness to send an envoy to Pyongyang. At that point, however, any interest in broader negotiations was derailed by intelligence uncovering North Korea's clandestine highly enriched uranium (HEU) program. Although there is still debate about how far along the program was, the fact that at least some centrifuges as well as designs had been transferred from the Pakistanis now seems beyond dispute.[10] Such transfers would have constituted a clear breach of a number of North Korea's international commitments, including to the NPT, the 1992 Joint [North-South] Declaration on the Denuclearization of the Korean Peninsula, and the Agreed Framework.

To this day, what happened during Assistant Secretary James Kelly's visit to Pyongyang in October 2002 remains the subject of dispute even to those who were present.[11] However, the key issue was not how far along the North Korean program was but what mix of sanctions, engagement, and inducements the United States would pursue to blunt it. The Bush administration opted for a punishment strategy. It exerted strong pressure on both Japan and Korea to concur with a KEDO resolution condemning the HEU program as a violation of the Agreed Framework, cutting off fuel oil shipments, and ultimately rescinding its commitment to the Agreed Framework altogether (Pollack 2003).

The North Korean response combined a stated willingness to negotiate with escalation. In October 2002, North Korea had proposed the negotiation of an agreement that would resolve all outstanding nuclear issues in return for three concessions: respect for North Korean sovereignty, a binding US commitment to nonaggression, and a promise from the United States that it would not "hamper" the country's economic development (presumably a reference to the lifting of sanctions and perhaps economic assistance).[12] This proposal was revived by the North Koreans following the cutoff of oil shipments in November.

When the United States failed to respond, Pyongyang escalated in a series of steps. In December 2002, Pyongyang asked the IAEA to unseal the Yongbyon facilities, and when the agency asked the government to reconsider, the IAEA inspectors were ejected. An IAEA board statement condemning the move was followed by North Korea's formal renunciation of its obligations under the NPT on January 10, 2003. Shortly thereafter, the regime resumed its reprocessing of spent nuclear fuel rods and took steps to generate new fissile material by refueling and restarting the reactor. At several points during the spring, North Korea either stated or hinted that it already had a nuclear capability or saw it as their right to develop one (for example, Pritchard 2007, 65).

The United States subsequently undertook other actions designed to pressure the North Koreans to reconsider, including the mobilization of military assets in the region. Two sets of economic measures are particularly relevant here. The first was the strengthening of interagency efforts to deter and stop North Korean engagement in illicit activities, including counterfeiting, the drug trade, and the financial transactions and money laundering associated with the country's weapons trade.[13] These efforts involved substantial financial forensics and ultimately rested on the ability of the Treasury Department to cut off foreign banks from correspondent banking relations in the United States using a set of tools that were brought into full play against North Korea in 2005 with the designation of Banco Delta Asia (BDA) as a bank of money-laundering concern.[14] Although not initially linked to the nuclear issue, the progenitors of these programs were well aware of their potential uses in the nuclear negotiations (Zarate 2013, 229, 232).

The second action, the initiation of the Proliferation Security Initiative (PSI) in May 2003, was a multilateral effort to cooperate in the interdiction of trade in WMD-related materials (Winner 2005; Wolf, Chow, and Jones 2008; Valencia 2010). Although the PSI did not specifically target North Korea, the December 2002 interdiction of a North Korean vessel transporting Scud missile parts to the Middle East provided an example of the type of activity the administration wanted to stem.[15] Multilateral cooperation on interdiction was targeted at what was deemed illicit trade,[16] but such measures were no doubt seen by the North Koreans as sanctions on legitimate activity and had little effect on the nuclear negotiations.

Effectively stymied, the administration undertook a third policy review in which divergent strategies from engagement through regime change were tabled (Funabashi 2007, 138–139; Chinoy 2008, 145–147). The chosen middle-ground approach, known as "tailored containment," explicitly eschewed any direct negotiation with North Korea while orchestrating economic and political pressure against it. Thanks to papers released by former Secretary of Defense Donald Rumsfeld, we have insight into the logic of tailored containment.[17] In a memo dated December 26, 2002,[18] Rumsfeld argued that "getting to the table is what Pyongyang seeks; for us to grant it in response to the latest nuclear provocations would only reinforce Pyongyang's weak hand and prove that bad behavior pays." Rumsfeld argued for new multilateral and bilateral sanctions and for "pressing China and Russia to ratchet up diplomatic pressure and constrict economic aid and development projects." The ultimate objective of these sanctions was to "train Kim Jong Il to understand that blackmail tactics that worked with the previous administration will no longer work." However, as we will see, Beijing and Moscow did not share Rumsfeld's priors about how to deal with North Korea, a classic example of the coordination problem. American efforts at behavior modification were doomed to failure.

In sum, the Bush administration's punishment strategy did not have the intended effect. Following the termination of heavy-oil shipments, North Korea escalated in ways that did not leave the United States with easy and effective responses. Given the trade patterns we described in Chapter 3, the sanctions strategy could only work by coordinating a multilateral approach. The Six Party Talks, which had their origin in a trilateral meeting hosted by Beijing in April 2003, appeared to serve American interests by providing a venue through which the five parties could coordinate pressure on the North. However, the new South Korean government of Roh Moo-hyun had doubts about the utility of pressure and was wedded to a strategy of wide-ranging engagement. Despite recurrent frustrations, China shared these views with respect to strategy (International Crisis Group 2006, 2009; Snyder 2009). Russia, too, had doubts about the utility of pressure (Funabashi 2007, 166–196; Toloraya 2008).

Rather than marshaling collective pressure on North Korea, then, the lack of success at the Six Party Talks gradually forced the Bush administration to consider the inducements it would be willing to offer for a settlement. To understand why, it is necessary to consider in more detail the Chinese and South Korean approaches to North Korea at the outset of the Six Party Talks. The strategic choices made by both countries not only had political effect in the negotiations; they also help explain the increases in trade, investment, and aid that we documented in Chapter 3 (see Figures 3.1, 3.6, 3.9).

Coordination Problems I: Chinese Strategy Toward the DPRK

China's approach to the informal three-party talks and then the formal Six Party Talks was initially facilitative.[19] After unsuccessful efforts with Russia to resolve the crisis in late 2002, Beijing's conception was that the three-party talks would provide a cover for the United States and North Korea to undertake the bilateral negotiations that the Bush administration was unwilling to conduct directly. Quite early, the Chinese Foreign Ministry made clear that it was opposed to North Korea's nuclear ambitions, and it backed that statement with multilateral diplomatic action—for example, voting in February 2003 for an IAEA resolution that identified North Korea's actions as a violation of NPT obligations and referring the issue to the UN Security Council (Liu 2003, 358).

However, China had a very different idea of how to curtail Pyongyang's nuclear program. Although its motives are subject to debate (Glaser, Snyder, and Park 2008; International Crisis Group 2006, 2009; Liu 2003; Wu 2005; Shambaugh 2003; Scobell 2003, 2004; Snyder 2009), Beijing consistently questioned the maximalist nature of US demands in the Six Party Talks, was opposed to sanctions on both principled and pragmatic grounds, and argued that the United States needed to formulate effective quid pro quos.

In effect, Chinese strategy focused on deep engagement, even if it sought to steer that engagement in a market-oriented direction. Moreover, this strategy was embedded in broader trends in China's domestic and foreign economic policy (Reilly 2014b). These included the "Go Out" (*zou chuqu* 走出去) policy encouraging Chinese state-owned enterprises (SOEs) to invest abroad, the "Revitalize Northeast China" (*zhenxing dongbei* 振兴东北) push, which envisioned a deepening of trade with North Korea, and the diplomatic effort to create a "an amicable, tranquil and prosperous neighborhood" (*mulin, anlin, fulin* 睦邻安邻富邻) through trade and investment on the principle of "mutual benefit" (*shuangying* 双赢).

How did this strategy of deep engagement unfold? Just as the second nuclear crisis was breaking, bilateral China-DPRK relations had already improved significantly following a period of stress that had begun early in the post–Cold War period and continued after the death of Kim Il-sung in 1994. The Chinese recognition of South Korea in 1992 and the demand for hard currency payment for exports were major shocks for Pyongyang, and the first nuclear crisis strained China-North Korea relations as well.[20] Whatever aid China extended during the early Kim Jong-il period for political purposes was clearly not adequate to blunt the ravages of famine. There is even evidence that a fall in Chinese exports in 1994, probably to conserve domestic supplies, was a precipitating cause of the famine itself. It was not until May 1996 that Chinese premier Li Peng and North Korean vice premier Hong Song-nam signed an agreement promising aid and wider economic cooperation (Noland 2000; Haggard and Noland 2007, 156).[21] Despite this initiative, however, and the growth of informal border trade during the famine, overall trade between the two countries mirrored the decline in diplomatic interaction, falling steadily over the second half of the 1990s.

A spate of high-level diplomatic exchanges in 1999 reversed the diplomatic freeze and set the stage for Kim Jong-il's first visit to China in May 2000, just prior to the North-South summit.[22] The visit was clearly designed to seek aid, but China had its objectives as well: to nudge North Korea toward a more rational economic strategy. The *Xinhua* account of the visit tells of Kim Jong Il lavishing praise on the Chinese economic model.[23] Kim Jong-il's second visit in January 2001 was similarly scripted to include visits to the Shanghai Stock Exchange, the Zhangjiang High-Tech Science Park, the Pudong development area, and even a Chinese–General Motors joint venture factory. Chinese and North Korean officials discussed the possible opening of a trade office in Shanghai, and Kim Jong-il was said to have expressed his intent to open an export-processing zone in Sinuiju that would mimic the Chinese zones he had seen.[24] As we noted in Chapter 2, the year 2002 was probably the highpoint, however brief, of open reformism in North Korea.

Not surprisingly, Kim Jong-il's 2004 visit replayed economic themes, but now such visits occurred in the context of an economic relationship that had begun to revive and a political relationship that was seeing more frequent high-level exchanges. These developments even captured the attention of the South Korean government, which took note of the tendency toward greater North Korean integration with China.

During the 2004 summit, Wen Jiabao publicly declared that the Chinese government positively encouraged investment in North Korea. This was followed by a bilateral investment agreement, formation of a joint committee on economic cooperation in March 2005, and the explicit articulation of a new framework for bilateral relations which was summarized in the complex phrase "government guidance with companies in the lead; market-based operations and mutual benefit" (Park 2009, 90; Freeman and Thomson 2009; Reilly 2014a, 2014b). These principles were restated in Hu Jintao's first visit to North Korea as president in October 2005. In his fourth trip to China in January 2006, Kim Jong-il sought large-scale "cooperation" in the face of financial sanctions that we discuss in more detail later. Wen Jiabao's response implied clearly that government support was designed as a complement to rather than a substitute for commercial engagement. North Korea would need to reform, Chinese firms would be the lead players, and these firms would need to profit from their ventures (Park 2009, 91; Reilly 2014a, 2014b). This message was again delivered pointedly during Jang Song-thaek's eleven-day "study tour" later in the year, accompanied by more than thirty high-ranking officials.

Nonetheless, the message was also clear that China was willing to allow a significant increase in bilateral economic cooperation. Thus, while the United States was seeking to form a multilateral coalition of restraint that included China as a crucial player, Beijing's diplomacy was moving in an altogether different direction. Although not extending aid on a large scale, China was effectively pursuing a strategy of "deep engagement" that was strikingly similar to South Korea's Sunshine Policy.

Coordination Problems II: The Sunshine Policy

South Korea's strategy with respect to North Korea posed significant diplomatic and economic challenges as well. These challenges to American strategy were rooted in divergent partisan cycles, beginning before the onset of the second nuclear crisis with the well-documented differences between the administrations of Kim Dae-jung (1998–2003) and President George W. Bush (2001–2009) (Oberdorfer and Carlin 2014, 249–251; Levin and Han 2002, 109–113). The Sunshine Policy has been subjected to extensive commentary (for example, Moon and Steinberg 1999; Levin and Han 2002; Kirk 2009; Moon 2012) as well as statements by the principles (Kim 1997; Lim 2012). We focus here on some of its distinctive economic components, how they related to conceptions of engagement outlined in our introduction in Chapter 1, and how they contributed to the coordination problems we have noted.

As Levin and Han (2002, 25–26) document, the Kim administration came into office with a quid pro quo conception of engagement in line with the principle of "mutual benefit." Yet as North Korea derided efforts to exchange humanitarian assistance for family reunions as "horse-trading," the Kim Dae-jung administration gradually shifted to a conception of "flexible reciprocity" that eschewed explicit quid pro quos. Nonetheless, the wider conception of engagement was defended—albeit delicately—on transformational grounds. The Sunshine Policy took its name from an Aesop fable in which the north wind and the sun debate which is more efficacious in getting a traveler to remove his coat; sunshine—a metaphor for persuasion—trumped wind's brute force. Although explicitly denying any intention to undermine or absorb the North Korean government, the underlying assumption of the Sunshine Policy, based in part on Kim's reading of the effects of the Helsinki Final Act of 1975,[25] was that gradual engagement would not only moderate North Korean behavior but also foster favorable policy and even institutional and cognitive shifts.

Economic exchanges played a critical role in this process. The idea of the "separation of politics and economics" was a crucial component of the Sunshine Policy. Private actors would have increasing freedom to engage in trade and investment with the North without government approval, or backing. Lim Dong-won's epigrammatic explanation of the policy to a Chinese audience used sixteen characters to summarize it, focusing heavily on diffuse reciprocity and economics: "Easy tasks first, difficult tasks later; private channel first, government channel later; economy first, politics later; give first, take later" (Lim 2012, 213). Yet Kim Dae-jung was consistent in his belief that the effect of such exchanges was "nudging North Korea towards a market economy and the democratic elements and environment [*sic*]" (Kim 1997, 131).

The separation of politics and economics proved extremely difficult to sustain for reasons pertaining to politics in both South and North. First, the very backwardness of the North Korean economy immediately raised the question of infrastructure investment to facilitate deeper integration. In his Berlin speech, President Kim noted that, despite the separation of economics and politics, "to realize meaningful economic collaboration, the social infrastructure, including highways, harbors, railroads and electric and communications facilities, must be expanded." Early projects in this vein included expensive road and rail links on both sides of the peninsula. Second, the humanitarian dilemmas outlined in Chapter 3 operated in force: a policy that sought to signal compassion with Korean compatriots was necessarily drawn to the extension of aid, which expanded sharply in the late Kim Dae-jung years (Figure 4.4).

Even achieving the separation of economics and politics required an overarching political-legal framework, however, and rested on a conception of North Korean counterparties that proved unrealistic if not dangerously misleading. The passage of the Inter-Korean Exchange and Cooperation Act in 1990 during the Roh Tae-woo presidency was the first effort to establish a legal foundation for North-South trade and investment, and was followed by the negotiation of a number of additional protocols that facilitated basic commercial exchanges (Chi 2004). But the National Assembly failed to ratify four key North-South agreements (on investment guarantees, avoidance of double taxation, procedures for resolution of commercial disputes, and clearing settlements), substantially reducing private-sector interest in pursuing commercial relations with the North.

In 2003 information broke about the negotiation of the summit. It became clear that the Kim Dae-jung government had extended large-scale cash assistance in anticipation of it. Early business ventures in the North led by the Hyundai Group were in fact not profitable but lost in a complex maze of subsidies if not outright bribery. Kim Dae-jung's policy and his award of the Nobel Prize became mired in scandal (Kirk 2006, 190–208). A number of small- and medium-sized firms did commercial business with the North, as we showed in Chapter 5, but presummit transfers and even some of those associated with Hyundai's business were channeled through South Korean government entities directly to accounts under the control of Bureau 39 and thus the Korean Workers' Party and ultimately the Kim family itself. It became increasingly clear that if commercial relations were to deepen, they would require a new model—exemplified in the Kaesong Industrial Complex (KIC)—for which the government would need to invest in both the physical and legal infrastructure required for firms to operate.

Finally, the shift toward "flexible reciprocity" almost of necessity was vulnerable to political challenges, which surfaced in the last year of Kim Dae-jung's presidency, continued throughout the Roh Moo-hyun administration, and culminated in the election of Lee Myung-bak in 2007. Not only did Pyongyang fail to reciprocate South Korean largesse—for example, failing to rebuild its side of the North-South rail links and missing scheduled meetings. It also made clear that it had no intention of discussing security issues with Seoul and even escalated tensions by provoking an incident along the Northern Limit Line (NLL), in June 2002, in which six South Korean sailors were killed.

Moreover, conservatives suspected—and at least one North Korean source subsequently confirmed—that this escalatory response constituted a self-conscious strategy of extortion. Jang Jin-sung's memoir *Dear Leader* (2014), based on his work in the United Front Department, argues that Kim Jong-il faced a dilemma at the outset of the engagement period. In desperate need of aid, he was concerned that pressure to pursue a more reciprocal approach might force him to choose between no aid and aid with political or even military concessions. To avoid this trade-off, the regime adopted the "NLL strategy" of self-consciously using provocations as blackmail. "The underlying logic was simple: South Korea must continue to provide unconditional aid and keep their engagement with the North separate from political issues, or give up peace again" (Jang 2014, 256).

Just as the nuclear crisis was breaking in December 2002, South Korea went to the polls and elected a reformist human rights lawyer, Roh Moo-hyun, as president. The election reflected both longer-run generational shifts and a sharp uptick in anti-Americanism following a tragic accident in which two Korean middle-school girls were run over and killed by a US army vehicle. However, the US approach to both South and North Korea in 2001–2002 was also implicated in the framing of the electoral campaign and arguably even in its outcome. The Bush administration did not hide its preference for the conservative candidate Lee Hoi-chang (Pritchard 2007, 74–76), and the American challenge to the Sunshine Policy became one of the dominant issues in the campaign. In a notorious speech in Los Angeles in 2004, President Roh stated openly that he believed that North Korea acquired nuclear weapons out of a sense of insecurity—emanating quite clearly from the United States— and that addressing that insecurity would resolve the nuclear weapons issue (Roh 2004).

Roh thus ran on a platform not only of continuing the Sunshine Policy of his predecessor but of deepening South Korean commitment to the North in significant ways. Interestingly, the first principle of his so-called Peace and Prosperity Policy, enunciated in his inaugural speech, was a commitment to resolve all outstanding issues through dialogue. This priority was a sharp departure from the first principle of the Sunshine Policy, which was no tolerance of provocations as well as maintenance of a robust deterrent. The commitment to dialogue was not simply a matter of principle: the administration sought to build a complex institutional structure of dialogues from the ministerial level down to functional working groups on particular issues.[26] Table 6.2 summarizes institutional developments during this heyday of North-South

TABLE 6.2

North-South talks, 2000–2007

	2000	2001	2002	2003	2004	2005	2006	2007
Total number of talks	26	9	33	38	25	36	24	20
Joint declaration	1	0	0	0	0	0	0	0
Joint statement	7	2	7	10	6	8	2	8
Agreement	3	1	10	17	10	10	4	3
Agreement and joint statement	1	0	0	0	0	0	0	1
Agreement or joint statement	12	3	17	27	16	18	6	12
No agreement or joint statement	14	6	16	11	9	18	18	8
Share with declaration, agreement or statement (%)	46.1	33.3	51.5	71.1	64.0	50.0	25.0	60.0

SOURCE: Ministry of Unification (n.d.).

talks, which began following the 2000 summit, accelerated in 2002, continued through the Roh administration, and culminated in the 2007 summit.

According to the South Korean ambassador at the time, the accommodating nature of Roh's approach to the North stemmed directly from fear that the United States might attack North Korea, precipitating a conflict that would engulf the peninsula (Han 2009, 194–196). But the approach was not simply the result of short-term concerns. At least some of Roh's top advisors believed that the transformative aspects of engagement should be abandoned altogether, that unification was a chimera, and that the purpose of engagement was to foster peaceful coexistence—in short, a policy that might well be considered a strategy of pure appeasement (Ra 2013).

As with the Sunshine Policy, however, the currency of the Peace and Prosperity Policy was clearly economic. Efforts at North-South cooperation included ambitious and ultimately stillborn plans to embed cooperation in a wider regional integration framework called the Northeast Asian Cooperation Initiative. Aid in the form of food and fertilizer was the most tangible and immediate way of signaling continuity with the Kim Dae-jung years. Despite the onset of the nuclear crisis, Roh's administration almost immediately committed 100,000 tons of food through the WFP before reverting to the bilateral Inter-Korean Economic Cooperation Promotion Committee for the discussion of aid commitments (see Chapter 4).

After June 2004, bilateral relations fell into a freeze that did not thaw until a year later, when a high level South Korean envoy met directly with Kim Jong-il in the hope of restarting both North-South talks and the broader Six Party effort. In a striking indicator of the disconnect between the nuclear and engagement tracks, North Korea made its largest aid request to the South only a month before its February 10, 2005, announcement that it was suspending its participation in the Six Party Talks and that it had nuclear weapons. Despite pressure from the United States and statements by President Roh that *additional* aid should await progress in the talks, *humanitarian* assistance—in which the government counted both its fertilizer and food aid shipments—was not made conditional.

The shift in US strategy in the second Bush administration, which we describe in more detail later, and the June 2005 resumption of both the bilateral and Six Party Talks aligned incentives between the United States and South Korea and thus mitigated the coordination problems that had plagued the talks up to that point. Inducements played a role in this process,[27] and they continued and even expanded into 2006 (*Agence France Press* 2006). Not until the missile and nuclear tests of July did the Roh administration condition aid on

North Korean behavior and, given the quick resumption of the talks on North Korea's dealings with Banco Delta Asia (BDA), that period was short-lived.

In addition to outright aid, the Roh administration remained strongly committed to a number of "cooperative projects" with the North, including most significantly the Mt. Kumgang tourist project and the Kaesong Industrial Complex. Kaesong had its origins in the vision of Hyundai chairman Chung Ju-yung and his 1998 visit to North Korea, but its realization was a direct outgrowth of the 2000 summit and it was announced immediately following the summit in August 2000. The initial business model was for Hyundai to lease the land rights in the zone for 50 years, develop the complex, and then sell or lease land or facilities to South Korean and other firms interested in locating there. At the October 2007 summit, Roh agreed to an agenda of additional joint projects, such as an industrial park at Haeju, but by this point he was a lame duck and his successor, Lee Myung-bak, did not honor this commitment when he took office four months later.

The South Korean government was intimately involved in Kaesong virtually from the outset, in part because of financial constraints at Hyundai Asan associated with the project. The government provided an estimated $223 million of the $374 million cost for the first stage alone (Manyin and Nanto 2011), not taking into account indirect project support. The channels of government involvement were multiple, ranging from the direct participation of the state-owned Korea Land Corporation and the Korea Electric Power Corporation to the provision of both financial incentives and political risk insurance for firms entering the zone.

By June 2004, lots were on sale, and by the end of the year products were rolling off the assembly lines of the first investors. Again, it is important to underscore the timing of the project, which started to generate significant foreign exchange earnings for the North just as negotiations in the Six Party Talks were stalling out. Although the regime placed a brief moratorium on new entrants into the zone following the missile tests of 2006, the foreign exchange earnings kept Kaesong going. Indeed, after the 2010 sanctions associated with the sinking of the *Cheonan* until the closure of the zone in 2016, it was virtually the only North-South trade left.

In sum, the Bush administration strategy of seeking to pressure the North Korea regime not only faced headwinds in the very different preferences of China and South Korea with respect to *diplomatic* engagement. It also faced the constraint that both China and South Korea were pursuing strategies of deep *economic* engagement. These strategies exhibited subtle, and ironic, differences. China sought to emphasize the significance of market-oriented reforms, commercial principles, and a lead role for firms. South Korean strategy—partly by design, partly of necessity—placed more weight on aid and joint projects such as infrastructure and the enclaves at Kaesong and Mt. Kumgang. Yet both provided an important economic lifeline to Pyongyang that effectively offset the sanctions that the United States sought to mobilize.

The First Three Rounds of the Six Party Talks: August 2003–January 2005

The United States came to the first round of the Six Party Talks (August 27–29, 2003) with a list of demands embodied in the acronym CVID: a *complete* (meaning plutonium and HEU), *verifiable* (meaning a return to the NPT and IAEA inspections), *irreversible dismantlement* of all facilities at Yongbyon (in contrast to the Agreed Framework, which had frozen North Korea's nuclear program but left it intact). Although inducements for compliance were not made explicit—in part because ongoing disagreements within the administration[28]—their sequencing was clear: any concessions from the United States would come only *after* these actions had been completed.

Pyongyang was willing to negotiate to get to CVID, but it had a very clear view of how the sequencing of inducements should unfold.[29] As a first step, the North Koreans would declare their intention to abandon their nuclear program, a costless step, in return for Washington's resumption of fuel oil supply and expanded humanitarian food aid. As a second step, North Korea would freeze its nuclear activities—but not dismantle them—and allow inspections if the United States signed a legally binding nonaggression treaty and compensated the North for lost energy supplies. In the third step, Pyongyang would accommodate US concerns about missiles in return for establishing diplomatic relations. Finally, at the point of completion of the two LWRs promised under the Agreed Framework, the North Koreans would verifiably dismantle the Yongbyon facilities. In a virtual mirror image of US proposals, the North Korean approach front-loaded the inducements it would receive while delaying irreversible actions until the distant future.

With US negotiators given little discretion to negotiate, the first talks ended with so little progress that the Chinese were forced to extend additional bilateral inducements of their own to convince the North Koreans to even return for the next round (Funabashi 2007, 320–321). This became a pattern as China, South Korea (through the Kaesong project), and Japan (through a second Koizumi-Kim summit in May 2004) extended various inducements to the North, both to improve prospects for the talks and to achieve diplomatic objectives altogether independent of the Six Party process.

Not until the third round of talks (June 23–26, 2004) did the United States place an offer on the table, one that constituted a virtual mirror image of the North Korean approach. North Korean commitments were heavily front-loaded, while American inducements would not be forthcoming until progress was made on a wide agenda of bilateral issues. In return for a North Korean statement of its willingness to dismantle all nuclear programs, South Korea and Japan would resume HFO shipments in line with their Agreed Framework commitments. The North would institute a freeze on all nuclear activities and provide the five parties with a detailed plan for disabling, dismantling, and eliminating all of its nuclear activities, including its HEU program, existing stocks of fissile material, weapons, and components. All of this work would take place under the auspices of international inspections.

Once agreement on the plan was reached, the United States and others would provide security assurances. Other economic inducements, such as meeting longer-run energy needs or removing sanctions, would be phased and subject to further negotiation. The path to normalization was more distant still and would require progress on the widened agenda of the June 2001 policy review and the so-called bold approach.

The North Koreans had little interest in these proposals and no doubt wanted to wait for the outcome of the US presidential election. The fourth round of talks scheduled to take place prior to September 2004 failed to materialize.

From Movement to Collapse: The Second Term of President George W. Bush

In her 2012 memoir *No Higher Honor*, Condoleezza Rice offers a surprisingly candid assessment of the limitations of the first Bush administration's strategy and the thinking that lead to a change of course in the second. She notes the sour taste left by the Kim Dae-jung–Bush summit, the costs of the "Axis of Evil" characterization, and how divisions within the administration had made policy making difficult. She focuses in particular on the dilemmas posed by dealing with a particularly hard target and a multilateral diplomatic setting in which the United States did not hold all the cards. Sanctions, she concludes, were unlikely to be effective: "If Kim Jong-il had to freeze his people to death in the face of a cutoff of fuel assistance, his view was 'So be it.' North Korea had plenty of ways to buy, steal and smuggle what it needed to ensure the relative comfort of the regime and its military" (159). Moreover, she is cognizant of US isolation and the coordination problem: "A U.S. policy of complete isolation of North Korea in the service of regime change was not, in the long term, one that others in the region, particularly China and South Korea, would likely abide" (159). She is also quite clear that the handling of intelligence on the HEU program not only was a missed opportunity but contributed to the problem. By constraining Kelly's opportunity to "fully explore what might have been an opening to put the program on the table" and moving to cut off heavy fuel oil shipments, the administration had contributed to the crisis (162–163). Although she recognized that the president was sympathetic to the hawks, she had come to the conclusion that, in the absence of a military option, negotiation—and the requisite quid pro quos—were necessary.

On becoming secretary of state, Rice sought "a longer-term framework that pointed the way toward denuclearization *and* a resolution of the underlying tensions in the region" (167). She contemplated the development of multilateral institutions for Northeast Asia that would complement alliance relationships, including a peace treaty (523–524). To pursue this path, she had to make the president comfortable with a diplomatic approach to North Korea and secure the latitude to negotiate without her envoy being "micromanaged."

This strategy involved three components. The first was more effective coordination among the five parties, meaning at least some accommodation to the positions of China and South Korea. Second, the United States would pursue sanctions, including financial ones, primarily as defensive measures to block proliferation rather than as tools that would necessarily bring pressure to bear. Indeed, she worried about the politicization of sanctions in a way that would scuttle diplomacy. Finally, Rice had to convince the president that a policy of seeking regime change was unlikely to work: "One can hardly negotiate successfully with a regime if one is publicly committed to its destruction" (159). Despite extraordinarily tough rhetoric from the North Koreans,[30] the second Bush administration was clearly more willing to engage North Korea. Chief US negotiator Christopher Hill was granted greater latitude to pursue the specific quid pro quos that had been lacking in the talks (Hill 2014, 197–204).

Through the "Road Map" Agreements of 2007

The September 2005 Joint Statement, the outcome of the prolonged fourth round of Six Party Talks,[31] was a breakthrough, remaining the touchstone document of the Six Party Talks process to this day. The statement of principles laid out the broad quid pro quo that had been implicit in earlier rounds of negotiations. It was unambiguous that the denuclearization of the peninsula was a shared goal and that North Korea was committed to "abandoning" its nuclear program, rejoining the NPT, and readmitting IAEA inspectors. In return, the United States affirmed that it had no intention of attacking or

invading North Korea. Moreover, both the United States and Japan committed to "tak[ing] steps" to normalize relations. The statement made reference
both to the negotiation of a peace regime on the Korean peninsula and to
exploration of wider multilateral cooperation on security issues.

The Joint Statement also outlined the inducements on offer. First, the five
parties would provide energy assistance, and South Korea reaffirmed its commitment to a very specific proposal made in July 2005 providing 2 million
kilowatts of electric power to the DPRK. The statement also contained a
euphemistic reference to the lifting of sanctions and the provision of other
economic assistance ("the Six Parties undertook to promote economic cooperation in the fields of energy, trade and investment, bilaterally and/or mul-
tilaterally.") The issue of LWRs, which had entered late in the negotiations
and threatened to derail them (Funabashi 2007, 398–402), was finessed by
the affirmation of North Korea's right to a civilian nuclear program, but the
provision of such reactors by the five parties would only be discussed "at an
appropriate time."

How would the exchange of inducements for policy actions actually work?
The Joint Statement was explicit on this point: the proposed measures would
be implemented in a phased fashion "in line with the principle of 'commitment for commitment, action for action.'" The sequencing problems of
"big deals" and "grand bargains" would be solved through incremental steps.
Implementation of this strategy was almost immediately muddied by ongoing differences within the Bush administration over the appropriate mix of
inducements and sanctions and particularly their timing (Hill 2012, 241–244;
Zarate 2013, 219–237). Hawks crafted a statement following the fourth round
of talks that parsed the agreement in a highly restrictive way so that it appeared
to require full compliance with NPT obligations *prior to* the provision of any
meaningful inducements.[32] Discussion on LWRs would only occur after these
actions had been taken, and normalization of relations remained contingent
on discussion of the full range of issues vetted in the 2001 policy review and
"bold approach." Not surprisingly, it took less than forty-eight hours for the
North Korean foreign ministry to reject this approach.[33]

The gradual refinement of the Illicit Activities Initiative into a host of new
financial restrictions on North Korea further complicated negotiations since
they were interpreted by the regime as little more than additional sanctions.[34]
The most significant of these new measures was the so-called "bad bank"
strategy. The US Treasury Department named Banco Delta Asia a "primary
money laundering concern" on September 15, 2005, at almost the exact moment that the fourth round of the Six Party Talks was reaching a conclusion.

The bad bank strategy was very different from traditional sanctions. Despite the fact that the United States conducted very limited direct trade, investment, or financial relations with North Korea, it could leverage the need for correspondent banking relations with American financial institutions to bring pressure to bear on Pyongyang. It remains unclear what share, if any, of BDA's North Korean accounts, which totaled about $25 million, were in fact illicit; at least some of the assets were held by entities engaged in commercial ventures with the North. Nonetheless, by April 2006 BDA had been driven into receivership by its money-laundering designation. Moreover, the effects of the designation were by no means limited to BDA. Other banks, from Europe to Southeast Asia, quickly saw the writing on the wall and moved to close North Korean accounts. In describing this episode, Juan Zarate (2013) notes that even Chinese banks did not want to participate in a resolution of the issue for fear that they would be held liable. A one-page notification had essentially isolated North Korea from international financial markets.

Despite the fact that the BDA affair is frequently seen as a success, the North Korean response to the restricted interpretation of the Joint Statement and Treasury's actions was in fact escalatory. The regime quickly abandoned the Six Party negotiations, which did not convene between November 2005 and December 2006. The BDA measures were sufficient to inflict significant financial and macroeconomic distress on North Korea, but they were not adequate to deter it from producing fissile material and undertaking the missile and nuclear tests of June and October 2006, even at the cost of a strongly worded Security Council resolution (UNSCR 1695) on its missile program and the first set of multilateral sanctions following the nuclear test (UNSC 1718). Indeed, in a pattern that would repeat in 2009, 2013, and 2016, the imposition of multilateral sanctions was a prelude—in clear stimulus-response fashion—to the conduct of nuclear and missile tests.

In what sense, then, can we say that the BDA actions and multilateral sanctions "worked"? The initial multilateral sanctions embodied in UNSCR 1718 did not have much material effect, as we showed in Chapter 3. This was because they required Chinese acquiescence and were limited to large-scale conventional weapons systems and WMD-related trade. However, there is ample evidence that the BDA actions did have a material effect, either on elite assets or, more probably given the small amount of money at stake, because of their wider consequences for North Korea's foreign economic relations. Victor Cha (2012, 268), a participant in the negotiations, reports that a North Korean delegate admitted openly, "You have finally found a way to hurt us." The markets' reaction was evident in a rapid collapse in the North Korean

exchange rate at the time that BDA went into receivership. The importance
of the issue was also signaled by a North Korean statement in April 2006 that
publicly tied a resumption of talks to a resolution of the BDA issue, which, as
we will see, was indeed required to move from the 2005 Joint Statement to the
operational agreements reached in 2007 to implement it.[35]

It is hard to make the case that the BDA actions alone were able to secure
North Korean concessions, however. The United States had to reciprocate.
Bilateral talks on BDA were held in March 2006 and resumed quickly following the October 2006 nuclear test in December 2006 and then in January 2007,
when a final deal was struck on the regime's BDA funds (National Committee
on North Korea 2007; Hill 2014, 245–262). Moreover, the BDA and UN
sanctions worked only by promising a return to the tightly phased "actions
for actions" approach contained in the Joint Statement of September 2005.
This approach was elaborated in the two "road map" agreements of 2007,[36]
which require scrutiny, since they embody a highly elaborate and phased set of
inducements. An analysis of this episode shows that the limitations on a sanctions strategy by no means guaranteed that inducements would work either.

Action for Action? The Road Map Agreements of 2007
and Their Implementation

The United States had an array of concerns with respect to North Korea's
nuclear program. These not only included existing stocks of fissile material and
the opportunities for reprocessing spent fuel from the Yongbyon reactor; they
also included the verification regime, the HEU program, and possible proliferation activities as well. Given the fact that the most immediate challenge was
to slow the accumulation of fissile material, the Bush administration developed
a strategy that focused in the first instance on Yongbyon.

The "Initial Actions for the Implementation of the Joint Statement" of
February 13, 2007, outlined a series of very short-run measures, inducements
for actions, designed to build confidence while having a material effect on the
visible program. In the first sixty days, a freeze on Yongbyon—an agreement
to "shut down and seal [the facility] for the purpose of eventual abandonment"—and allow the return of IAEA inspectors was to be exchanged for
delivery of oil. North Korea also agreed to begin discussions on a declaration
of its activities, although not to complete the declaration or provide it in
full. The United States committed to set in motion a number of diplomatic
processes, although also not necessarily to complete them: to "start" bilateral
talks aimed at normalization; to "begin" the process of removing North Korea
from the list of state sponsors of terrorism; and to "advance the process" of

lifting sanctions under the Trading with the Enemy Act. During the first and second phases, a complete declaration of all nuclear programs and disablement of all existing nuclear facilities would be exchanged for economic, energy, and humanitarian assistance up to the equivalent of 1 million tons of heavy fuel oil. However, this large package—in excess of what was offered under the Agreed Framework—would depend on the full disablement of the nuclear facilities at Yongbyon. In the short run, a shipment of 50,000 tons of heavy fuel oil was the only actual inducement on offer.

The October 2007 agreement—the "Second-Phase Actions for the Implementation of the September 2005 Joint Statement"—reiterated these commitments and set out a more precise timetable. The agreement appears to have stated that the disablement of the reactor, the reprocessing plant and the fuel fabrication facility would be completed by the end of 2007 and that North Korea would provide a full declaration. It also stated explicitly that removing North Korea from the list of state sponsors of terrorism would be conditional on actions with respect to disablement. Not stated explicitly, but implied by the "actions for actions" approach, is that the North Koreans expected disablement to also be phased to the provision of the HFO shipments, suggesting a timetable likely to run well past the end-2007 deadline.

As we saw in Chapter 4, a major US food aid package, including new monitoring arrangements, was finalized during this phase of the negotiations. It suggested a tacit linkage between progress in the talks and humanitarian assistance, albeit under cover of a WFP appeal.[37] To meet domestic requirements that there be a "substantial improvement in monitoring and access" for the aid package to go ahead, North Korea negotiated the new monitoring regime outlined in detail in Chapter 4.

The United States also responded as required by proceeding to lift restrictions on North Korea associated with the Trading with the Enemy Act and through President Bush's formal notice to Congress of his intention to remove Pyongyang from the list of state sponsors of terrorism after forty-five days. During the July 2008 round of talks, the six parties agreed to fulfill "in parallel" their agreed commitments with respect to HFO shipments and complete disablement by the end of October.

Did the phased inducements in the "actions for actions" approach work? The February 2007 agreement to freeze the North's nuclear facilities was delayed as a result of technical difficulties in resolving the BDA issue, but oil shipments commenced in July and the freeze was in place by October 2007, when second-phase actions were to commence. North Korea began implementing the October 3 Agreement by shutting down the five-megawatt nuclear reactor at Yongbyon, and although it missed the year-end deadline for disablement, completing eight of the eleven steps necessary to make the reactor inoperable for at least a year, this deviation was partly technical and not viewed by the United States as serious.[38]

Two issues—the North Korean declaration of its programs and the linked issue of verification—ultimately posed stumbling blocks. An early declaration in November fell well short of US and other intelligence estimates of the likely stock of fissile material. It was lacking in detail and made no mention of either HEU or proliferation activities, which had become an issue of increasing concern following the September 2007 Israeli bombing of a reactor in the Syrian desert that had been constructed with North Korean support. In the absence of a robust declaration, verification and monitoring became more important both politically and substantively.

Following three further rounds of negotiations in early 2008, in April of that year the United States and North Korea reached a face-saving agreement in Singapore. North Korea promised a new declaration of its plutonium-based program. The United States would provide a bill of particulars on its suspicions with respect to proliferation activities and HEU—which the North Koreans continued to deny—and North Korea would confidentially "acknowledge" them—in other words, "We didn't do it and we are not going to do it again." A massive compilation of documents was delivered to the United States in May and formally delivered to the Chinese as chair of the Six Party Talks in June.

The September 2005 statement of principles made reference to the fact that denuclearization would be "verifiable" and that North Korea would return to the NPT and IAEA inspections. However, management of verification issues had been delegated to the nuclear working group in the February 2007 agreement, implying that it was not a component of the first two phases of implementation outlined in the two 2007 road map agreements. Following bilateral negotiations on the issue, the parties issued a joint communiqué on July 12 outlining broad principles, including agreement that at least the initial inspection mechanism would involve experts from the six parties, with the IAEA limited to "consultancy and assistance."

Both domestic political constraints within the United States and increasing disaffection on the part of South Korea and Japan (which refused to supply fuel oil at all because of the Pyongyang's failure to address the abductee issue)—in short both credibility and coordination problems—undermined the tightly scripted exchange of inducements for North Korean actions. As criticism of the integrity of the North Korean declaration and the utility of the entire Six Party process mounted, the Bush administration sought to mollify critics by undertaking an outside review of the declaration that the North Koreans had provided and by moving verification efforts into the second phase.[39] Moreover, it demanded that IAEA inspectors ultimately lead the implementation of the protocol, in line with expectations stated in the September 2005 Joint Statement that North Korea would return "at an early date" to the NPT and to IAEA safeguards. When North Korea rejected these efforts, claiming that full verification would come only at the end of the denuclearization process, the administration chose to step back from an important inducement: rescinding North Korea's designation as a state sponsor of terrorism.

These events occurred exactly at the time that Kim Jong-il was subsequently believed to have suffered a stroke, compounding the difficulty of reaching any agreement. On August 26, a foreign ministry statement announced that North Korea would stop and then reverse the disablement process at Yongbyon and, in a thinly veiled reference to the military, restore facilities "as strongly requested by its relevant institutions."[40] On September 24, in a virtual replay of the events of early 2003, it removed IAEA seals and surveillance cameras from its reprocessing facility and restricted international inspectors from its reactor site. South Korean intelligence leaks suggested that North Korea was also restoring an undeclared underground nuclear site at Punggye, suggesting a hard-line response to the US change in course that would extend into the Obama administration.

Realizing that the entire Six Party process was now in jeopardy, the Bush administration reversed course and sent Christopher Hill to Pyongyang to negotiate a face-saving protocol in early October that would permit North Korea to be taken off the terrorism list.[41] But nearly a month after this last-minute concession, North Korea questioned its precise terms with respect to the taking of samples, once again providing an entry point for critics of the deal. Two further rounds of negotiations in December proved unsuccessful. The United States believed that the North Koreans had reneged on verbal assurances of verification that had been given in October and stated that further energy assistance under the agreement would not be forthcoming, thus effectively ending the implementation process. The Six Party Talks—and the implementation agreements that they had ultimately generated in 2007—were dead.

Conclusion: Inducements and Constraints in the Six Party Talks

Several conclusions emerge from this chapter's consideration of the rise and fall of the Six Party Talks. First, the history of the talks confirms the significance of the coordination problems outlined in our introduction in Chapter 1.

The United States had limited success in turning the Six Party Talks into a five-party cartel that would use economic-cum-political pressure to bring North Korea to the table and elicit concessions. China's commitment to deep engagement was a constant, and Beijing exercised influence both within the Six Party Talks and through its capacity to influence UN Security Council action in 2006. Japan (roughly through the second Koizumi-Kim summit in 2004) and particularly South Korea (though the end of the Roh administration in 2007) were also seeking to engage North Korea, even at times when the talks were not progressing. As Rumsfeld himself was forced to admit in a memo to the president only days before the first nuclear test, in October 2006, "It is not only difficult, but possibly impossible, for the US to gain the international diplomatic support sufficient to impose the leverage on Iran and/or North Korea required to cause them to discontinue their nuclear programs."[42] As we have seen, Secretary of State Rice had already reached this conclusion based on her analysis of the first administration's record.

The strategy of pressuring North Korea was not only futile; it was counterproductive. North Korea responded to both military threats and economic pressure by accelerating its pursuit of weapons, most notably in early 2003 and in 2006, and again in 2009 in a second round of missile and nuclear tests in the first year of the Obama administration.

This conclusion about the counterproductive nature of sanctions is more complicated with respect to the use of financial instruments, but it ultimately appears to pertain as well. We have evidence that the BDA actions had diplomatic effect because of the weight that the North Koreans put on them in the resumption of negotiations. But these apparent gains were fleeting. The timing of the BDA announcement undermined the momentum of the September Joint Statement and resulted in a suspension of the talks for over a year, during which the North Koreans tested both missiles and a nuclear weapon. The BDA sanctions and the multilateral UN sanctions that followed were effective only because the United States was willing to resolve the BDA issue and resume negotiations by returning to an "action for action" inducements approach.

Were inducements successful? On the positive side of the ledger, they appear crucial to the negotiations leading to the 2005 breakthrough, the resumption of talks in 2006, and the two road map agreements in 2007. Critics such as Sigal (2009a, 2009b) argue that the problem was not that inducements did not work; it was that the United States did not follow through on its commitments. Sigal argues that the Bush administration moved the goalposts by including issues that were assigned to a third phase and then punished North Korea by reneging on the lifting of sanctions when Pyongyang balked. Domestic political constraints and the increasing divergence between US strategy and the changed foreign policies of the Lee Myung-bak and Abe, Fukuda, and Aso governments also impinged on the ability of the United States to maintain its commitments.

But the question must then be asked: was North Korea ultimately interested in negotiating and implementing the agreements? Christopher Hill's strategy in 2008 was to focus on the inducements required to stop production of plutonium in Yongbyon through an agreement on disabling the facility. He self-consciously sought to finesse the issues of proliferation, HEU, accumulated stocks of fissile material, and the weapons themselves. Once the North Koreans saw the benefits of concessions and once trust was built, it was hoped that they would be willing to deal on these questions as well.

Still, it is not clear that North Korea was willing to deal on these questions. A less charitable interpretation of the events of 2008 suggests that the North Korean regime was divided on the issue, engaged in strategic deception, or perhaps rendered incapable of action by the deterioration in Kim Jong-il's health and a preoccupation with the succession. North Korea never publicly acknowledged either its proliferation activities—despite overwhelming evidence on the Syrian reactor—or its HEU program. If taken in good faith, the proliferation and HEU deal could be treated as an acknowledgment that North Korea had engaged in such behavior in the past but would not do so in the future. However, the bitter fight over verification, even though technically not a part of the second phase of implementation, raised broader questions about the regime's intentions.

Even had the 2007 agreements been fully implemented, a prolonged round of further negotiations—and side payments—would be required to address verification, reentry into the NPT, the readmission of IAEA inspectors, and the question of existing stocks of fissile material and weapons, as well as HEU and nuclear cooperation with Syria, Iran, and other states. During these negotiations, North Korea would effectively maintain a nuclear capability, in effect arming through strategic delay. The least charitable interpretation is that the North Koreans sought throughout negotiations to maintain at least a minimal nuclear deterrent.

Based on the evidence on offer from the negotiations, it is impossible to distinguish between these more and less charitable interpretations of North Korean intent; they are observationally equivalent. But the regime's reaction must be read not only against the evidence from the negotiations but also against the domestic developments in North Korea described in Chapter 2, particularly in the wake of Kim Jong-il's stroke and the onset of the succession.

Internal political developments provided no evidence of more accommodating political forces within the regime or evidence of complementary actions toward reform and opening that would have sent credible signals of North Korea's type. To the contrary, as we have seen the regime was moving in the opposite direction after 2005. Further evidence for this more skeptical interpretation of the utility of inducements can be found by outlining developments during the first Obama administration.

7

Negotiating on Nuclear Weapons II
Permanent Crisis, 2009–2016

The Obama administration came to office committed to a strategy toward its foreign adversaries almost diametrically opposed to that of the first Bush administration. At least as a matter of declaratory policy, the new administration signaled a willingness to engage, including with North Korea. In his inaugural address, President Obama offered to "extend a hand" to adversaries willing to "unclench their fist." In an important interview in 2015, the president elaborated on the so-called Obama Doctrine, arguing that the overwhelming capabilities enjoyed by the United States substantially reduced the risks of engagement.[1]

Did this strategy have effect with respect to North Korea? The short answer is no. The initial North Korean response to the new administration was escalatory, quickly launching a satellite in April 2009 that was widely seen as a stalking horse for the country's long-range missile program. The regime undertook a second nuclear test in May and then withdrew "permanently" from the Six Party Talks. With the effective collapse of the talks, negotiations moved from the more or less institutionalized format of the 2003–2008 period, albeit with significant pauses, to less structured diplomatic signaling and recurrent crisis bargaining (Table 7.1).

These episodes unfolded in recurrent cycles during the 2009–2016 period. In response to the early 2009 tests, the Obama administration resorted to a two-track policy reminiscent of the so-called Perry approach of the late Clinton years (Perry 1999, 2015). Although greater emphasis was put on a tightening of multilateral sanctions against North Korea through the UN Security

TABLE 7.1

Economic statecraft 2009–2016: Post–Six Party Talks phase

Timeline	Economic and other inducements	Sanctions and constraints	North Korean response
To satellite launch (April 5, 2009) and second nuclear test (May 25, 2009)	Initial stated willingness by Obama administration to engage; maintenance of food aid program	No change from status quo ante	Satellite launch and nuclear tests of April–May 2009
From 2009 satellite and nuclear tests to sinking of *Cheonan* and shelling of Yeonpyeong Island	Onset of strategic patience: downplaying significance of Six Party Talks and holding out prospective benefits only	Active pursuit of multilateral sanctions following missile and nuclear tests (UNSC Presidential Statement April 13, 2009; UNSC Resolution 1874, June 12 2009)	Further missile tests (July 2009); withdrawal from Six Party Talks
Sinking of *Cheonan* and shelling of Yeonpyeong Island (2010–2011) through death of Kim Jong Il	Strategic patience modified in 2011 through negotiations over freeze agreement	Additional ("May 24") sanctions from South Korea following sinking of *Cheonan*; negotiation of US-ROK Counter-Provocation Plan	
Collapse of Leap Day Deal (March–April) through fourth (January 6, 2016) and fifth (September 9, 2016) nuclear tests	Leap Day Deal (February 29, 2012), followed by return to strategic patience, prospective benefits only	Additional multilateral and bilateral sanctions in wake of April and December 2012 satellite launches and third nuclear test (UNSC Presidential Statement; April 16, 2012; UNSC Resolutions 2087, January 22, 2013, and UNSCR 2094, March 7, 2013); military signaling during March–April 2013 crisis; sanctions following missile tests in 2015, and fourth and fifth nuclear tests in 2016 (UNSCR 2270, March 2, 2016, and UNSCR 2321, November 30, 2016)	North Korean satellite launches (April/December 2012); third nuclear test (February 2013); rollout of *byungjin* line (March/April 2013) committing to nuclear program; sustained increase in missile tests and of new types and two additional nuclear tests

Council, the United States restated its willingness to reengage through the Six Party Talks on the basis of the September 2005 Joint Statement.

This basic strategy persisted through the entire period examined here. Except for the failed Leap Day Deal of February 2012, however, the benefits on offer were all prospective. The administration specifically rejected additional incentives solely for talks or for any North Korean actions that were viewed as obligations under UN Security Council resolutions or prior agreements. Indeed, it even insisted that a return to the talks would require advance or "up-front" actions on the part of North Korea to show seriousness of intent; not until 2016 were these preconditions gradually relaxed. Nonetheless, efforts to restart negotiations faced the credibility or sequencing problems that we outlined in our introduction in Chapter 1.

The Lee Myung-bak government, which had come into office in February 2008, took a similar approach to engagement. It made promises of substantial assistance, conditional on a settlement of the nuclear issue and the pursuit of reforms by the North. In the short run, as we saw in Chapter 3 (Figure 3.9), aid dropped to virtually nothing. Although nominally different, President Park Geun-hye (who came into office in February 2013) pursued quite similar policies. In principle, her conception of *Trustpolitik* involved small reciprocal steps, but as we showed in Chapter Four it also rested largely on benefits that were contingent on North Korean moves.

This two-track strategy, dubbed "strategic patience" in the United States, had little success in resuming talks. At each step that sanctions were imposed or aid withdrawn, North Korea responded by escalating tensions. It largely eschewed the Six Party process altogether or advanced proposals at complete odds with the American approach. These included parallel or even prior negotiation of a "peace regime" that would replace the armistice and a resumption of the Six Party Talks "without preconditions," meaning that North Korea would take no actions beforehand. In the interim, North Korea would remain—de facto if not de jure—a nuclear power, a position which no doubt influenced the country's interest in negotiating (Landau 2012). In early 2013, the rollout of the *byungjin* line formally committed the regime to the twin goals of economic development and continued pursuit of its nuclear weapons program. Not surprisingly, this was a political nonstarter from the perspective not only of the United States but of the other four parties as well.

The pattern of escalation, mutual recriminations, sanctions, and further escalation unfolded in several cycles during the second Obama administration, and we trace them in this chapter. Following a naval skirmish along the Northern Limit Line (NLL) in November 2009, Pyongyang undertook one of the more egregious provocations of the post–Korean War period by sinking a South Korean naval vessel, the *Cheonan*, causing the loss of 46 sailors in March 2010. In November, North Korea shelled Yeonpyeong Island, sovereign territory of the Republic of Korea. These events shifted the US and South Korean policy focus from negotiations back to sanctions and strengthening of the deterrent.[2]

During 2011 the United States pursued a modest softening of strategic patience through the negotiation of a "food for freeze" deal, which was finalized just before Kim Jong-il's death on December 17, 2011, and announced publicly on February 29, 2012. But this so-called Leap Day Deal fell apart almost immediately with the announcement by Kim Jong-un of the intention to launch a satellite that was seen as a thinly veiled step in the buildup of the country's long-range missile program.

Although the April 13, 2012, test failed, it set in train a sequence of events that bore an uncanny similarity to those of early 2009: international condemnation and sanctions; a second, more successful satellite launch in December 2012; another expression of multilateral concern and sanctions; a third nuclear test in April 2013; a third UNSC sanctions resolution; and a taut period of military confrontation in the spring of 2013. Although the level of tensions eventually subsided from their early 2013 peak, little progress was made during 2013–2016 in resuming negotiations and the North Korean nuclear and missile programs continued to march forward.

In early 2016, this cycle repeated yet again with the fourth nuclear test in January, another successful satellite launch in February, and passage in March of the most sweeping UN Security Council resolution (UNSCR) to date. Yet these measures were met by a marked acceleration of missile tests and signs of substantial increases in capability, capped by the fifth nuclear test in September 2016. We take up this last episode in more detail in our conclusions in Chapter 8.

As during the Bush era, both policy and scholarly debate during the two Obama administrations revolved around the utility of sanctions and inducements. Sigal (2009) argues that North Korea's behavior in the first half of 2009 was largely a response to the failure of negotiations in late 2008. Just as North Korea had offered an escalatory response to the cutoff of heavy fuel oil (HFO) shipments in 2002, it responded similarly to the joint decision of the United States, South Korea, and Japan to suspend HFO shipments in December 2008.[3] The bellicose language and the missile and nuclear tests were simply tactics designed to increase the regime's bargaining leverage. Subsequent analyses in this vein repeatedly returned to the failure of sanctions and Obama's unwillingness to take initiatives or to offer inducements of adequate scope to influence North Korean behavior (see, for example, Asia Society 2009; Wit 2009; Lewis, Hayes, and Bruce 2011; Sigal 2012, 2016; Hayes and Tanter 2012; Halperin 2012; Moon 2012; Frank 2012; Gurtov 2014; von Hippel and Hayes 2014).

The evidence that sanctions did not have their intended effect is fairly ample, and once again both coordination and sequencing issues appear to play a crucial role. China maintained its declaratory commitment to denuclearization and even sharpened it following the 2013 and 2016 nuclear tests. China also signed on to new multilateral sanctions during this period (2009, 2013, and 2016), at least initially implementing some of them in a high-profile way. Yet the deep economic engagement with North Korean continued unabated and when challenged, Beijing generally came to North Korea's defense.

We can say with some confidence that the prospective approach of the Obama and Lee administrations did not prove effective—vaguely worded inducements did not bring North Korea back to the table. However, we do have the important episode of the Leap Day Deal, and not enough has been made of what it reveals about the effectiveness of inducements. A modest trust-building exercise fell apart when the new regime chose to prioritize a satellite test over a significant humanitarian aid package and return to the Six Party Talks. Similar conclusions can be drawn about the modest efforts of the Park Geun-hye administration (Park was inaugurated in February 2013) to pursue so-called *Trustpolitik*, and about a partial lifting of Japanese sanctions over the abduction issue in mid-2014. Neither did China's efforts at deep engagement secure North Korean cooperation or serve to restart the Six Party Talks; on the contrary, the period under consideration was punctuated by further nuclear and missile tests.

It is hard to avoid the conclusion that domestic political dynamics in North Korea associated with the succession, both before and after Kim Jong-il's death, had pushed the regime toward a harder line that made it impervious to both sanctions and inducements, and certainly of a largely prospective sort. These domestic political constraints included, among others, continuing insecurity following Kim Jong-il's stroke in August 2008 and the complex politics of the succession itself, which demanded careful attention to the interests of the military and security apparatus (Chapter 2). However, we do not need to rely on speculation about the internal dynamics of the regime to draw conclusions about North Korean intent. By early 2013, the regime had rolled out the *byungjin* line, committing the country openly to pursuit of its nuclear and missile program, and had written these commitments into its constitution; the *byungjin* line was only reinforced by the May 2016 Party Congress. The principal offer by the North Koreans throughout this period was for bilateral negotiations on a peace regime, but in advance of nuclear negotiations, an offer that was impossible for the United States to take up for both domestic and international political reasons.[4]

Engagement Manqué: January 2009–March 2010

In a controversial CNN/YouTube debate in July 2007, Barack Obama answered affirmatively to a question of whether he would be willing to meet "separately, without preconditions, in the first year of [his] administration with the leaders of Iran, Syria, Venezuela, Cuba, and North Korea." Of political necessity, that offer was subsequently modified (Bader 2012, 29), but the administration signaled at least a general willingness to build on the engagement strategy that the Bush administration had pursued prior to the breakdown of the Six Party Talks in 2008. According to Stephen Bosworth, the president's North Korean envoy, this commitment was communicated not only through public statements but directly to North Korea in the president's first few days in office.[5]

The stated willingness to talk did not imply the extension of concessions ex ante; in the words of Jeffrey Bader (2012, 7), senior director for Asian affairs at the National Security Council, policy required "breaking the cycle of North Korean provocation, extortion and accommodation (by China, Japan, Russia, South Korea and the United States), and reward." A crucial issue that was to persist throughout 2009–2010 was therefore the sequencing of the Six Party Talks and any quid pro quos that might be associated with them. At her secretary of state nomination hearings, Hillary Clinton suggested, although she did not state, that the United States would not negotiate normalization of relations prior to complete denuclearization. The North Koreans furiously responded that normalization was not a reward for disarming and that their "status as a nuclear weapons state" would remain unchanged as long as North Korea was exposed "even to the slightest U.S. nuclear threat."[6] Even before the missile test of April, North Korean statements introduced demands that it would be physically as well as politically impossible to meet, such as removing South Korea from the US nuclear umbrella or extended deterrent.

The Obama administration's shift from prospective engagement to the embrace of sanctions and a return to the "two-track" approach came as early as February, with intelligence foreseeing the launch of a three-stage "space launch vehicle" that ultimately took place on April 5. North Korea protested vigorously that it had a right to the peaceful use of outer space and was in any case not a state party to the Missile Technology Control Regime. These legal protests notwithstanding, the launch was seen by the United States, South Korea, Japan, and ultimately China and Russia as adequately cognate to an intercontinental missile test and therefore a violation of UNSC 1718.[7] After efforts by Japan to secure support for a Security Council resolution failed, a compromise was reached on a Presidential Statement, which although viewed as a weaker signal, nonetheless condemned the launch as a violation of UNSC 1718, closing the "missile-satellite" distinction that North Korea had sought to exploit and marginally expanding sanctions.

A classic escalatory cycle followed, but North Korean capabilities were now well advanced from what they had been, giving rise to a corresponding in-difference to the resumption of talks or to quid pro quos involving security guarantees. Within hours of the Presidential Statement, North Korea "perma-nently" withdrew from the Six Party Talks, declared all commitments under the talks null and void, and threatened to resume the reprocessing of spent fuel rods, pursue construction of a light-water reactor (LWR), and boost its nuclear deterrent.[8] International Atomic Energy Agency (IAEA) and US inspectors who had been on the ground at Yongbyon were ejected. On April 24, 2009, the UN Sanctions Committee issued the "adjustments" to sanctions under UNSCR 1718 requested by the Presidential Statement, and thus three ad-ditional North Korean firms were designated. The North Korean Foreign Ministry quickly affirmed that reprocessing had begun, suggested that the imposition of sanctions would constitute a nullification of the armistice, and threatened both further missile tests and a second nuclear test.

That second test came on May 25. Following a prolonged and difficult dip-lomatic process, the UN Security Council passed Resolution 1874 on June 12, calling on Pyongyang to cease and desist development of its nuclear and missile programs and to return to the Six Party Talks, the Non-Proliferation Treaty (NPT), and the IAEA safeguards. It is worth outlining the corresponding sanc-tions in some detail. Even though American policy makers did not believe that they would induce a change in course (Bader 2012, 39), the sanctions were important both for their economic effects and for the political signal they sent, including from China.[9]

UNSCR 1874 went beyond UNSCR 1718 in both the scope of products covered and the means of enforcement.[10] It did not constitute a trade embargo on North Korea; humanitarian assistance was explicitly excluded, and the de-sign of the sanctions excluded the vast majority of commercial trade, as we saw in Chapter 3. Nonetheless, it extended UNSCR 1718 to include all arms-related trade as well as training or assistance related to such sales. The signifi-cance of these sanctions appear small given the likely decline in the weapons trade (Chapter 3), but they had bite through their effect on so-called dual-use technologies with both civilian and potential military uses (Abt 2014, 77–93). Moreover, the resolution called on both international institutions and member states not to undertake new grants, financial assistance, or concessional loans to North Korea and asked that they maintain "vigilance" with respect to current aid programs.

The most interesting features of the resolution had to do with enforcement. UNSCR 1874 came close to making the American-led Proliferation Security Initiative (PSI) a formal multilateral effort. It called upon member states to inspect all cargo on their territory, including at both seaports and airports, believed to contain prohibited items, and it contained a number of additional provisions that would affect shipping if rigorously enforced.[11] The resolution provided the basis for an increase in interdictions (Table 3.1), starting with the shadowing of a North Korean ship (the *Kang Nam I*) in June of 2009, ultimately forcing its return to North Korea. Significant shipments of weapons were also interdicted in 2009 and 2010 in France, the United Arab Emirates, Thailand, and South Africa.[12]

In addition to interdiction, the UNSCR 1874 explicitly provided for the use of financial means to stop WMD-related trade. These measures were potentially more sweeping than trade sanctions since the resolution permitted the blocking of transfers and even the freezing of any assets that "could contribute" to North Korea's weapons programs or activities.[13] As with the Banco Delta Asia (BDA) sanctions, the United States was willing to implement these measures aggressively on its own—for example, by designating new entities and individuals under existing statutes and issuing an additional bank advisory with respect to North Korea (US Department of the Treasury 2009).[14] Nor was it alone; between them, the United States, the European Union, Japan, and Australia made twenty-nine "autonomous designations" of North Korean firms: these were undertaken outside of the UN sanctions designation process. The United States also engaged in active sanctions enforcement diplomacy in Asia-Pacific to encourage others to do so as well. Following the passage of UNSCR 1874, the United States appointed an ambassador for sanctions enforcement who traveled to the region and consulted with officials in China, Malaysia, Thailand, Singapore, and Russia on sanctions enforcement.

As the Obama administration pursued its multilateral approach to sanctions, it also made clear that no further inducements, including a relaxation of sanctions, would be offered to North Korea in advance of resumption of the talks. In a widely cited comment at the ASEAN Regional Forum in Singapore in May 2009, Secretary of Defense Robert Gates said that the United States was "tired of buying the same horse twice" and expressed opposition to "the notion that we buy our way back to the status quo ante."[15] The United States also argued (and rightly from a legal point of view) that it was in any case not in a position to relax multilateral sanctions; any such change would be contingent on North Korea taking the actions called for under multilateral UN Security Council resolutions.

Yet if the United States was unwilling to offer inducements for the purpose of bringing North Korea back to the Six Party Talks, the question remained of what *prospective* benefits the five parties might offer. The Obama administration was unwilling to commit to finalizing normalization prior to complete denuclearization, and for good political reasons; it seemed implausible that such a process could even begin let alone reach a conclusion while North Korea remained a de facto nuclear power. However, it also clearly recognized, in the words of a senior official, that "if North Korea is to take major steps to dismantle its nuclear capabilities there must be a corresponding set of initiatives on the part of not only the United States but South Korea, China, and Japan."[16] Given the difficulties of implementing all components of the agenda outlined in the September 2005 Joint Statement all at once, it seemed inevitable that the talks would have to focus on the phasing of inducements and reciprocal actions.

The issue of inducements was initially made moot, however, because the passage of UNSCR 1874 in June was met almost immediately by North Korean escalation. In June the Foreign Ministry announced that the country would weaponize all newly extracted plutonium, commence a uranium enrichment program, and provide a "decisive military response" to any "blockade." According to the announcement, it had "become an absolutely impossible option for the DPRK to even think about giving up its nuclear weapons."

At the same time that North Korea was escalating, however, it too began to signal a willingness to reengage. Bilateral talks were held between an American delegation and its North Korean counterparts in December 2009. It is possible that sanctions and deteriorating economic circumstances had some effect in this regard. Indirect evidence of this can be gleaned from Pyongyang's extraordinary proposal to South Korea that it pay for a third bilateral summit.[17]

North Korean counterproposals with respect to the Six Party Talks cast doubt on the regime's seriousness. The diplomatic to and fro centered on the format under which negotiations would take place, but the proposals only served to disguise much more fundamental disagreements about the agenda. The United States repeatedly stated its willingness to engage with North Korea, including bilaterally, as long as the talks were held "within the framework" of the Six Party Talks. Not only did the Six Party Talks provide a multilateral venue for coordinating with Japan, South Korea, China, and Russia; holding negotiations under their aegis also ensured that diplomacy would focus on denuclearization as one objective. The United States repeated its opposition to "talks for talks' sake" and sought to reconfirm Pyongyang's commitment to agreements made in prior rounds of the talks. Most notably these included the September 2005 Joint Statement and the implementation accords of February and October 2007.

Over the course of late 2009, a new North Korean strategy emerged that was deeply at odds not only with US and South Korean views but also with the views of the other three parties. North Korea appeared to support a return to multilateral talks through initial bilateral talks and promised the high-level access that would permit indirect contact with the leadership; lack of access had plagued the late-2008 negotiations. However, multilateral talks among the armistice parties and bilateral talks with the United States were now advanced as a precondition for even resuming, let alone completing, the agenda spelled out in the Six Party Talks process.[18] Moreover, the objectives of the talks would not be limited to bargaining over North Korean denuclearization but would include "denuclearization of the entire peninsula." Given that the President George H. W. Bush had announced the withdrawal of all tactical nuclear weapons from the peninsula in 1991 and that South Korea had no nuclear weapons program, this formulation implied a reconsideration of the extended deterrent and even US possession of nuclear weapons.

China sought to bridge the divide through intense diplomatic activity in February and March 2010. However, its efforts were preceded by an even more crucial high-level visit that brought a rich array of incentives to bear. Rightly seen as an inflection point in Beijing's approach to North Korea, this visit effectively ratified Beijing's "deep engagement" approach outlined in Chapter 6 and extended a host of new direct and indirect supports.

In October 2009, Premier Wen Jiabao became the first Chinese premier in nearly two decades to visit Pyongyang, bringing with him a high-level delegation of economic officials. This diplomatic effort set the stage for a succession of visits by Kim Jong-il to China in May and August 2010 and in May 2011. Although taking place against the backdrop of ongoing North Korean reluctance to engage in the Six Party Talks and the clashes with South Korea we describe later, each visit was scripted by China with a strong economic agenda, suggesting the benefits of reform. However, as Reilly (2014a, 2014c) summarizes, the most consequential effect of these meetings was increased

Chinese engagement (see also Li 2016). During his visit, Wen promised to build a new bridge across the Yalu River (at an estimated cost of US$150 million); signed a number of diplomatic accords, including a new aid agreement (Reilly 2014c); designated 2010 as the "Year of Sino-Korean Friendship"; and agreed to establish two new joint economic development zones on islands in the Yalu. A host of Chinese initiatives followed these diplomatic exchanges, including use of the Chinese ambassador in Pyongyang to mobilize foreign investment in North Korea, announced support for Chinese firms, the creation of a Fund for Investment in North Korea through the Chinese Overseas Investment Federation, and commitments to the provision of infrastructure.

But what really mattered was the signal that these measures sent to Chinese firms in sectors such as mining, including national-level state-owned enterprises (SOEs) (China Minmetals Corporation), provincial-level SOEs (Tonghua Iron and Steel), and large private groups (Wanxiang). Firms from the Northeast showed a particular interest in the opening, an outcome that fit with the 2002 national campaign to "revitalize the north-east" (*zhenxing dongbei*). Provincial and even municipal officials in cities such as Dandong and Jilin jumped on the bandwagon set in motion by the Wen and Kim Jong-il visits, a phenomenon that Reilly dubs "local liberalism" (2014b, 7). The rapid exploitation of the signals sent by the central government generated not only deeper cross-border ties but an effective lobby for closer North Korean relations and the provision of supporting infrastructure on the Chinese side of the border (Reilly 2014a, 2014b).

We have no smoking gun to prove that China's "deep engagement" efforts had the direct effect of undermining prospects for resumption of the Six Party Talks. But whatever the intent of the Chinese initiatives, they clearly had that effect. Indeed, as we see in the next section they unfolded against a backdrop of North Korean provocations vis-à-vis the South. A procedural proposal by the Chinese would have granted North Korea another round of bilateral meetings with the United States, but it was to be followed by a preparatory six-party meeting in anticipation of a full resumption of the Six Party Talks. Accepting the Chinese proposal, the United States saw the steps as linked, with the bilateral meetings tied to a commitment to resume the talks. Despite early Chinese optimism about the proposal, North Korea remained silent on it. Before a North Korean envoy could go to New York to explore the diplomatic options, the *Cheonan* incident occurred, turning policy in both the United States and South Korea in a harder direction.

From the Sinking of the *Cheonan* to the Leap Day Deal

In contrast to the Obama administration's initial willingness to engage, the Lee Myung-bak administration had explicitly run on a platform that rejected the approach to the North of the Kim Dae-Jung and Roh Moo-hyun eras. These differences initially put Seoul and Washington at odds, even at the end of the Bush administration (Sigal 2009). With the events of 2009 and the sinking of the *Cheonan* and shelling of Yeonpyeong Island in 2010, however, the two governments converged around a steadily tightening sanctions regime.

In March 2008, the Lee administration outlined a quite comprehensive set of economic inducements for North Korea under the rubric of "Mutual Benefits and Common Prosperity" policy, or "Vision 3000 through Denuclearization and Opening," the latter because of its stated objective of lifting North Korea's per capita income to $3,000 (Suh 2009). Three features of Lee Myung-bak's policy constituted a departure from that of his predecessors, all centered on demands that North Korea reciprocate. The first was its insistence that progress on denuclearization be made a condition for progress on North-South relations. The economic incentives on offer were initially linked to a return to the 2007 road map agreements that came out of the Six Party Talks, a linkage that North Korea had always rejected.

The second departure was the implicit assumption that the aid on offer from the South would be conditional on reform and opening in the North, an assumption that was increasingly divergent from North Korean realities (Chapter 2). On completion of the second phase of the 2007 road map, the South Korean government would initiate five wide-ranging economic development programs with the North, all premised, however, on sweeping reforms. The program included creating new free-trade zones and building up export-oriented firms; major investment in infrastructure, including a North-South highway; education and vocational training aimed at increasing productivity and international competitiveness; and both government and NGO involvement in improvement of social infrastructure. These were to be backed by the fifth initiative: the orchestration of a massive $40 billion fund to be disbursed over ten years and financed by the Inter-Korean Cooperation Fund, international financial institutions (which North Korea would enter), foreign investment, and the aid package that was expected from normalization of diplomatic relations with Japan.

Third, and implicit in the other two components of the program, was a shift away from providing relatively unconditional aid. Even humanitarian support was made conditional on much tighter monitoring of actual conditions, transparency in distribution, and North Korean conformity with international standards governing humanitarian assistance. As we have seen, a rapid decline in South Korean assistance was the effect of these new standards.

North Korea's response to Lee's initiative, which was particularly vitriolic, was to reject the demands for denuclearization and opening and to argue for a return to the principles articulated in the two North-South summit declarations (June 15, 2000, and October 4, 2007). Reference to these declarations from the engagement era were to be a leitmotif of North Korean diplomacy toward the South through the entire period considered here. The Lee administration's approach was softened marginally in an important National Assembly speech on July 11, 2008, delivered in the immediate aftermath of the murder of a tourist by the North Korean military at the Mt. Kumgang resort. President Lee acknowledged the progress being made through the Six Party Talks and called for dialogue in order to implement the joint declarations. North Korea quickly rejected that initiative.[19] Even before the events of 2010 discussed later, virtually all aspects of North-South relations went into abeyance, including the elaborate structure of North-South meetings built up over the previous decade (see Table 6.2).

The North Korean response was not simply rhetorical. It extended to a significant restructuring of the military units responsible for the South[20] and to a series of military encounters along the Northern Limit Line (NLL), the de facto maritime border in the West Sea (Roehrig 2009).[21] In early 2009, Pyongyang began a sustained escalation around the NLL. In January, it declared its intention to protect its own version of the maritime border and suggested that it would not be bound by the armistice. Tensions around the issue escalated when South Korea joined the Proliferation Security Initiative in the wake of the North's second nuclear test in May 2009. The North Korean military responded by declaring that it could not guarantee the "legal status" of five South Korean islands that the NLL had been drawn to incorporate. For the remainder of the year and into early 2010, North Korea repeatedly conducted short-range missile and artillery tests off both coasts. Particularly important in this pattern of escalation was a skirmish in November that resulted in damage to a North Korean vessel and loss of life; this event was almost certainly the precursor to the subsequent sinking of the *Cheonan* the following March.

How the Lee Myung-bak government handled the investigation of the *Cheonan*, whether it was used for political purposes, and whether the North Koreans were culpable as charged became contested political questions in South Korea (Civilian-Military Joint Investigation Group 2010; Suh and Lee 2010; Lee and Yang 2010; You 2014). From our perspective, however, the most important consequence was the effect of this incident on the strategies of both South Korea and the United States. In a nationally televised address from the Korean War Memorial on May 24, 2010, President Lee announced a sweeping new sanctions regime against the North, which became known as the "May 24 measures."[22] The sanctions included prohibition of both general and processing-on-commission trade, which effectively limited North-South trade to the Kaesong Industrial Complex (KIC),[23] and the suspension of humanitarian aid except for that targeting vulnerable groups such as children, which effectively fell off as well. Nor was the South Korean response limited to economic instruments. A host of changes in military strategy and force posture were initiated as well, particularly following the shelling of Yeonpyeong Island later in the year (Jackson 2016, 186–187).[24]

United States policy followed suit. Even before the full report of the incident had been made public, Secretary of State Hillary Clinton endorsed the Lee administration's approach, including its intention to bring the issue before the Security Council, and hinted at a full review of all US policies toward North Korea. The Joint Communique of the 42nd U.S.-ROK Security Consultative Meeting in October contained a particularly explicit commitment to extended deterrence, including reference to the nuclear umbrella, and the creation of an Extended Deterrence Policy Committee.

In a highly symbolic press conference at the demilitarized zone (DMZ) in July 2010, Clinton, accompanied by the secretary of defense, Robert Gates, announced the administration's intention to levy new sanctions on North Korea. Less than a month later, President Obama signed a new executive order (EO 13551) targeting any entity that facilitated North Korean arms trafficking, import of luxury goods, or other illicit activity on behalf of Pyongyang. This included money laundering, counterfeiting of goods and currency, and cash smuggling associated with the notorious "Office 39" of the Korean Workers' Party, long believed to be a source of slush funds to the top leadership, including through receipts from illicit activities (UN Panel of Experts 2010; Gause 2015, 175–218).

The North Koreans again responded to sanctions by escalating. After American scientist Siegfried Hecker visited Yongbyon at Pyongyang's invitation in November 2010, he reported witnessing an estimated one thousand centrifuges at the nuclear complex (Hecker 2010). Hecker's visit was clearly a pointed North Korean signal, and it raised questions about the extent of North Korean cooperation with third parties such as Iran and Pakistan. It also revealed effective North Korean circumvention of UNSCR 1718 (2006) and UNSCR 1874 (2009).

Only a few days after the release of Hecker's report, on November 23, 2010, North Korea shelled Yeonpyeong Island near the disputed NLL, killing two South Korean military personnel, two South Korean civilians, injuring an additional score, and damaging the island's infrastructure. The stated justification was the ongoing North Korean rejection of the legitimacy of the NLL and threats by joint US-South Korean military exercises in its vicinity.

Even more clearly than in the past, China's actions suggested an extreme unwillingness to take sides against North Korea, let alone impose material costs. After issuing bland calls for calm "on both sides," and blocking UN Security Council action on the matter, the Chinese called for an "emergency session" of the Six Party Talks. Their proposal was quickly rejected by South Korea, the United States, and Japan. Instead, the United States outlined in more detail that the talks could only restart on the basis of prior North Korean actions that signaled seriousness of intent. These preconditions included an announced freeze on nuclear tests; a freeze on missile tests; a verifiable freeze on the enrichment program, to be monitored by IAEA inspectors; a commitment to the 2005 Joint Statement; and a commitment to abide by the armistice.

On the military front, in November 2010, the United States and South Korea went forward with planned joint naval exercises in the Yellow (West) Sea involving the US aircraft carrier *George Washington*, despite earlier Chinese objections (Bader 2012, 90–91). President Lee Myung-bak replaced his defense minister, and he and the new defense minister made public comments about more forceful military responses to future North Korean provocations. South Korea undertook the largest civil defense drill in decades. The US chairman of the Joint Chiefs of Staff Admiral Mike Mullen re-enforced this message by visiting Seoul and signaling support for a marked relaxation of South Korean rules of engagement.

In both the United States and South Korea, a minority argued that the two allies were caught in the same dynamic that had ensnared the Bush Administration, in which sanctions served to escalate rather than mitigate tensions and the only way out was some form of engagement.[25]

In neither country, however, was the political configuration favorable to reengagement. Public opinion in South Korea swung strongly behind the Lee administration's strategy of further sanctions and demands for strict reciprocity. In the United States, the November 2010 Congressional elections resulted in a Republican majority in the House of Representatives and a narrowed Democratic majority in the Senate—a political configuration strongly reminiscent of the one facing President Clinton when Republicans took control of Congress in 1994 and proceeded to cudgel the administration with its North

Korea policy (Noland 2000; Hathaway and Tama 2004). Nonetheless, a deepening food crisis in 2011 (Chapter 4) and a Chinese diplomatic initiative set the stage for the final effort in the period covered here to deploy inducements vis-à-vis North Korea.

The Rise, Fall, and Aftermath of the Leap Day Deal

As we showed in Figure 4.1, the reemergence of food problems can be seen in the secular decline in aggregate food supply that began in late 2005. Partly a result of reversals of reform, such as the ban on private trading in grain and efforts to revive the public distribution system (PDS) (Haggard and Noland 2009), high politics played an important role in the shortages. Following the North's missile and nuclear tests in 2006, South Korea suspended fertilizer shipments and, because of general donor fatigue, multilateral food aid dried up. With global food prices rising sharply from late 2007, the regime's capacity to import grain on commercial terms was also seriously impaired. The aid deal of 2008 was some help, but by March of 2009 less than a third of the aid promised had been shipped because of ongoing conflicts over access. Following the tensions of early 2009, North Korea decided to walk away from the aid program altogether. Later in the year, the disastrous currency reform of November 2009 set in train an inertial inflation that was to persist for over three years, exacerbating the challenges facing North Korean households.

Over the first half of 2011, signs of increasing distress mounted. They included a number of exogenous shocks: extreme cold during the 2010 planting season, floods in August and September prior to the harvest (Food and Agriculture Organization 2010), and the continuing rise in world food prices. An NGO assessment found food rations at near famine-era levels (Weingartner 2011).[26] North Korean behavior also showed rising concern—for example, in aggressive requests for bilateral aid and ultimately in approaches to both the South and the United States.

This sequence of events posed all of the humanitarian dilemmas outlined in the introduction in Chapter 1 and in Chapter 4. Should humanitarian assistance be separated from politics? Or might aid provide an opening wedge to dialogue? These dilemmas were on ample display in 2011–2012 in the negotiation of the Leap Day Deal. Yet no sooner had a deal been reached, which effectively offered food in exchange for a freeze, than the regime signaled its priorities by attempting a satellite launch. The launch not only scuttled the initiative but set in train an escalatory cycle from which the parties did not emerge until mid-2013.

In parallel to these developments, China engaged in a diplomatic initiative designed to offer an exit from the stalemate generated by the sinking of the *Cheonan* and the shelling of Yeonpyeong Island in 2010. Its three-step formula consisted of a reopening of North-South channels followed by bilateral talks with the United States and then a full resumption of the Six Party Talks. Following a breakthrough meeting between the South Korean chief nuclear negotiator and his North Korean counterpart on the sidelines of the ASEAN Regional Forum in July, North Korea expressed willingness to implement the September 2005 Joint Statement and to make joint efforts to resume the talks. This initiative was followed by two more rounds of North-South talks, although bilateral relations soured badly after the death of Kim Jong-il (Foster-Carter 2012). Bilateral discussions with the United States took place in July and October 2011 and February 2012, supplemented by separate talks on humanitarian assistance (Clinton 2011). An important meeting between Chinese vice premier Li Keqiang and Kim Jong-il in Pyongyang in October appeared to bless these efforts at rapprochement at the highest level (Zhang 2011).

The central product of these diplomatic efforts came in the so-called Leap Day Deal, codified in subtly different but largely congruent statements by the US State Department (US Department of State 2012) and the North Korean Ministry of Foreign Affairs on February 29, 2012. The core quid pro quo, and a controversial one, was that the United States would provide 240,000 metric tons of nutritional assistance based on an appropriate monitoring protocol "with the prospect of additional assistance based on continued need."[27] The United States also included a statement of nonhostile intent and a willingness to allow people-to-people exchanges. For its part, the North would implement a series of steps that conformed broadly to US preconditions to restarting the Six Party Talks: a moratorium on long-range missile launches, nuclear tests, and nuclear activities at Yongbyon, including uranium enrichment activities; and an agreement to allow IAEA inspectors to verify and monitor the moratorium and confirm the disablement of the five-megawatt reactor and associated facilities. Despite their differences, the two statements[28] clearly reflected an agreement rooted ultimately in a "food for freeze" quid pro quo, notwithstanding Obama administration claims to the contrary.

On March 16—with the regime now firmly under the leadership of Kim Jong-un—North Korea announced its intention to launch a satellite to commemorate Kim Il-sung's one hundredth birthday. The announcement came barely two weeks after the Leap Day Deal was rolled out, the attempted launch on April 13, 2012, about six weeks after that. Theories proliferated on why the new leadership chose to test, including the symbolic value of the

Kim Il-sung centenary launch, the need to carry out a legacy project inherited from Kim Jong-il, and the need for the Kim Jong-un regime to show resolve to both foreign and domestic audiences, particularly in the military. The regime may also have simply miscalculated, believing that it could diminish opposition to the launch by proceeding with the terms of the nuclear component of the deal; only three days after the satellite launch announcement, the IAEA confirmed that it had in fact been invited back into North Korea to inspect facilities.

Whatever the domestic circumstances that generated the launch, and the legalistic justification that North Korea offered,[29] three conclusions are germane here. The first is that inducements were not able to secure even a freeze of North Korea's nuclear and missile programs; nor were they able to offset whatever domestic political dynamics were at work to generate the launch.

Second, the announcement of the launch led not only to the collapse of the Leap Day Deal but to further sanctions and another escalatory cycle. The United States immediately withdrew its offer of food aid, and North Korea responded by rescinding its invitation to IAEA inspectors. The launch not only scuttled the resumption of negotiations but raised the bar on them and generated pressure for more sanctions. Condemnation was not limited to the United States, South Korea, and Japan. Both Russia and China denounced the launch as well and quickly agreed to an April 16 UNSC President's Statement that outlined stronger actions than those proposed in the tepid compromise Presidential Statement of April 13, 2009. For example, the 2012 statement subjected new companies to the asset freeze, banned new technologies for transfer to North Korea, and promised more intensive monitoring of enforcement through an updated work program for the sanctions committee.[30]

The third conclusion centers on the complex coordination and moral hazard problems surrounding China's relationship with its North Korean client. A collection of Chinese documents on the late Kim Jong-il period (Cathcart and Madden 2012) shows that the late leader had sought assiduously to solidify economic, political, and security ties with China in his last months: presiding over additional economic initiatives, meeting with and introducing his son to the incoming Chinese premier, and holding discussions with a top People's Liberation Army general. With his death, China maintained its declaratory policy vis-à-vis North Korea's nuclear and long-range missile programs, but was simultaneously forced to define its position with respect to the succession.

Thanks to another dossier assembled by Adam Cathcart (2012a), we have a near complete record of all official Chinese pronouncements surrounding the succession as well as press and expert commentary. The immediate political reaction was unambiguous: the Chinese leadership, at the very highest levels, both blessed the succession[31] and summoned ambassadors from the other parties to reassure them that the succession was going smoothly and to warn against external meddling.[32] Moreover, while the magnitude of support provided is still debated, the Chinese stance was backed by a substantial injection of financial and material aid, including food through the WFP at the peak of the lean season; support for the hundredth anniversary celebration of the birth of Kim Il-sung (Cathcart and Madden 2012; He 2013; Reilly 2014b, 2014c)[33]; and a virtual restatement of the "deep engagement" approach by Jang Song-thaek during a visit to Beijing later in the year. The Wen Jiabao–Jang Song-thaek joint communiqué and other statements emanating from this trip contained ample evidence of Chinese pique at North Korean reluctance to undertake more wide-ranging reform and opening (Cathcart 2012b). Nonetheless, deep engagement was reaffirmed.

"Déjà Vu All Over Again": The December 2012 and February 2013 Missile and Nuclear Tests

The North Koreans' failed satellite launch in April 2012 had brought with it the worst of all possible worlds for the new leadership: a spectacular technological failure, on full international and domestic media view, as well as the loss of a nontrivial aid package. It was thus a virtual certainty that the regime would try again, which it did with the second satellite on December 12 of that year. This test set in train another cycle of sanctions, a third nuclear test on February 12, 2013, and still further efforts to constrain North Korean behavior. These efforts included not only incremental changes in the sanctions regime but some of the most overt military posturing on the peninsula since the onset of the second nuclear crisis in late 2002. As we saw in Chapter 2, North Korea became even more explicit than ever in its commitment to retain its nuclear capability and develop a variety of delivery systems for it.

The December satellite test generated more than a month of contentious negotiations at the UN Security Council. Beijing and Washington finally struck a deal on UNSCR 2087 (January 22, 2013), which represented a step up from the President's Statement following the April launch. This resolution made marginal adjustments to the sanctions regime,[34] but US negotiators extracted a stated commitment to additional actions in case of subsequent tests, a commitment it sought to cash in on following the fourth nuclear test in January 2016. Beijing also engaged in quite visible bilateral diplomacy, summoning North Korea's ambassador several times in late January and publicly warning against the risks of a third nuclear test.

The North Korean response was almost immediate, and its statement, is-sued in the name of the National Defense Commission, constituted a clear indication of the shift in political direction that would be codified following the nuclear test in the *byungjin* line.[35] The statement effectively said that North Korea would never denuclearize; the only condition under which it would do so would be global denuclearization. In the interim, the Six Party Talks were again declared dead, this time permanently ("There will no longer exist the six-party talks."). The statement also disavowed North Korean commit-ment to the September 2005 Joint Statement that had been the single most significant achievement of the Six Party Talks process, and openly declared that North Korea would undertake a third nuclear test and satellite launches "one after another." Moreover, while the statement noted that UNSCR 2087 was "worked out through backstage dealing with the U.S. as a main player" it was adopted by the UNSC with "blind hand-raising by its member nations," a particularly defiant statement vis-à-vis China. The next day, a similar state-ment regarding the South was released[36] aimed at the incoming Park govern-ment, which had been elected in December 2012 and had, like Barack Obama, articulated a more forthcoming posture toward the North (Park Geun-hye 2011, 2012). This statement formally disavowed the North-South denucle-arization agreement of 1991 and threatened attacks on the South if sanctions were implemented.

The nuclear test of February 12, 2013, once again set in motion nego-tiations at the UN Security Council that effectively codified the multilateral sanctions regime that would remain in place through North Korea's fourth nuclear test that would come in January 2016. The new sanctions contained in UNSCR 2094 (March 7, 2013) can be seen as "punitive," aimed at changing the regime's behavior (mainly a codification of sanctions on luxury goods),[37] and "defensive," aimed at impeding the North Korean nuclear weapons pro-gram and its proliferation. In addition to designation of new individuals and entities subject to travel bans and asset seizures, China agreed for the first time to language urging member states to prohibit any financial flows that might be associated with these programs—for example, by blocking the establishment of correspondent relationships with banks in their jurisdictions. Although the language effectively excluded a range of North Korean accounts in China, they set the stage for US sanctions against North Korea's Foreign Trade Bank in an effort to send a warning to Chinese commercial banks.[38] The new resolution also called on member states to deny ports and overflight rights to ships and airplanes believed to be involved in military programs or evasion of sanctions, and even called for "enhanced vigilance over DPRK diplomatic personnel" to prevent them from engaging in proliferation activities.

Because of the opacity of the underlying connections to the weapons programs, these measures were bounded by a "credible information" clause: that governments can refuse to implement sanctions if they claim lack of "reasonable grounds" to do so, which grants them substantial discretion in enforcement. Yet the test had clearly come as a surprise to China, unleashing a domestic debate on the issue (Beauchamp-Mustafaga 2013) and highly visible signaling of enforcement. This included the decision to join US sanctions against the Foreign Trade Bank and publication in September of a detailed dual-use technologies list (Cavazos, Hayes and von Hippel 2013).

What followed the new sanctions resolution—before it could take material effect—was a succession of particularly escalatory moves (Table 7.2). To be sure, many North Korean "actions" were rhetorical, of dubious credibility, and broadly in line with past responses to regularly scheduled joint US-ROK military exercises.[39] Moreover, careful reading suggests that most of these actions were defensive and designed to deter. However, threats to preempt and launch attacks on the United States were novel and met with sharper responses than in the past. The United States initially augmented deployed forces in a way designed to signal resolve, including through mock bombing runs by nuclear-capable B-52 and B-2 bombers.[40] In the midst of the exercises, secretary of defense Chuck Hagel announced a major ballistic-missile defense initiative, including installation of fourteen additional interceptors. The United States and South Korea finalized a Combined Counter-Provocation Plan that defined new rules of engagement to ensure a more rapid response to North Korean military probes.

In addition to conventional military signaling, North Korea was quick to play the nuclear card. On April 2, 2013, the General Department of Atomic Energy announced concrete steps to restart both enrichment and reprocessing at Yongbyon explicitly for weapons purposes. Through the end of the period considered here, ongoing analysis of satellite imagery coupled with statements by the regime itself suggested continual augmentation of the country's nuclear capabilities: in evidence that the five-megawatt reactor had in fact been restarted; in completion of a LWR; in expansion of the enrichment facility; in evidence of reprocessing; and in the stocks of fissile material already accumulated (International Atomic Energy Agency 2014; Albright 2015). In March 2014, the Foreign Ministry announced that the country was considering a "new form of nuclear test for bolstering up its nuclear deterrence," and subsequent statements reiterated the right to conduct further nuclear tests.[41] The

TABLE 7.2

North Korean Response to UN Security Council Resolution 2094 (March–April 2013)

Date	Statement/action (source)
March 5	Threatens nuclear retaliation for any US action; claims miniaturization of nuclear warhead; nullifies Armistice; discontinues Panmunjon mission of the KPA; severs US-DPRK hotline (Supreme Command of the Korean People's Army)
March 7	Declares "right" to launch preemptive nuclear strike (Foreign Ministry)
March 8	Nullifies all agreements on non-aggression between North and South as well as joint declaration on denuclearization (Committee for the Peaceful Unification of the Fatherland)
March 10	Declares right to launch preemptive nuclear strike if Key Resolve exercises proceed (Foreign Ministry)
March 11	Calls Key Resolve an effective declaration of war (Supreme Command of the Korean People's Army)
March 11–12	Kim Jong-un visits two military units opposite ROK's Baengnyeong Island, near where *Cheonan* sunk and declares DPRK will turn the island into "sea of fire"
March 14	Live fire drills near the Northern Limit Line
March 21	Statement that Anderson Air Force Base on Guam and Okinawa "within striking range of our precision strike means" (Supreme Command of the KPA)
March 27	Severing of hotline used to coordinate movement of goods and people into and out of Kaesong Industrial Complex (Supreme Command of the KPA)
March 29	Kim Jong-un pictured in "operational meeting" of strategic rocket commanders, with maps showing strike plans against US targets; rocket forces placed on "standby"
March 30	North-South relations put on a "state of war" basis ("The government, political parties and organizations of the DPRK")
March 31–April 2	Plenary of WPK Central Committee introduces *byungjin* line of simultaneous development of economy and nuclear weapons; ratified by 7th Session of 12th Supreme People's Assembly
April 2	5-megawatt reactor at Yongbyon and "enrichment plant" will be restarted with objective to further nuclear weapons program (General Department of Atomic Energy)
April 4	Musudan missiles moved to east coast launch site
April 8	All North Korean workers withdrawn from Kaesong Industrial Complex (statement by Kim Yang-gon, secretary of the Central Committee of the Workers' Party of Korea)
April 9	Foreigners warned to leave Seoul to avoid war (Korea Asia-Pacific Peace Committee)
April 15–26	Threat to attack South "without notice" for insults to the leadership on Kim Il-sung's birthday ("Ultimatum" from Supreme Command of the KPA); repeated rejection of both US and South Korean offers of dialogue (including statements by Policy Department, National Defense Commission)

SOURCE: Cha and Kim (2013), Haggard (2013c), various Korean Central News Agency reports.

steps in the nuclear program were also matched by a sharp increase in missile testing (Lewis 2015), including evidence of an effort to develop a submarine-launched ballistic missile (SLBM) capability.

Finally, as we showed in Chapter 2, these developments unfolded against broader political and doctrinal developments. Most significantly, the crisis overlapped with the rollout of the *byungjin* line, which committed the regime to both economic reconstruction and continuing development of its nuclear program.

Subsequent diplomatic efforts to engage occurred along two axes: efforts by the five parties, particularly China, to restart the Six Party Talks; and efforts to resume North-South talks as a prelude or complement to broader reengagement. With respect to the Six Party Talks, North Korea moved toward a policy of talks "without preconditions," effectively demanding that the United States drop its insistence on up-front actions. While such offers initially conceded denuclearization as an ultimate objective, they also asserted "the legitimate status of the DPRK as a nuclear weapons state" in the interim and suggested a range of prior actions the United States would have to take before denuclearization could proceed or talks could even start. Moreover, North Korea continued to link denuclearization on the peninsula to wider global steps toward nuclear disarmament or an explicit rejection on the part of the United States of its long-standing policy of extended deterrence.[42] An offer made in January 2015 to trade a suspension of joint exercises for a moratorium on nuclear testing was a clear nonstarter: the offer in fact required no action on North Korea's part and provided no assurances on the further program development.[43] Over the course of 2015 and in the run-up to the fourth nuclear test in 2016, North Korea appeared to show less and less interest in the Six Party Talks, emphasizing the need to negotiate a peace regime first.[44]

For its part, the United States, as well as South Korea and Japan, continued to hew to "strategic patience": no up-front inducements were on offer and North Korea had to signal intent by meeting existing obligations before talks could commence (for example, Davies 2013). Yet in intense diplomatic exchanges in September–November 2014, signals were sent that these preconditions could be moderated at least in part—for example, by undertaking some actions after talks had been reconvened.[45] In addition to several Track 2 exercises, these signals included two public US offers of direct bilateral talks and an invitation to a high-level Track 1.5 dialogue with all lead five-party negotiators, effectively a meeting "without preconditions." Yet despite these concessions, orchestrated in part by China's persistence, North Korea continued to demur with respect to the Six Party Talks, even engaging in a massive and highly public hack of Sony Pictures Entertainment that brought forth additional US sanctions (Haggard and Lindsay 2015). Insistence on negotiation of a peace regime—a proposal that was a complete nonstarter for any American president—had become the centerpiece of North Korea's strategy.

The tribulations of President Park Geun-hye's *Trustpolitik* followed a similarly dispiriting path. Although complex and involving many discrete components (Ministry of Unification 2013), as we argued in Chapter 4 the conceptual underpinning of *Trustpolitik* was the effort to find a middle ground between the largely unconditional engagement of the Kim-Roh years and the "prior expectations" of the Lee Myung-bak administration (Park 2011, 2012). The middle-ground approach was embedded in a larger regional initiative, the Northeast Asia Peace and Cooperation Initiative (Lee 2014), that looked surprisingly similar to its Roh Moo-hyun predecessor. But descriptions of the process always focused first on small, incremental, and easily reversible steps that would solve the bargaining problems described in the introduction in Chapter 1 by building trust: resuming dialogue, humanitarian assistance, and small-scale projects. Links to the nuclear program were not explicit; rather, only as trust was built—including through North Korean moderation in its weapons program—could "Vision Korea" projects be launched. These included more capital-intensive efforts such as large-scale infrastructure projects and support for new investment zones as well as South Korean support for North Korean entry into the international financial institutions with its presumption of financial assistance.

The actual contours of *Trustpolitik*, however, were continually revised by the shifting landscape between North and South and as a result of actions taken by both sides. As with the United States in 2009, the inauguration of a more forthcoming administration in South Korea did not elicit cooperation. Even after the tensions of early 2013 had subsided, early efforts to provide small-scale humanitarian assistance quickly gave way to a standoff over the closure of Kaesong in April. Understanding the strategic mistake of walking away from the foreign exchange generated by the KIC, and with the May 24 measures still firmly in place, the North tacked back to negotiations in early June.[46] The status of Kaesong was only resolved when the Park administration sent surprisingly strong signals of its willingness to close the zone altogether.[47] However, subsequent offers on the part of the North were aimed, as they long had been, at getting the South to stop its joint exercises with the United States and were quickly rejected.[48] A round of conciliatory signals in early 2014, including the North Korean New Year's speech, one-off resumption of family reunions, and a modest aid initiative in February 2014 all failed to generate wider momentum for talks.

In an important speech in Dresden on March 28, President Park once again restated the logic of *Trustpolitik* with proposals very similar to those made in the past (Park 2014). In an important turn, however, the speech addressed the issue of unification in a surprisingly frank way, leaving little doubt that any re-unification would occur on Southern terms; the choice of a German venue for this speech could hardly by lost on Pyongyang. Prior to the Dresden speech, Park had also formed a Presidential Commission to consider the issue of uni-fication in greater detail. The North Korean response was swift and unequivo-cal.[49] A major negotiation in August 2015, triggered by a land mine that badly maimed two South Korean soldiers, resulted in a surprising agreement that, like so many in the past, failed to sustain forward momentum.[50] Following the nuclear and missile tests of 2016, Park gave a speech to the National Assembly that seemed to write the obituary on the *Trustpolitik* experiment. She even raised the possibility of unification via the collapse of the Kim regime and the absorption of the North by the South.

Conclusion: Hard Target Redux

During the two administrations of Barack Obama, negotiations over North Korea's nuclear program moved from the loosely structured format of the Six Party Talks to tacit bargaining among the major parties and episodic nego-tiations following the North's satellite launches and nuclear tests through the UN Security Council. The lessons we draw from the succession of bargaining "rounds" outlined in Table 7.1 are relatively easy to restate.

First, as in the Six Party Talks, tacit negotiations were hampered by the se-quencing and credibility problems outlined in the introduction in Chapter 1. The United States, as well as Korea and Japan, were increasingly reluctant to return to negotiations in the absence of prior signals of intent on the part of North Korea. North Korea, too, repeatedly sought actions that would signal an end to the US "hostile policy" or a show of South Korean "sincerity." Yet all parties were generally loath to move first, and the only significant agreement that was reached during the period, the Leap Day Deal, quickly collapsed.

Second, neither the imposition of sanctions nor the use of broader military signals had much effect on North Korean behavior. Three partial exceptions are worth noting. It is possible that the economic and food constraints that surfaced in 2010–2011 had some bearing on the willingness of North Korea to reengage following the *annus horribilis* of 2010. It is also possible that American and South Korean willingness to escalate and use pointed military signals in the spring of 2013 contributed to the deescalation of the crisis. Finally, it appears that the Park administration's willingness to close Kaesong induced North Korea's return to the table at least on that narrow issue.

However, none of these measures had any effect on the core issue of resuming nuclear talks, let alone making progress in them. In fairness, we have evidence that the principals were well aware of the fact that sanctions were unlikely to return North Korea to the table (for example, Bader 2012, 39; Campbell 2016, 173–174). But a review of the period certainly confirms that North Korean responses to sanctions tended to be escalatory rather than conciliatory, a point raised repeatedly by the prominent "doves" cited in the introduction to this chapter (Asia Society 2009; Wit 2009; Lewis, Hayes, and Bruce 2011; Sigal 2012, 2016; Hayes and Tanter 2012; Halperin 2012; Moon 2012; Frank 2012; Gurtov 2014; von Hippel and Hayes 2014).

Nonetheless, we also noted that any effects that sanctions might have had were dampened by Chinese behavior and the resulting coordination problems in both sanction design and implementation. Because of its concern about limiting downside risk from a North Korean collapse or outside intervention on the peninsula, Beijing repeatedly signaled limits on its willingness to bring pressure to bear. Signals of support were particularly strong around the succession despite evidence that policy preferences sharply diverged. In each subsequent round of conflict, the Chinese showed repeated reluctance to fully exercise its leverage.

Not only did China discount the effectiveness of sanctions, it also showed a revealed preference for a strategy we have called "deep engagement." Although largely commercial, deep engagement involved positive signals to Chinese firms with respect to trade and investment, complementary investments, and ongoing provision of aid, particularly following Kim Jong-un's succession in December 2011. Yet China's strategies of engagement did not work, either; over time, North Korea's interest in returning to talks on the nuclear issue showed a secular decline.

Nor did other strategies of engagement work to bring North Korea back to the table. We considered several phases of the 2009–2016 cycle as reflecting signs of US willingness to engage: the early days of the Obama administration; the negotiations leading up to the Leap Day Deal; the political configuration that North Korea faced vis-à-vis the South with the election of President Park Geun-hye in December 2012; and the diplomatic initiatives of the first half of 2015. In each case, it could be argued that engagement also suffered from coordination problems. Parties were reluctant to lift sanctions that had accumulated during the prior period, and negotiations were complicated over the course of 2014 by complex human rights politics associated with the UN Commission of Inquiry. Like those favoring more sanctions, critics can argue that the five parties were not forthcoming enough. But the Leap Day Deal is an important disconfirming case, suggesting the willingness to take risks with an agreement placing extraordinarily modest constraints on North Korea's nuclear and missile program, not a single one of them irreversible. It took mere weeks for North Korea to effectively walk away from the arrangement.

We close with the central conclusion reached in Chapter 2: the play of external sanctions and inducements vis-à-vis a hard target like North Korea appear to have much weaker effect than is thought. Are there either "smart engagement" or "smart sanctions" measures that were not tried but might nonetheless "work"? These issues were raised once again in the aftermath of the fourth and fifth nuclear tests, satellite launch, and accelerating missile tests of 2016, developments we address in our Conclusions in Chapter 8.

8

Conclusion

Whither North Korea? Whither Economic Statecraft?

For a small, opaque country, North Korea has generated a surprisingly rich body of research. This literature ranges from strategic accounts of the nuclear weapons issue to the humanitarian and human rights challenges posed by its oppressive political system and the attendant refugee problem. Most of this work grasps at elusive straws of external influence, arguing for strategies to constrain North Korea's options through deterrence and sanctions, through diplomatic and economic engagement, or through complex carrot-and-stick combinations of the two.

In this book, we have attempted to focus a unifying political-economic lens on these issues. In effect, we follow "Deep Throat's" injunction to Watergate reporters Woodward and Bernstein: "Follow the money." Without an understanding of the political economy of North Korea, including both its domestic coalitional foundations and its evolving external economic relations, it is hard to reach any meaningful conclusions about the efficacy of sanctions and engagement. In sum, we need a theory of the case.

In this conclusion, we start by looking back at our core findings, measuring them against some of the analytic expectations established in our introduction in Chapter 1. We then turn in a more prospective direction by addressing two clusters of issues. First, what if North Korea were to change? How might that affect the conclusions drawn here? Second, what if the major parties undertook different strategies with respect to North Korea? Can we imagine policies that might be more effective? Although necessarily speculative, these questions permit comparisons with other relevant cases, most notably Iran. We also consider a spate of new diplomatic initiatives—including both sanctions and proposals for engagement—that were introduced in the wake of the fourth nuclear test in early 2016.

We argue that the prospects for fundamental political change are limited. However, there is evidence that a de facto, if not de jure, economic reform process is under way. We assess the prospects for reform, which rest not only on internal reforms of agriculture and industry but on further opening of the external sector as well. Does such an opening make the country more vulnerable to sanctions and inducements? The answer is yes. But, as we have shown, the effects of this opening are ultimately conditional on how key states—most notably China—respond to this process.

We then ask in what ways these partial reforms may be affected by more refined sanctions and inducement strategies. Sanctions negotiated at the multilateral level and through independent efforts by other parties in early 2016 seemed quite sweeping in their intent and, if fully implemented, would clearly have impact. Yet coordination problems persisted and even intensified as the United States and its allies responded to the North Korean nuclear and missile tests with defensive actions that were viewed by China as hostile. The process and outcome of the 2016 sanctions efforts raises quite fundamental questions about whether an increasingly divided world order—split between authoritarian and liberal governments—can find common ground in controlling "hard targets" like North Korea.

Inducements face similar constraints. We now have a long list of proposals for how economic integration might be used to underpin a new security architecture in Northeast Asia. However, functionalist arguments that economic integration might facilitate political settlements have repeatedly failed. It appears, rather, that deeper economic integration rests on reaching a political settlement. As we have seen, the bargaining problems in such a settlement are great, requiring the five parties to essentially accept—and even recognize—a nuclear North Korea, a highly unlikely prospect. The default is not simply a repeat of past cycles, in which North Korea tested new capabilities and its neighbors sought to contain the attendant risks. By late 2016, the North Korea problem was morphing into a broader issue of contention between China and the United States and its Northeast Asian allies.

Findings: The Political Economy of Inducements and Constraints

In this book, we cast our inquiry in a framework that considered two possible ways in which sanctions and inducements might work. In addition to the standard bargaining model, centered on quid pro quos and a cost-benefit calculus, we considered the broader question of how sanctions and particularly engagement might have transformative effects. Following the work of Etel Solingen (1998, 2007), we began our analysis in Chapter 2 with the underlying political structure and coalitional foundations of the North Korean regime. This was important for providing a baseline with respect to political and economic change, but it was also important for addressing the endogenous nature of countries' foreign policies. Solingen argues that external economic relations are in the first instance a function of regime characteristics, social bases of support, and policy choices rather than the other way around. We argued that North Korea has to date been the paradigmatic hard target: a repressive one-party familial regime based on an inward-oriented political coalition with significant representation of the military, the military-industrial complex, and the security apparatus. These factors not only make the regime relatively impervious to sanctions but shape how it engages with the world economy and thus its responsiveness to economic inducements as well.

In the next section, we consider in more detail whether and how North Korea might be changing, both politically and economically. However, the political system appears to have undergone only marginal changes despite the succession and has even regressed. The country continues to present a near-classic example of what Solingen calls a "backlash coalition" and power appears to be, if anything, even more concentrated. The marketization born out of state failure has not been followed by proactive top-down reform. Commitment to reform—and commitments that would require a reassessment of the country's broader foreign and military policy—has been limited at best. Indeed, the *byungjin* line openly rejects the very idea at the core of liberal models: that economic development and militarized foreign policies work at cross-purposes.

We argued that the narrowness of the regime's key constituencies has affected the government's responses to sanctions and inducements and the extent to which growing openness would have transformative effects. The regime has managed to insulate itself from the effects of sanctions, in part through its deepening economic ties to China. It has imposed the costs of its autarkic policies on the nonelite groups that constitute the vast majority of the population and devised sophisticated sanctions evasion strategies. Inducements, in contrast, have been most attractive not when having wider effect—as a broader opening to trade and investment might—but when captured and used by the state and politically connected groups, including through illicit activities, weapons sales, and even by the rents generated by sanctions. This finding pertains to food as well as other forms of external support, as we showed in Chapter 4.

We also followed the existing sanctions literature in underlining how the efficacy of sanctions and inducements depend on external coordination issues (Martin 1992; Hufbauer et al. 2007). And we demonstrated that these coordination problems had a dynamic component (Caruso 2003; Kaempfer and Ross 2004). North Korea has been pulled into China's orbit not only by the latter's extraordinary rapid growth but also by political factors. On the one hand, sanctions pushed the North's external trade toward its least punctilious partners. On the other hand, China's commitment to a strategy of engagement had a similar pull effect. We demonstrated this in detail with a closer consideration of North Korea's trade with both China and South Korea, a case study of trade in sanctioned luxury goods, and a detailed consideration of other sources of income ranging from illicit activities to aid and foreign investment.

An obvious point emerging from this story is that not all forms of "engagement" are likely to have a transformative effect. The state controls the connections between the foreign and the domestic economy, and it has been engaged in activities that have negative rather than positive externalities in the form of exports of drugs and weapons and counterfeiting. The regime is also engaged in complex sanctions evasion strategies that we outline in more detail further on.

In Chapter 5, we looked at these issues through a micro-lens, reporting the results of firm-level surveys of Chinese and South Korean firms doing business in North Korea. The objective was to determine whether engagement—in the form of increased cross-border exchange—was having the transformative effects postulated by engagement models. Perhaps our most important finding is descriptive: at the time of the survey, cross-border transactions remained to a significant extent under state control. Although this could be changing, we suggest how sanctions evasion strategies continue to rest on the operations of state trading companies to a significant degree. We found that the institutions of a market economy were weak, with uncertainty over property rights and dispute settlement and faint indicators of the emergence of trust, such as the extension of credit. Chinese firms in particular report the necessity to bribe to do business, and we provided evidence that outside of larger state and private entities, firm size itself might be limited by the risks of predation.

The important exception that proves the rule is the import of South Korean institutions into the Kaesong Industrial Complex (KIC). Chinese firms operated a relatively unsubsidized frontier-style capitalism while South Korean firms operated in an enclave that was ultimately the result of political negotiations between Seoul and Pyongyang and an effective set of risk-sharing subsidies or guarantees for South Korean firms. We outlined the skeptical case for the transformative effects of these enclaves by considering in detail the tight controls exercised by the North Korean government over the KIC and its workers and suppliers, and the absence of backward and forward linkages. The KIC could "spread" only by replicating more such enclaves, but North Korean behavior limited the appeal of such efforts.

Chapters 6 and 7 took up the diplomatic dimension of sanctions and engagement, focusing on the period since the onset of the second nuclear crisis in 2002. In these chapters, we considered hypotheses about the effectiveness of sanctions and inducements in generating quid pro quos. First, we found that the coordination issues we highlighted with respect to North Korea's external economic relations were replicated in the diplomacy of the five parties: South Korea, China, Japan, Russia, and the United States, surfacing first in the institutionalized mechanism of the Six Party Talks and then outside it when the talks collapsed in 2008. We found strong evidence of constraints on the five parties from their heterogeneous diplomatic strategies: both tough stances and more proengagement approaches continually ran into difficulties associated with the other parties' divergent diplomatic approaches. Both those seeking effective sanctions and those seeking more engagement were blocked from their favored strategies.

We also found, as a result, that while sanctions appeared to have surprisingly little effect on the course of negotiations, inducements hardly fared better. Even when coordinated, these inducements were caught up in the bargaining and sequencing problems that we outlined in our introduction in Chapter 1. Negotiations both before and after the collapse of the Six Party Talks in 2008 foundered repeatedly on mirror-image credible commitment problems. The United States and South Korea showed reticence to extend benefits given past history, a reticence neatly summed up by US secretary of defense Robert Gates' reluctance to "pay for the same horse twice." North Korea for its part saw little reason to abandon a cheap and effective deterrent for benefits that were highly uncertain, particularly given the political environment in the United States, Japan, and South Korea.

Finally, we sought to address the humanitarian dilemmas that surround economic statecraft, emphasizing once again that these problems arise not only with respect to sanctions but with respect to inducements as well. Multilateral food assistance began in 1995 during the famine, and the aid program subsequently grew into the area of most sustained interaction between North Korea and the international community. In trying to ameliorate this disaster, however, the humanitarian community faced a fundamentally hostile environment. The North Korean government would not permit independent distribution of food;

rather, food aid was channeled through the public distribution system (PDS) with severe constraints on assessment and monitoring activities. Yet even in the face of chronic shortages, the regime has been unwilling to reprioritize its external relations to put greater emphasis on human security, particularly by generating adequate foreign exchange to import food and medicine on commercial terms. This history has contributed to profound fatigue among donors. The World Food Program (WFP) initiatives of the 2010s have been funded at only a fraction of their proposed levels and are at risk of being rolled up altogether despite ongoing evidence of malnutrition in North Korea (UNICEF 2013).

In sum, we concluded from the evidence available over the course of the second nuclear crisis that the United States and its allies should not overestimate the degree of influence it has on North Korea. There are good theoretical reasons to believe that the pattern of North Korea's engagement with its key partners—South Korea, China, Japan, the United States, and Russia—could tilt its trajectory toward a more open market economy. Yet such engagement could also reinforce existing tendencies toward state socialism or even the kind of kleptocratic resource-based economy sadly common in Central Asia and Sub-Saharan Africa. These outcomes depend in large measure on China, on which North Korea is increasingly dependent. But they are ultimately endogenous to North Korea's political economy, grounded in key features of the regime and the strategic choices of the leadership. While the rest of the world can influence incentives at the margin, our research should be seen in large part as a cautionary tale: the way North Korea turns will depend on decisions made in Pyongyang.

That said, our account so far has necessarily been backward looking. It is at least possible that the North Korean political system will change and that the processes of cross-border marketization from below may simply not have had adequate time to generate their predicted effects; this sort of engagement may be a long game. What if North Korea were to change politically or economically, either more suddenly or through an evolutionary process?

Prospects for Political and Economic Change

In Chapter 2, we characterized core features of the political and economic system through mid-2016. Here we assess the prospects for change, a more dynamic but obviously more speculative undertaking. We look first at the prospects for political change, which we deem limited, and then at the prospects for incremental economic reforms, which are more likely and in fact already in train. But these reforms face fundamental limitations that are ultimately rooted in both the regime's foreign policy and its domestic political economy.

Prospects for Political Change

We argue that the transition from Kim Jong-il to Kim Jong-un did not mark a fundamental shift in the nature of the regime and indeed might have buttressed some of its core features. Successions in personalist systems generate substantial churning as the incoming leadership expands its discretion and engages in coup proofing by purging potential rivals, advancing the careers of followers, and consolidating bases of support. However, the very uncertainty of the succession favored a complex of the same institutional forces that had been in place under the ancien regime. This remained true—and perhaps even more true—after the unveiling of the *byungjin* line in March 2013. Frank (2014) argues that this new orientation marked a subtle shift from *songun* ("military first") because of its suggestion that economic development would be elevated to a par with national security. But for our purposes here—which are to understand North Korea's foreign policy behavior—the departures of *byungjin* seem to pale before the commitment to maintain and further develop the country's nuclear capability. Moreover, the *byungjin* line underscored that the regime did not see the objectives of economic development and pursuit of a nuclear program to be in tension; indeed, they could even operate as complements. Such views are at direct odds with the expectations of "transformative engagement" models.

Is the political system stable, or is it vulnerable to change or even collapse? To answer this question, it is worthwhile to consider possible transition paths. Magaloni and Kricheli (2009) calculated a transition matrix for changes from different types of authoritarian rule over the 1950–2006 period. They find that single-party systems were the most stable authoritarian form, and would have shown themselves to be more stable still had many not fallen in tight sequence following the collapse of the Soviet Union. The fact that North Korea survived this external shock along with a handful of other communist systems is a reminder of authoritarian resilience and the variety of tools—both repressive and accommodating—that such regimes can deploy to retain power (Dimitrov 2013).

When single-party regimes did transition, it was most likely to military (38.6 percent) or dominant party systems (33.3 percent), with democracy a distant third (19.3 percent, accounted for mostly by the anomalous Eastern European transitions, which had the advantages of proximity to Europe). Transitions to "anarchy"—that is, the "collapse" scenario often discussed in the literature on North Korea (for example, Bennett and Lind 2011)—were relatively rare (8.8 percent). Were it not for the ongoing legitimation challenge posed by North Korea's junior status on a divided peninsula and the possibility of unification, it would be puzzling why the country's collapse is deemed such a likely possibility.

Given the regime's leaderist and monolithic nature, a political opening from the top that would allow constrained competition, let alone democracy, seems highly unlikely. The risks would therefore appear to be greatest that the system would become more explicitly military, perhaps by an overt or subtle coup in which military actors became even more prominent than they currently are. We outlined in Chapter 2 how the regime has met these risks, including through a legitimation strategy that has for decades successfully identified the country with the Kim family. It is far from clear how a challenger would justify a departure from this ideological order, but the fundamental point is that the most likely regime transition path "from above" is not one that would result in competitive authoritarianism or democracy but one in which the military would play an even more significant role.

What about the possibility of some kind of transition "from below"? In addition to the sheer repressiveness of the system and its spotty economic performance, two particular grievances are worth noting that could spark dissent: corruption and inequality. Rising corruption can be documented both in refugee surveys (Kim 2010; Haggard and Noland 2011a), the firm surveys discussed in Chapter 5, and most recently case studies (Noland 2014a). The emergent market economy is characterized by pervasive rules and regulations that are subject to arbitrary and capricious change, effectively placing all economic agents out of compliance with some rule or another. Such a system invites shakedown and extortion and raises bribe prices.[1] There have been sporadic reports of confrontations between officials and market traders that could in theory spiral into more substantial challenges, as they did in Tunisia, for example.

Second, both anecdotal accounts and surveys suggest that inequality in North Korea is rising, with the phenomenon having both spatial and class dimensions (Kim and Kim 2012). There is also considerable complementary evidence from refugee surveys for a collapse of the social welfare system, at least for nonelite households in the hinterlands (Kim et al. 2012). Growth could even be following the relatively unusual path of "the rich getting richer and the poor getting poorer," in part because of the growing centrality of resource rents in the economy. A combination of poor economic performance and rising inequality might also breed resentments that could manifest themselves in protest.

The extraordinary repressive apparatus of the state, the continued reach of "organizational life" (Lankov, Kwak, and Cho 2012), and the low level of societal trust revealed in refugee surveys make the likelihood of collective action from below limited. The mass mobilization that unseats authoritarian regimes occurs in capital cities and typically rests on the existence of independent organizations that the regime cannot fully control, such as churches, ethnic associations, or unions (Haggard and Kaufman 2016). The regime is clearly aware of these risks. Pyongyang has seen a flood of public and private investment, generating what might be called "the Pyongyang illusion."[2] Those connected with the regime and in the protected private sector are doing well, and some are in fact becoming rich. Independent organizations outside the government are, to date, nonexistent. Because of the neighborhood in which North Korea is located, the prospects of mass mobilization or insurgency moving in from the periphery of the country are also limited. The greatest risk would therefore seem to arise from spontaneous, "prairie fire" protests that spiral beyond control. Yet the absence of a capacity to coordinate, for example through social media, the pervasiveness of the security apparatus, and the willingness to use overwhelming force would probably guarantee that such movements would be effectively deterred and crushed if they did surface.

In looking at prospects for change, then, we need to think about a North Korean political system that is broadly structured as it currently is. Yet even if we preclude changes *of* the regime, or at least see them as unlikely, changes *in* the regime, as happened in China and Vietnam, cannot be ruled out. Economic policy would clearly be a major way in which the system might change.

Prospects for Economic Reform

The most likely course of economic policy change would be for the regime to initiate a gradual process of reform and opening conforming, at least in broad outlines, with the Chinese approach. Three questions are germane. To what extent are such changes feasible? Could they yield a sustainable growth path? And could such a reform path lead to a moderation of North Korea's foreign policy behavior?

Reforms would unfold along three key axes, setting aside a complex set of macroeconomic questions: a continuation of the so-called June 28 (2012) agricultural reforms and the May 30 (2014) measures with regard to state-owned enterprises and, most important for our purposes, an external opening to greater trade and investment.[3]

As of this writing, there is growing evidence that the North Korean pilot reforms in agriculture have in fact been continuing (Ireson 2014). Although important for the livelihoods of cultivators, there are significant reasons that North Korean reforms are unlikely to be led by rural reforms to the same extent that they were in China and Vietnam. In China, productivity-increasing agricultural reforms led to an increase in agricultural output and a movement of extremely low-productivity agricultural labor to the nascent light-manufacturing sector. From a political economy perspective, each of the three principal groups in the economy benefited: farmers saw rising incomes; the migrants who moved to the emerging light-manufacturing sector earned higher wages than on the farm; and even the urban proletariat in the state-owned manufacturing sector saw an improvement in real wages as the implicit terms of trade between food and industrial products fell. Reform under these circumstances constituted a "happy equilibrium": no large group came out an obvious loser.

The share of the workforce in agriculture in North Korea when reforms were first contemplated in the late 1990s, around 35 percent, was roughly half that of China and Vietnam (more than 70 percent) at the time they undertook reform (Noland 2000, table 3.7). Also, agriculture in North Korea is more industrial input dependent. Agricultural reforms would most likely have large effects if complemented by substantial increases in the availability of fertilizer and energy for irrigation. To date, such an allocation of resources by the regime has not been forthcoming and appears out of line with its current coalitional emphasis on the interests of the military, party, and capital city rather than those of the countryside. Such reforms would undoubtedly increase the welfare of farmers, but even with large increases in productivity and substantial gains for the farmers themselves, agriculture will not be the "leading sector" of a major transformation.

The flip side of the small agricultural sector is a large industrial sector. Despite its much lower level of income, reform in this sector on the surface more closely resembles the difficult processes of transition in highly industrialized Eastern European countries such as Slovakia, Belarus, or Romania. Much of the capital stock in these countries was effectively worthless and largely had to be closed down altogether, with painful adjustments for displaced workers.

In these sectors, however, marketization from below might make transitional processes easier in North Korea, both economically and politically, than they were in Eastern Europe; indeed, they could even be easier than they would be on the cooperatives, where party and state functionaries could sabotage incentives favoring cultivators. The decline in the industrial sector in North Korea has been so substantial, and the social benefits provided by employment in the state sector already so eroded, that tremendous gains could arise from simply letting managers do business as they see fit, as is already occurring on a de facto basis (Kim and Yang 2015; Lankov 2016). We can even imagine quite fundamental sectoral changes as former managers of heavy industry shift into a variety of more profitable light-manufacturing activities, exploiting their control over land and labor in league with the emerging private and even underground financial sector. As we showed in Chapter 3, there is some evidence that such shifts may already be spilling over into the external sector in the form of increasing exports of light labor–intensive manufactures (see Li 2016).

North Korea is also no exception to the tendency of socialist economies to ignore the service sector. We already observe, under the current degree of marketization, the growth of small-scale activities such as restaurants, hauling and transportation services, and small shops. With deeper reforms—or simply a more laisser-faire government approach to the state sector—we can imagine the growth of larger-scale commercial enterprises in such areas as construction, transportation, and even finance and telecommunications (Kim and Yang 2015).

Given its small size and geographical position, however, it is clear that the foreign sector has to play an even larger role in the North Korean transition than it has played in China, with its continental size and huge domestic market. Interestingly, the regime's renewed effort to attract foreign direct investment is a tacit recognition of this fact. In addition to the extraordinary demand for investment because of North Korea's poverty and lack of a functioning financial system, foreign firms also represent a kind of neural synapse between the latent productive potential of the North Korean economy and the world economy. Foreign firms have the blueprints for the products that the rest of the world wants to buy, as well as the global distribution and marketing networks to bring those products to potential consumers.

In the industrial sector, North Korea would be exporting minerals but also light- and medium-tech labor-intensive manufactures. It would import capital goods, intermediates, and food. The composition of employment would shift toward emerging export-oriented manufacturing sectors, and potentially millions of North Korean workers would change jobs as they did in the earlier East Asian miracles. The prevalence of subscale manufacturing establishments and the excessive geographic dispersion of existing facilities mean that this process of restructuring would have its own distributional consequences, to be sure. Some existing industrial towns could be depopulated, but others with more favorable geographic locations—near ports, near China, or near the road and rail links with South Korea and Russia—would expand dramatically. Interactions with the outside world would increase exponentially, with the share of international trade in the economy multiples of what it is today. The strategy naturally faces some risks with respect to the future of the Chinese economy (Laing 2013) and the end of the boom in commodity prices (Hendrix and Noland 2015).[4] But China's growth continues to outpace that of other countries in the Asia-Pacific, and in this regard China's proximity is a plus.

Such an economic transformation would not be without its own distinctive political risks, most notably with respect to South Korea. As documented in Chapter 3, North Korea's external economic relations are characterized by an extraordinary dependence on China. But conventional gravity model results indicate that South Korea, not China, is North Korea's natural primary trade partner (Noland 2015). If North Korea traded as though it were a "normal" country, South Korea would naturally account for most of its external commerce, followed by China, Japan, the United States, and Russia. There may well be legacy or hysteresis effects that boost China's prominence relative to what the models predict. Nevertheless, the implications are clear: a truly reformed North Korea would be pulled into South Korea's orbit, an outcome that the current regime would surely regard as unacceptable.

This observation suggests that any opening would take place through tentative steps amenable to political control, reversible and oriented largely toward China and perhaps a handful of middle-income countries willing to take the political and economic risk; recall that multilateral sanctions do not prohibit all commercial trade. A series of announcements since November 2013 would suggest an intention to pursue such an approach through the creation of new special economic zones (SEZs).[5] The success of these efforts could be measured along two dimensions. The first would be purely economic spillovers. Would the zones generate backward and forward linkages? Would local firms become suppliers of inputs to foreign firms operating in the zones? Would the products produced in the zones be used in the broader economy by local businesses or consumers? Would technology, broadly defined to include new management approaches or ways of doing business, diffuse beyond the confines of the zones?

Equally if not more important are the sorts of policy spillovers related to what we call the transformational model of engagement. Would SEZs come to drive broader economic policy as in China in the 1980s? Would the government effectively commit to strong property rights in these enclaves, or would such rights be subject to political manipulation, as occurred in the KIC in 2013? Would the more liberal rules in the SEZs eventually broaden to the whole economy?

We do not need to look at North Korea's foreign economic policy to date to be skeptical. The World Bank undertook a comprehensive review of SEZs around the world and found that most fail to generate these policy spillovers (Farole 2011): they do not generate much investor interest nor, as a result, do they act as a catalyst for changes in the broader economy.[6] Put differently, a SEZ strategy generally cannot substitute for a broader reform effort and this is particularly true with respect to a country with such an overweening state and weak history of protecting private property rights. But the underlying problems with the export-oriented model are political. As long as the regime is committed to the *byungjin* line, this transformational strategy would have to be oriented almost entirely toward China. To break out of that constraint would require significant and credible concessions with respect to the country's nuclear program, which to date have not been in evidence.

Political and Economic Change: A Reprise

In sum, the prospects for political and economic change in North Korea appear constrained. At the political level, the Kim family franchise seems surprisingly hard to dislodge, even if it is underperforming. The combination of strong institutions of repression and social control and a coalition of family, party, and military-security-industrial complex makes authoritarian persistence a real possibility. Moreover, we can outline an adaptive, trial-and-error partial reform path that may generate not only economic but political benefits for the regime, as happened in other communist regimes that have survived (Dimitrov 2013).

At the same time, we have traced a number of constraints on this gradual reform process. There are important gains from reforms in the agricultural and industrial sectors, although agriculture is less likely to lead the North Korean transition than it did in China. We can identify a strategy that focuses resources on Pyongyang and permits a gradual expansion of the service sector from Pyongyang to provincial capitals, spreading into real estate and development.

The most substantial gains, however, and the ones most likely to have transformative effect, are those of the external sector. But North Korea's existential situation—the smaller, poorer member of a divided state surrounded by larger, richer countries—means that the political leadership is rightly hesitant to fully embrace reforms that would make it a distinctly second-class version of its southern neighbor. And while North Korea has mineral resources that confer some natural comparative advantage, the country does not exist in a commercial vacuum. Why would a foreign investor locate in a North Korean startup SEZ rather than in Vietnam or even Morocco, Myanmar, or Zambia, whose governments are making serious efforts to roll out the welcome mat to foreign investors without similar political risks (and have various forms of preferential access to the United States market to boot)?

Most important for our purposes, however, is the regime's expressed intention of moving toward a cautious economic opening. Quite contrary to the transformative engagement model, the hints of interest in an SEZ strategy have had little or no effect on the conduct of foreign policy. Indeed, if we take the *byungjin* line seriously, it reflects the regime's belief, at least, that economic development and pursuit of nuclear weapons can go hand in hand. A key question is therefore how accommodating the rest of the world will be to North Korea's efforts. This question returns us to our interest in the role of sanctions and engagement.

The Role of Economic Statecraft I: Sanctions

As we have emphasized throughout this book, North Korea's trade is heavily politicized. In considering the possible consequences of any North Korean reform effort, we also need to consider the likely path of both future sanctions and engagement strategies.

At the time of the fourth nuclear test in January 2016, North Korea was under multilateral economic sanctions via four United Nations Security Council resolutions (UNSCRs): 1695 (2006) following North Korean missile tests; 1718 (2006) following North Korea's first nuclear test; 1874 (2009) following the second nuclear test; and 2094 (2013) following the third nuclear test. In addition to these multilateral sanctions, individual countries, including the United States, South Korea, and Japan, maintained or instituted additional unilateral or so-called autonomous sanctions. In some cases, these additional sanctions were also directly connected to North Korea's nuclear efforts—for example, restrictions on particular products, entities, or individuals.[7] In some cases, they were tied to altogether different issues, including human rights.

Sanctions related to North Korea's weapons programs can be thought of as having two components. The first is essentially "defensive," seeking to disrupt the North Korean military program and protect against, and limit, North Korea's proliferation activities and the financial and trade networks that support them.[8] These measures include bans on the export of military hardware, on the importation of most kinds of military goods, and on dual-use technologies that have both military and civilian uses. Also, they target specific individuals engaged in the country's weapons program and proliferation activities. Each new resolution has expanded or tightened these measures at the margin, and they now extend into restrictions on finance, aid, and shipping as well.[9]

The metric for measuring the success of such sanctions is not altogether clear. On the one hand, critics deem them a failure because they have not prevented North Korea from continuing to make progress on its nuclear and missile programs. North Korea has done this in part through the ongoing use of deception to evade sanctions, for example, through the use of shell companies (see UN Panel of Experts 2015, 2016; Mailey 2016; Park and Walsh 2016; Center for Advanced Defense Analysis 2016).[10] The country has also relied on purely internal capacities and reverse engineering. And in large measure, North Korea has survived as a result of China's tacit support and the coordination problems we have noted throughout the book. Even if we set aside China's growing economic influence, sanctions depend heavily on exporting countries' maintenance of successful export control regimes and complementary controls on third parties that might help evade sanctions or finance such activities. These regimes are administratively difficult and require significant resources that a number of states may be unwilling to invest. Multilateral measures in support of interdiction also have "credible information" clauses, which allow a government that does not want to enforce them to say that it lacks credible information or that the information provided to it does not meet the standard of "reasonable grounds" for action.

On the other hand, it is widely recognized that sanctions are never going to plug all leaks and that the objective is ultimately to raise the costs and limit the product choices associated with the nuclear and missile programs rather than shut them down altogether. Moreover, some sanctions, most notably those pertaining to dual-use technologies, do have spillover effects on purely commercial trade and investment and perhaps even on humanitarian programs (Abt 2014). As a result, they also have the effect of raising costs.

In addition to "defensive" sanctions, both UN sanctions and particular bilateral sanctions, such as those imposed by the United States, Japan, and South Korea, are strategic: they impose costs in the hope of changing North Korean behavior and, in particular, bringing it back to talks that will lead to concessions on its nuclear program. Our skepticism about these sanctions is twofold. First, China appears largely uninterested in supporting them or, when they do support them, enforcing them fully. We showed in our case study in Chapter 3 that even nuisance restraints on luxury trade were weakly implemented. Until imposition of multilateral sanctions in the wake of the fourth nuclear test in 2016, China resisted any effort to increase pressure on North Korea by sanctioning its commercial trade. Our second source of skepticism stems from our arguments about North Korea's ability to both circumvent these restraints through increasingly complex sanctions evasion strategies (Park and Walsh

2016; Center for Advanced Defense Analysis 2016) and absorb their costs. North Korea is the paradigmatic "hard target."

Two innovations in the sanctions regime would change the prospects for influencing North Korea going forward. The first would be for China to become sufficiently disaffected to use the vast economic leverage over North Korea that it so clearly possesses. Following the fourth nuclear test in January 2016, the relevant parties once again engaged in a contentious negotiation over a new Security Council resolution, finally passed on March 2 as UNSCR 2270. For the first time since the onset of the nuclear crisis in 2002, China agreed to provisions that would affect North Korea's commercial trade, including a conditional ban on coal imports that accounted for about a third of North Korea's total exports, a ban on Chinese exports of aviation fuel, a variety of restraints that would affect its shipping, and new financial sanctions.[11] Yet despite China's willingness to use punitive measures, the resolution was written with caveats that granted the Chinese significant discretion in implementation. These included provisions that could be read to require a link between the sanctioned activity and the country's weapons program and a second, potentially larger reservation that referenced humanitarian concerns: the sanctions were not to affect "transactions that are determined to be exclusively for livelihood purposes" (UNSCR 2270, para. 29b). As of this writing in late 2016, analysis of trade and other measures of the economic relationship, such as the stability of the exchange rate and prices, suggest that Chinese implementation of UNSCR 2270 has been less than vigorous.[12]

As with all sanctions, much depends on the capacity of North Korea to adjust to these new measures, assuming that they are implemented. Such adjustments would include shifting toward unsanctioned activities (Li 2016), turning to more forgiving jurisdictions, exploiting sanctions leakage, black markets and third-party brokers, and simply imposing the costs on the population as necessary. Yet it is hard to escape the conclusion that a complete ban on coal exports—coming on top of the $130 million a year in cash payments associated with the closure of the KIC—not only would affect income accruing to the elite but would have wider implications as the country faced severe balance-of-payments constraints.

The parallels to Iran are worth noting, as they demonstrate the significance of the coordination problem and how it can even trump the domestic political economy factors we have highlighted. Iran was exposed to sanctions precisely because it was so dependent on oil exports. The P5+1 (the permanent members of the Security Council, plus Germany and EU representation) could not shut down Iranian oil exports completely, nor did it seek to do so.

Agreements allowed a number of critical importers, including China, to continue to purchase oil. However, US sanctions against Iran's central bank and the EU boycott of Iranian oil exports dramatically squeezed other purchasers, and total oil exports declined from 2.8 million barrels per day in July 2011 to less than 1 million barrels per day by July 2012.

North Korea is less open, less dependent on any one commodity, and less dependent on foreign investment, which was also affected by the Iran sanctions. As we noted in Chapter 3, however, its export profile increasingly resembles that of a rentier state, with coal and proscribed mineral exports topping 50 percent of total trade. When multilateral sanctions against Iran coalesced around restricting the country's oil exports, the Iranian economy contracted sharply (2012–2013). Moreover, the Iranian rial experienced a sharp depreciation on the black market that spread the effects of the sanctions broadly across the population (see World Bank 2015; Samore 2015; Katzman 2016).

It is not coincidental that the tightening of the sanctions regime against Iran appeared to be directly related to its leadership's decision to come back to the bargaining table through the secret negotiations that began in March 2013, almost exactly when the sanctions' effects were becoming evident. It is noteworthy that this channel was opened by the supreme leader, Ayatollah Ali Khamenei, even before the change in government in August 2013 that brought a more moderate president, Hassan Rouhani, into office.[13] In sum, it is entirely within the realm of possibility that a more exposed North Korea could in fact find itself politically vulnerable to sanctions were the Chinese weak link in the sanctions regime strengthened.

A second route through which external constraints might have effect, partly offsetting the coordination problem, would be more aggressive pursuit of secondary sanctions, including on designated financial institutions. To implement such measures, the United States and other parties would in particular need to impose secondary sanctions against noncompliant Chinese financial institutions and the growing network of Chinese and other brokers on which North Korea has relied to evade sanctions, denying them access to the lucrative US market (Park and Walsh 2016; Center for Advanced Defense Analysis 2016). Beijing has vociferously opposed such measures. The United States and other parties would also need to contend with the evasive adaptations that North Korea has pursued in the past. These include shifting its banking and commercial operations deeper into the international gray market available to it in Russia, the Middle East, and elsewhere and using diplomatic channels for sanctions evasion, money laundering, and illicit activities (UN Security Council 2016). Nonetheless, such measures arguably "worked" in the BDA case, as we saw in Chapter 6 both from testimony of North Koreans and from actions the regime took to get back to talks.

In the wake of the fourth nuclear test, the United States passed, and the president threatened to implement, precisely such secondary sanctions; in the wake of the fifth test, a first step in implementing such secondary sanctions was actually taken.[14] If implemented aggressively, such sanctions might constrain North Korea even in the absence of cooperation by the Chinese government, effectively solving the coordination problem by limiting the ability of Chinese banks and brokers to sustain North Korea's lifeline. Even if it pushed North Korea further into the world's gray economy, it is difficult to sustain an entire country on the basis of such networks alone.

In sum, the limited effect of sanctions that we have seen to date does not simply reflect the capacity of the North Korean regime to absorb costs. It also reflects the fact that sanctions will not work as long as China is committed to sustaining North Korea and its ongoing weapons programs.

However, even were China to cooperate more fully on the issue of secondary sanctions, to have effect the endgame would ultimately involve negotiations. As we noted in Chapter 6, the "success" of the BDA sanctions involved the circuitous route of suspension of the Six Party Talks and North Korea's first nuclear test, and ultimately required not simply a complex resolution of the BDA issue but also additional incentives from the five parties.

Again, comparison to the Iranian case is germane. Iran did not unilaterally undertake commitments to scale back its nuclear program; rather, the secret bilateral talks noted previously led to reconvening the so-called P5+1 negotiations, and it was these that generated both the interim agreement of November 2013 and the final conclusion of the framework agreement in July 2015. As comparisons of Iran and North Korea suggest, sanctions need to be considered in the broader framework of negotiations and the trade-offs and inducements that they might ultimately generate.

The Role of Economic Statecraft II: Multilateral Strategies for Engagement

In the early stages of the nuclear crisis, the question of inducements was often quite central to negotiations, as for example in the quid pro quos of 2007 that led to a brief period of progress in the Six Party Talks. Following the collapse of the talks, North Korea's economic interests became simpler and have since been restated in virtually all of the regime's pronouncements on the nuclear crisis. The sanctions regime is illegitimate, it fails to take into account North Korea's security interests, and it is part and parcel of a "hostile policy" orchestrated against the country by the United States and its allies.[15] For these reasons, the sanctions should be lifted.

Functional proposals for getting North Korea back to the talks have at times gone well beyond lifting sanctions, however, and have included a variety of proposals aimed at embedding North Korea in a larger Northeast Asian security and economic architecture or simply linking it to existing international institutions. These prospective inducements have not had any discernible effect in moving the regime toward negotiations. Nonetheless, it is worth considering three clusters of options as a way of reviewing the pros and cons of engagement strategies with countries such as North Korea. First would be efforts to include the country in existing multilateral institutions, most notably the Asian Development Bank (ADB), the World Bank, the International Monetary Fund (IMF), and the nascent Asian Infrastructure Investment Bank (AIIB). A second cluster of proposals centers on fostering economic integration through a regional free-trade area or wider economic community. Finally, options for deeper integration could develop out of the Six Party Talks were they to resume.

We conclude in this section that none of these options are particularly appealing to North Korea, and for reasons we have noted throughout: not only do they rest on a commitment to reform and opening but they also involve substantial outside scrutiny of North Korea's economic system. In the following section, we invert the logic. Rather than consider how economic inducements might lead to a settlement of the nuclear question, we address wider political proposals for the negotiation of a peace regime. As we will see in both discussions, economic and political forms of engagement are laced through with the moral hazard and bargaining problems that have been a focus of the book.

Accession to Existing Institutions: The Asian Development Bank, the World Bank, the International Monetary Fund, and the Asian Infrastructure Investment Bank

Beyond the lifting of sanctions, the case for drawing on existing institutions is straightforward. North Korea is in need of depoliticized technical assistance on a panoply of issues running from the mundane but critical, such as developing meaningful national statistical capabilities, through basic agricultural and health technologies, to the social infrastructure of a modern economy: institutions for managing macroeconomic policy, including through reform of the central bank; specification of property rights and means for resolving commercial disputes; regulatory structures; and international trade and investment.

This is what the World Bank, the IMF, the WTO, and regional development banks, including the ADB, do for a living. Why create new institutions when existing ones are perfectly well suited for the job? Moreover, these institutions have the political advantage of independence and standard operating procedures. As a result, they are less vulnerable to risks of moral hazard and politicization.

Were the underlying political issues surrounding North Korea's nuclear program resolved, the legal and procedural barriers to incorporating the country into international financial institutions would be much less of a problem than commonly thought.[16] One model of multilateral engagement would be to allow the World Bank to play a coordinating role as the administrative arm of a consultative group. It would engage in more detailed analysis of the North Korean economy and become the repository for a dedicated North Korea fund that would initially support technical assistance and the building of local institutional capacity. These early actions would eventually support the country's entry into international financial institutions (IFIs), direct lending, and guarantee investment activity through the International Finance Corporation. Japanese postcolonial claims payments could be one source of financing for such a facility as the two countries normalized relations.[17] Additional funds might be available via the ADB and the newly created AIIB.

The central difficulty is that North Korea has shown little interest in joining these multilateral financial institutions. In 1997, in the midst of economic collapse and famine, it hosted an informational mission by the IMF and released to it macroeconomic data that had been constructed with the assistance of the local United Nations Development Program (UNDP) office. However, members of the mission indicated privately that when their North Korean interlocutors realized that additional data would have to be provided and that immediate financial assistance would not be forthcoming, they lost interest. Rather than being seen as an inducement, the regime has to date treated these institutions as carriers of the same type of intrusive outside scrutiny that they have sought to evade with respect to their weapons programs.

New Institutions: A Northeast Asian Free-Trade Area

An alternative to reliance on existing organizations would be to develop a new entity, either with or without North Korea initially, that might serve as a strong inducement for deeper integration with the regional economy. The most encompassing idea would be some form of a Northeast Asian free-trade area (FTA). Grand initiatives of this sort, albeit with different titles, have been proposed by a succession of South Korean presidents, and not only during the engagement years of the Kim and Roh administrations. Most recently Park Geun-hye proposed a Northeast Asia Peace and Cooperation Initiative (Ministry of Foreign Affairs 2015). Such an initiative could emerge from efforts already well under way. South Korea has a free-trade agreement with the United States and one with China. China, Japan, and South Korea also began negotiating a trilateral FTA in 2013 that could become the nucleus of a wider agreement.

Under current conditions, however, it is inconceivable that the North Korean regime would opt for inclusion in a preferential trade agreement. In addition to the transparency issues outlined previously, such a venture would require at least some commitment on its part to fundamental liberalization of its external sector, which is anathema as we have seen. Participation in a FTA would clearly rest on the willingness of the other parties to tolerate North Korean exceptionalism—an arrangement under which North Korea would enjoy some benefits of preferential trade without making substantial commitments of its own. We return to this possibility in a moment, but only note that such an exceptional arrangement could substantially limit the transformative effect it is designed to have.

"North Korea Plus": The Economic Dimension of
a Northeast Asia Peace and Security Mechanism

If existing multilateral institutions or arrangements like a FTA are not likely to be of interest to North Korea, is their scope for an altogether new mechanism likely to grow out of the Six Party Talks? Although the talks are clearly in abeyance, the five parties all remain committed, at least as a matter of declaratory policy, to the multilateral cooperation outlined in the Joint Statement of September 19, 2005, and in the two 2007 "road map" agreements. These include a variety of possible cooperative arrangements on issues such as maritime and air transport; cross-border environmental issues; and technical trade and investment facilitation measures, such as customs clearance and regional support for new export-oriented industrial parks in the North.

Two issues that deserve somewhat greater attention are ground transport and energy, both of which raise the crucial question of external financing of North Korean reforms. These sectors have repeatedly been vetted as opening wedges to wider cooperation between the North and its neighbors and are exemplary of the functional integration that some have argued can be used to reach wider bargains. The continued economic growth of Northeast Asia clearly depends in part on the ongoing development of the major transportation corridors in the region (Tsuji 2003; Na 2007), two of which are directly related to the integration of the Korean peninsula: the western corridor, or Gyeongui line, which would not only link North and South but provide a rail link for South Korea to China; and the eastern corridor, which could link both Koreas to each other and, through Russia, to Europe. The latter was a focal point of Park Geun-hye's Eurasia Initiative.[18] Rail transport might therefore constitute a useful early issue for discussion, particularly given the fact that it would be relatively undemanding of North Korea but could nonetheless yield easy rents even if not linked to wider reforms. Similarly, multilateral support for road improvement would garner strong support from the DPRK, China, South Korea, and Russia.

Energy shipments to the DPRK have played a crucial role as a short-run inducement in the Six Party Talks (Chapter 6).[19] Beyond the rehabilitation of the North Korean energy sector, broader energy cooperation is often highlighted as one area that could benefit from multilateral cooperation, particularly given the strategic jockeying over energy supplies in the region. The most significant ideas in this vein are power grid interconnection and the development of oil or gas pipeline networks (Babson 2002; Gulidov and Kim 2007; von Hippel and Hayes 2008). These ideas face not only daunting technical constraints (for example, with respect to interconnection) but also extraordinarily high capital costs and very long time frames for public and private investment to gel. As a result, both pipelines and a grid interconnection remain vulnerable to the holdup problem: North Korea could easily disrupt and render worthless extraordinarily large investments, as it did with the KEDO light-water reactor projects. As we noted in Chapter 3, ambitious Russian investment projects in North Korea have come to naught precisely over such concerns.

The common thread running through all of these proposals—using existing institutions, developing altogether new ones, embedding a settlement of the nuclear issue in complementary economic agreements—is the objective of integrating North Korea into broader regional and global economies. We have argued that such opening is a prerequisite to the country's economic renewal and resolution of its chronic humanitarian problems. We are perfectly cognizant that there is a critical role for the public sector in providing depoliticized technical assistance and financing infrastructure. However, earlier ventures such as the Tumen River project and the Korean Peninsula Energy Development Organization (KEDO)—which was created in the wake of the Agreed Framework—are reminders of the costs of using a multilateral vehicle as a funnel for aid in the absence of complementary reforms. China and South Korea may extend support on a bilateral basis as a hedge against North Korea's collapse or as inducements in talks. But the development of more permanent multilateral structures is unlikely in the absence of a North Korean shift in course. Institutions, in short, are not a solution to fundamental heterogeneity among the interests of the parties that seek to form them. Nor can they break down the barriers posed by North Korea's grand strategy. Rather, North Korea's grand strategy is a block to such institutions forming in the first place.

Conclusion: Negotiation as Engagement

By the time of the fourth and fifth nuclear tests in 2016, the prospect that any of the five parties would extend additional economic inducements to moderate North Korean behavior had become vanishingly small. South Korea's skepticism about engagement strategies can be dated to the election of conservative governments in the region beginning in 2008. Japan began to wind down its North Korea trade at around this time. The United States declared its unwillingness to "pay for the same horse twice" in 2009. Even China seemed to reach the limits of its patience following the third test in 2013. Although trade continued apace, specific initiatives associated with its "deep engagement" period seemed to have gone into abeyance (Li 2016). By 2016 "inducements" had been reduced to the possibility that sanctions might be lifted in the context of a revived negotiation; all else on offer was strictly prospective.

As a result, the debate about engagement has also substantially narrowed from the question of economic inducements to how negotiations might be restarted. As we saw in Chapter 7, North Korea has shown decreasing interest in the Six Party Talks, floating peace regime proposals as a prior step required to build confidence. China has endorsed resumption of the talks, and has floated ideas for the simultaneous pursuit of nuclear and peace regime talks. The United States, for its part, has no interest in peace regime talks unless coupled with a commitment to denuclearization. These divergent approaches to negotiations are an obvious recipe for continued stalemate. Facing the limited interest of North Korea in talks, and in response to accelerating nuclear and missile testing, the pendulum has naturally swung back toward a consideration of defense, deterrence, and more forceful military signals designed either to get North Korea's attention or to directly degrade its capabilities (see, for example, Council on Foreign Relations 2016).[20] As belief in the willingness of North Korea to disarm falls, strategy discussions necessarily shift toward containment and limiting the damage associated with a de facto nuclear North Korea.

China clearly has the capability to alter these dynamics, but as of this writing has shown little interest in doing so. The extent of North Korea's dependence on Chinese trade and investment belies Beijing's claim of lacking effective influence. In the absence of Chinese support, North Korea would clearly face daunting economic difficulties and would need to rethink its willingness to negotiate—and perhaps quite quickly. Yet the acceleration of the regime's nuclear and missile programs has had the perverse effect of driving deeper wedges between China and the United States, South Korea, and Japan, most notably around questions of missile defense. Without cooperation among the five parties toward a common approach to negotiations—involving both Chinese leverage and US and South Korean willingness to make concessions—North Korea will continue to exercise outsized influence over the region's future.

In closing, we can therefore only ask the North Korean leadership, "Quo vadis?" In 2013 the young and untested leader of North Korea faced an interesting choice. When given the opportunity to meet Google chairman Eric Schmidt, leader of one of the world's most dynamic and innovative companies, Kim Jong-un declined. Yet on multiple occasions—totaling six visits—he managed to find time to spend hours partying with former Chicago Bulls basketball player Dennis Rodman. This simple and revealing choice, as much as the complexities of the economic and diplomatic relations addressed in this book, suggests that decision making in an authoritarian regime is subject not only to institutional and economic constraints but to the discretion and even whim of its leadership. Rather than pursue security through negotiations on denuclearization and economic reform, the regime has opted for the opposite: a *byungjin* line that clings to nuclear weapons and a flawed economic strategy, enabled by China's acquiescence.

In dealing with such regimes—and North Korea on many dimensions is admittedly an extreme case—both sanctions and engagement have become favored instruments of different foreign policy constituencies. For those seeking to avoid the risks of military escalation, sanctions provide a relatively costless foreign policy tool, at least against smaller parties. If we set aside its political dimensions, engagement, too, is a relatively costless policy, particularly for a large country like the United States. This observation was at the heart of the so-called Obama doctrine. But perhaps the central lesson of our analysis is that the outside world should be modest in its expectations for influence through such tools. The restraints on economic statecraft hinge not only on well-known coordination problems and the bargaining issues we have emphasized but also on the internal features of hard targets such as North Korea. Without an understanding of the domestic political economy of such states and the quite distinctive external economic relations to which it gives rise, the United States and its allies will be operating in a policy world characterized by wishful thinking rather than effective influence.

REFERENCE MATTER

Notes

1. It is important to note that engagement as we define it thus encompasses the relaxation of prior sanctions or controls.

2. During the Kim Jong-il era, foreign influences were likened by the leadership to "germs," "mosquitoes," and other vermin to be kept at bay. "Reform" was described as "honey-coated poison"; "opening," as "a Trojan horse tasked with destabilizing socialism" (Noland 2001). Similar descriptions have been used by Kim Jong-un, who was quoted by the official press agency as stating, "We must set up mosquito nets with two or three layers to prevent capitalist poison being persistently spread by enemies after seeping across the border into our territory." ("N. Korean Leader Condemns Cultural 'Invasion,'" *Global Post*, February 26, 2014, http://www.globalpost.com/dispatch/news/afp/140226/nkorean-leader-condemns-cultural-invasion).

3. Drezner (2000) has added some nuance by distinguishing bargaining over sanctions from the enforcement phase and by showing that the *nature* of coordination matters. Ad hoc coalitions—such as those forged through the Six Party Talks convened to address the North Korean nuclear issue—face greater challenges than those organized through enduring multilateral institutions.

4. This statement by Kim Dae-jung is exemplary in this regard: "With deepening economic exchanges and cooperation . . . the North Korean economy will . . . show greater vitality in its economic relations with the outside world. As the planned economic system gradually turns toward a market economy, the North Korean economy is expected to experience rapid growth, and the economic disparity with South Korea will begin to narrow. When and if such developments occur, along with improved living standards for its citizens and the inevitable change in their world view and/or perception of the outside world, we would project that there would inevitably be demands for changes even in their political system. As these trends take root, it would be unavoidable for the North Koreans to tolerate or even accept the multi-party system and the principle of free elections" (1997,

121). Although the policies of the two "progressive" governments of Kim Dae-jung and Roh Moo-hyun bore significant similarities, there were differences as well. The Sunshine Policy of the Kim era, which derived its name from the Aesop fable of the sun and the wind, saw engagement as a means to transform North Korea. The "peace and prosperity" strategy of Roh-era policy was explicitly noninstrumental and sought to defuse tension via reassurance (Ra 2013).

CHAPTER TWO

1. The literature on authoritarian regimes is vast, but examples of recent efforts to categorize such systems can be found in Bueno de Mesquita et al. 2003; Gandhi and Prze-worski 2007; Myerson 2008; Magaloni and Kricheli 2010; Levitsky and Way 2010; Svolik 2012; and Geddes 2016. Weeks 2012 and 2014 considers the effects of regime type on foreign policy behavior.

2. For the debate over estimates of famine deaths, see Goodkind and West 2001; Lee 2003, 2011; Haggard and Noland 2007a; Goodkind, West, and Johnson 2011; and Spooren-berg and Schwekendiek 2012.

3. As we show in Chapter 3, the result has been a surprising reliance on exports of raw materials, mainly from larger Chinese investments that can secure political protection and mitigate financial risks through countertrade.

4. For example, the well-known Polity IV data set codes all regimes on a scale from −10 to +10 on the basis of a number of discrete institutional features, including the com-petitiveness and openness of leadership selection, constraints on the executive, and the competitiveness of, regulation or control of political participation. From 1948 through 1956, the country was ranked at −7; from 1957 through 1966, at −8; and since 1967, at −9.

5. The Supreme People's Assembly (SPA) is nominally an elected legislative body and the ultimate source of state power. In line with the concept of democratic centralism, however, the party nominates a single slate of candidates that is then elected with virtual unanimity. The SPA is undoubtedly one of the more minimalist legislatures in the world, in recent years meeting for no more than a couple of days a year.

6. The regime held ad hoc party conferences in 2010 and 2012 to anoint Kim Jong-un as the successor, but the first formal party congress was not convened until 2016.

7. The Political Committee (renamed the Politburo in 1980); the Central Military Af-fairs Commission; and the Standing Committee (replaced by the Secretariat in 1966). The core governing body under the 1972 constitution was the Central People's Committee (CPC), but that body was dominated by party officials, thereby weakening ministerial and technocratic influence (Yang 1999).

8. The 1992 constitution separated command over the military from the president and stipulated that the NDC was "the highest military leadership body of state power" (Article 111) and that its chairman "commands and directs all the armed forces" (Article 112).

9. At the time of his father's death, Kim Jong-il was both chairman of the National Defense Commission and commander-in-chief of the KPA, and he had effective control of the Organization and Guidance Department. He probably ruled through his personal secretariat and ad hoc structures consisting of select members of the Politburo and military and security apparatus leaders who belonged to the KWP Central Military Affairs Com-mittee and the NDC (Koh 1997, 5).

10. Membership in each body shown in Figure 2.1 and in Tables 2.1 and 2.2 for a given year is as of December 31.

11. Trends toward increased military participation in core institutions even extended to the Party Secretariat (Haggard, Herman, and Ryu 2014).

12. Among the most comprehensive treatments of the repressive apparatus is the annual publication of the Korean Institute for National Unification (KINU) *White Paper on Human Rights in North Korea*. See also UN Human Rights Office of the High Commissioner's 2014 *Report of the Commission of Inquiry on Human Rights in the Democratic People's Republic of Korea*.

13. In comparison with other communist systems, the North Korean party is relatively large, with membership estimated as about 12 percent of the population (Lankov, Kwok, and Cho 2012). It can by no means be equated with the elite, but recruitment is selective, subject to rigorous screening and particularly close oversight. Because membership is a prerequisite for access to the perks and rents of higher office, recruitment generates high-powered incentives for loyalty.

14. For example, Articles 110 and 111 of the 2004 criminal code provide for up to two years of labor training for individuals and firms engaging in "illegal commercial activities, therefore gaining large profits." Article 118 extends similar punishment to "gaining large profits through usury." Article 119 prohibits "illegally giving money or goods in exchange for labor."

15. See Stephan Haggard, Marcus Noland, and Jaesung Ryu, "Cells Phones and Jamming Failures: A Combustible Mix," *North Korea: Witness to Transformation* (blog), February 28, 2012, http://blogs.piie.com/nk/?p=5145.

16. See Kevin Stahler, "North Korea's Cell Phone Growth in Context," *North Korea: Witness to Transformation* (blog), September 30, 2014, http://blogs.piie.com/nk/?p=13504.

17. See Stephan Haggard, "Controlling the Border," *North Korea: Witness to Transformation* (blog), August 21, 2014, http://blogs.piie.com/nk/?p=13432. Also see Stephan Haggard, "Slave to the Blog: IT Edition," *North Korea: Witness to Transformation* (blog), August 8, 2014, http://blogs.piie.com/nk/?p=13391.

18. An example is provided by the leaked "Panama Papers." A British banker resident in Pyongyang allegedly set up a shell company in the British Virgin Islands which, in cooperation with several North Korean state entities, was used to evade international sanctions. See Juliette Garside and Luke Harding, "British banker set up firm used by North Korea to sell weapons,'" *The Guardian*, April 4, 2016, http://www.theguardian.com/news/2016/apr/04/panama-papers-briton-set-up-firm-allegedly-used-by-north-korea-weapons-sales. See also UN Security Council (2016).

19. Choi and Lecy (2011) mention a wonderful bit of historical engineering. In order to justify discussion of reform—however marginal—the argument was advanced that Korea had begun to develop capitalism as early as the seventeenth century but its evolution was disrupted by Japanese colonialism.

20. The antimarket campaigns began with the imposition of escalating age restrictions on market traders in the fall of 2007 and were followed by stepped-up inspections of the general markets and a dramatic reduction in their days of operation (Haggard and Noland 2010).

21. This explanation rests on the idea that authorities were spooked by the ongoing inflation associated with the reforms. They had no ability to control prices of consumer goods entering the country from China, but believed that they could control the price of grain, which loomed large in the consumption basket.

22. See "Kim Jong Un Speaks at Military Parade," Korean Central News Agency (KCNA), April 15, 2012, http://www.kcna.co.jp/index-e.htm.

23. According to the official Korean Central News Agency, on April 6, 2012, in a meeting with the Central Committee of the Korean Workers' Party, Kim Jong-un stated,

"[We should focus] all the issues arising in the economy on the Cabinet and establishing strict discipline and order of solving them under the unified command of the Cabinet," KCNA, April 19, 2012, http://www.kcna.co.jp/item/2012/201204/news19/20120419 -07ee.html.

24. For example, Choi Song Min, "Rich Traders Invest in Chongjin Construction," *DailyNK*, August 10, 2012, http://www.dailynk.com/english/read.php?cataId= nko1500&num=9662.

25. The new line was rolled out at the Plenum of the Workers' Party Central Committee at the end of March 2013 and institutionalized in a number of laws passed in the SPA meetings that immediately followed. See "Report of Plenary Meeting of WPK Central Committee," KCNA, March 31, 2013, and "Seventh Session of the 12th SPA of DPRK Held," KCNA, April 1, 2013. On nuclear weapons in particular, see "Law on Consolidating Position of Nuclear Weapons State Adopted," KCNA April 1, 2013, and especially "Nuke and Peace 1" and "Nuke and Peace 2," KCNA, April 26 and 27, 2013.

26. Food shortages and rising prices meant that enterprises could not pay adequate wages, and of course the agricultural reforms could not be expected to yield short-term payoffs given that planting decisions had already been made for the crop cycle.

27. The most celebrated of these expropriations was of the Chinese mining firm Xiyang. See Stephan Haggard, "Chinese Investment in the DPRK: Shanghaied!" *Witness to Transformation* (blog), August 12, 2012, http://blogs.piie.com/nk/?p=7158. Also see Stephan Haggard, "Ripping Off Foreigners II: China Edition," *Witness to Transformation* (blog), October 24, 2015, http://blogs.piie.com/nk/?p=7909.

28. The effort to establish multiple channels for the approval of foreign direct investment was reversed, raising doubts about which agencies were actually in charge of investment screening and in a position to make authoritative commitments. See Institute of Far Eastern Studies, "North Korea to Announce New Economic Development Plan and Organizational Restructuring," *NK Briefs*, February 29, 2012, http://ifes.kyungnam.ac.kr/ eng/FRM/FRM_0101V.aspx?code=FRM120229_0001.

29. Orascom accumulated significant cash balances in North Korea as a result of its operation of the cell phone network, but faced effective expropriation of these profits when the regime sought to allow repatriation only at the market, not the official, exchange rate.

30. A revised law governing the Rason zone gave extraordinary power and discretion to the Rason City People's Committee relative to previous rules. In 2012 the Chinese surfaced the dirt road linking Hunchun and Rason and committed to extending the four-lane road to Chongjin and extending power lines into the zone. The Russians have refurbished the rail link connecting Rason and Russia, and both Russia and China have invested in improving the harbor.

CHAPTER THREE

1. A full discussion of sources and estimation strategy can be found in Haggard and Noland 2007b; we extend that exercise through 2011 here.

2. It is important to underscore that not all of North Korea's military exports can be technically considered illicit. As a nonmember of the Missile Technology Control Regime, North Korea has the right to export such weapons. But after 2006 such sales were proscribed by a succession of UN Security Council resolutions that restricted export and import of major weapons systems. Light arms exports were banned by UNSCR 2270 only in 2016.

3. For mirror statistics, one uses the bilateral exports (imports) of a partner country as an estimate of North Korea's imports (exports) from that partner (Noland 2000).

4. The timing of this trough in trade corresponded to the Asian financial crisis and a slowdown in Japan, but given the closed nature of the North Korean economy it is not clear that the regional financial crisis mattered; political factors seem more significant.

5. Such collateral damage is a theme of Abt (2014), which describes efforts to do business in North Korea.

6. A similar modeling of the North-South trade relationship found that the 2006 sanctions had no effect, in part because relations improved somewhat in 2007 and through early 2008. However, unilateral sanctions imposed by South Korea did have a depressing effect on trade following the sinking of the *Cheonan* in 2010.

7. See UN Panel of Experts (2010, 2012, 2013, 2014, 2015, 2016).

8. In Figure 3.2, "Australian list—SITC 3" takes the Australian list and maps the verbal descriptions of the sanctioned luxury products to Standard International Trade Classification (SITC 3) categories. The "Japanese list" is based on KOTRA, which attempted to map the Japanese sanctions list to detailed product categories using the Harmonized System (HS) (Kim 2006). The third variant ("Australian list—HS 2") reconstructs the Australian list using KOTRA's HS codes, which tend to be more narrowly drawn than the SITC-based categories used to construct the Australian list. This analysis is based on UN Comtrade-reported data so trade that is intentionally misclassified (for example, luxury watches labeled as industrial machinery) is not detected.

9. It is worth noting that the drop in luxury exports in 2009 under the Australian HS designation was less steep than the drop in overall Chinese exports during that year. Put differently, the *share* of luxury goods in overall Chinese exports, which constituted 5 to 7 percent of Chinese exports to the DPRK, actually *increased* in that year.

10. See Marcus Noland, "European Luxury Goods Exports to North Korea," *North Korea: Witness to Transformation* (blog), October 18, 2012, http://www.piie.com/blogs/nk/?p=7867.

11. North Korea's largest imported commodity group has been mineral products, which includes crude oil. Textiles and animal/vegetable products made up the second and third largest import categories, respectively, in 2014.

12. Kevin Stahler "How Has the Commodity Bust Affected North Korea's Trade Balance? (part 1)," *North Korea: Witness to Transformation* (blog), January 20, 2015, http://blogs.piie.com/nk/?p=13778; also see Kevin Stahler "How Has the Commodity Bust Affected North Korea's Trade Balance? (Part 2)," *North Korea: Witness to Transformation* (blog), January 21, 2015, http://blogs.piie.com/nk/?p=13796.

13. The Soviets, who were a source of technology in the 1980s, also began to terminate technology transfer in the military sphere.

14. See Stephan Haggard, "More Debt Follies: DPRK Debt to Russia," *North Korea: Witness to Transformation* (blog), July 19, 2012, https://piie.com/blogs/north-korea-itness-transformation/more-debt-follies-dprk-debt.

15. KOTRA has a reasonable track record in eliminating obvious discrepancies, but it probably underestimates the growth of North Korea's trade with the developing world. For example, we add North Korea's bilateral trade with Myanmar to KOTRA-reported total trade data from 1990 to 2011. In a separate exercise (Haggard and Noland 2010b), we developed some alternative estimates based on International Monetary Fund (2006) and KOTRA and UN Comtrade data for the period 1990–2008.

16. Stephan Haggard, "Orascom in North Korea: Don't Leave Me Hanging," *North Korea: Witness to Transformation* (blog), December 10, 2013. http://blogs.piie.com/nk/?p=12505.

17. These two commodities are appropriate for several reasons. First, both are relatively undifferentiated and so permit such head-to-head comparisons. Second, if the Chinese are extending support to North Korea, such support is typically assumed to take the form of "friendship prices" on key commodities of central concern to the regime.

18. We found similar patterns with respect to corn and wheat (not reproduced here).

19. For more on South Korean assistance to North Korea see Stephan Haggard, Kent Boydston, and Jaesung Ryu, "South Korean Aid to the North I: An Accounting 1991–2015," *North Korea: Witness to Transformation* (blog), July 20, 2015, http://blogs.piie.com/nk/?p=14284; "South Korean Aid to the North II: An Accounting, 1991–2015," July 21, 2015, *North Korea: Witness to Transformation* (blog), http://blogs.piie.com/nk/?p=14289; "South Korean Aid to the North III: An Accounting, 1991–2015," *North Korea: Witness to Transformation* (blog), August 12, 2015, http://blogs.piie.com/nk/?p=14365; and "South Korean Aid to the North IV: An Accounting, 1991–2015," September 1, 2015, http://blogs.piie.com/nk/?p=14424.

20. The KIC was closed by President Park following the nuclear test and satellite launch in early 2016, with the implication that North-South trade would fall to nothing except for possible humanitarian assistance.

21. It should be noted, however, that this trade is not necessarily entirely under the central government's control. It may be a net addition to foreign exchange earnings when viewed from the perspective of the country as a whole, but accrues, for example, to individual military units, trading companies, or rogue drug dealers.

22. Missiles, for example, can be misreported as fabricated metal products; illicit drugs, as medicine or, as in one infamous case, honey.

23. The *So San* was interdicted on the high seas by a Spanish warship, and the boarding itself was legal because there was no ship under that name in the North Korean registry. However, because US and Spanish authorities had no legal basis to seize the cargo, which included Scud missiles purchased by Yemen, an American ally, the ship had to be released.

24. The PSI was not based on any fundamental changes in international law, but developed common principles, sharing of intelligence and protocols, full exploitation of national legal authorities, and ship-boarding agreements with major flag-of-convenience countries. The United States also pursued diplomatic efforts to restrict overflight by aircraft suspected of carrying North Korean weapons. From an initial membership of eleven, the PSI had nearly one hundred members by 2013, with predictable holdouts including not only China, Iran, and Syria but other potential intermediaries such as Malaysia and Pakistan (Pollack 2011, 414; UN Panel of Experts 2010, 2013; also see Table 3.1 in this chapter).

25. The resolution "called upon" (but again did not require) member states to inspect all cargo on their territory, including at both seaports and airports, if it was believed to contain prohibited items. Moreover, it authorized members to inspect vessels on the high seas or to escort them to port if there were reasonable grounds to suspect that they carried prohibited cargo. It also precluded the provision of bunkering services to any ship suspected of prohibited trade, providing an additional constraint. An important loophole was that such interdiction had to have the consent of the country under which the vessel is flagged. If the flag state does not consent, "the flag state shall direct the vessel to proceed to an appropriate and convenient port for the required inspection."

26. For example, states could block the establishment of correspondent relationships with banks in their jurisdictions, setting the stage for US sanctions against North Korea's Foreign Trade Bank.

27. Although drugs almost certainly dominate North Korea's smuggling activity, there is evidence, in the form of diplomatic expulsions, of trade in other sanctioned items, including so-called conflict diamonds from civil war zones in Africa, along with rhino horns, and ivory (Noland 2000; Asher 2005; Prahar 2006). North Korea has also been accused of insurance fraud (Kim Kwang-jin 2011).

28. For example, Peter Prahar (2006) testified before Congress on both the purchase of 60 kilos of amphetamines by Japanese crime syndicates for $1 million (or $17,000 per kilo) in 1998 and a Japanese seizure of 565 kilograms in 1999 with a street value of $347 million (or $615,000 per kilo)! Clearly, the former rather than the latter are closer to what we would consider export prices.

29. The US Department of State's *International Narcotics Control Strategy Report* (1999) estimated the area under opium cultivation in North Korea at 4,200 to 7,000 hectares in 1998, which would yield 30 to 44 metric tons of opium, or 4.6 to 6.8 metric tons of heroin at a conversion rate of 6.5 to 1. In 2002, according to the UN Office on Drugs and Crime's *World Drug Report* (2006), the farm gate price of opium ranged from a low of $142 per kilo (in Afghanistan) to a high of $234 per kilo (in Myanmar). If we take the generous estimate of $200 per kilo, this yields a total farm gate value for opium production of $6–9 million. The UN Office of Drugs and Crime (2003) reports 2001 wholesale prices of heroin in China at approximately $20,000 per kilo, yielding a total value of approximately $92–135 million. But this assumes that North Korea was capable of collecting street prices for wholesale transactions. Prices of heroin on other markets also underwent a sharp decline following the collapse of the Taliban regime in Afghanistan and the resurgence of production in that country.

30. Sovacool (2009) estimates annual average seizures involving North Korea between 1996 and 2006 of only 30 kilograms of heroin, 2 kilograms of opium, and 120 kilograms of methamphetamine. *The International Narcotics Control Strategy Reports* for 2004 through 2011 reported no large-scale drug trafficking involving the DPRK state or its nationals, and the 2011 *World Drug Report* makes no mention whatsoever of North Korea in its detailed discussion of the international heroin and opium markets.

31. The North Korean regime itself has begun to show signs of concern over drug trafficking because of growing domestic use (US Department of State 2005b, 68; Lankov and Kim 2013).

32. In addition to the sources cited later, this section draws on outstanding reporting by Kevin Hall. Hall, whose articles include "Treasury Casts a Wide Net Under Patriot Act," *ArkansasOnline*, March 12, 2016, http://www.arkansasonline.com/news/2007/mar/18/ treasury-casts-wide-net-under-patriot-act-20070318; "U.S. Challenged on Action Against Keybank," McClatchy Newspapers, April 16, 2007, http://www.realcities.com/mld/ krwashington/news/columnists/kevin_g_hall/; "Money Laundering Allegations by U.S. False, Report Says," *McClatchyDC*, April 16, 2007, http://www.mcclatchydc.com/latest -news/article24462799.html; "Gold sales may have spurred Macau bank's blacklisting," *PoliticalHotwire*, April 17, 2007, http://politicalhotwire.com/political-discussion/14477-swiss -authorities-question-u-s-counterfeiting-charges-against-north-korea.html; and "Bank owner disputes money-laundering allegations," *McClatchyDC*, May 16, 2007, http://www .mcclatchydc.com/news/nation-world/world/article24463246.html.

33. In the wake of the finding, the bank experienced a severe run on deposits. Under pressure not only from the United States but from correspondent banks in Japan, Korea, and Europe, Banco Delta Asia severed connections with fifty North Korean individuals or businesses, many believed to be military or party related; replaced several managers; and allowed a panel named by Macau's government to administer its operations (Demick and Meyer 2005).

34. There have been no fresh discoveries of North Korean supernotes in recent years, leading some experts to conclude that North Korea has significantly scaled back its counterfeit currency operations (Walter 2016). However, counterfeiting has not been limited to currency. Evidence also exists of North Korean involvement in counterfeiting of cigarettes and pharmaceuticals (Chestnut 2007, 2014; Asher 2006). In the mid-2000s, the US tobacco industry put potential gross revenues from counterfeiting on the order of $520–720 million annually based on the prices of counterfeit cigarettes in Asian ports such as Pusan, Manila, and Kaohsiung (Coalition of Tobacco Companies 2005). However, this estimate is also a wild exaggeration because it reflects the street value of the cigarettes once they have been sold to criminal gangs.

35. For precise estimates for each category of illicit trade by year, see Haggard and Noland (2007b).

36. Some illicit activities are almost surely subject to central control; others are probably conducted by state entities but without direction from central authorities (or perhaps even without their specific knowledge); and some may be conducted by what amount to local criminal gangs. As a result, even our best guess of the total returns to the *country* should be further discounted by the fact that not all of those resources flow to the *regime*.

37. In addition to remittances, labor exports, and tourism, North Korea earns unknown revenue from other service sector activities such as animation, overseas construction, and the Mansudae Studio's production of statues, murals, and other cultural artifacts overseas.

38. These remittances were initially funneled through credit unions and firms affiliated with the Chosen Soren, a powerful organization of Korean residents in Japan with a decidedly pro-Pyongyang tilt. The dominant financial channel for remittances from 1975 to 2002, the Ashikaga Ginko, canceled its correspondent relations with the Foreign Trade Bank of North Korea in 2002 and failed in the following year. As a result, remittances had to rely either on transfers through third parties, such as the Macao banks targeted by the United States after 2005 or on cash carried by travelers that was subject to a ¥1 million limit.

39. Lee Tae-hoon, "Most N. Korean defectors send money home," *Korea Times*, October 10, 2010, http://www.koreatimes.co.kr/www/news/nation/2010/10/116_74335 .html.

40. "Defectors Send $10 Million a Year to N. Korea," *Chosun Ilbo*, February 7, 2011, http://english.chosun.com/site/data/html_dir/2011/02/07/2011020700405.html.

41. A recent defector account suggested that predation not only is personal but reflects quotas allocated to National Security Agency (NSA) agents to secure desirable luxury items for higher-ups. See Im Jeong Jin, "Defector Families Are Moneybags for NSA Agents," *DailyNK*, January 27, 2011, http://www.dailynk.com/english/read .php?cataId=nk01500&num=7303.

42. Originally conceived as helping the North pay off Soviet-era debts, the model of organizing contract workers replicates models in a much wider array of countries, including China, Kuwait, Mongolia, Qatar, and the United Arab Emirates (Cho and Kim 2007).

43. Marcus Noland, "Spiritual Pollution and the Export of Labor," *North Korea: Witness to Transformation* (blog), August 7, 2013, http://blogs.piie.com/nk/?p=11127.

44. Lee (2015) asserts that the revenues earned by these workers amount to $1.2–2.3 billion per year, implying revenues of $20,000–46,000 per worker—between two and four and a half times world per capita income of roughly $10,000.

45. After an initial boom, the flow of visitors slackened, in part because of North Korean provocations, and Hyundai was unable to make the payment schedule specified in the original agreement. In 2001 the contract was renegotiated, effectively cutting Hyundai's obligation in half. The South Korean government, in the form of the Korean National Tourism Organization, assumed a greater operational role by effectively providing a subsidy.

46. There has been some Chinese activity in the zone since 2008, but the legal ramifications of using Hyundai Asan's property appears to have deterred both China and private operators from entering. In any case, the location of the site and poor transportation deter serious Chinese tourism.

47. Koryo Group provides these estimates on its Travel Advice FAQ page, http://www.koryogroup.com/tips/.

48. A brief word should be said about the aid associated with the 1994 Agreed Framework and the Korean Peninsula Energy Development Organization (KEDO). KEDO's remit was to construct two nuclear reactors to replace the nuclear facilities shut down under the Agreed Framework. In addition, it provided 500,000 metric tons of heavy fuel oil per year to compensate for the loss of electricity generation capacity from the closed reactor. More than $4 billion was pledged to this effort, principally by the governments of South Korea and Japan. The United States was mainly responsible for the provision of heavy fuel oil. However, the lion's share of KEDO funds was both raised and spent outside of North Korea—for example, for the design and procurement of reactor components. In considering the capital account, we are interested solely in what was actually transferred to North Korea, which appears to have consisted only of the heavy fuel oil and whatever funds were used for site construction, including payment for workers and shipped construction materials such as cement. The project was effectively suspended with the onset of the nuclear crisis in October 2002. Shipments of heavy fuel oil were stopped in December 2002. Light-water reactor construction slowed to a halt in 2003–2004, and KEDO itself was formally terminated in 2005.

49. See Stephan Haggard and Weiyi Shi, "Chinese investment in North Korea: Some data (part 1)," *North Korea: Witness to Transformation* (blog), June 30, 2014, http://blogs.piie.com/nk/?p=13223 and "Chinese investment in North Korea: Some data (part 2)," *North Korea: Witness to Transformation* (blog), July 1, 2014, http://blogs.piie.com/nk/?p=13265.

50. In theory, the current account and capital account should sum to zero; any imbalance in transactions in goods and services is exactly offset by a corresponding financial flow. In reality, however, this never holds, generating a balancing term known as the "statistical discrepancy." Unsurprisingly, in the North Korean case this discrepancy has been large at times (in 1990, at the onset of its financial crisis, and in 1997, at the peak of the famine), in most years having a negative value. The implication is that North Korea has resources that are unaccounted for; that is, it generates more revenue than is accounted for by spending and saving (Haggard and Noland 2007b). If this implication is correct, there are a variety of possible explanations, none mutually exclusive. The North Korean central bank may be accumulating official reserves, or we may have overestimated revenues: perhaps even our skeptical guesses about unconventional revenues are generous, and the earnings from these activities are even less than our best guesses. Or perhaps spending has been underestimated;

that is, imports have been undercounted. It is quite possible that North Korea is importing dual-use technologies or even weapons systems that are unreported. Or it may be that other items, such as luxury goods, are not accounted for in existing statistics.

Another possibility is that we have underestimated saving and investment abroad. There could also be unaccounted for capital outflows. We have assumed that North Korea is not engaged in any substantial FDI of its own, but there is certainly some, such as in labor-contracting companies or North Korean–themed restaurants. More significantly, it is highly likely that the top circles of the North Korean elite, particularly the Kim family, have accumulated perhaps substantial foreign assets. The location of these assets remains one of the most intriguing puzzles of North Korea's external economic relations and a matter of great interest to future sanctions efforts.

51. Our low and high estimates represent an aggregate deficit of $13.0 billion and a surplus of $4.2 billion, respectively, underlining the uncertainty in these efforts.

52. See Marcus Noland, "Hugely important: North Korea running a current account surplus?" *North Korea: Witness to Transformation* (blog), March 18, 2013, http://blogs.piie .com/nk/?p=9647.

53. In some of the regressions, there is evidence of autocorrelated residuals, which means that estimated standard errors are likely to be downwardly biased and, as a consequence, the reported level of statistical significance is exaggerated. For obvious reasons, this is a bigger issue for the regressions on monthly data.

54. Although the estimated effects may be overstated, there is no reason to believe that the signs of the coefficients would be biased.

55. Trade with China (and South Korea) looms sufficiently large in the North Korean economy for China (and South Korea) to presumably face an upward-sloping North Korean supply curve (i.e., the magnitude of their demands are such that external demand shifts actually affect North Korean internal prices). In modeling terms, this possibility implies the need to estimate demand and supply simultaneously.

56. This model can be formulated algebraically as

$$\log M_t^d = \alpha_0 + \alpha_1 \log (PM/P)_t + \alpha_2 \log Y_t \tag{1}$$

where M_t^d = quantity of imports demanded; PM/P = relative price of imports; and Y_t = an index of domestic activity.

57. One technical benefit of including this term is that it renders the time trend insignificant and reduces the autocorrelation of the residuals to an acceptable level.

58. Tests for autocorrelation suggest that we can take the significance levels as indicated.

CHAPTER FOUR

1. This is seen most clearly in the case of Saddam Hussein–era Iraq. See Marcus Noland, "Sanctions and the Ghosts of Iraq, part 1," *North Korea: Witness to Transformation* (blog), April 16, 2013, http://www.piie.com/blogs/nk/?p=10076.

2. For a more detailed discussion of the difficulties in estimating food balances, see Haggard and Noland (2007a, 41–49) and Haggard and Noland (2008a).

3. In addition to the logistical problems of moving and distributing grain in this fashion, we know that food is not distributed equally in North Korea because of the political claims of the regime and the military. Widening inequality coupled with an increasing reliance on the market for food also means that some are better positioned to gain access to food than others.

4. See Food and Agriculture Organization, "The Democratic People's Republic of Korea: Outlook for Food Supply and Demand in 2014/15 (November/October)," February 3, 2015, http://www.ncnk.org/resources/publications/20150203DPRK.pdf.

5. See Haggard and Noland (2007a) for a fuller treatment of this point.

6. These include increases in prices for oil, water, and fertilizer, which are inputs to food production; increased demands for grain directly and indirectly through higher meat consumption in many emerging markets, most notably China; diversion of stocks to the production of ethanol; growth of financial speculation in food commodity markets; and disruption of international trade, primarily due to export embargos, to name a few (Hendrix 2011).

7. Our data are assembled primarily from observations reported in the *DailyNK*, and other Korean-language academic and media sources. As with all data on and from North Korea, these publications should be treated with caution. Markets are fragmented, and we have little information on quality differences; also, prices may vary depending on such factors as proximity to the Chinese border or rice-growing areas. See Haggard and Noland (2009) for a more complete exploration of these issues.

8. This is not to say that prices in local currency terms are determined entirely in the global market, as North Korean authorities have at times alleged. Domestic food price inflation was clearly driven in the first instance by the badly managed November 2009 currency reform and may have subsequently been influenced by the extended period of military tensions that followed the breakdown of the Six Party Talks.

9. The UNICEF survey reported three measures of childhood malnutrition: wasting (low weight to height), stunting (low height for age), and underweight (low weight for age). The two age-related measures (stunting and underweight) can be interpreted as reflecting the effects of chronic malnutrition. Wasting, can be interpreted as signaling immediate, acute malnutrition. This measure tends to be more volatile and may fluctuate with seasonal variability in food availability. For a discussion of possible sources of bias in the 2012 survey, see Marcus Noland, "UNICEF 2012 Nutritional Survey," *North Korea: Witness to Transformation* (blog), January 3, 2013, http://www.piie.com/blogs/nk/?p=8768.

10. The 2009 survey reports relevant population percentages in three groups: moderate malnutrition, severe malnutrition, and the global rate that sums the two. Global acute malnutrition is defined as an individual being two standard deviations or more below the median. Moderate acute malnutrition is defined as being between two and three standard deviations below the median. Severe acute malnutrition is defined as being more than three standard deviations below the median.

11. Screenings in the most seriously affected counties showed 14.6 percent of adults presenting with moderate and 2.8 percent presenting with severe acute malnutrition; this compares with the 2009 survey estimating 4.7 percent moderate and 0.5 percent severe acute malnutrition.

12. Predictably, the data show strong regional effects. The privileged capital city of Pyongyang had a severe-stunting rate of only 4 percent. Ryanggang was the worst affected province, with an overall stunting rate of more than 12 percent. The low scores for Ryanggang, a kind of North Korean Appalachia, can be rationalized by its isolated rural population. Not so South Hamgyong, however. Moreover, it is notable that South Hamgyong does worse than North Hamgyong, which is farther from Pyongyang but closer to China. These general patterns were confirmed in a postharvest security assessment in 2013 (World Food Program 2013a).

13. Haggard and Noland (2007a) provide estimates of the extent of diversion. Haggard and Noland (2011a) found that in two large scale surveys, refugees overwhelmingly

believed that the aid went primarily to the military. In a more recent survey of 500 refugees conducted by a South Korean NGO, 78 percent of respondents reported not receiving international food aid while in North Korea and some said that after they received aid they were forced to return it following the departure of monitors. When asked where the aid went, large majorities thought that it went to the military or other connected groups. See "78% of N. Korean Defectors Never Saw Foreign Food Aid," *Chosun Ilbo*, April 6, 2011, http://english.chosun.com/site/data/html_dir/2011/04/06/2011040600985.html.

14. A WFP audit (World Food Program 2014) provides the latest recitation of monitoring problems.

15. In the wake of the famine, early WFP appeals were formally nested in a broader combined humanitarian appeal under the OCHA. However, food was always the overwhelming share of total aid extended to North Korea, in part because of concerns that more fungible forms of assistance would be diverted.

16. Initially designed to run through March 2008, the program was subsequently extended through the end of August 2008. It would feed roughly 1.9 million beneficiaries, less than one-third of the previously targeted population, requiring to do so 150,000 metric tons of commodities at a cost of approximately $102 million. Distribution focused on fifty vulnerable counties jointly selected by the WFP and the government. Foods enriched with vitamins and minerals produced at WFP-supported factories were distributed to young children and pregnant and nursing women, and cereal rations were supplied to underemployed workers through food-for-community-development schemes aimed at rehabilitating agricultural and other infrastructure.

17. North Korea demanded a reduction in staff to ten or fewer, closure of the regional offices outside Pyongyang, and confinement of this staff to Pyongyang with only quarterly opportunities to visit project sites in the field.

18. Devastating floods in major cereal-growing provinces in August 2007 provided an opening for a short-term emergency program, but it was small and targeted at those directly displaced.

19. The bulk of the US contribution was to be channeled through the WFP (up to 400,000 tons), with the remainder distributed by a consortium of five US NGOs (up to 100,000 tons). The US contribution constituted over 60 percent of the WFP program and nearly 80 percent if the NGO contribution is included.

20. The program was designed to provide food assistance to an estimated 6.2 million beneficiaries in 131 counties/districts in 8 provinces.

21. Since the NGOs were completely dependent on US approval for access to the 100,000 tons of food they were to deliver, the USAID coordinator effectively exercised a veto over negotiations between the NGOs and USAID's North Korean counterpart organization, the Korea-America Private Exchange Society (KAPES). This agreement would become the foundation for the WFP's negotiation with the more hardline National Coordinating Committee (NCC). Revealingly, both of these organizations fell under the Ministry of Foreign Affairs.

22. Information from a variety of sources had already suggested an aggressive push on the part of North Korean embassies to secure grain in the face of increasing foreign exchange constraints and high world-market prices. As a WFP official put it privately, "[WFP] policy is: No access, no food. But the North Koreans are saying: No food, no access."

23. Marcus Noland, "Slave to the Blog: More Updates!" *North Korea: Witness to Transformation* (blog). March 26, 2011, http://blogs.piie.com/nk/?p=720; *Good Friends*, "North

Korea Today No. 413." July 27, 2011, http://goodfriendsusa.blogspot.com/2011/08/north-korea-today-no-413-july-27-2011.html.

24. *Good Friends*, "North Korea Today No. 387." January 26, 2011; *Good Friends*, "North Korea Today No. 395." March 23, 2011, http://goodfriendsusa.blogspot.com/2011/04/good-friends-aims-to-help-north-korean_11.html.

25. For details on this last program, see World Food Program, "Korea, DPR Country Brief," n.d., http://documents.wfp.org/stellent/groups/public/documents/ep/wfp276263.pdf.

26. A memo written to the UN Emergency Relief Coordinator covering events in July 2009 makes the perceived links clear. "There has been a general slow-down in funding for all agencies since the May nuclear tests and the July missile launch . . . In addition to calls from some donors on making humanitarian aid conditional on political progress, more conservative media outlets have started to question the role of the UN in DPRK. Some traditional donors with operations in DPRK are currently stalling contributions in part due to domestic concerns about providing resources to DPRK."

27. This aid ended with the decision in December 2002 to terminate heavy-oil shipments in response to intelligence on North Korea's highly enriched uranium (HEU) program. KEDO was dissolved in 2005.

28. In each announcement, the administration emphasized that food aid decisions would be made on the basis of demonstrated need, competing demands, and "donors' ability to access all vulnerable groups and monitor distribution" (US Department of State 2004). In February 2003, the administration promised 40,000 tons of food, with another 60,000 conditional on further progress with respect to monitoring. In December 2003, and again in July 2004, the State Department announced contributions to the WFP (the proposed 60,000 tons and a 50,000-ton contribution to the 2004 appeal, respectively).

29. These included removal from the State Department's terrorism list, lifting of restrictions under the International Emergency Economic Powers Act (successor to the Trading with the Enemy Act), and a resumption of heavy-oil shipments.

30. US Department of State, "North Korea: Response to Flooding," press statement, August 31, 2007, http://2001-2009.state.gov/r/pa/prs/ps/2007/aug/91669.htm.

31. At the end of 2009, Congress went so far as to require that expended food aid deemed unmonitored at the end of the NGO and WFP programs be either paid back or deducted from any future aid on offer! (Public Law 111-117 [2010 Consolidated Appropriations Act], Sec. 7071 (f) (6), December 16, 2009).

32. The Kim Young-sam administration had agreed to provide 150,000 tons of food aid in unmarked bags and acquiesced to Japanese support as well. However, North Korean authorities forced the ship carrying the first load of rice to fly a North Korean flag and even detained the crew. The Kim administration shifted to making all aid conditional on the opening of talks, which did not transpire, until relenting in 1997 as evidence of distress mounted (Noland 2000, 194–196).

33. Under the Kim Dae-jung administration, NGOs that managed to establish a consistent record of raising funds and conducting humanitarian operations for a year were entitled to apply for a license that designated them a "North Korea support group" eligible for support through the Inter-Korean Cooperation Fund. Over time, the relationship between the government and the NGOs became more institutionalized, including through the formation of a policy council that sought to identify joint projects among NGOs and with the government.

34. At the time of the April request, the Roh government had committed to shipping 150,000 tons of fertilizer but had not made a decision on the remaining 300,000 tons included in Pyongyang's initial request.

35. The $230 million aid package included 100,000 tons of rice, which accounted for just over $200 million of the total. The North Koreans responded to the regular aid cutoff by suspending ministerial talks and halting family reunions.

36. The resumption of rice aid initially proved contentious, but the final resolution of the Banco Delta Asia problem and apparent progress in the Six Party Talks led to resumption of large-scale aid in July (400,000 tons of rice), for the first time sent overland.

37. For example, in the spring of 2011, a period of acute distress, a spokeswoman for the Ministry of Unification could state that "decisions on large-scale aid funded by the government would be made not only on the basis of humanitarian situations in North Korea (DPRK) but also on our assessment on inter-Korean relations in general." The administration subsequently sought to tie US food aid to resumption of North-South talks. See "S. Korea remain [sic] lukewarm on food aid to DPRK," Xinhua, May 18, 2011, http://news.xinhuanet.com/english2010/world/2011-05/18/c_13881050.htm.

38. For example, "UM Opposes Large Scale Food Aid to NK," KBS World, http://world.kbs.co.kr/english/news/news_IK_detail.htm?No=75763).

39. For more on South Korean assistance to North Korea, see the blog North Korea: Witness to Transformation's four-part series from Stephan Haggard, Jaesung Ryu, and Kent Boydston: "South Korean Aid to the North I: An Accounting 1991–2015," July 20, 2015, http://blogs.piie.com/nk/?p=14284; "South Korean Aid to the North II: An Accounting, 1991–2015," July 21, 2015, http://blogs.piie.com/nk/?p=14289; "South Korean Aid to the North III: An Accounting, 1991–2015," August 12, 2015, http://blogs.piie.com/nk/?p=14365; "South Korean Aid to the North IV: An Accounting, 1991–2015," September 1, 2015, http://blogs.piie.com/nk/?p=14424.

40. At a press conference in April 2011, China's vice commerce minister, Fu Ziying, claimed that China had provided support for North Korean agriculture in the form of fertilizer and fuel but had made no explicit mention of food and specifically denied any cash assistance. See "China Released Details on Aid to North Korea," Arirang News, April 27, 2011, http://www.arirang.co.kr/News/News_View.asp?code=Ne2&nseq=115383. At the other end of the spectrum are claims of regular yearly assistance of 100,000 tons of grain, which exceeded total annual quantities shipped over the entire crisis period. See "Scale of Yearly Unconditional Aid to N. Korea Unveiled," Dong-a Ilbo, June 24, 2012, http://english.donga.com/srv/service.php3?biid=2012062508548, which cites unnamed sources. However, multiple named sources did confirm that there were large shipments made in the immediate aftermath of Kim Jong-il's death, and this is confirmed in the data. See, for example, Kim Tae-hong, "China Aids North Korea," DailyNK, January 30, 2012, http://www.dailynk.com/english/read.php?cataId=nk00100&num=8736. For a review of conflicting Chinese statements see Yan (2016).

41. The most intriguing source to emerge in this regard is the publication in Japanese of China's Secret File on Relations with North Korea (Takitachosen Chugoku Kimitsu Fairu), which was edited and translated by Satoshi Tomisaka and purportedly written largely by an official of the International Department of the Chinese Communist Party's Central Committee. Regardless of the veracity of this report, its findings comport closely both with other academic studies and with contemporaneous press accounts and Chinese statements.

42. "China Ships 10,000 Tons of Heavy Oil to North Korea," Yonhap News Agency, October 26, 2005; "North Korea, China Sign Economic Cooperation Agreement," Korean

Central News Agency, October 11, 2005; "North Korea Agrees to Open All Railways to Chinese Train Companies," Yonhap News Agency, October 25, 2005.

43. Starting on September 30, 2007, UN relief agencies, which warehouse supplies in China, were not allocated the wagons required to make aid shipments in the wake of the August floods because of the loss of eighteen hundred rail wagons in North Korea. Beginning on the weekend of October 13–14, North Korea began returning the cars and Chinese authorities began allocating them to the relief agencies on a one-for-one basis before aid finally resumed in more substantial quantities.

44. In mid-December 2007, China's Ministry of Finance announced that it was eliminating a 13 percent tax rebate on grain exports. This change in policy affected eighty-four categories of grain and included wheat, corn, rice, and soybeans. At the end of December, it went further, declaring that over the course of 2008 it would impose further export taxes ranging from 5 to 25 percent on grain exports. In early January 2009, the Ministry of Commerce announced discretionary quotas on the export of milled grain.

45. "Kim Jong Il Restores North-China Relations," DailyNK, March 3, 2008. See also USDA Foreign Agricultural Service (2012).

46. An alternative paradigm in international relations, largely from Canada, Northern Europe, and the developing world, emphasizes that "security" should be reconceptualized to focus on "human security," taking the individual rather than the state or regime as the unit of analysis (United Nations Development Program 1994; Buzan, Waever, and de Wilde 1998; Smith 2005 on North Korea; Paris 2001 for a critique).

CHAPTER FIVE

1. See Johnson, Ostry, and Subramanian (2007) for an example of the claim of the institution-enhancing impact of international trade in a non-North Korean context.

2. For example, see Moon (2008).

3. We also surveyed a control group of firms in both countries that were not conducting business in North Korea at the time: 53 in the Chinese survey and 50 in the South Korean survey. We estimate that at that time of the South Korean survey about four hundred firms were engaged in economic activities in the North outside of the Kaesong Industrial Complex (KIC), meaning that our sample constituted a significant share of the universe.

4. More recent case studies of Chinese firms investing in North Korea suggest that the basic findings from our formal survey still hold. See Marcus Noland, "Case Studies on Chinese Business in North Korea," North Korea: Witness to Transformation (blog), February 5, 2014, http://blogs.piie.com/nk/?p=12854. We discuss the continued Chinese policy of "deep integration" with the North in Chapter 7.

5. The vast majority of the enterprises in the sample doing business in North Korea were Chinese (98 percent), although around 20 percent of the control group reported being headquartered outside of China, mostly in Japan or South Korea. Forty percent of the respondents reported that their chief executive officer (CEO) spoke Korean. This share was virtually identical across firms currently doing business and those not doing business in North Korea.

6. In contrast, the "not doing business" sample included a different mix of ownership structures, with 38 percent reporting foreign ownership, mostly Japanese or South Korean, and only 28 percent accounted for as private enterprises and sole proprietorships. Interestingly, there were not many pure SOEs in either sample (5 percent in the "doing business" sample; 4 percent in the "not doing business" sample), although joint stock companies,

which frequently have government participation, accounted for about 21 percent of the first group and 26 percent of the second group.

7. For exporters, the major products were quite diversified and included construction materials (including upholstery; 13 percent), apparel and clothing (11 percent), grain and edible oils (10 percent), and chemicals and electrical equipment (8 percent each). On the import side, the product mix was much more concentrated, with aquatic products (30 percent), metal and metal products (27 percent), and wood and wood products (18 percent) accounting for almost 75 percent of the top imports from the dominant supplier.

8. We obtained a similar pattern of responses to a question asking when the respondent established a relationship with its most significant counterparty. Most of these relationships were established after 2004.

9. The firms included public companies, private enterprises, and individual proprietorships. The majority (58 percent) reported access to outside finance via commercial banks, but 7 percent identified public-sector financial institutions as their primary funding source. The role of the public sector, however, was probably larger than these answers would suggest because the government offered a loan guarantee program for KIC entrants that went through commercial banks; we return to this point later.

10. The remaining responses were equally divided among selling to the North Korean market, exporting to third-country markets, or exploiting natural resources.

11. For the sample as a whole, a plurality of the firms were engaged directly in manufacturing (47 percent) followed by trade (33 percent), agriculture, forest, and fisheries (13 percent), and other activities.

12. The number of firms that reported the KIC as their main location of business (26 percent) exceeded the number of firms answering that they "operated a factory" in the KIC (17%). Given that, to our knowledge, there were no other economic activities at Kaesong outside of the zone, we interpreted the 26 percent in the sample as all operating in the KIC.

13. Also of interest is what did *not* appear to matter. Variables relating to sources of funding were statistically uncorrelated with entry. Neither the provincial location of the firms' headquarters nor having headquarters in a border town significantly correlated with entry. Nor did having a chief executive officer (CEO) who spoke Korean. These characteristics—proximity and language skills—might be associated with being more informed about the North Korean business environment or being able to make more nuanced risk assessments, yet they inclined firms neither toward nor away from doing business. With respect to business activity, service providers were deterred from entry. This could be because of North Korean regulations that create explicit entry barriers, but it could also be because service activities require a local presence that is riskier than merchandise trade transactions.

14. Among the variables that appeared uncorrelated with the decision to enter the North Korean market or that were correlated but not robustly so in a multivariate context, as reported by Haggard and Noland (2012a), were legal status (listed, unlisted, sole proprietorship, foreign); sources of private funding; major product revenue share; location of headquarters other than Seoul; and the ability of the CEO to speak languages other than Korean and Chinese.

15. Among those who did report assistance, assistance took the form of trade preferences (23 percent), special financing (8 percent), export-import insurance (4 percent), and investment guarantees (3 percent).

16. An interesting finding in the South Korean sample was that the CEO's ability to speak Chinese was a significant correlate of entry, in part because most of the POC trade runs through China. As shown in Table 5.3, Chinese networks play some introductory role.

17. Among the control groups of Chinese and South Korean firms not doing business in North Korea, by far the most frequently cited reason was lack of familiarity with the country itself (55 percent agreed or strongly agreed in the China survey; 58 percent in the South Korea survey) or with the North Korean market (87 percent agreed or strongly agreed in the China survey; 48 percent in the South Korea survey). In the China survey, 57 percent cited the weakness of the North Korean economy; 51 percent, the poor reputation of DPRK policies; and 45 percent, the poor reputation of North Korean firms. These concerns were more muted in the South Korea survey: 34 percent cited the weakness of the North Korean economy; 40 percent, the poor reputation of North Korea's policies; and 38 percent, the poor reputation of North Korean firms.

18. Since the survey was conducted, the ban on domestic use of cell phones has been lifted, with the Egyptian firm Orascom introducing domestic cellular service through most of the country (Noland 2009). Whether foreign firms' needs for international connections have been fully addressed by subsequent relaxations is unknown. China has made cross-border use of cell phones a negotiating demand in establishing the rules for China-oriented SEZs.

19. Problems with arbitrary and capricious implementation of regulations paralleled the responses reported by North Korean market participants in refugee surveys (Haggard and Noland 2011a).

20. Relative to firms outside the zone, they quite naturally did not regard infrastructure quality as much of an issue. But even on this question, 70 percent viewed it as a problem. Again, this could be interpreted as a motivation to avoid North Korean risk by locating in the KIC.

21. Multiple responses for dispute resolution modalities were permitted. If the modality figures are calculated as a share of total responses (not number of enterprises), the exporter results are as follows: Chinese government officials (13 percent), other Chinese firms or business associations (12 percent), and Chinese courts (11 percent). For importers, the results are as follows: private negotiation (23 percent), North Korean local officials (12 percent), and Chinese officials (9 percent). For investors, the results are as follows: private negotiation (21 percent), local North Korean officials (18 percent), and Chinese officials (13 percent). In no case did the North Korean court system's share of responses reach 10 percent.

22. Investors who experienced disputes showed a greater proclivity to pursue resolution of future disputes through appeals to local officials (32 percent for those experiencing disputes versus 19 percent for those not) and provincial officials (25 percent versus 7 percent).

23. For importers, the most frequently cited reason for dispute was defective goods (43 percent), followed by declining quality (33 percent) and late shipments (14 percent).

24. For example, the percentages of respondents reporting disputes with non–North Korean counterparties were 14 percent for arm's-length exporters and 5 percent for arm's-length importers. A possible reason for the lower dispute rates for KIC firms is the frequency of contact with a counterparty. Nearly all of the KIC firms indicated that they communicated with their primary counterparty on a daily basis, whereas for a handful of non-KIC firms communication was as infrequent as once a year.

25. Among importers, for example, 57 percent reported that they were "not satisfied at all," 33 percent were "not satisfied," and only 10 percent were "basically satisfied."

26. The more frequent use of US dollars in import trade may reflect the preferences of sellers who wanted to be paid in home or conveniently usable currencies. It could also reflect the distinctive preferences of North Korean SOEs (more highly represented among Chinese importers' counterparties) and/or the North Korean government, which may have wanted to earn convertible currency that did not have to be spent in China.

27. These results parallel those obtained in the China survey, where less than 5 percent of the firms reported extending credit to their partners, with most of these (60 percent) involving Chinese SOEs extending loans to their North Korean SOE counterparties.

28. It could be that having access to state support made firms more relaxed about payment terms, or it could be that counterparties, acknowledging state backing, were more relaxed about eventual payment. Intriguingly, transactions involving firms that had access to South Korean dispute resolution employed relatively stricter terms. It is worth noting what was not robustly correlated with payment terms: firm size, CEO ability to speak Chinese, introduction networks, duration of the relationship, views on bribery, and perceptions of the business environment.

CHAPTER SIX

1. We now have numerous accounts of the progress and lack of progress in the Six Party Talks. Several stand out for the thoroughness of their reporting including Sigal (2005), Funabashi (2007), Pritchard (2007), Mazarr (2007), Chinoy (2008), Bechtol (2010), and Pollack (2011).

2. Following the onset of the crisis, the United States clearly had reason to doubt North Korean commitments under the Agreed Framework, which, however, also called for a process of normalization of relations with the United States that had made limited progress during the Clinton administration.

3. Similarly, admission into international financial institutions (IFIs) does not necessarily ensure lending because of the conditional nature of IFI programs. The problem with these inducements is even more pronounced if we believe that important actors in North Korea simply seek delay or are indifferent or even hostile to increased trade, investment, or involvement with IFIs in the first place.

4. On the eve of Kim Dae-jung's visit to Washington, Powell told reporters that the Bush administration would build on the Clinton momentum regarding North Korea. The White House publicly rebuked Powell, who later admitted that he had leaned "too forward in my skis." The first statement of a willingness to engage, however vague and hedged, came following the completion of the policy review. See George Bush, "Statement by the President," June 13, 2001, http://georgewbush-whitehouse.archives.gov/news/releases/2001/06/20010611-4.html.

5. These remarks were made at the Asia Society Annual Dinner, June 10, 2002, http://asiasociety.org/policy-politics/colin-powell-remarks-asia-society-annual-dinner-2002.

6. In the words of Manyin and Jun (2003, 17) the administration "gave conflicting signals about whether it would continue donating food aid to North Korea and, if so, how much and whether it should be conditioned on North Korean actions in the humanitarian and/or security areas."

7. Most notable in this regard was the Nuclear Posture Review submitted to Congress in December 2001, to which the North Koreans responded strongly, and the National Strategy to Combat Weapons of Mass Destruction issued in December 2002.

8. Particularly John Bolton, then undersecretary of state for arms control and international security. See John Bolton, "Beyond the Axis of Evil: Additional Threats from Weapons of Mass Destruction," May 6, 2001, Heritage Foundation, http://www.heritage.org/Research/Lecture/Beyond-the-Axis-of-Evil. Also see his speech, "North Korea: A Shared

Challenge to the U.S. and ROK," before the Korean-American Association, Seoul, August 29, 2002, https://2001-2009.state.gov/t/us/rm/13219.htm.

9. See Korean Central News Agency, "Spokesman of DPRK Foreign Ministry on Bush's Statement on Resuming Negotiations with DPRK," June 21, 2001, http://www.kcna.co.jp/index-e.htm; and "KCNA on U.S.-Proposed Resumption of DPRK-U.S. Negotiations," June 28, 2001, http://www.kcna.co.jp/index-e.htm.

10. Moreover, such transfers took place well before the Bush administration came to office. On the debate over the extent of the program, see Hersh (2003); the exchange between Harrison (2005a, 2005b) and Reiss, Gallucci et al. (2005); and Zhang (2009). In his 2006 memoir, Pervez Musharraf states that a 1996 deal included "nearly two dozen P-1 and P-2 centrifuges" (296), as well as specialized equipment such as a flowmeter and oils and training at Pakistani facilities. Other intelligence in the public domain includes purchases of equipment, including aluminum tubes, that could have been used in a HEU program as well as traces of HEU on documents subsequently submitted to the United States in 2008 (Zhang 2009).

11. Did the North Koreans admit to having a HEU program, only claim the right to have one, or deny that they had one altogether? And even if they did deny having a HEU program, was an opportunity missed because of tight instructions that prohibited the United States from signaling a willingness to negotiate? Jannuzi (2003) reports a North Korean version of the Kelly visit and Pyongyang's expectation of an offer to negotiate. See also Struck (2002) and Pritchard (2007, 34–40).

12. Interestingly, this proposal made explicit reference to the economic reforms of 2002 as a sign of the regime's good intent. See "Foreign Ministry Statement at Conclusion of Non-Aggression Treaty Between DPRK and U.S. Called For," Korean Central News Agency, October 25, 2002, http://www.kcna.co.jp/index-e.htm.

13. This set of measures came to be called the Illicit Activities Initiative. See Asher (2007) and particularly Zarate (2013, 219–237) for an overview of the program.

14. The core authority for undertaking these actions was Section 311 of the USA PATRIOT Act. See "Fact Sheet: Overview of Section 311 of the USA Patriot Act," http://www.treasury.gov/press-center/press-releases/Pages/tg1056.aspx.

15. The *So San* had been tracked by the United States; when it was off the coast of Yemen, the United States sought cooperation from Spain in boarding the ship and inspecting it. Scud missile parts were found hidden under cement, but the ship was released when Yemen, a US ally in the war on terror, acknowledged that it was the purchaser.

16. An early success was the Australian interdiction of the *Pong Su*, carrying an estimated $50 million worth of heroin. See Michael Richardson, "Crimes Under Flags of Convenience," *Yale Global*, May 19, 2003, http://yaleglobal.yale.edu/content/crimes-under-flags-convenience.

17. The release of Rumsfeld's 2011 memoir was accompanied by the launch of a website, *Rumsfeld's Rules*, http://www.rumsfeld.com/, which has a searchable database of documents.

18. Donald Rumsfeld to Richard Cheney, Colin Powell, George Tenet, Spencer Abraham, and Condoleezza Rice, "Remaining Firm on North Korea," December 26, 2002, *Rumsfeld's Rules*, http://www.rumsfeld.com/.

19. On China's early approach to the talks, see Scobell (2003), Liu (2003), International Crisis Group (2004), Wu (2005); in particular see Funabashi (2007, 300–346) and Acuto (2012).

20. Although China took a similarly critical position during the first nuclear crisis with respect to the utility of sanctions, it showed increasing exasperation with North Korea as the crisis escalated in the spring of 1994. China acquiesced to strong UN Security Council statements and sought to exercise influence bilaterally to convince North Korea to stand down (Lee 1996; Wit, Poneman, and Galucci 2004, 196–199, 209; Kim 2007; Oberdorfer and Carlin 2014, 251–252).

21. "China's Li Pledges to Help Flood-Stricken North Korea," *Japan Economic Newswire*, July 9, 1996.

22. In June, Kim Yong-nam, a member of the Politburo and chairman of the Supreme People's Assembly, visited Beijing. In October, Chinese foreign minister Tang Jiaxuan reciprocated by visiting Pyongyang, setting the stage for the first summit: Kim Jong-il's visit of May 2000. Overall, during the 1990s Chinese officials made nine official visits to North Korea; North Korea made only seven to China. In the 2000s, in contrast, these numbers rose to thirty-three and twenty-seven, respectively (Reilly 2014b, 4).

23. "President Jiang Holds Talks with Visiting North Korean Leader," *Xinhua*, June 1, 2000.

24. "Kim Jong-il said to order development of Sinuiju special economic zone," *Joongang Ilbo*, January 31, 2001.

25. The "third basket" emphasized human rights, including freedom of emigration and reunification of families, cultural exchanges, and freedom of the press. Derided as a sop by the Soviets that they had no intention of honoring, the third basket played an embarrassing role as groups formed in Eastern Europe to pursue its premises (Kim Dae-jung, personal communication, July 15, 2008).

26. The main forums included so-called interministerial talks, interministerial defense talks (largely moribund), economic talks that addressed aid and cooperation projects, and working-level talks on particular projects such as Kaesong, rail and road links, Imjin River flood control, and maritime agreements.

27. The restart of negotiations was facilitated by promises of generous economic assistance, including commitments to provide energy in the form of electric power, the deepening of commercial relations, and expansion of government-to-government projects. These commitments can be seen in the agreement reached following the 10th meeting of the Economic Cooperation Committee described in Rhee (2005), which also contains quite frank assessments of the continuing limits on commercial relations.

28. Again, the Rumsfeld papers provide interesting insight. In a memo with wide distribution among the top leadership, NSC advisor Condoleezza Rice outlines a broad strategy for dealing with North Korea. Her draft says, "We have proposed multilateral talks to North Korea and remain prepared to engage in such talks. In this multilateral format, we are prepared to discuss all issues, including DPRK interest in security assurances." Rumsfeld responds by striking out the second sentence. Even Rice's inducements are couched in vague terms: "Should North Korea verifiably eliminate its nuclear weapons program . . . it will find that the international community, including the United States, is prepared to respond." Condoleezza Rice to Vice President Richard Cheney et al., "North Korea Policy Points," March 4, 2003, *Rumsfeld's Rules*, http://library.rumsfeld.com/doclib/sp/2628/2003-03-04%20from%20Condoleezza%20Rice%20re%20North%20Korea%20Policy%20Points.pdf.

29. Ser Myo-ja, "North Korea Details Its Plan to End Crisis," *Joongang Daily,* August 28, 2003, http://joongangdaily.joins.com/article/view.asp?aid=2025739.

30. The North Koreans greeted the new administration with a statement of their intent to withdraw from the Six Party Talks declaring their possession of nuclear weapons (February 10) followed by an offer to negotiate "disarmament" with the United States "on an equal footing" (March 31).

31. The fourth round of talks consisted of two phases, July 26–August 7 and September 13–19, 2005.

32. The statement noted that the benefits promised to North Korea "will only accrue in the context of the denuclearization of the Korean Peninsula," the meaning of which was outlined in detail: "that the DPRK would return, at an early date, to the NPT and come into full compliance with IAEA safeguards, including by taking all steps that may be deemed necessary to verify the correctness and completeness of the DPRK's declarations of nuclear materials and activities." See "Assistant Secretary of State Christopher R. Hill's Statement at the Closing Plenary of the Fourth Round of the Six-Party Talks," US Department of State, *Archive*, September 19, 2005, http://2001-2009.state.gov/r/pa/prs/ps/2005/53499.htm.

33. The DPRK issued its own poison pill by threatening that the United States "should not even dream of the issue of the DPRK's dismantlement of its nuclear deterrent before providing LWRs." See"Spokesman for DPRK Foreign Ministry on Six-Party Talks," Korean Central News Agency, September 20, 2005, http://www.kcna.co.jp/index-e.htm.

34. Executive Order 13224 of September 2001 and Title III of the USA PATRIOT Act were crucial statutory starting points. These were followed by Executive Order 13382 of June 2005, which authorized seizure of any US assets of WMD proliferators and their supporters, named three North Korean entities, and authorized executive agencies to list others as warranted. On October 21, 2005, the US Treasury Department added eight North Korean entities to the sanctions list, and on April 6, 2006, it issued a provision prohibiting any US person from "owning, leasing, operating or insuring any vessel flagged by North Korea." See National Committee on North Korea (2009).

35. "N. Korean Offers Nuclear Talks Deal," *BBC News*, April 13, 2006, http://news.bbc.co.uk/2/hi/asia-pacific/4905308.stm.

36. "Initial Actions for the Implementation of the Joint Statement," February 13, 2007, Ministry of Foreign Affairs of Japan, http://www.mofa.go.jp/region/asia-paci/n_korea/6party/action0702.html, and "Second-Phase Actions for the Implementation of the September 2005 Joint Statement," October 3, 2007, U.S. Department of State, *Archive*, https://2001-2009.state.gov/r/pa/prs/ps/2007/oct/93217.htm.

37. The appeal gave cover to the United States's very large-scale and rapidly disbursing aid program of 500,000 tons over the course of one year beginning in June 2008; 400,000 tons would be channeled through the WFP, with 100,000 tons going through a consortium of NGOs.

38. The North Koreans would subsequently modulate their disablement efforts, complaining about the pace at which the fuel oil was being delivered. The HFO shipments of 1 million tons or equivalent were to be divided equally by the five parties: 200,000 each. Over the next fourteen months, HFO shipments were slowed in part because of disagreements among the parties and in part because of logistical issues. See Haggard and Noland (2011b, app. 3) for information on the HFO delivery by the five parties and their timing. By March 2009, the DPRK had received 500,000 tons of oil and equipment and 245,110 tons of fuel-equivalent assistance (Manyin and Nikitin 2010).

39. Following the July 12 joint communiqué, the United States circulated a very tough draft verification protocol that included full access to all materials and all sites regardless

of whether or not included in the North's declaration. This, in effect, was the equivalent of the IAEA special inspections protocol. A sense of the intense political pressure on the administration's policy and a clear statement of the use of verification to address it can be found in Condoleezza Rice's "Remarks at Heritage Foundation on U.S. Policy in Asia," June 18, 2008, http://www.america.gov/st/texttransenglish/2008/June/20080619140227e aifaso.8862574.html.

40. "Foreign Ministry's Spokesman on DPRK's Decision to Suspend Activities to Disable Nuclear Facilities," Korean Central News Agency, August 26, 2008, http://www.kcna .co.jp/index-e.htm.

41. The new agreement, critical components of which were transmitted only in verbal form, allowed "sampling and other forensic measures" at the three declared sites at Yongbyon—the reactor, the reprocessing plant, and the fuel fabrication plant—and access to undeclared sites but only by mutual consent.

42. Donald Rumsfeld to George W. Bush, "Declaratory Policy and the Nuclear Programs of North Korea and Iran," October 5, 2006, *Rumsfeld's Rules*, http://www.rumsfeld .com/.

CHAPTER SEVEN

1. In an interview with *New York Times* correspondent Thomas Friedman, the approach was subsequently dubbed "the Obama Doctrine." See Thomas Friedman, "Iran and the Obama Doctrine," *New York Times*, April 2, 2015.

2. North Korea contests the legal status of the islands, arguing that both the drawing of the NLL and the inclusion of the islands to the south of it were unilateral actions by the UN Command. See International Crisis Group (2011).

3. According to Sigal, these problems were compounded by the failure of the Obama administration to engage Pyongyang with sufficient alacrity and by the "crime and punishment" strategy of imposing sanctions in the wake of the missile test of April. Sigal (2009) notes open references by Secretary Clinton to the succession, labeling North Korea a "tyranny," and appointing a special envoy, Stephen Bosworth, who concurrently held a full-time position outside government.

4. In addition to the domestic political constraints of negotiating a peace regime with a de facto nuclear North Korea, bilateral negotiations for a peace regime would have sidelined South Korea's role in the process.

5. See Stephen Bosworth, "Remarks at the Korea Society Annual Dinner, Washington, DC, June 9, 2009; also see Hillary Rodham Clinton, "Statement before the Senate Foreign Relations Committee," January 13, 2009, http://www.state.gov/secretary/ rm/2009a/01/115196.htm, and "Secretary Clinton's Interview with Asahi Shimbun in Tokyo," February 17, 2009, http://iipdigital.usembassy.gov/st/english/texttrans/2009/02/ 20090219163832eaifaso.5075342.html#axzz4JnIyvxhX. And see Sigal (2016).

6. "DPRK Foreign Ministry's Spokesman Dismisses U.S. Wrong Assertion," Korean Central News Agency, January 13, 2009 (and as amended following Hillary Clinton's nomination hearings on January 17, 2009), http://www.kcna.co.jp/index-e.htm. North Korea's commitment to denuclearization was signaled only very indirectly through Chinese sources following the visit of Wang Jiarui, chief of the International Liaison Department of the Chinese Communist Party (CCP) to Pyongyang in January 2009. See "Top DPRK Leader Kim Jong-il Meets with Visiting CPA Official, *Xinhua*, January 23, 2008, http://news.xinhuanet .com/english/2009-01/23/content_10707546.htm.

7. Paragraph 2 "Demands that the DPRK not conduct any further nuclear test or launch of a ballistic missile." In UNSCRs 1874 and 2094, the ambiguity was removed by prohibiting launches using "ballistic missile technologies."

8. "DPRK Foreign Ministry Vigorously Refutes UNSC's 'Presidential Statement,' Korean Central News Agency, April 14, 2009, http://www.kcna.co.jp/index-e.htm.

9. For an overview of China's bilateral response to the test, see Kenji Minemura, "N. Korea Squirms after China Raps Test," *Asahi Shinbun*, February 24, 2010, http://www.asahi.com/english/TKY201002230434.html.

10. The resolution also established a new process for overseeing the sanctions effort by creating the Independent Panel of Experts to oversee the implementation of both UNSCR 1718 and UNSCR 1874, monitor efforts on the part of member states, and provide more independent recommendations to the UN Security Council than could be provided by the Intergovernmental Sanctions Committee. See UN Independent Panel of Experts (2010, 2012, 2013, 2014, 2015, 2016).

11. The resolution authorized members to inspect vessels on the high seas or to escort them to port if there were reasonable grounds to believe that they were carrying prohibited cargo. It also precluded the provision of bunkering services to any ship suspected of prohibited trade, placing an additional constraint on any suspect ship.

12. An important loophole is that interdiction must have the consent of the country under which the vessel is flagged. Acting under Article 41 (as opposed to Article 42) of Chapter VII, UNSCR 1874, does not authorize the use of force.

13. The ability to attach financial transactions was also a more flexible instrument than the designation of particular firms because of the ability of North Korea to proliferate shell companies not technically designated by the UN Sanctions committee.

14. Financial Crimes Enforcement Network Advisory, "North Korean Government Agencies' and Front Companies' Involvement in Illicit Financial Activities," FIN-2009-A002, June 18, 2009, Washington, DC.

15. "North Korea is Warned by Gates on Testing," *New York Times*, May 29, 2009.

16. Assistant Secretary of State Kurt M. Campbell, "Press Availability in Beijing, China," October 14, 2009, U.S. Department of State, Washington, DC.

17. According to Lee Myung-bak's memoir, the North Koreans asked for 100,000 tons of corn, 400,000 tons of rice, 300,000 tons of fertilizer, $100 million worth of asphalt, and $10 billion to capitalize a North Korean development bank. See Choe Sang-hun, "North Korea Sought Talks and Attached a Hefty Price Tag, South's Ex-Leader Says," *New York Times*, January 29, 2005, http://www.nytimes.com/2015/01/30/world/asia/north-korea-sought-talks-and-attached-a-hefty-price-tag-souths-ex-leader-says.html.

18. In an early formulation of the proposal by the Foreign Ministry, for example, North Korea allowed that talks on a peace regime may be held "either at a separate forum as laid down in the September 19 Joint Statement or in the framework of the six-party talks for the denuclearization of the Korean Peninsula like the DPRK-US talks now under way." See "DPRK Proposes to Start of Peace Talks," Korean Central News Agency, January 11, 2010, http://www.kcna.co.jp/index-e.htm. After a meeting with the Chinese leadership in October 2009, Kim Jong-il stated, "We expressed our readiness to hold multilateral talks, depending on the outcome of the DPRK-U.S. talks. The six-party talks are also included in the multilateral talks." This suggests both the importance of bilateral talks and the fact that multilateral talks must not be limited to the Six Party Talks. See "Kim Jong-il Visits Wen Jiabao at State Guest House," Korean Central News Agency, October 5, 2009, http://www.kcna.co.jp/index-e.htm.

19. "Lee Myung-bak's 'Policy Speech' under Fire," *Korean Central News Agency*, July 13, 2008, http://www.kcna.co.jp/index-e.htm.

20. The General Reconnaissance Bureau integrated a number of intelligence agencies and operational units under the Workers' Party—the Operations Department, the Overseas Intelligence Investigation Department (Office 35), and the Reconnaissance Bureau of the Ministry of the People's Armed Services. It is assumed that the General Reconnaissance Bureau had responsibility for the sinking of the *Cheonan* and that Kim Jong-il visited the unit shortly after the incident.

21. The NLL was drawn unilaterally by the United Nations Command following failure to agree on a maritime border during the armistice negotiations. The NLL had effectively served as the de facto maritime boundary in the West Sea for decades, but North Korea began to contest it in the 1970s for a combination of strategic and economic reasons. Armed clashes occurred around the NLL in 1999, 2002, and 2004.

22. The sanctions regime can be found in Ministry of Unification, "Announcement of Measures Against North Korea," May, 24, 2010, http://nautilus.org/wp-content/uploads/2011/12/2010MOU.pdf.

23. New investments in the country, including into Kaesong, were also proscribed, and the number of South Korean personnel in the zone was reduced. The sanctions also prohibited North Korean ships from entering South Korean waters and banned all South Korean visits to the North outside of the Kaesong and Mt. Kumgang projects.

24. These included a wide-ranging defense reform plan, the declaration of a new military doctrine of "proactive deterrence"—suggesting disproportionate responses to provocations—the development of longer-run ballistic missiles, and the creation of a Northwest Islands Command and a corresponding military buildup on the islands.

25. Interestingly, Siegfried Hecker (2010) held this view.

26. See Marcus Noland, "Slave to the Blog: Updates Galore!" *North Korea: Witness to Transformation* (blog), February 24, 2011, http://blogs.piie.com/nk/?p=463; Stephan Haggard, "Food Backgrounder," *North Korea: Witness to Transformation* (blog), March 15, 2011, http://blogs.piie.com/nk/?p=657; Stephan Haggard and Marcus Noland, "Blog Post on *38 North*: 'Logic and Illogic of Food Aid,'" *North Korea: Witness to Transformation* (blog), April 13, 2011, http://blogs.piie.com/nk/?p=870; Marcus Noland and Stephan Haggard, "Parsing the WFP/FAO Report," *North Korea: Witness to Transformation* (blog), April 5, 2011, http://blogs.piie.com/nk/?p=826.

27. "DPRK Foreign Ministry Spokesman on Result of DPRK-U.S. Talks," *Korean Central News Agency*, February 29, 2012, http://www.kcna.co.jp/index-e.htm. Also see Victoria Nuland, U.S.-DPRK Bilateral Discussions, press statement, February 29, 2012, http://www.state.gov/r/pa/prs/ps/2012/02/184869.htm.

28. The North Korean statement made explicit mention of the fact that this interim step was a prelude to resumption of the multilateral talks in which the lifting of sanctions, a peace regime, and even the provision of LWRs would be on the table. The American statement was silent on the resumption of talks and only noted that sanctions were not targeted at the welfare of the North Korean people.

29. Pyongyang claimed that the Leap Day Deal made no explicit mention of satellite launches and that North Korea had the right to peaceful use of outer space as a signatory to the Outer Space Treaty. However, UNSC Resolution 1874 was quite explicit in "deciding," with the force of international law, "that the DPRK shall suspend all activities related to its ballistic missile programme" and "that the DPRK not conduct any further nuclear

test or any launch using ballistic missile technology." US negotiators, concerned about intelligence regarding a possible launch, claimed that they had made it clear to their North Korean counterparts that the test of a satellite would be seen as a violation of the agreement.

30. "Statement by the President of the Security Council," S/PRST/2012/13, UN Security Council, April 16, 2012, http://www.mofa.go.jp/region/asia-paci/n_korea/missile_12/pdfs/state_120416.pdf.

31. In its condolence message, China stated its expectation that North Korea "will remain united as one with the leadership of the Workers' Party of Korea (WPK) and comrade Kim Jong Un." When condolences were expressed at the DPRK embassy, virtually the entire top Chinese leadership was present: Hu Jintao, president; Xi Jinping, vice president; Wu Bangguo, chairman of the Standing Committee of the National People's Congress, Li Changchun, propaganda chief; Guo Boxiong, vice chairman of the Central Military Commission; Yang Jiechi, foreign minister; and Wang Jiarui, head of the CPC International Department. Wen Jiabao, Jia Qinglin, Li Keqiang, He Guoqiang, and Zhou Yongkang visited the embassy the next day.

32. Editorials reflecting the official position—in some cases differing in their Chinese and English versions—emphasized that China must signal its intention to protect North Korea's independence, not meddle in its internal affairs, and take a strong stance against instability or "upheaval" (Cathcart 2012, 23–26).

33. In an important essay on China's aid relationship with the DPRK by a leading expert with high-level access, Fang He (2013) claimed that China gave unconditional aid to the new regime in 2012 and the first half of 2013 totaling 600 million renminbi (approximately $100 million), which in his view was an unprecedented amount.

34. The resolution expanded travel bans and asset freezes to four additional individuals and six additional entities; urged vigilance vis-à-vis the activities of North Korean officials abroad; including bulk cash transactions; and promised clarification of protocols for inspecting ships if the flag country or the DPRK refuses permission.

35. "DPRK NDC Issues Statement Refuting UNSC Resolution," Korean Central News Agency, January 24, 2013, which simply cites the National Defence Commission (NDC) statement in full.

36. "S. Korean Authorities Accused of Fabricating UN 'Resolution' with Foreign Forces," Korean Central News Agency, January 25, 2013, http://www.kcna.co.jp/index-e.htm, reproducing a statement from the Committee for the Peaceful Reunification of Korea.

37. Although it established for the first time a common definition of the term, the list was shortened at Chinese insistence and had in any case proven leaky, as we saw in Chapter 3. The common list, consisting only of jewelry, yachts, luxury autos, and racing cars, was far shorter than individual lists that had been produced by Australia, the European Union, Japan, or even Russia.

38. See Stephan Haggard, "Financial Sanctions: The Devil in the Details," *North Korea: Witness to Transformation* (blog), March 12, 2013, http://blogs.piie.com/nk/?p=9679.

39. Key Resolve is a computer-assisted simulation exercise that ran from March 11 to March 21, 2013. Foal Eagle consists of combined field-training exercises involving approximately 10,000 US and 200,000 South Korean troops.

40. Adam Entous and Julian E. Barnes, "U.S. Dials Back on Korean Show of Force," *Wall Street Journal*, April 3, 2013.

41. "DPRK FM Blasts UN for Taking Issue with DPRK over Its Justifiable Rocket Launching Drills," Korean Central News Agency, March 30, 2014, http://www.kcna

.co.jp/index-e.htm; "WPK's Line on Simultaneously Carrying On Economic Construction, Building of Nuclear Forces Is Justifiable," Korean Central News Agency, April 3, 2014, http://www.kcna.co.jp/index-e.htm.

42. The first of these offers, and one of the more complete in its justification, was made in a statement issued by the NDC in June 2013. See "DPRK Proposes Official Talks with U.S.," Korean Central News Agency, June 16, 2013, http://www.kcna.co.jp/index-e.htm. By early 2014, the stance of the regime had hardened significantly, with virtual rejection of denuclearization and threats to continue testing both nuclear weapons and missiles: "NDC of DPRK Clarifies Stand on U.S. Hostile Policy Towards It," Korean Central News Agency, March 14, 2014, http://www.kcna.co.jp/index-e.htm.

43. Stephan Haggard, "More New Year's Initiatives," *Witness to Transformation* (blog), January 13, 2015, http://blogs.piie.com/nk/?p=13772.

44. See for example "Letter dated 19 October 2015 from the Permanent Representative of the DPRK to the United Nations Addressed to the President of the Security Council," S/201/799. UN Security Council, October 19, 2015. Sigal (2016) dissects these proposals.

45. Yi Yong-in and Choi Hyun-june, "U.S. Six Party Talks Envoy Gives Strong Message on Dialogue with North Korea," *Hankyoreh*, October 30, 2014; Anna Fifield, "U.S. and North Korea Have Been Secretly Having 'Talks about Talks,'" *Washington Post*, February 2, 2015.

46. "CPRK [Committee for the Peaceful Unification of Korea] Special Statement Proposes Talks between Authorities of North, South." Korean Central News Agency, June 6, 2013, http://www.kcna.co.jp/index-e.htm.

47. Talks had been on and off until August 7, when the Ministry of Unification (MOU) authorized payment of insurance compensation to 109 firms in the complex totaling more than $250 million. Within a week, the North had called for a resumption of talks and reached an agreement addressing Southern concerns about the zone.

48. "NDC of DPRK Advances Crucial Proposals to S. Korean Authorities," Korean Central News Agency, January 16, 2014, http://www.kcna.co.jp/index-e.htm.

49. "Pyongyang slams South Korean president's reunification speech" *South China Post*, April 12, 2014, http://www.scmp.com/news/asia/article/1478279/n-korea-blasts-souths-reunification-offer-daydream-psychopath; "NDC of DPRK Sends Special Proposal to S. Korean Authorities," *South China Post*, June 30, 2014.

50. Stephan Haggard, "Tensions Update IV: The Agreement," *North Korea: Witness to Transformation* (blog), August 24, 2015, http://blogs.piie.com/nk/?p=14422.

CHAPTER EIGHT

1. These developments have a gender dimension as well. Women have been disproportionately shed from state-affiliated employment and thrust into a market environment characterized by weak institutions and corruption. Among the most recent cohort of refugees to leave North Korea surveyed by Haggard and Noland (2011a), 95 percent of female traders report paying bribes to avoid the penal system. In short, the increasingly male-dominated state preys on the increasingly female-dominated market.

2. See Stephan Haggard, "The Pyongyang Illusion," *North Korea: Witness to Transformation* (blog), November 5, 2011, http://blogs.piie.com/nk/?p=463. See also Collins (2016).

3. The following draws on Haggard and Noland (2007a, chap. 7).

4. For more on the effect of commodity prices on North Korea–China trade, see Kevin Stahler, "North Korea-China Trade Update: Coal Retreats, Textiles Surge," *North Korea: Witness to Transformation* (blog), October 27, 2014, http://blogs.piie.com/nk/?p=13578.

5. Most of these planned venues are quite small—on the order of four square kilometers or less—making them more like "bonded warehouses" than SEZs as commonly understood. See Stephan Haggard and Kent Boydston, "Slave to the Blog: Foreign Investment Edition," *North Korea: Witness to Transformation* (blog), June 10, 2015, http://blogs.piie .com/nk/?p=14178.

6. Indeed, if there were "leakage" of finished products intended for export out of the SEZs and into the local market, enterprises outside of SEZs operating under more onerous rules might rightly regard it as a competitive threat and demand that SEZs be shuttered.

7. In other cases, these sanctions addressed concerns ranging from human rights to particular North Korean actions, such as the sinking of the *Cheonan* in the case of South Korea's May 24 sanctions.

8. These sanctions have also been aimed at nonmilitary illicit activities of various sorts, as described in Chapter 3, including counterfeiting, smuggling, drug trafficking, insurance fraud, and the like. We argue that the share of North Korean trade accounted for by these activities is actually declining. The expansion of commercial trade in recent years has made North Korea less dependent on criminal activities and thus less vulnerable to their disruption.

9. For example, UNSCR 2094 increased the number of individuals and entities subject to travel bans and asset seizures, urged member states to prohibit financial flows that might be associated with nuclear and missile programs, and urged denial of port or overflight rights to ships and airplanes believed to be involved in military programs or evasion of sanctions.

10. See also Juliette Garside and Luke Harding, "British banker set up firm 'Used by North Korea to sell weapons,'" *The Guardian*, April 4, 2016, http://www.theguardian .com/news/2016/apr/04/panama-papers-briton-set-up-firm-allegedly-used-by-north -korea-weapons-sales.

11. For a full analysis of the sanctions, see Stephan Haggard, "The Sanctions Resolution," *North Korea: Witness to Transformation* (blog), March 3, 2016, http://blogs.piie.com/ nk/?p=14880.

12. See Stephan Haggard, "Sanctions Watch I," *North Korea: Witness to Transformation* (blog), October 24, 2016, https://piie.com/blogs/north-korea-witness-transformation/ sanctions-watch-i; and William Brown, "China's North Korea Trade Surges in August: Are sanctions busted?" *Korea Economic Institute of America* (blog), October 4, 2016, http:// blog.keia.org/2016/10/chinas-north-korea-trade-surges-in-august-are-sanctions-busted/.

13. See Laura Rozen, "Inside the Secret U.S-Iran Diplomacy that Sealed Nuke Deal," *Al Monitor*, August 11, 2015, http://www.al-monitor.com/pulse/originals/2015/08/iran -us-nuclear-khamenei-salehi-jcpoa-diplomacy.html#.

14. For more detailed analysis of US sanctions legislation and executive orders, see National Committee on North Korea, "Summary of the North Korea Sanctions and Policy Enhancement Act of 2016," February 18, 2016, http://www.ncnk.org/resources/publica tions/HR757_Summary_Final.pdf. On President Obama's executive order in the wake of this legislation, see Stephan Haggard, "Executive Order 13722," *North Korea: Witness to Transformation* (blog), March 21, 2016, http://blogs.piie.com/nk/?p=14915. On secondary sanctions, see Office of Foreign Asset Control Specially Designated Nationals

List Update, September 26, 2016, https://www.treasury.gov/resource-center/sanctions/OFAC-Enforcement/Pages/20160926.aspx.

15. See "Letter dated 4 March 2016 from the Permanent Representative of the Democratic People's Republic of Korea to the United Nations addressed to the Secretary-General," http://docbox.un.org/DocBox/docbox.nsf/GetFile?OpenAgent&DS=A/70/776&Lang=E&Type=DOC; Korean Central News Agency, "DPRK Government Denounces U.S., S. Korea Sophism about "Denuclearization of the North," *KCNA Watch*, July 7, 2016, https://kcnawatch.co/newstream/1467857429-986878332/dprk-government-denounces-u-s-s-koreas-sophism-about-denuclearization-of-north/.

16. Joining the IMF is a prerequisite for membership in the World Bank, but both are universal institutions, have relatively limited and vague requirements for membership, and do not require consensus or supermajority votes to take on new members (Feinberg 2011, 64–67). IMF membership is not a prerequisite for joining the ADB, which might thus be the appropriate starting point for North Korea.

17. Correlation with Vietnam's experience in joining the World Bank suggests that the North Koreans might expect an eventual lending program on the order of $150–250 million annually. Given South Korea's interest in revitalizing North Korea and the prospects of Japanese postcolonial payments, actual lending might be substantially larger. In the past, Japanese officials signaled that normalization could include a multiyear package of grants, low-interest-rate loans, and trade credits of as much as $10 billion, consistent with the value of Japan's 1965 settlement with South Korea appropriately adjusted for inflation and other factors.

18. For more details on Park's 2015 Eurasia Initiative, see South Korea Ministry of Unification, "EurAsia Initiative," http://www.mofa.go.kr/ENG/image/common/title/res/0707_eurasia_bro.pdf.

19. The February 2007 Joint Statement promised an initial shipment of "emergency energy assistance" in the form of 50,000 tons of heavy fuel oil (HFO) to be followed in the next phase by up to 1 million tons of HFO or its equivalent following denuclearization.

20. The most significant measure in this vein taken by the time this book was in press was the decision by the United States and South Korea to deploy the Terminal High-Altitude Area Defense system to South Korea, a decision that China vociferously opposed and which has made cooperation among China, South Korea, and the United States more difficult.

References

Aaltola, Mika. 1999. "Emergency Food Aid as a Means of Political Persuasion in the North Korean Famine," *Third World Quarterly* 20(2):371–386.

Abbott, Kenneth W., and Duncan Snidal. 1998. "Why States Act Through Formal International Organizations." *Journal of Conflict Resolution* 42(1):3–32.

Abrahamian, Andray. 2012. "A Convergence of Interests: Prospects for Rason Special Economic Zone." KEI Academic Paper Series— On Korea, February 24. http://www.keia .org/publication/convergence-interests-prospects-rason-special-economic-zone.

Abt, Felix. 2014. *A Capitalist in North Korea: My Seven Years in North Korea.* Tokyo: Tuttle Publishing.

Acharya, Amitav. 2000. *Constructing a Security Community in Southeast Asia: ASEAN and the Problem of Regional Order.* London: Routledge.

———. 2009. *Whose Ideas Matter? Agency and Power in Asian Regionalism.* Ithaca, NY: Cornell University Press.

Acuto, Michele. 2012. "Not Quite the Dragon: A 'Chinese' View on the Six Party Talks, 2002–8," *International History Review* 34(1):1–17.

Agence France Presse. 2006. "South Korea Doubles Fund for Aid to North Korea." January 18.

Aggarwal, Vinod, and Min Gyo Koo, eds. 2008. *Asia's New Institutional Architecture: Evolving Structures for Managing Trade, Financial and Security Relations.* Berlin: Springer-Verlag.

Aggarwal, Vinod, and Shujiro Urata, eds. 2006. *Bilateral Trade Agreements in the Asia-Pacific: Origins, Evolution, and Implications.* London: Routledge.

Ahmed, Faisal. 2012. "The Perils of Unearned Foreign Income: Aid, Remittances, and Government Survival," *American Political Science Review,* 106(1):146–165.

Albright, David. 2010. *Peddling Peril: How the Secret Nuclear Trade Arms America's Enemies.* New York: Free Press.

———. 2015. "North Korean Plutonium and Weapon-Grade Uranium Inventories." Institute for Science and International Security paper, October 7. http://www.isis -online.org/uploads/isis-reports/documents/North_Korean_Fissile_Material_Stocks_ Jan_30_2015_revised_Oct_5_2015-Final.pdf.

Alesina, Alberto, Ignazio Angeloni, and Federico Etro. 2005. "International Unions," *American Economic Review* 953 (June):602–615.

Allen, Susan Hannah. 2005. "The Determinants of Economic Sanctions Success and Failure," *International Interactions* 31:117–138.

———. 2008a. "Economic Sanctions and Political Constraints," *Foreign Policy Analysis* 4:255–274.

———. 2008b. "The Domestic Political Costs of Economic Sanctions," *Journal of Conflict Resolution*, 52:916–944.

Anderson, James E., and Oriana Bandera. 2006. "Traders, Cops, and Robbers," *Journal of International Economics* 70:197–215.

Anderson, James E., and Douglas Marcouiller. 2002. "Insecurity and the Pattern of Trade: An Empirical Investigation," *The Review of Economics and Statistics* 84(2):342–352.

Anderson, Penelope, and Paul Majarowitz. 2008. "Rapid Food Security Assessment North Pyongan and Chagang Provinces, Democratic People's Republic of Korea." Report prepared by Mercy Corps, World Vision, Global Resource Services, Samaritan's Purse, June 30.

Andreas, Peter. 2005. "Criminalizing Consequences of Sanctions: Embargo Busting and Its Legacy," *International Studies Quarterly*, 49:335–360.

Armstrong, Charles. 2013. *Tyranny of the Weak: North Korea and the World, 1950–1992.* Ithaca, NY: Cornell University Press.

Asahi Shimbun. 2010. "N. Korea Squirms After China Raps Test." February 24. http://www.asahi.com/english/TKY201002230434.html.

Asher, David. 2005. "NAPSNet Policy Forum 05-92A: The North Korean Criminal State, Its Ties to Organized Crime and Possibility of WMD Proliferation." November 15. http://nautilus.org/napsnet/napsnet-policy-forum/the-north-korean-criminal-state-its-ties-to-organized-crime-and-the-possibility-of-wmd-proliferation/#axzz2gUcYcPR2.

———. 2006. "Statement Before the Subcommittee on Federal Financial Management, Government Information, and International Security, Senate Homeland Security and Government Affairs Committee, US Senate." Washington, DC, April 25. http://www.hsgac.senate.gov/download/042506asher.

———. 2007. "The Impact of U.S. Policy on North Korean Illicit Activities." Statement before a joint hearing of the House Committee on Foreign Affairs Subcommittee on Terrorism, Nonproliferation, and Trade and the House Committee on Financial Services Subcommittee on Domestic and International Monetary Policy, April 18. http://www.heritage.org/research/lecture/the-impact-of-us-policy-on-north-korean-illicit-activities.

Asia Society. 2009. "North Korea Inside Out: The Case for Economic Engagement." Asia Society Center for U.S.-China Relations and University of California Institute on Global Conflict and Cooperation Task Force. http://asiasociety.org/files/pdf/North_Korea_Inside_Out.pdf.

Assistant Secretary of State Kurt M. Campbell. 2009. "Press Availability in Beijing, China, October 14, 2009." http://www.state.gov/p/eap/rls/rm/2009/10/130578.htm.

Babson, Bradley O. 2002. "Searching for the Right Side of History in Northeast Asia: Potential Role of Energy Cooperation with North Korea," Economic Research Institute for Northeast Asia Report 46 (June).

Bader, Jeff. 2012. *Obama and China's Rise.* Washington, DC: Brookings Institution Press.

Baldwin, David. 1971. "The Power of Positive Sanctions," *World Politics*, 24(1):19–38.

————. 1985. *Economic Statecraft*. Princeton, NJ: Princeton University Press.

Baldwin, Richard. 1997. "The Cause of Regionalism," *The World Economy* 20:865–888.

Barbieri, Katherine. 1996. "Economic Interdependence: A Path to Peace or a Source of Interstate Conflict?" *Journal of Peace Research*, 33(1):29–49.

————. 2002. *The Liberal Illusion: Does Trade Promote Peace?* Ann Arbor, MI: University of Michigan Press.

Bauer, John. 2009. "Unlocking Russian Interests on the Korean Peninsula," *US Army War College Quarterly Parameters* (Summer). http://www.strategicstudiesinstitute.army.mil/pubs/Parameters/Articles/09summer/bauer.pdf.

BBC News. 2006. "North Korea Offers Nuclear Talks Deal." April 13. http://news.bbc.co.uk/2/hi/asia-pacific/4905308.stm.

Beauchamp-Mustafaga, Nathan. 2013. "China and UN Security Council Resolution 2094: Is the Third Time the Charm?" *SinoNK.com*, March 11. http://sinonk.com/2013/03/11/china-and-un-security-council-resolution-2094-is-the-third-time-the-charm/.

Bechtol, Bruce. 2010. *Defiant Failed State: The North Korean Threat to International Security.* Washington, DC: Potomac Books.

Bechtol, Bruce, Paul Rexton Kan, and Robert Collins. 2010. "Criminal Sovereignty: Understanding North Korea's Illicit International Activities." Letort Paper, Strategic Studies Institute, Carlisle Barracks, PA. https://nkleadershipwatch.files.wordpress.com/2010/04/pub975.pdf.

Bennett, Bruce, and Jenner Lind. 2011. "The Collapse of North Korea: Military Missions and Requirements," *International Security* 2(3):84–119.

Berglof, Erik, Mike Burkart, Guido Friebel, and Elena Paltseva. 2008. "Widening and Deepening: Reforming the European Union," *American Economic Review: Papers & Proceedings* 98(2):133–137.

Berkofsky, Axel. 2010. *Japan-North Korea Relations: Bad and Not Getting Better.* Istituto per gli Studi di Politica Internazionale Policy Brief No. 193, July 15.

Bermudez Joseph S., Jr. 2004. "Information and the DPRK's Military and Power-Holding Elite." In *North Korean Policy Elites.* Edited by Kong Dan Oh. Alexandria, VA: Institute for Defense Analyses.

Bhagwati, Jagdish. 2008. *Termites in the Trading System: How Preferential Agreements Undermine Free Trade.* New York: Oxford University Press.

Bhatia, Shyam. 2008. *Goodbye Shahzadi: A Political Biography of Benazir Bhutto.* New Delhi: Roli Books.

Bolton, John. 2001. "Beyond the Axis of Evil: Additional Threats from Weapons of Mass Destruction." Paper presented at the Heritage Foundation, Washington, DC, May 6. http://www.heritage.org/Research/Lecture/Beyond-the-Axis-of-Evil.

————. 2002. "North Korea: A Shared Challenge to the U.S. and ROK." Remarks to the Seoul Korean-American Association, August 29.

————. 2007. *Surrender is Not an Option: Defending America at the United Nations.* New York: Threshold Editions.

Bosworth, Stephen. 2009. "Remarks to the Korea Society Annual Dinner." Washington, DC, June 9.

Bradley, Curtis, and Judith Kelly. 2008. "The Concept of International Delegation," *Law and Contemporary Problems* 71(1):1–36.

Brooks, Risa A. 2002. "Sanctions and Regime Type: What Works, and When?" *Security Studies* 11(4):1–50.

Brown, William. 2016. "Is Byungjin Working? A Look at North Korea's Money," *The Peninsula* (blog). http://blog.keia.org/2016/09/is-byungjin-working-a-look-at-north -koreas-money/.

Brownlee, Jason. 2007. "Hereditary Succession in Modern Autocracies," *World Politics* 59 (July):595–628.

Bueno de Mesquita, Bruce, Alistair Smith, Randolph Siverson, and James D. Morrow. 2003. *The Logic of Political Survival*. Cambridge, MA: MIT Press.

Bumiller, Elisabeth. 2009. "North Korea Is Warned by Gates on Testing." *New York Times*, May 29. http://www.nytimes.com/2009/05/30/world/asia/30military.html?_r=0.

Bush, George W. 2001. "Statement of the President." June 13. http://georgewbush -whitehouse.archives.gov/news/releases/2001/06/20010611-4.html.

———. 2010. *Decision Points*. New York: Broadway Books.

Buzan, Barry, Ole Wæver, and Jaap De Wilde. 1998. *Security as a New Framework for Analysis*. Boulder, CO: Lynne Reiner.

Buzo, Adrian. 1999. *The Guerilla Dynasty: Politics and Leadership in North Korea*. Boulder, CO: Westview Press.

Calder, Kent, and Min Ye. 2004. "Regionalism and Critical Junctures: Explaining the "Organization Gap" in Northeast Asia," *Journal of East Asian Studies* 4:191–226.

Campbell, Kurt. 2016. *The Pivot: The Future of American Statecraft in Asia*. New York: Twelve.

Carlin, Robert, and Joel Wit. 2006. *North Korean Reform: Politics, Economics and Security*. London: International Institute for Strategic Studies.

Caruso, Raul. 2003. "The Impact of International Economic Sanctions on Trade: An Empirical Analysis," *Peace Economics, Peace Science and Public Policy* 9(2): Article1.

Cathcart, Adam, ed. 2012a. "China and the North Korean Succession." *SinoNK.com*, January 19. http://sinonk.com/2012/01/19/china-north-korea-dossier-no-1-china-and -the-north-korean-succession/.

Cathcart, Adam. 2012b. "Translating Jang Song Taek in Beijing: A Communique Troika." *SinoNK.com*, August 18. http://sinonk.com/2012/08/18/translating-jang-song-taek -in-beijing-a-communique-troika/.

Cathcart, Adam, and Michael Madden, eds. 2012. "'A Completely Different Blueprint': North Korea's Relations with China at the End of the Kim Jong Il Era." *SinoNK. com*, August 20. http://sinonk.com/wp-content/uploads/2012/08/sinonk-dossier -no-3-chinanorth-korean-relations-at-the-end-of-kim-jong-il-era.pdf.

Cavazos, Roger, Peter Hayes, and David von Hippel. 2013. "Technical Bulletin #59 on Prohibition of Dual Use Exports to North Korea." *NAPSNet* special report, September 26. http://us4.campaign-archive2.com/?u=0de7e0e84dc3aff619f936a70&id=3e07e153 6b&e=1e6a801eb5.

Center for Advanced Defense Analysis, 2016. *In China's Shadow: Exposing North Korean Overseas Networks*. Seoul: Asan Institute for Policy Studies.

Central Bureau of Statistics (North Korea). 2002. "Korea, North Nutrition Assessment 2002." http://ghdx.healthdata.org/organizations/central-bureau-statistics-north-korea.

———. 2005. "Data Set Records." http://ghdx.healthdata.org/organizations/central -bureau-statistics-north-korea.

Cha, Victor. 2009/2010. "Powerplay: Origins of the U.S. Alliance System in Asia," *International Security* 34(3):158–196.

———. 2012. *The Impossible State: North Korea, Past and Future*. New York: HarperCollins.

Cha, Victor, and David Kang. 2003. *Nuclear North Korea: A Debate on Engagement Strategies.* New York: Columbia University Press.

Cha, Victor, and Ellen Kim. 2013. "U.S. Korea Relations: Crisis de Jour," *Comparative Connections* 15(1):41–55. http://csis.org/files/publication/1301qus_korea.pdf.

Chang, Yoonok, Stephan Haggard, and Marcus Noland. 2006. "North Korean Refugees in China: Evidence from a Survey." In *The North Korean Refugee Crisis: Human Rights and International Response.* Edited by Stephan Haggard and Marcus Noland. Washington, DC: US Committee for Human Rights in North Korea.

Changyong, Choi, and Jesse D. Lecy. 2012. "A Semantic Network Analysis of Changes in North Korea's Economic Policy," *Governance,* 25(4):589–616.

Chayes, Abram, and Antonia Handler Chayes. 1993. "On Compliance," *International Organization,* 47(2):175–205.

Cheney, Richard. 2011. *In My Time: A Personal and Political Memoir.* New York: Threshold Editions, Simon and Schuster.

Cheong, Seong-chang. 2000. "Stalinism and Kimilsungism: A Comparative Analysis of Ideology and Power," *Asian Perspective* 24(1):133–161.

Chestnut, Sheena. 2005. "The 'Soprano State'? North Korean Involvement in Criminal Activity and Implications for International Security." Honors thesis. Stanford University.

———. 2007. "Illicit Activity and Proliferation: North Korean Smuggling Networks," *International Security* 32(1):80–111.

———. 2014. *Illicit: North Korea's Evolving Operations to Earn Hard Currency.* Washington, DC: Committee on Human Rights in North Korea.

Chinoy, Michael. 2008. *Meltdown: The Inside Story of the North Korean Nuclear Crisis.* New York: St. Martins.

Cho, Myongchul, and Jiyeon Kim. 2007. "Overseas North Korean Workers and Implications," *KIEP Global Economy Today* 7(31):1–11.

Choe, Sang-Hun. 2015. "North Korea Sought Talks and Attached a Hefty Price Tag, South's Ex-Leader Says," *New York Times,* January 29. http://www.nytimes.com/2015/01/30/world/asia/north-korea-sought-talks-and-attached-a-hefty-price-tag-souths-ex-leader-says.html?ref=topics&_r=1.

Chosun Ilbo. 2011. "Defectors Send $10 Million a Year to N. Korea." February 7, http://english.chosun.com/site/data/html_dir/2011/02/07/2011020700405.html.

Chung, Chin O. 1978. *Pyongyang Between Peking and Moscow.* Tuscaloosa, AL: University of Alabama Press.

Civilian-Military Joint Investigation Group. 2010. "Joint Investigation Report on the Attack Against ROK Ship *Cheonan.*" http://www.cheonan46.go.kr/.

Clay, Karen. 1997a. "Trade, Institutions and Credit," *Explorations in Economic History* 34:495–521.

———. 1997b. "Trade Without Law: Private-Order Institutions in Mexican California," *Journal of Law, Economics and Organization* 13(1):202–231.

Clemens, Walter. 2010. "North Korea's Quest for Nuclear Weapons: New Historical Evidence," *Journal of East Asian Studies* 10:127–154.

Clinton, Hillary. 2011. "Visit of North Korean Vice Foreign Minister Kim Kae-gwan to New York." Press statement, July 24. http://www.state.gov/secretary/20092013clinton/rm/2011/07/169003.htm.

Coalition of Tobacco Companies. 2005. *Production of Counterfeit Cigarettes in the Democratic People's Republic of Korea (DPRK).* June 29.

Collins, Robert. 2016. *Pyongyang Republic: North Korea's Capital of Human Rights Denial.* Washington, DC: Committee for Human Rights in North Korea. https://www.hrnk .org/uploads/pdfs/Collins_PyongyangRepublic_FINAL_WEB.pdf.

Committee on Foreign Relations. 2009. "Nomination of Hillary R. Clinton to Be Secretary of State: Hearing Before the Committee on Foreign Relations, United States Senate, One Hundred Eleventh Congress, First Session, January 13, 2009." http://www.gpo .gov/fdsys/pkg/CHRG-111shrg54615/pdf/CHRG-111shrg54615.pdf.

Copeland, Dale. 2014. *Economic Interdependence and War.* Princeton, NJ: Princeton University Press.

Corera, Gordon. 2006. *Shopping for Bombs: Nuclear Proliferation, Global Insecurity, and the Rise and Fall of the A. Q. Khan Network.* New York: Oxford University Press, 2006.

Cornell, Erik. 2002. *North Korea under Communism: Report of an Envoy to Paradise.* London: Routledge.

Cortright, David, and George A. Lopez. 2000. *The Sanctions Decade: Assessing UN Strategies in the 1990s.* Boulder, CO: Lynne Rienner.

———. 2002. *Sanctions and the Search for Security: Challenges to UN Action.* Boulder, CO: Lynne Rienner.

Council on Foreign Relations. 2016. *A Sharper Choice on North Korea: Engaging China for a Stable Northeast Asia.* New York: Council on Foreign Relations Independent Task force Report No. 74, http://www.cfr.org/north-korea/sharper-choice-north-korea/p38259.

Creekmore, Marion. 2006. *A Moment of Crisis: Jimmy Carter, The Power of a Peacemaker, and North Korea's Nuclear Ambitions.* New York: Public Affairs Publishing.

Crumm, Eileen M. 1995. "The Value of Economic Incentives in International Politics," *Journal of Peace Research* 32(3):313–330.

Cuddington, John T, and Daniel Jerrett. 2008. "Super Cycles in Real Metals Prices?" *IMF Staff Papers* 55:541–565.

DailyNK. 2008. "Kim Jong Il Restores North-China Relations [sic]." March 3.

———. 2011. "Defector Families Are Moneybags for NSA Agents." January 27. http:// www.dailynk.com/english/read.php?cataId=nk01500&num=7303.

Davies, Glyn T. 2013. Keynote Address, 2013 IFES-WWICS Washington Forum on Korea, Washington, DC, June 14. http://www.wilsoncenter.org/event/2013-ifes-wwics -washington-forum-korea.

Demick, Barbara. 2010. *Nothing to Envy: Ordinary Lives in North Korea.* New York: Spiegel & Grau.

Demick, Barbara, and Josh Meyer, 2005. "U.S. Accuses North Korea of Conspiracy to Counterfeit," *Los Angeles Times*, December 18.

Dent, Christopher M. 2006. *New Free Trade Agreements in the Asia-Pacific.* Basingstoke, UK: Palgrave McMillan.

———. 2008. *East Asian Regionalism.* London: Routledge.

Dimitrov, Martin, ed. 2013. *Why Communism Did Not Collapse.* New York: Cambridge University Press.

Dong-a Ilbo. 2012. "N. Korea Jacks Up Imports of luxury goods Under New Leader." October 4. http://english.donga.com/srv/service.php3?biid=2012100422928.

Downs, Chuck. 1998. *Over the Line: North Korea's Negotiating Strategy.* Washington, DC: American Enterprise Institute Press.

Drezner, Daniel W. 1999. *The Sanctions Paradox.* Cambridge, UK: Cambridge University Press.

————. 2000. "Bargaining, Enforcement, and Multilateral Economic Sanctions," *International Organization* 54 (Winter):73–102.

————. 2003. "The Hidden Hand of Economic Coercion," *International Organization* 57 (Summer):643–659.

————. 2011. "Sanctions Sometimes Smart: Targeted Sanctions in Theory and Practice," *International Studies Review* 13:96–108.

Drury, A. Cooper, and Yitan Li, 2006. "U.S. Economic Sanction Threats against China: Failing to Leverage Better Human Rights," *Foreign Policy Analysis* 2(4):307–324.

East Asia Study Group. 2002. "Final Report of the East Asia Study Group." ASEAN + 3 Summit, Phnom Penh, November 4. http://www.mofa.go.jp/region/asia-paci/asean/pmv0211/report.pdf.

Eaton, Jonathan, and Maxim Engers. 1992. "Sanctions," *Journal of Political Economy*100(5):899–928.

Eberstadt, Nicholas. 1996. "How Much Money Goes from Japan to North Korea?" *Asian Survey* 36(5):523–542.

————. 1999. *The End of North Korea*. Washington, DC: American Enterprise Institute Press.

————. 2007. *The North Korean Economy: Between Crisis and Catastrophe*. Piscataway, NJ: Transaction Books.

————. 2011. "Outside Aid Has Failed. Only an 'Intrusive Aid' Approach Will Work," *Global Asia* 6(3):42–44.

Eberstadt, Nicholas, Marc Rubin, and Albina Tretyakova. 1995. "The Collapse of Soviet and Russian Trade with the DPRK, 1989–1993," *Korean Journal of National Reunification* 4:87–104.

Elliott, Kimberly Anne. 1998. "The Sanctions Glass: Half Full or Completely Empty?" *International Security* 23(1):50–65.

Embassy of the People's Republic of China. 2011. "Zhang Zhijun Talks About the Outcome of Vice Premier Li Keqiang's Visit to DPRK, ROK." October 27. http://www.china-embassy.org/eng/zgyw/t873490.htm.

Epstein, David, and Sharon O'Halloran. 2008. "Sovereignty and Delegation in International Organizations," *Law and Contemporary Problems* 71(1):77–92.

Escribà-Folch, Abel. 2012. "Authoritarian Responses to Foreign Pressure: Spending, Repression, and Sanctions," *Comparative Political Studies* 45(6):683–713.

Escribà-Folch, Abel, and Joseph Wright. 2010. "Dealing with Tyranny: International Sanctions and the Survival of Authoritarian Regimes," *International Studies Quarterly* 54(2):335–359.

Farole, Thomas. 2011. "Special Economic Zones: What Have We Learned?" World Bank Poverty Reduction and Economic Management Network Economic Premise 64, September. http://siteresources.worldbank.org/INTPREMNET/Resources/EP64.pdf.

Fearon, James D. 1995. "Rationalist Explanations for War," *International Organization* 49(3):379–414.

Federovskiy, Alexander. 2013. "Russia's Policy Toward North Korea," *Russian Analytical Digest* 132. http://www.css.ethz.ch/publications/pdfs/RAD-132-4-7.pdf.

Feenstra, Robert C., Chang Hong, Hong Ma, and Barbara J. Spencer. 2012. "Contractual Versus Non-Contractual Trade: The Role of Institutions in China." National Bureau of Economic Research Working Paper 17728, January.

Feinberg. Richard. 2011. *Reaching Out: Cuba's New Economy and the International Response.* Washington, DC: Brookings Institution.

Fifield, Anna. 2006. "North Korea Passed Tens of Millions via Macao Bank," *Financial Times*, December 18. http://www.ft.com/intl/cms/s/0/bb96a2c2-8e3c-11db-aeoe -0000779e2340.html#axzz3bHVPaVLa.

Flake, L. Gordon, and Scott Snyder, eds. 2003. *Paved with Good Intentions: The NGO Experience in North Korea.* Westport, CT: Praeger.

Food and Agriculture Organization. 2010. "Special Report: FAO/WFP Crop and Food Security Assessment Mission to the Democratic People's Republic of Korea." November 16. http://www.fao.org/docrep/013/al968e/al968e00.htm.

———. 2012a. "Overview of Needs and Assistance in DPRK 2012." http://www.wfp.org/ sites/default/files/DPRK%20Overview%20Of%20Needs%20And%20Assistance%20 2012.pdf.

———. 2012b. "Project 200114 Resource Situation." February 6.

———. 2013a. "Special Report: FAO/WFP Crop and Food Security Assessment Mission to the Democratic People's Republic of Korea." November 28 http://www.fao.org/ docrep/019/aq118e/aq118e.pdf.

———. 2013b. "Protracted Relief and Recovery Operation (PRRO) 200114 'Nutrition Support for Women and Children in DPRK.'" *PRRO 200114 Quarterly M&E Bulletin*, January–March 2013. http://www.wfp.org/sites/default/files/PRRO%20200114%20 bulletin%202013%201st%20quarter%20version%20FINAL.pdf.

———. 2014. "Internal Audit of WFP Operations in the Democratic People's Republic of Korea (DPRK)." Office of the Inspector General Internal Audit Report AR/14/01, January. http://documents.wfp.org/stellent/groups/public/documents/reports/wfp263 172.pdf.

Foster-Carter, Aidan. 2012a. "North-South Relations: Plumbing the Depths," *Comparative Connections* 14(1):89–106.

———. 2012b. "Party Time in Pyongyang," *38 North*, April 22. http://38north .org/2012/04/afostercarter042212/.

Frank, Ruediger. 2005. "Economic Reforms in North Korea (1998–2004): Systemic Restrictions, Quantitative Analysis, Ideological Background," *Journal of the Asia Pacific Economy* 10(3):278–311.

———. 2012. "Why Now Is a Good Time for Economic Engagement of North Korea." *Asia-Pacific Journal* 11(14):1–5.

———. 2014. "Can North Korea Prioritize Nukes and the Economy at the Same Time?" *Global Asia* Spring 9(1):38–42.

Freeman, Carla, and Drew Thomson. 2009. "The Real Bridge to Nowhere." US Institute of Peace working paper, April 22.

Friedman, Thomas. 2015. "Iran and the Obama Doctrine." *New York Times*, April 2.

Funabashi, Yoichi. 2007. *The Peninsula Question: A Chronicle of the Second North Korean Nuclear Crisis.* Washington, DC: Brookings Institution.

Funabashi, Yoichi, and Yoichi Kato. 2009. "Interview with Secretary Hillary Clinton." *Asahi Shimbun* (Tokyo), February 17. http://www.state.gov/secretary/20092013clinton/ rm/2009a/02/117626.htm.

Gandhi, Jennifer, and Adam Przeworski. 2007. "Authoritarian Institutions and the Survival of Autocrats," *Comparative Political Studies* 40(11):1279–1301.

Gartzke, Eric. 2006. *The Affinity of Nations Index, 1946–2002.* http://dss.ucsd.edu/~egartzke/ datasets.htm.

Gartzke, Erik, Quan Li, and Charles Boehmer. 2001 "Investing in the Peace: Economic Interdependence and International Conflict," *International Organization* 55(2):391–438.

Gause, Ken E. 2011. *North Korea under Kim Chong-Il: Power, Politics, and Prospects for Change.* Santa Barbara, CA: Praeger Security International.

———. 2012. *Coercion, Control, Surveillance, and Punishment: An Examination of the North Korean Police State.* Washington, DC: Committee for Human Rights in North Korea.

———. 2013. *Coercion, Control, Surveillance, and Punishment: An Examination of the North Korean Police State,* 2nd ed. Washington, DC: Committee for Human Rights in North Korea.

———. 2015. *North Korean House of Cards: Leadership Dynamics Under Kim Jong-un.* Washington, DC: Committee on Human Rights in North Korea (forthcoming).

Gibbons, Elizabeth D. 1999. *Sanctions in Haiti: Human Rights and Democracy under Assault.* Westport, CT: Praeger.

Gibson, Clark C. et al. 2005. *The Samaritan's Dilemma: The Political Economy of Development Aid.* Oxford, UK: Oxford University Press.

Glaser, Bonnie, Scott Snyder, and John S. Park. 2008. "Keeping an Eye on an Unruly Neighbor: Chinese Views of Economic Reform and Stability in North Korea." Center for Strategic and International Studies and US Institute of Peace working paper, January 3.

Goldstein, Avery. 2005. *Rising to the Challenge: China's Grand Strategy and International Security.* Stanford, CA: Stanford University Press.

Goldstein, Judith, Miles Kahler, Robert Keohane, and Anne-Marie Slaughter, eds. 2000. *Legalization and World Politics.* Cambridge, UK: Cambridge University Press.

Good Friends. 1998. "The Food Crisis of North Korea—Witnessed by 1,694 Food Refugees," December 12, http://www.goodfriends.or.kr.eng/report/1019e/htm.

———. 2011. "North Korea Today No. 387." Good Friends Research Institute for North Korean Society, January 26. http://goodfriendsusa.blogspot.com/2011/02/north-korea-today-no-387-january-26.html.

———. 2011. "North Korea Today No. 395." Good Friends Research Institute for North Korean Society, March 23.

———. 2011. "North Korea Today No. 413." Good Friends Research Institute for North Korean Society, July 27.

Goodkind, Daniel, and Loraine West. 2001. "The North Korean Famine and Its Demographic Impact," *Population and Development Review* 27(2):219–238.

Goodkind, Daniel, Loraine West, and Peter Johnson. 2011. "A Reassessment of Mortality in North Korea, 1993–2008." US Census Bureau, Population Division, March 28.

Gourevitch, Peter. 1986. *Politics in Hard Times: Comparative Responses to International Economic Crises.* Ithaca, NY: Cornell University Press.

Green, Michael, and Bates Gill, eds. 2009. *Asia's New Multilateralism: Cooperation, Competition and the Search for Community.* New York: Columbia University Press.

Greif, Avner. 1993. "Contract Enforceability and Economic Institutions in Early Trade: The Maghribi Traders' Coalition," *American Economic Review* 83(3):525–548.

Greif, Avner, Paul Milgrom, and Barry R. Weingast. 1994. "Coordination, Commitment, and Enforcement: The Case of the Merchant Guild," *Journal of Political Economy* 102(4):745–776.

Grieco, Joseph. 1997. "Systemic Sources of Variation in Regional Institutionalization in Western Europe, East Asia, and the Americas." In *The Political Economy of Regionalism.* Edited by Helen Milner and Edward Mansfield. New York: Columbia University Press.

Grimes, William. 2009. *Currency and Contest in East Asia: the Great Power Politics of Financial Regionalism*. Ithaca, NY: Cornell University Press.

Grimmet, Richard F. 2006. "Conventional Arms Transfers to Developing Nations, 1998–2005." Congressional Research Service, Washington, DC.

Gunjal, Kisan, Swithun Goodbody, Siemon Hollema, Katrien Ghoos, Samir Wanmali, Krishna Krishnamurthy, and Emily Turano. 2013. *Special Report: FAO/WFP Crop and Food Security Assessment Mission to the Democratic People's Republic of Korea*. November 28. http://documents.wfp.org/stellent/groups/public/documents/ena/wfp261353.pdf.

Gunjal, Kisan, Swithun Goodbody, Joyce Kanyangwa Luma, and Rita Bhatia. 2010. *Special Report: FAO/WFP Crop And Food Security Assessment Mission to the Democratic People's Republic of Korea*. November 16. http://www.fao.org/docrep/013/AL968e/AL968e00.htm.

Gurtov, Mel. 2014. "Why the U.S. Should Engage North Korea Right Now." *Foreign Policy in Focus*, August 13. http://fpif.org/u-s-engage-north-korea-right-now/.

Haass, Richard, and Meghan O'Sullivan. 2000. "Terms of Engagement: Alternatives to Punitive Policies," *Survival* 42(2):113–135.

Haggard, Stephan. 1997. "Regionalism in Asia and the Americas." In *The Political Economy of Regionalism*. Edited by Edward D. Mansfield and Helen V. Milner. New York: Columbia University Press.

———. 2013a. "The Devil in the Details: Financial Sanctions." *North Korea: Witness to Transformation* (blog), March 12. http://blogs.piie.com/nk/?p=9679.

———. 2013b. "Orascom in North Korea: Don't Leave Me Hanging." *North Korea: Witness to Transformation* (blog), December 10. http://blogs.piie.com/nk/?p=12505.

———. 2013c. "What Are the North Koreans Doing?" *North Korea: Witness to Transformation* (blog), April 1. http://blogs.piie.com/nk/?p=9889.

Haggard, Stephan, Luke Herman, and Jaesung Ryu. 2014. "Political Change in North Korea: Mapping the Succession," *Asian Survey* 54(4):773–800.

Haggard, Stephan, and Robert Kaufman. 2016. *Dictators and Democrats: Elites, Masses and Regime Change*. Princeton, NJ: Princeton University Press.

Haggard, Stephan, and John Lindsay. 2015. "North Korea and the Sony Hack: Exporting Instability through Cyberspace." East-West Center AsiaPacific Issues Series 117, May. http://www.eastwestcenter.org/node/35164.

Haggard, Stephan, and Marcus Noland. 2007a. *Famine in North Korea: Markets, Aid, and Reform*. New York: Columbia University Press.

———. 2007b. "North Korea's External Economic Relations." Peterson Institute for International Economics Working Paper 07-7.

———. 2008a. "Authors' Response: Famine in North Korea—A Reprise," *Asia Policy* 5:203–221.

———. 2008b. "North Korea's Foreign Economic Relations," *International Relations of the Asia-Pacific* 8(2):219–246.

———. 2009. "Famine in North Korea Redux?" *Journal of Asian Economics* 20(4):384–395.

———. 2010a. "The Winter of Their Discontent: Pyongyang Attacks the Market." Peterson Institute for International Economics Policy Brief PB10-1. https://www.piie.com/publications/pb/pb10-01.pdf.

———. 2010b. "Reform from Below: Behavioral and Institutional Change in North Korea," *Journal of Economic Behavior and Organization* 73(2):133–152.

———. 2011a. *Witness to Transformation: Refugee Insights into North Korea*. Washington, DC: Peterson Institute for International Economics.

———. 2011b. "Engaging North Korea: The Role of Economic Statecraft." East-West Center Policy Studies 59. http://www.eastwestcenter.org/sites/default/files/private/ps059_0.pdf.

———. 2011c. "Monitoring Aid," *North Korea: Witness to Transformation* (blog), May 17. https://piie.com/blogs/north-korea-witness-transformation/monitoring-aid.

———. 2012a. "The Microeconomics of North–South Korean Cross-Border Integration," *International Economic Journal* 26(3):407–430.

———. 2012b. "Networks, Trust, and Trade: The Microeconomics of China-North Korea Integration." Peterson Institute for International Economics Working Paper Series 12-8. http://www.iie.com/publications/wp/wp12-8.pdf.

———. 2012c. "China-DPRK Economic Relations: Evidence from a Firm-level Survey." In *Reordering Chinese Priorities on the Korean Peninsula*. Washington, DC: Center for Strategic and International Studies.

Haggard, Stephan, Marcus Noland, and Jennifer Lee. 2012. "Integration in the Absence of Institutions: China-North Korea Cross-Border Exchange," *Journal of Asian Economics* 23(2):130–145.

Haggard, Stephan, Marcus Noland, and Erik Weeks. 2008. "North Korea on the Precipice of Famine." Peterson Institute for International Economics Policy Brief PB08-6, May. http://www.iie.com/publications/pb/pb08-6.pdf.

Haidar, Jamal Ibrahim. 2017. "Sanctions and Export Deflection: Evidence from Iran." *Economic Policy* (forthcoming).

Hall, Kevin G. 2007. "Money Laundering Allegations by U.S. False, Report Says." *McClatchyDC*, April 16. http://www.mcclatchydc.com/latest-news/article24462799.html.

Halperin, Morton H. 2012. "Promoting Security in Northeast Asia: A New Approach." *NAPSNet Policy Forum*, October 30. http://nautilus.org/napsnet/napsnet-policy-forum/promoting-security-in-northeast-asia-a-new-approach/.

Han, In Sup. 2006. "The 2004 Revision of Criminal Law in North Korea: A Take-off?" *Santa Clara Journal of International Law* 5(1):122–133.

Han, Sung-joo. 2009. "Han Sung-joo: ROK Ambassador to the USA, 2003–2005." In *Ambassadors' Memoir: U.S.-Korea Relations through the Eyes of the Ambassadors*. Washington, DC: Korea Economic Institute.

Harden, Blaine, and Glenn Kessler. 2008. "Dispute Stalls U.S. Food Aid To N. Korea; A Third of Population Needs Help, U.N. Says." *Washington Post*, December 9.

Harrison, Selig. 2001. *Korean Endgame: A Strategy for Reunification and U.S. Disengagement*. Princeton, NJ: Princeton University Press.

———. 2005a."Did North Korea Cheat?" *Foreign Affairs* 84(1):99–110.

———. 2005b. "Harrison Replies," *Foreign Affairs* 84(2):146–148.

Harvey, David I., Neil M. Kellard, Jakob B. Madsen, and Mark E. Wohar. 2013. "Trends and Cycles in Real Commodity Prices: 1610–2010." http://www.nottingham.ac.uk/~lezdih/commod.pdf.

Hastings, Justin. 2014. "The Economic Geography of North Korean Drug Trafficking Networks," *Review of International Political Economy* (February):162–193.

Hathaway, Robert, and Jordan Tama. 2004. "The U.S. Congress and North Korea during the Clinton Years," *Asian Survey* 44(4):711–733.

Hawkins, Darren, David Lake, Daniel Nielson, and Michael Tierney, eds. 2006. *Delegation and Agency in International Organizations*. Cambridge, UK: Cambridge University Press.

Hayes, Peter, and Richard Tanter. 2012. "Key Elements of Northeast Asia Nuclear-Weapons Free Zone (NEA-NWFZ)." *Nautilus Institute*, September 26. http://nautilus.org/wp -content/uploads/2012/10/Hayes-Tanter-NWFZ-2-pager-Oct1-2012.pdf.

He, Fang. 2013. "The Gains and Losses from the War to Resist American Aggression and Aid Korea," *Yan Huang Chun Qiu* 12:11–17 (in Chinese).

Hecker, Siegfried. 2010. "A Return Trip to North Korea's Yongbyon Nuclear Complex." Center for International Security and Cooperation, Stanford University, November 20. http://iis-db.stanford.edu/pubs/23035/HeckerYongbyon.pdf.

Hellman, Joel S. 1998. "Winners Take All: The Politics of Partial Reform in Postcommunist Transitions," *World Politics* 50(2):203–234.

Hendrix, Cullen. 2011. "Markets vs. Malthus: Food Security and the Global Economy." Peterson Institute for International Economics Policy Brief 11-12, July. https://piie .com/publications/policy-briefs/markets-vs-malthus-food-security-and-global -economy.

Hendrix, Cullen, and Marcus Noland. 2014. *Confronting the Curse: The Economics and Geopolitics of Natural Resource Governance*. Washington, DC: Peterson Institute for International Economics.

———. 2015. "Myanmar: Cross-Cutting Governance Challenges." Peterson Institute for International Economics Working Paper Series WP15-2, March.

Henning, Randall. 2009. "The Future of the Chiang Mai Initiative: An Asian Monetary Fund?" Peterson Institute for International Economics Policy Brief PB09-5, February 5.

Hersh, Seymour. 2003. "The Cold Test: What the Administration knew about Pakistan and the North Korean nuclear program," *The New Yorker*, January 27.

Hill, Christopher. 2011. "Food for Thought in North Korea." *Project Syndicate*, February 22. http://www.project-syndicate.org/commentary/food-for-thought-in-north-korea.

———. 2014. *Outpost: Life on the Frontlines of American Diplomacy*. New York: Simon and Schuster.

Hix, Simon. 2010. "Institutional Design of Regional Integration: Balancing Delegation and Representation." Asian Development Bank Regional Economic Integration working paper, November.

Hotham, Oliver. 2014. "Inside the Kim Family Business: Office 39." *NK News*, September 17. http://www.nknews.org/2014/07/inside-the-kim-family-business-office-39/.

Hufbauer, Gary Clyde, and Jeffrey J. Schott. 2007. "Fitting Asia-Pacific Agreements into the WTO System." Paper presented at the New Asia-Pacific Trade Initiatives Joint Conference of The Japan Economic Foundation and the Peterson Institute for International Economics. Washington, DC, November 27.

Hufbauer, Gary Clyde, Jeffrey J. Schott, Kimberly Ann Elliott, and Barbara Oegg. 2007. *Economic Sanctions Reconsidered*, 3rd ed. Washington, DC: Peterson Institute for International Economics.

Hughes, Christopher W. 2005. "Japan-North Korea Relations and the Political Economy of Sanctions." Unpublished manuscript. University of Warwick.

———. 2006. "The Political Economy of Japanese Sanctions Towards North Korea: Domestic Coalitions and International Systemic Pressures," *Pacific Affairs* 79(3):455–481.

Human Rights Watch. 2015. "North Korea: Harsher Punishments for Contact with South." February 9. http://www.hrw.org/news/2015/02/09/north-korea-harsher -punishments-contact-south.

Hunter, Helen-Louise. 1999. *Kim Il-song's North Korea*. Westport, CT: Praeger.

Hymans, Jacques E. C. 2006. *The Psychology of Nuclear Proliferation: Identity, Emotions, and Foreign Policy*. Cambridge, UK: Cambridge University Press.

Ikenberry, John. 2003. "America in East Asia: Power, Markets, and Grand Strategy." In *Beyond Bilateralism: The Emerging East Asian Regionalism*. Edited by T. J. Pempel and Ellis Kraus. Stanford, CA: Stanford University Press.

Ikenberry, John, and Chung-in Moon, eds. 2008. *The United States and Northeast Asia: Debates, Issues and New Order*. London: Rowman and Littlefield.

Institute for Far Eastern Studies. 2010. "DPRK Strengthens Control Mechanisms with Revised Law on the People's Economy." NK Brief No. 10-11-26-1, November 26.

———. 2012. "North Korea to Announce New Economic Development Plan and Organizational Restructuring." February 29. http://ifes.kyungnam.ac.kr/eng/FRM/FRM_0101V.aspx?code=FRM120229_0001.

International Atomic Energy Agency. 2014. "Application of Safeguards in the Democratic People's Republic of Korea." Report GOV/2014/42-GC (58)/21, September 3. https://www.iaea.org/sites/default/files/gc58-21_en.pdf.

International Crisis Group. 2006. "China and North Korea: Comrades Forever?" Asia Report No. 112, February 1.

———. 2009. "Shades of Red: China's Debate over North Korea." Asia Report No. 179, November 2. http://www.crisisgroup.org/en/regions/asia/north-east-asia/north-korea.aspx#

———. 2011. "China and Inter-Korean Clashes in the Yellow Sea." Asia Report No. 200, January 27.

International Institute for Strategic Studies. 2007. *Nuclear Black Markets: Pakistan, A. Q. Khan, and the Rise of Proliferation Networks—A Net Assessment*. London: International Institute for Strategic Studies.

International Monetary Fund. n.d. *International Financial Statistics Online*. https://www.google.com/search?q=IMF+Direction+of+Trade+Statistics&oq=IMF+Direction+of+Trade+Statistics&aqs=chrome..69i57j0l5.1778j0j4&sourceid=chrome&ie=UTF-8#q=IMF+International+Financial+Statistics+Online.

———. 2006. *Direction of Trade Statistics*. https://www.imf.org/external/pubs/cat/longres.aspx?sk=19305.0.

Jackson, Van. 2016. *Rival Reputations Coercion and Credibility in US-North Korea Relations*. New York: Cambridge University Press.

Jang, Jin-sung. 2014. *Dear Leader: Poet, Spy, Escapee—A Look Inside North Korea*. New York: Atria Publishing.

Jannuzi, Frank. 2003. "North Korea: Back to the Brink? In *George W. Bush and Asia: A Midterm Assessment*. Edited by Robert M. Hathaway and Wilson Lee. Washington, DC: Woodrow Wilson International Center for Scholars. http://www.wilsoncenter.org/sites/default/files/BushMidterm.pdf.

Jing, Ran, and Mary E. Lovely. 2015. "A View Through the Trade Window: North Korean Exports as an Indicator of Economic Capabilities." *World Economy*, 30(1):P1–20, January 2015.

Johnson, Simon, John McMillan, and Christopher Woodruff. 1999. "Contract Enforcement in Transition." European Bank for Reconstruction and Development Working Paper 45, November.

———. 2002. "Courts and Relational Contracts," *Journal of Law, Economics, and Organization* 18(1):221–277.

Johnson, Simon, Jonathan Ostry, and Arvind Subramanian. 2007. "The Prospects for Sustained Growth in Africa." International Monetary Fund Working Paper 07/52, May.

Johnson, Tim, and Kevin Hall. 2007. "Owner of Macau Bank Denies Illegal Dealings with N. Korea." *McClatchyDC*, March 27. http://www.mcclatchydc.com/2007/03/27/15996/owner-of-macau-bank-denies-illegal.html.

Jones, David Martin, and Michael L. R. Smith. 2007. "Making Process, Not Progress: ASEAN and the Evolving East Asian Regional Order," *International Security* 32(1):148–184.

Joongang Ilbo. 2001. "Kim Jong-Il Said to Order Development of Sinuiju Special Economic Zone." January 31.

Kaempfer, William, and Anton Lowenberg. 1988. "The Theory of International Economic Sanctions: A Public Choice Approach," *American Economic Review* 78(4):786–793.

———. 1992. *International Economic Sanctions: A Public Choice Perspective*. Boulder, CO: Westview Press.

Kaempfer, William H., Anton Lowenberg, and William Mertens. 2004. "International Economic Sanctions Against a Dictator," *Economics and Politics* 16(1):29–51.

Kaempfer, W., and Martin T. Ross. 2004. "The Political Economy of Trade Sanctions Against South Africa: A Gravity Model Approach." In *The Political Economy of Trade, Aid and Foreign Investment Policies*. Edited by Devashish Mitra and Arvind Panagariya. Amsterdam: Elsevier North-Holland.

Kahler, Miles. 2001. "Legalization as Strategy: The Asia-Pacific Case," *International Organization* 54(3):549–571.

Kahler, Miles, and Scott Kastner. 2006. "Strategic Uses of Economic Interdependence: Engagement Policies on the Korean Peninsula and Across the Taiwan Strait," *Journal of Peace Research* 43(5):523–541.

Kahneman, Daniel, and Amos Tversky. 1979. "Prospect Theory: An Analysis of Decision under Risk, *Econometrica* 47(2):263–291.

Kalyvitis, Sarantis, and Irene Vlachaki. 2011. "Misued Financial Aid, Political Aid, and Regime Survival." *Social Science Research Network*, January. http://papers.ssrn.com/sol3/papers.cfm?abstract_id=1489897.

Kan, Paul, Bruce Bechtol, and Robert Collins. 2010. "Criminal Sovereignty: Understanding North Korea's Illicit International Activities." Strategic Studies Institute, March. http://www.strategicstudiesinstitute.army.mil/pdffiles/pub975.pdf.

Kang, Chol-hwan. 2005. *The Aquariums of Pyongyang*. New York: Basic Books.

Katzenstein, Peter. 2005. *A World of Regions: Asia and Europe in the American Imperium*. Ithaca, NY: Cornell University Press.

Katzman, Kenneth. 2016. "Iran Sanctions." Congressional Research Service, Washington, DC, March 23.

Kelley, Judit. 2009. "The Role of Membership Rules in Regional Organizations." Paper presented at the Asian Development Bank Workshop on Institutions for Regionalism in Asia and the Pacific, Honolulu, August 9–10.

Keohane, Robert O. 1984. *After Hegemony: Cooperation and Discord in the World Political Economy*. Princeton, NJ: Princeton University Press.

Kim, Byung-Yeon. 2010. "Markets, Bribery, and Regime Stability in North Korea." East Asia Institute Asia Security Initiative Working Paper No. 4, April.

Kim, Dae-jung. 1997. *Three Stage Approach to Korean Reunification*, 3rd rev. ed. Los Angeles: University of Southern California Center for Multiethnic and Transnational Studies.

Kim, Kap-sik. 2008. "Suryong's Direct Rule and the Political Regime in North Korea Under Kim Jong Il," *Asian Perspective* 32(3):87–109.

Kim, Kwang-jin. 2011. "The 'Defector's Tale: Inside North Korea's Secret Economy," *World Affairs* (September/October). http://www.worldaffairsjournal.org/article/ defector%E2%80%99s-tale-inside-north-korea%E2%80%99s-secret-economy.

Kim, Samuel S. 2007. "Sino-North Korean Relations in the Post-Cold War World." In *North Korea: The Politics of Regime Survival.* Edited by Young Whan Kihl and Hong Nack Kim. Armonk, NY: M. E. Sharpe.

Kim, Samuel S., and Tai Hwan Lee. 2002. "Chinese-North Korean Relations: Managing Asymmetrical Interdependence." In *North Korea and Northeast Asia.* Edited by Samuel Kim and Tai Hwan Lee. New York: Rowman and Littlefield.

Kim, Suk Hi, and Semoon Chang. 2007. *Economic Sanctions Against a Nuclear North Korea: An Analysis of United States and United Nations Actions Since 1950.* Jefferson, NC: MacFarland.

Kim, Suk-Jin, and Moon-Soo Yang. 2015. "The Growth of the Informal Economy in North Korea." Korea Institute for National Unification Studies Series 15-2, October.

Kim, Sung Chull. 2006. *North Korea Under Kim Jong Il: From Consolidation to Systemic Dissonance.* Albany: State University of New York Press.

Kirk, Donald. 2009. *Korea Betrayed: Kim Dae Jung and Sunshine.* New York: Palgrave MacMillan.

Kirshner, Jonathan. 1997. "The Microfoundations of Economic Sanctions," *Security Studies* 6 (Spring):32−64.

Koh, B. C. 2005. "'Military-First Politics' and Building a 'Powerful And Prosperous Nation' In North Korea." Nautilus Institute Policy Forum 05-32A, April 14. http://www .nautilus.org/fora/security/0532AKoh.html.

Korea Institute for National Unification. 2009. "White Paper on Human Rights in North Korea." http://www.kinu.or.kr/eng/pub/index.jsp.

Korean Central News Agency. 2002. "Foreign Ministry Statement at 'Conclusion of Non-Aggression Treaty between DPRK and U.S. Called For.'" October 25. http://www .kcna.co.jp/index-e.htm.

———. 2008. "Lee Myung Bak Regime's Sycophancy towards U.S. and Anti-DPRK Confrontation Hysteria Blasted." April 1. reprinted from *Rodong Shinmun.* http://www .kcna.co.jp/index-e.htm.

———. 2010. "Foreign Ministry on UN Presidential Statement on 'Cheonan.'" July 10. http://www.kcna.co.jp/index-e.htm.

Koremenos, Barbara, Charles Lipson, and Duncan Snidal. 2001. "The Rational Design of International Institutions," *International Organization* 55(4):761−799.

Koremenos, Barbara, Charles Lipson, and Duncan Snidal, eds. 2003. *The Rational Design of International Institutions.* New York: Cambridge University Press.

Kricheli, Ruth, and Beatriz Magaloni. 2010. "Political Order and One-Party Rule," *Annual Review of Political Science* 13 (June):123−143.

Lacy, Dean, and Emmerson Niou. 2004. "A Theory of Economic Sanctions and Issue Linkage," *Journal of Politics,* 66(1):25−42.

Laing, Jonathan R. 2013. "Where Will It End," *Barron's,* June 24. http://online.barrons .com/article/SB50001424052748704878904578541251070413678.html#articleTabs_ article%3D1.

Lake, David. 2007. "Delegating Divisible Sovereignty: Sweeping a Conceptual Minefield," *Review of International Organizations* 2:219−237.

Landau, Emily. 2012. "Decade of Diplomacy: Negotiations with Iran and North Korea and the Future of Nuclear Nonproliferation." Institute for National Security Studies, INSS Memorandum No. 115, March.

Lankov, Andrei. 2002. *From Stalin to Kim Il Sung: The Formation of North Korea, 1945–1960.* New Jersey: Rutgers University Press.

———. 2007. *Crisis in North Korea: The Failure of De-Stalinization, 1956.* Honolulu: University of Hawaii Press.

———. 2014. "The Shadowy World of North Korea's Palace Economy." *Al Jazeera,* September 3. http://www.aljazeera.com/indepth/opinion/2014/09/shadowy-world -north-korea-palac-201493132727658119.html.

———. 2016. "The Resurgence of the Market Economy in North Korea." Carnegie Moscow Center, February 3. http://carnegie.ru/2016/02/03/resurgence-of-market-eco nomy-in-north-korea/ithc.

Lankov, Andrei, In-ok Kwak, and Choong-Bin Cho. 2012. "The Organizational Life: Daily Surveillance and Daily Resistance in North Korea," *Journal of East Asian Studies* 12(3):193–214.

Lankov, Andrei, and Seok-hyang Kim. 2013. "A New Face of North Korean Drug Use: Upsurge in Methamphetamine Abuse Across the Northern Areas of North Korea," *North Korean Review* 9(1):45–60.

Lee, Chae-Jin. 1996. *China and Korea: Dynamic Relations.* Stanford, CA: Hoover Press.

Lee, Karin, and Julia Choi. 2009. *North Korea: Unilateral and Multilateral Economic Sanctions and U.S. Department of Treasury Actions 1955–April 2009.* Washington, DC: National Committee on North Korea. http://www.ncnk.org/resources/publications/DPRK_ Sanctions_Report_April_2009.doc/file_view.

Lee, Myung-bak. 2008. Speech to the National Assembly. July 11. http://www.korea .net/Government/Briefing-Room/Presidential-Speeches/view?articleId=90998&pag eIndex=20.

Lee, Rensselaer. 2013. "The Russian Far East and China: Thoughts on Cross-Border Integration." *Foreign Policy Research Institute E-Notes,* November. http://www.fpri.org/ docs/Lee_-_Russia_and_China.pdf.

Lee, Sang-Hyun. 2014. "The Northeast Asia Peace and Cooperation Initiative (NAPCI): A Vision toward Sustainable Peace and Cooperation in Northeast Asia," *Asan Forum* 2(6). http://www.theasanforum.org/the-northeast-asia-peace-and-cooperation-initiative -napci-a-vision-toward-sustainable-peace-and-cooperation-in-northeast-asia/.

Lee, Sang Yong. 2012. "6.28 Agriculture Policy on the Back Foot." *DailyNK,* October 12. http://www.dailynk.com/english/read.php?cataId=nk09002&num=9907.

Lee, Seung-Hun, and Panseok Yang. 2010. "Were the 'Critical Evidence' Presented in the South Korean Official Cheonan Report Fabricated?" *Arxiv.* http://arxiv.org/ftp/arxiv/ papers/1006/1006.0680.pdf.

Lee, Seung-ju. 2015. "Human Rights Conditions of Overseas Laborers from North Korea." Unpublished paper. Database Center for North Korean Human Rights, Seoul.

Lee, Suk. 2003. "Food Shortages and Economic Institutions in the Democratic People's Republic of Korea." Ph.D. dissertation, Department of Economics, University of Warwick, Coventry, UK.

———. 2011. "Analysis and Issues of the 2008 North Korean Census." Korea Development Institute. http://m.kdi.re.kr/front/report_view.jsp?pub_no=12403#origin FileDownload.

Lee Tae-hoon. 2010. "Most N. Korean defectors Send Money Home." *Korea Times,* October 10. http://www.koreatimes.co.kr/www/news/nation/2010/10/116_74335.html.

Letzkian, David, and Mark Souva. 2007. "An Institutional Theory of Sanctions Onset and Success," *Journal of Conflict Resolution*, 51(6):848–871.

Levchenko, Andrei A. 2007. "Institutional Quality and International Trade," *Review of Economic Studies* 74(3):791–819.

———. 2011. "International Trade and Institutional Change." National Bureau of Economic Research Working Paper 17675, December.

Levin, Norman D, and Yong-Sup Han. 2002. *Sunshine in North Korea: The South Korean Debate over Policies toward North Korea*. Santa Monica CA: Rand Corporation.

Levitsky, Steven, and Lucan Way. 2010. *Competitive Authoritarianism: Hybrid Regimes after the Cold War*. Cambridge, UK: Cambridge University Press.

Levy, Jack S. 1997. "Prospect Theory, Rational Choice, and International Relations," *International Studies Quarterly* 41:87–112.

Lewis, Jeffrey, Peter Hayes, Scott Bruce. "Kim Jong Il's Nuclear Diplomacy and the US Opening: Slow Motion Six-Party Engagement," *Asia-Pacific Journal* 9(43):1–13.

Li, Dunqiu. 2006. "Policy Forum 06-70A: DPRK's Reform and Sino-DPRK Economic Cooperation," *NAPSNet Policy Forum*, August 23. http://nautilus.org/napsnet/napsnet -policy-forum/dprks-reform-and-sino-dprk-economic-cooperation/.

Li, Yitlan, and Cooper Drury. 2004. "Threatening Sanctions When Engagement Would Be More Effective: Attaining Better Human Rights in China," *International Studies Perspectives*, 5(4):378–394.

Lim, Dong-won. 2012. *Peacemaker: Twenty Years of Inter-Korean Relations and the North Korean Nuclear Issue*. Palo Alto, CA: Shorenstein Asia-Pacific Research Center.

Lim, Jae-cheon. 2012. "North Korea's Hereditary Succession Comparing Two Key Transitions in the DPRK," *Asian Survey* 52(3):550–570.

———. 2009. *Kim Jong-Il's Leadership of North Korea*. New York: Routledge.

Lind, Jennifer. 1997. "Gambling with Globalism: Japanese Financial Flows to North Korea and the Sanctions Policy Option," *Pacific Review* 10(3):391–406.

Lind, Jennifer, and Daniel Byman. 2010. "Pyongyang's Survival Strategy: Tools of Authoritarian Control in North Korea," *International Security* 35(1):44–76.

Lintner, Bertil. 2005. *Great Leader, Dear Leader: Demystifying North Korea Under the Kim Regime*. Chiang Mai, Thailand: Silkworm Books.

Litwak, Robert. 2000. *Rogue States and U.S. Foreign Policy: Containment after the Cold War*. Washington, DC: Woodrow Wilson Center Press.

Liu, Ming. 2003. "China and the North Korean Crisis: Facing Test and Transition," *Pacific Affairs* 76(3):347–373.

Long, William J. 1996. "Trade and Technology Incentives and Bilateral Cooperation," *International Studies Quarterly* 40(1):77–106.

Lyne, Mona, Daniel Nielson, and Michael J. Tierney. 2006. "Who Delegates? Alternative Models of Principals in Development Aid." In *Delegation and Agency in International Organizations*. Edited by Darren Hawkins, et al. Cambridge, UK: Cambridge University Press.

Mailey, J. R. 2016. "Hiding in Plain Sight: Cowboys, Conmen and North Korea's $6 Trillion Natural Resource Prize." *38 North* special report, April. http://38north.org/ wp-content/uploads/2016/04/201604_HIDING-IN-PLAIN-SIGHT_JRMailey.pdf.

Major, Solomon. 2012. "Timing Is Everything: Economic Sanctions, Regime Type, and Domestic Instability. *International Interactions* 38(1):79–110.

Mansfield, E. D., and B. M. Pollins. 2003. *Economic Interdependence and International Conflict: New Perspectives on an Enduring Debate.* Ann Arbor, MI: University of Michigan Press.

Mansfield, Edward, and Jon Pevehouse. 2008. "Democratization and the Varieties of International Organizations," *Journal of Conflict Resolution* 52(2):269–294.

Mansourov, Alexandre. 2012. "Part I: A Dynamically Stable Regime." *38 North*, December 17. http://38north.org/2012/12/amansourov121712/.

———. 2013. "North Korea: The Dramatic Fall of Jang Song Thaek," *38 North*, December 9. http://38north.org/2013/12/amansourov120913/.

———. 2014. "North Korea: Leadership Schisms and Consolidation During Kim Jong-un's Second Year in Power," *38 North*, January 22.

Manyin, Mark, and Dick K. Nanto. 2011. *The Kaesong North-South Industrial Complex.* Washington, DC: Congressional Research Service.

Manyin, Mark E, and Ryun Jun. 2003. "U.S. Assistance to North Korea." Congressional Research Service, Washington, DC, March 17.

Manyin, Mark, and Mary Beth Nikitin. 2010. "Foreign Assistance to North Korea." Congressional Research Service, Washington, DC, June 1.

———. 2013. "Foreign Assistance to North Korea." Congressional Research Service, Washington, DC, June 11.

———. 2014. "Foreign Assistance to North Korea." Congressional Research Service, Washington, DC, April 2.

Marinov, Nikolay. 2005. "Do Economic Sanctions Destabilize Country Leaders?" *American Journal of Political Science* 49(3):564–576.

Marshall, Monty G., and Benjamin R. Cole. 2011. "Global Report 2011: Conflict, Governance, and State Fragility." Center for Systemic Peace Global Report Series. http://www.systemicpeace.org/polity/polity4.htm.

Martin, Bradley K. 2006. *Under the Loving Care of the Fatherly Leader: North Korea and the Kim Dynasty.* New York: St. Martin's Press.

Martin, Lisa A. 1992. *Coercive Cooperation: Explaining Multilateral Economic Sanctions.* Princeton, NJ: Princeton University Press.

Martin, Lisa, and Beth A. Simmons. 1998. "Theories and Empirical Studies of International Institutions," *International Organization* 52(04):729–757.

Mazarr, Michael. 2007. "The Long Road to Pyongyang," *Foreign Affairs* 86(5):75–94.

McCormack, Gavan. 2004. *Target North Korea: Pushing North Korea to the Brink of Nuclear Catastrophe.* New York: Nation Books.

McEachern, Patrick. 2010. *Inside the Red Box: North Korea's Post-Totalitarian Politics.* New York: Columbia University Press.

McMillan, John, and Christopher Woodruff. 1999a. "Interfirm Relationships and Informal Credit in Vietnam," *Quarterly Journal of Economics* 114(4):1285–1320.

———. 1999b. "Dispute Prevention Without Courts in Vietnam," *Journal of Law, Economics and Organization* 15(3):637–658.

Michishita, Narushige. 2009. *North Korea's Military-Diplomatic Campaigns, 1966–2008.* London: Routledge.

Milgrom, Paul R., Douglas C. North, and Barry R. Weingast. 1990. "The Role of Institutions in the Revival of Trade: The Law Merchant, Private Judges, and the Champagne Fairs, *Economics and Politics* 2(1):1–23.

Miller, Terry, Kim R. Holmes, James M. Roberts, and Anthony B. Kim. 2012. "2012 Index of Economic Freedom." Heritage Foundation. http://www.heritage.org/index/download.

Milner, Helen V., and Keiko Kubota. 2005. "Why the Move to Free Trade? Democracy and Trade Policy in the Developing Countries," *International Organization* 59(1):107–143.

Ministry of Foreign Affairs. 2015. "Northeast Asia Peace and Cooperation Initiative." http://www.mofa.go.kr/ENG/North_Asia/res/eng_2015_0310.pdf.

Ministry of Unification. n.d. "Chronology of Inter-Korean Dialogue." http://eng.unikorea.go.kr/content.do?cmsid=3033#.

———. 2011. "Announcement of Measures against North Korea." Special report, May 24. http://nautilus.org/wp-content/uploads/2011/12/2010MOU.pdf.

———. 2013. "Trust-Building Process on the Korean Peninsula." September 23. http://eng.unikorea.go.kr/content.do?cmsid=1920.

Moenius, Johannes, and Daniel Berkowitz. 2011. "Law, Trade, and Development," *Journal of Development Economics* 96:451–460.

Moltz, James, and Alexandre V. Mansourov, eds. *The North Korean Nuclear Program: Security, Strategy, and New Perspective from Russia*. New York: Routledge.

Monde diplomatique. 2000. "Address by President Kim Dae-jung of the Republic of Korea, Lessons of German Reunification and the Korean Peninsula." March 9. http://www.monde-diplomatique.fr/dossiers/coree/A/1904.

Moon, Chung-in. 2008. "Managing the North Korean Nuclear Quagmire: Capability, Impact, Prospects." In *The United States and Northeast Asia: Debates, Issues, and New Order.* Edited by G. John Ikenberry and Chung-in Moon. New York: Rowman and Littlefield.

———. 2012. *The Sunshine Policy: In Defense of Engagement with North Korea.* Seoul: Yonsei University Press.

Moon, Chung-in, and Jong-Yun Bae. 2003. "The Bush Doctrine and the North Korean Nuclear Crisis," *Asian Perspective* 27(4):9–45.

Moon, Chung-in, and David Steinberg. 1999. *Kim Dae-Jung Government and Sunshine Policy.* Seoul: Yonsei University Press.

Moravcsik, Andrew. 1997. "Taking Preferences Seriously: A Liberal Theory of International Politics," *International Organization* 51(4):513–553.

Morrow, James D. 1999. "How Could Trade Affect Conflict?" *Journal of Peace Research*, 36(4):481–489.

Muico, Norma Kang. 2007. *Forced Labor in North Korean Prison Camps.* London: Anti-Slavery International. http://www.antislavery.org/includes/documents/cm_docs/2009/n/1_nk_2007.pdf.

Musharraf, Pervez. 2006. *In the Line of Fire: A Memoir.* New York: Free Press.

Myers, B. R. 2010. *The Cleanest Race: How North Koreans See Themselves and Why It Matters.* Brooklyn, NY: Melville Publishing.

———. 2015. *North Korea's Juche Myth.* Busan, South Korea: Sthele Press.

Myerson, Roger B. 2008. "The Autocrat's Credibility Problem and Foundations of the Constitutional State," *American Political Science Review* 102(1):125–139.

Na, H.-S. 2007. "Regional Cooperation on Transportation in Northeast Asia." In *New Linkages in Northeast Asian Regional Cooperation.* Edited by Kyuryoon Kim. Seoul: Korea Institute for National Unification.

National Committee on North Korea. 2007. "In the News: North Korea and Banco Delta Asia." NCNK Issue Brief: BDA. http://www.ncnk.org/resources/briefing-papers/all-briefing-papers/ncnk_issue_brief_bda.

Nanto, Dick K. 2009. "North Korean Counterfeiting of U.S. Currency." Congressional Research Service, Washington, DC, June 12.

Nanto, Dick K., Mark E. Manyin, and Kerry Dumbaugh. 2010. "China-North Korea Relations. Congressional Research Service, Washington, DC, January 22.

Natsios, Andrew S. 2001. *The Great North Korean Famine*. Washington, DC: US Institute for Peace.

Niblock, Tim. 2001. *Pariah States and Sanctions in the Middle East: Iraq, Libya, Sudan*. Boulder, CO: Lynne Rienner.

Nielson, Daniel, and Michael Tierney. 2003. "Delegation to International Organizations: Agency Theory and World Bank Environmental Reform," *International Organization* 57(2):241–276.

Nikitin, Mary Beth. 2011. "Proliferation Security Initiative." Congressional Research Service, Washington, DC, June 15.

Nincic, Miroslav. 2005. *Renegade Regimes: Confronting Deviant Behavior in World Politics*. New York: Columbia University Press.

———. 2010. "Getting What You Want: Positive Inducements in International Relations," *International Security* 35(1):138–183.

———. 2011. *The Logic of Positive Engagement*. Ithaca, NY: Cornell University Press.

Noh, Moo-hyun. 2004. "Speech at the World Affairs Council, Los Angeles." November 12.

Noland, Marcus. 2000. *Avoiding the Apocalypse: The Future of the Two Koreas*. Washington, DC: Peterson Institute for International Economics.

———. 2001. "Between Collapse and Revival: A Reinterpretation of the North Korean Economy." Paper presented at the Economic Development in North Korea and Global Partnership Conference, Cheju, South Korea, March 15–16.

———. 2009. "Telecommunications in North Korea: Has Orascom Made the Connection?" *North Korea Review* (Spring) 5:62–74.

———. 2013. "The Elusive Nature of North Korean Reform," *AsiaPacific Issues* (108). http://www.eastwestcenter.org/sites/default/files/private/api108.pdf.

———. 2014. "A Study to Analyze Cost-Benefits of the Reunification of Korean Peninsula to the United States." Korea Institute for International Economic Policy Research Paper, pages 9–21, Seoul.

Noland, Marcus, and L. Gordon Flake. 1997. "Opening Attempt: North Korea and the Rajin-Sonbong Free Trade and Economic Zone," *Journal of Asian Business* 13(2):99–116.

Noland, M., S. Robinson, and T. Wang. 2000. "Modeling Korean Unification," *Journal of Comparative Economics*, 28:400–421.

Nooruddin, Irfan. 2002. "Modeling Selection Bias in Studies of Sanctions Efficacy," *International Interactions* 28(1):59–75.

North Korea Leadership Watch. 2012. "Third Floor." October 18. https://nkleadershipwatch.wordpress.com/kji-2/third-floor/.

Nuland, Victoria. 2012. "U.S.-DPRK Bilateral Discussion." US Department of State press release, February 29. http://www.state.gov/r/pa/prs/ps/2012/02/184869.htm.

Oberdorfer, Don. 1997. *The Two Koreas: A Contemporary History*. Reading, MA: Addison-Wesley.

Oberdorfer, Don, and Robert Carlin. 2014. *The Two Koreas: A Contemporary History*. 3rd rev. ed. New York: Basic Books.

O'Neal, John R., and Russett, Bruce. 1997. "The Classical Liberals Were Right: Democracy, Interdependence, and Conflict, 1950–1985," *International Studies Quarterly* 41:267–294.

Pape, Robert A. 1997. "Why Economic Sanctions Do Not Work," *International Security* 22(2):90–136.

Park, Byung-kwang. 2009. "China-North Korea Economic Relations During the Hu Jintao Era," *Korea Focus* (Autumn):89–98.

Park, Geun-hye. 2011. "A New Kind of Korea: Building Trust between Seoul and Pyongyang," *Foreign Affairs* September/October:13–18.

———. 2012. "Trustpolitik and the Making of a New North Korea." November 15. https://piie.com/blogs/north-korea-witness-transformation/park-geun-hye-north-south-relations.

———. 2014. "An Initiative for Peaceful Unification on the Korean Peninsula." Speech delivered at the Dresden University of Technology, Dresden, March 24. http://english1.president.go.kr/activity/speeches.php?srh%5Bview_mode%5D=detail&srh%5Bseq%5D=5304&srh%5Bdetail_no%5D=27.

Park, Hyeong-jung. 2011. "The Hereditary Succession and Mass Replacement of Officials from Top to Bottom." Korea Institute for National Unification Online Series CO 11-32. http://repo.kinu.or.kr/bitstream/2015.oak/1896/1/0001447731.pdf.

———. 2013. "North Korea's 'New Economic Management System': Main Features and Problems." Korea Institute for National Unification. http://www.koreafocus.or.kr/design2/layout/content_print.asp?group_id=105092.

Park, John. 2009. "North Korea Inc.: Gaining Insights into North Korean Regime Stability from Recent Commercial Activities." US Institute of Peace working paper, April 22.

Park, John, and John Walsh. 2016. "Stopping North Korea Inc.: Sanctions Effectiveness and Unintended Consequences." MIT Security Studies Program. http://web.mit.edu/ssp/people/walsh/Stopping%20North%20Korea%20Inc_Park%20%20Walsh_FINAL.pdf.

Peksen, Dursun. 2009. "Better or Worse? The Effect of Economic Sanctions on Human Rights," *Journal of Peace Research* 46(1):59–77.

Peksen, Dursun, and A Cooper Drury. 2010. "Coercive or Corrosive: The Negative Impact of Economic Sanctions on Democracy," *International Interactions* 36(3):240–264.

Perl, Raphael. 2005. "CRS Report for Congress: Drug Trafficking and North Korea—Issues for US Policy." Congressional Research Service, Washington, DC, March 4.

———. 2006. "North Korean Counterfeiting of U.S. Currency." Congressional Research Service, Washington, DC, March 22.

Perl, Raphael, and Dick Nanto. 2007. "CRS Report for Congress: North Korean Crime-for-Profit Activities." Congressional Research Service, Washington, DC, February 16. http://fpc.state.gov/documents/organization/81342.pdf.

Perry, William. 1999. "Review of United States Policy Toward North Korea: Findings and Recommendations." US Department of State, Office of the North Korea Policy Coordinator report, October 12. http://belfercenter.hks.harvard.edu/files/1997%20NKPR.pdf.

Perry, William J. 2015. *My Journey to the Nuclear Brink.* Palo Alto, CA: Stanford University Press.

Polachek, Solomon William. 1980. "Conflict and Trade," *Journal of Conflict Resolution,* 24(1):55–78.

Pollack, Jonathan. 2003. "The United States, North Korea, and the End of the Agreed Framework," *Naval War College Review,* 56(3):11–49. https://www.usnwc.edu/getattachment/d65ed211-2e16-4ef3-828d-5308248ab652/United-States,-North-Korea,-and-the-End-of-the-Agr.aspx.

———. 2011. *No Exit: North Korea, Nuclear Weapons and International Security.* London: International Institute for Strategic Studies.

Pollack, Joshua. 2011. "Ballistic Trajectory: The Evolution of North Korea's Ballistic Missile Market," *Nonproliferation Review* 18(2):411–429.

Powell, Colin. 2002. "Remarks at Asia Society Annual Dinner." New York, June 10. http://asiasociety.org/policy-politics/colin-powell-remarks-asia-society-annual-dinner-2002.

Prahar, Peter A. 2006. "North Korea: Illicit Activity Funding the Regime." Statement before the Federal Financial Management, Government Information, and International Security Subcommittee of the Homeland Security and Government Affairs Committee, US Senate, Washington, DC, April 25.

Pritchard, Charles L. 2007. *Failed Diplomacy: The Tragic Story of How North Korea Got the Bomb*. Washington, DC: Brookings Institution Press.

Quinones, Kenneth C. 2002. "Beyond Collapse: Continuity and Change in North Korea," *International Journal of Korean Unification Studies* 11(2):25–62.

Ra Jong-Yil. 2013. "Living with Two Nations Under One Roof." *38 North*, January 7. http://38north.org/2013/01/jyra010713/.

Rapoport, Hillel, and Frédéric Docquier. 2005. "The Economics of Migrants? Remittances." IZA Discussion Paper Series No. 1531. Bonn: Institute for the Study of Labor. http://www.econstor.eu/bitstream/10419/21307/1/dp1531.pdf.

Ravenhill, John. 2001. *APEC and the Construction of Pacific Rim Regionalism*. Cambridge, UK: Cambridge University Press.

———. 2007. "Fighting Irrelevance: An Economic Community 'with ASEAN Characteristics.'" Australian National University Department of International Relations Working Paper 2007/3, August 22.

———. 2009. "The Political Economy of Asian Regionalism." Paper prepared for the Asian Development Bank Workshop on Institutions for Regionalism in Asia and the Pacific, Shanghai, December 2–3.

Reilly, James. 2014a. "China's Market Influence in North Korea," *Asian Survey*, 54(5):894–917.

———. 2014b. "China's Economic Engagement in North Korea," *China Quarterly* (November):1–21.

———. 2014c. "The Curious Case of China's Aid to North Korea," *Asian Survey* 54(6):1158–1183.

Reiss, Mitchell, Robert Gallucci, et al. 2005. "Red-Handed: The Truth about North Korea's Weapons Program," *Foreign Affairs* (March/April):142–148.

Rhee, Bong-jo. 2005. "Policy on Inter-Korean Cooperation and Exchanges," *Korea Policy Review* 1(2):16–20.

Rice, Condeleeza. 2003. "North Korea Policy Points." Memorandum to Richard Cheney et al., *Rumsfeld's Rules*, March 4. http://www.rumsfeld.com/.

———. 2008. "Remarks at the Heritage Foundation on U.S. Policy in Asia." June 18. http://iipdigital.usembassy.gov/st/english/texttrans/2008/06/20080619140227eaifaso.8862574.html#axzz3e7577Yuv.

———. 2011. *No Higher Honor: A Memoir of My Years in Washington*. New York: Crown Publishers.

Richardson, Michael. 2003. "Crimes Under Flags of Convenience." *Yale Global Online*, May 19. http://yaleglobal.yale.edu/content/crimes-under-flags-convenience.

Roehrig, Terence. 2009. "North Korea and the Northern Limit Line," *North Korean Review* 5(1):8–22.

Rose, David. 2009. "North Korea's Dollar Store," *Vanity Fair*, August. http://www
.vanityfair.com/politics/features/2009/09/office-39-200909.

Ross, Michael. 2013. *The Oil Curse: How Oil Wealth Shapes the Development of Nations.*
Princeton, NJ: Princeton University Press.

Rotberg, Robert I. 2007. *Worst of the Worst: Dealing with Repressive and Rogue Nations.* Washington, DC: Brookings Institution Press and World Peace Foundation.

Rowe, David M. 2001. *Manipulating the Market: Understanding Economic Sanctions, Institutional
Change and the Political Unity of White Rhodesia.* Ann Arbor: University of Michigan
Press.

Rozman, Gilbert. 2004. *Northeast Asia's Stunted Regionalism: Bilateral Distrust in the Shadow of
Globalization.* New York: Cambridge University Press.

Rumsfeld, Donald. 2002. "Remaining Firm on North Korea." Memorandum to Richard
Cheney, Colin Powell, George Tenet, Spencer Abraham, and Condoleeza Rice. *Rumsfeld's Rules*, December 26. http://www.rumsfeld.com/.

———. 2006. "Declaratory Policy and the Nuclear Programs of North Korea and Iran."
Letter to George W. Bush. *Rumsfeld's Rules*, October 5. http://www.rumsfeld.com/.

Russett, Bruce M., and John R. O'Neal. 2001. *Triangulating Peace: Democracy, Interdependence,
and International Organizations.* New York: WW Norton.

Samore, Gary, ed. 2015. *Sanctions Against Iran: A Guide to Targets, Terms and Timetables.*
Cambridge, MA: Belfer Center for Science and International Affairs.

Schloms, Michael. 2004. *North Korea and the Timeless Dilemma of Aid: A Study of Humanitarian Action in Famines.* Munich: Lit.

Schumpeter, Joseph. 1919. "State Imperialism and Capitalism." *Panarchy.* http://www
.panarchy.org/schumpeter/imperialism.html.

Scobell, Andrew. 2003. "China and North Korea: The Limits of Influence," *Current History*
(September):274–278.

———. 2004. *China and North Korea: From Comrades in Arms to Allies at Arm's Length.*
Carlisle Barracks, PA: Strategic Studies Institute. http://2001-2009.state.gov/r/pa/prs/
ps/2007/oct/93217.htm.

Ser, Myo-ja. 2003. "North Korea Details Its Plan to End Crisis." *Joongang Daily*, August 28.
http://joongangdaily.joins.com/article/view.asp?aid=2025739.

Severino, Rodolfo C. 2006. *Southeast Asia in Search of an ASEAN Community.* Singapore:
Institute for Southeast Asian Studies.

Shambaugh, David. 2003. "China and the Korean Peninsula: Playing for the Long Term,"
Washington Quarterly, 26(2):43–56.

Shin Chang-Hoon, 2014. *Beyond the UN COI Report on Human Rights in North Korea.*
Seoul: Asan Institute. http://en.asaninst.org/contents/asan-report-beyond-the-coi
-dprk-human-rights-report/.

Shin Gi-wook, and Daniel Sneider. 2007. *Cross Currents: Regionalism and Nationalism in
Northeast Asia.* Stanford, CA: Walter H. Shorenstein Asia-Pacific Research Center.

Shinn, James. 1996. *Weaving the Net: Conditional Engagement with China,* 35th ed. New York:
Council on Foreign Relations Press.

Shirk, Susan. 1993. *The Political Logic of Economic Reform in China.* Oakland, CA: University
of California Press.

Sigal, Leon V. 1998. *Disarming Strangers: Nuclear Diplomacy with North Korea.* Princeton, NJ:
Princeton University Press.

———. 2002. "North Korea Is No Iraq: Pyongyang's Negotiating Strategy, Arms Control Association, December. https://www.armscontrol.org/act/2002_12/sigal_dec02.

———. 2005. "Misplaying North Korea and Losing Friends and Influence in Northeast Asia." *The North Korean Nuclear Crisis: Regional Perspectives*, July 12. http://northkorea .ssrc.org/Sigal/.

———. 2009. "Punishing North Korea Won't Work," *Bulletin of the Atomic Scientists*, May 28.

———. 2009a. "Policy Forum 09-046: Why Punishing North Korea Won't Work . . . and What Will." *NAPSNet Policy Forum*, June 10. http://www.nautilus.org/fora/ security/09046Sigal.html.

———. 2009b. "North Korea Policy on the Rocks: What Can Be Done to Restore Constructive Engagement? *Global Asia* 4(2):8–12.

———. 2010. "Looking for Leverage in All the Wrong Places. *38 North*, May 1. http://www.38north.org/?p=545.

———. 2012. "In Deep Denial on North Korea and Prospects for US-North Korea Negotiations," *Asia-Pacific Journal* 10(34):1–10.

———. 2016. "Getting What We Need from North Korea," *Arms Control Today* 46(3):8–13.

Smith, Hazel. 2005. *Hungry for Peace*. Washington, DC: US Institute for Peace.

———. 2015. *North Korea: Markets and Military Rule*. New York: Cambridge University Press.

Smith, Heather. 1998. "The Food Economy: Catalyst for Collapse?" In *Economic Integration of the Korean Peninsula*. Edited by Marcus Noland. Washington, DC: Institute for International Economics.

Smith, James McCall. 2000. "The Politics of Dispute Settlement Design: Explaining Legalism in Regional Trade Pacts," *International Organization* 54(1):137–180.

Snyder, Scott. 1999. *Negotiating on the Edge: North Korean Negotiating Behavior (Cross-Cultural Negotiation Books)*. Washington, DC: US Institute of Peace.

———. 2008. "China-Korea Relations: Lee Myung-bak Era: Mixed Picture for China Relations," *Comparative Connections* 10(1). https://csis-prod.s3.amazonaws.com/s3fs -public/legacy_files/files/media/csis/pubs/0801qchina_korea.pdf.

———. 2009. *China's Rise and the Two Koreas: Politics, Economics, Security*. Boulder, CO: Lynne Rienner.

Solingen, Etel. 1994. "The Political Economy of Nuclear Restraint," *International Security* 19(2):126–159.

———. 1998. *Regional Orders at Century's Dawn: Global and Domestic Influences on Grand Strategy*. Princeton, NJ: Princeton University Press.

———. 2001. "Mapping Internationalization: Domestic and Regional Impacts," *International Studies Quarterly* 45:517–555.

———. 2007. *Nuclear Logics: Contrasting Paths in East Asia and the Middle East*. Princeton, NJ: Princeton University Press.

Solingen, Etel, ed. 2012. *Sanctions, Statecraft, and Nuclear Proliferation*. New York: Cambridge University Press, 2012.

Sovacool, Benjamin. 2009. "North Korea and Illegal Narcotics: Smoke but No Fire?" *Asia Policy* 7 (January):89–111.

Spoorenberg, Thomas, and Daniel Schwekendiek. 2012. "Demographic Changes in North Korea: 1993–2008." *Population and Development Review* 38(1):133–158.

Struck, Doug. 2002. "North Korean Program Not Negotiable, U.S. Told N. Korea," *Washington Post*, October 20.

Suh, Dae-Sook. 1988. *Kim Il Sung*. New York: Columbia University Press.

Suh, Jae Jean. 2009. *The Lee Myung-bak Government's North Korea Policy: A Study on Its Historical and Theoretical Foundation*. Seoul: Korean Institute for National Unification. https://www.kinu.or.kr/upload/neoboard/DATA05/suh.pdf.

Suh, Jae-Jung, and Seunghun Lee. 2010. "Rush to Judgment: Inconsistencies in South Korea's Cheonan Report," *Asia-Pacific Journal* 8(28).

Suominen, Kati. 2009. "The Changing Anatomy of Regional Trade Agreements in East Asia," *Journal of East Asian Studies* 9:29–56.

Svolik, Milan W. 2012. *The Politics of Authoritarian Rule*. Cambridge, UK: Cambridge University Press.

Szalontai, Balázs. 2005. *Kim Il Sung in the Khrushchev Era: Soviet-DPRK Relations and the Roots of North Korean Despotism, 1953–1964*. Cold War International History Project Series. Stanford, CA: Stanford University Press.

Szalontai, Balázs, and Changyong Choi. 2013. "China's Controversial Role in North Korea's Economic Transformation: The Dilemmas of Dependency," *Asian Survey* 53(2): 269–291.

Szalontai, Balázs, and Sergey Radchenko. 2006. "North Korea's Efforts to Acquire Nuclear Technology and Nuclear Weapons: Evidence from Russian and Hungarian Archives." Woodrow Wilson International Center for Scholars Cold War International History Project Working Paper #53, August.

Toloraya, Georgy. 2008. "Russia's East Asian Strategy: The Korean Challenge." *Russia in Global Affairs*, March 2. http://eng.globalaffairs.ru/number/n_10359.

Tomisaka, Satoshi, ed. and trans. *China's Secret File on Relations with North Korea [Takitachosen Chugoku Kimitsu Fairu]*. Purportedly written largely by an official of the International Department of the Chinese Communist Party's Central Committee.

Transparency International. 2011. "Corruption Perception Index 2011: Long Methodological Brief." http://www.transparency.org/cpi2011/in_detail.

———. 2014. "Corruption Perceptions Index 2014." http://www.transparency.org/cpi2014/results.

———. 2015. "Corruption Perceptions Index 2015." http://www.transparency.org/cpi2015#results-table.

Tsuji, Hisako. 2003. "An International Logistics Infrastructure for Northeast Asia." Economic Research Institute for Northeast Asia Discussion Paper No. 0307e, November. http://www.erina.or.jp/en/wp-content/uploads/2014/11/0307e.pdf.

UN Development Program. 1994. *Human Development Report 1994*. Oxford, UK: Oxford University Press.

———. 2009. "DRAFT Monthly Note to the Emergency Relief Coordinator."

UNICEF. 2010. "Multiple Indicator Cluster Survey 2009." https://mics-surveys-prod.s3.amazonaws.com/MICS4/East%20Asia%20and%20the%20Pacific/Korea%2C%20Democratic%20People%27s%20Republic%20of/2009/Final/Korea%20DPR%202009%20MICS_English.pdf.

———. 2012. "Democratic People's Republic of Korea: Final Report of the National Nutrition Survey 2012." https://www.unicef.org/eapro/DPRK_National_Nutrition_Survey_2012.pdf.

————. 2013."Democratic People's Republic of Korea: Final Report of the National Nutrition Survey 2012." http://kp.one.un.org/content/dam/unct/dprk/docs/Executive%20Summary%20DPRK%20Nutrition%20survey%202012.pdf.

UN Office on Drugs and Crime. 2003. "Global Illicit Drug Trends 2003." https://www.unodc.org/unodc/en/data-and-analysis/global_illicit_drug_drug_trends.html.

————. 2006. *World Drug Report 2006, Volume 1: Analysis.* https://www.unodc.org/pdf/WDR_2006/wdr2006_volume1.pdf.

UN Panel of Experts. 2010. "Report of the Panel of Experts Established Pursuant to Resolution 1874 (2009)." S2010-571. http://www.un.org/ga/search/view_doc.asp?symbol=S/2010/571.

————. 2012. "Report of the Panel of Experts Established Pursuant to Resolution 1874 (2009)."S2012-422.http://www.un.org/ga/search/view_doc.asp?symbol=S/2012/422.

————. 2013. "Report of the Panel of Experts Established Pursuant to Resolution 1874 (2009)."S2013-337.http://www.un.org/ga/search/view_doc.asp?symbol=S/2013/337.

————. 2014. "Report of the Panel of Experts Established Pursuant to Resolution 1874 (2009)."S2014-147.http://www.un.org/ga/search/view_doc.asp?symbol=S/2014/147.

————. 2015. "Report of the Panel of Experts Established Pursuant to Resolution 1874 (2009)."S2015-131.http://www.un.org/ga/search/view_doc.asp?symbol=S/2015/131.

————. 2016. "Report of the Panel of Experts Established Pursuant to Resolution 1874 (2009)."S2016-157.http://www.un.org/ga/search/view_doc.asp?symbol=S/2016/157.

UN Security Council. 2009. "Statement by the President of the Security Council." S/PRST/2009/7, April 13. http://www.un.org/en/ga/search/view_doc.asp?symbol=S/PRST/2009/7.

————. 2012. "Statement by the President of the Security Council," S/PRST/2012/13, April 16. http://www.mofa.go.jp/region/asia-paci/n_korea/missile_12/pdfs/state_120416.pdf.

————. 2016. "Letter dated March 4, 2016, from the Permanent Representative of the Democratic People's Republic of Korea to the United Nations addressed to the Secretary-General." March 7.

US Arms Control and Disarmament Agency. 1997. "World Military Expenditures and Arms Transfers 1997." Washington, DC, January 29. http://dosfan.lib.uic.edu/acda/wmeat97/wmeat97.htm.

USDA Foreign Agriculture Service. 2012. "People's Republic of China Grain and Feed Annual 2012." Global Agricultural Information Network Report CH 12022, March 2.

US Department of State. 1999. *International Narcotics Control Strategy Report.* Washington, DC.

————. 2004. "North Korea: US Food Donation." Press statement, July 23. http://2001-2009.state.gov/r/pa/prs/ps/2004/34653.htm.

————. 2005. *International Narcotics Control Strategy Report.* Washington, DC.

————. 2007. "Initial Actions for the Implementation of the Joint Statement." Media note, February 13. http://2001–2009. state.gov/r/pa/prs/ps/2007/february/80479.htm.

————. 2007. "Second-Phase Actions for the Implementation of the September 2005 Joint Statement." Media note, October 3.

US Department of the Treasury. 2009. "North Korean Government Agencies' and Front Companies Involvement in Illicit Financial Activities." Financial Crimes Enforcement Network Advisory, June 18. http://www.fincen.gov/statutes_regs/guidance/html/fin-2009-a002.html.

———. 2010. "Fact Sheet: New Executive Order Targeting Proliferation and Other Illicit Activities Related to North Korea." August 30. http://www.treasury.gov/press-center/press-releases/Pages/tg839.aspx.

———. 2011. "Fact Sheet: Overview of Section 311 of the USA Patriot Act." Press release, February 10. http://www.treasury.gov/press-center/press-releases/Pages/tg1056.aspx.

Valencia, Mark J. 2010. "*38 North* Special Report: North Korea and the Proliferation Security Initiative." *38 North*. http://38north.org/wp-content/uploads/2010/07/38north_SR_PSI.pdf.

Vaubel, Roland. 2006. "Principal-Agent Problems in International Organizations," *Review of International Organizations* 1:125–138.

Verdier, Daniel, and Byungwon Woo. 2011. "Why Rewards Are Better Than Sanctions," *Economics and Politics*, 23(2):220–238.

Voeten, Erik. 2010. "Regional Judicial Institutions and Economic Cooperation: Lessons for Asia?" Asian Development Bank Regional Economic Integration working paper, November.

von Hippel, David, and Peter Hayes. 2014. "Assessment of Energy Policy Options for the DPRK Using a Comprehensive Energy Security Framework." *NAPSNet* special report, January 30. http://nautilus.org/napsnet/napsnet-special-reports/assessment-of-energy-policy-options-for-the-dprk-using-a-comprehensive-energy-security-framework/.

Voronstov, Alexander. 2007. "Current Russia–North Korea Relations: Challenges and Achievements." Brookings Institution CEAP Visiting Fellows working paper, February 1.

Wallace, Robert. 2007. *Sustaining the Regime: North Korea's Quest for Financial Support.* Lanham, MD: University Press of America.

Walters, Greg. 2016. "North Korea's Counterfeit Benjamins Have Vanished," *Vice News*, March 16. https://news.vice.com/article/north-koreas-counterfeit-benjamins-have-vanished.

Weathersby, Kathryn. 2005. "Enigma of The North Korean: Back to the Future?" In "Challenges Posed by the DPRK for the Alliance and the Region." Korea Economic Institute newsletter, October.

Weeks, Jessica L. P. 2012. "Strongmen and Straw Men: Authoritarian Regimes and the Initiation of International Conflict," *American Political Science Review* 106(2):326–347.

———. 2014. *Dictators at War and Peace. Cornell Studies in Security Affairs Series.* Ithaca, NY: Cornell University Press.

Wei, Shang-Jin. 2000. "How Taxing Is Corruption on International Investors? *Review of Economics and Statistics* 82(1):1–11.

Weingartner, Miranda. 2011. "Food Security Assessment by 5 US NGOs." *CanKor*, February 28. https://vtncankor.wordpress.com/2011/02/28/food-security-assessment-by-5-us-ngos/.

Weisman, Steven. 2007. "How U.S. Turned North Korean Funds into a Bargaining Chip." *New York Times*, April 12. http://www.nytimes.com/2007/04/12/world/asia/12bank.html.

Weissmann, Mikael. 2014. "Keeping Alive: Understanding North Korea's Supply Lines and the Potential Role of Sanctions," Swedish Institute of International Affairs UL Paper No. 6, September 29.

Wertz, Daniel, J. J. Oh, and Insung Kim. 2016. "DPRK Diplomatic Relations." National Committee on North Korea issue brief, August.

Williams, Martyn. 2012. "English Transcript of Kim Jong Un's Speech." *North Korea Tech*,

April 15. http://www.northkoreatech.org/2012/04/18/english-transcript-of-kim
-jong-uns-speech/.

Winner, Andrew C. 2005. "The Proliferation Security Initiative: The New Face of Interdiction," *Washington Quarterly* 28(2):129–143.

Wit, Joel. 2009. *U.S. Strategy toward North Korea: Rebuilding Dialogue and Engagement*. Washington, DC: U.S.-Korea Institute at the School of Advanced International Studies.

Wit, Joel S., Daniel B. Poneman, and Robert L. Galucci. 2005. *Going Critical: The First
North Korean Nuclear Crisis*. Washington, DC: Brookings Institution Press.

Wolf, Charles, Jr., Brian G. Chow, and Gregory S. Jones. 2008. *Enhancement by Enlargement:
The Proliferation Security Initiative*. Santa Monica, CA: RAND Corporation.

Wood, Reed. 2008. "A Hand upon the Throat of the Nation: Economic Sanctions and State
Repression, 1976–2001," *International Studies Quarterly* 52:489–513.

World Bank. 2010. *World Development Indicators*. http://databank.worldbank.org/ddp/
home.do.

———. 2015. "MENA Quarterly Economic Brief: Economic Implications of Lifting
Sanctions on Iran." World Bank Middle East and North Africa Region, No. 5, July 23.

World Food Program. 2006. "WFP Governing Body Approves North Korea Aid Plan."
ReliefWeb, February 26. http://reliefweb.int/node/200814.

———. 2008. "Special Report: Crop and Food Security Assessment Mission to the Democratic People's Republic of Korea." December. http://www.fao.org/docrep/011/
ai475e/ai475e00.htm.

Wu, Anne. 2005. "What China Whispers to North Korea," *Washington Quarterly* 28(2):35–48.

Wu, Xinbo. 2009. "Chinese Perspectives on Building an East Asian Community in the
Twenty-First Century." In *Asia's New Multilateralism: Cooperation, Competition and the
Search for Community*. Edited by Michael Green and Bates Gil. New York: Columbia
University Press.

Xinhua. 2000. "President Jiang Holds Talks with Visiting North Korean Leader." June 1.

———. 2008. "Top DPRK Leader Kim Jong Il Meets with Visiting CPA Official." January 23. http://news.xinhuanet.com/english/2009-01/23/content_10707546.htm.

Yan, Yuye. 2016. "On China's Humanitarian Aid to North Korea Post-Cold War." Unpublished paper. Shanghai Finance University.

Yang, Moon-soo, and Kevin Sheppard. 2009. "Changes in North Korea's Corporate Governance." In *The Dynamics of Change in North Korea: An Institutionalist Perspective*. Edited
by Phillip Park. Seoul: Kyungnam University Press.

Yang, Sung-chul. 1999. *The North and South Korean Political System: A Comparative Analysis*.
Seoul: Hollym.

Yoon, Dae-Kyu. 2009. "Economic Reform and Institutional Transformation: A Legal Perspective." In *The Dynamics of Change in North Korea: An Institutionalist Perspective*. Edited
by Phillip H. Park. Seoul: Kyungnam University Press.

You, Jong-sung. 2014. "The *Cheonan* Dilemmas and the Declining Freedom of Expression in South Korea." Paper prepared for presentation at the 2014 International Studies Annual Convention, Toronto, March 26–29. https://papers.ssrn.com/sol3/papers
.cfm?abstract_id=2505777.

Yun, Minwoo, and Eunyoung Kim. 2010. "Evolution of North Korean Drug Trafficking:
State Control to Private Participation," *North Korean Review* 6(2):55–64.

Zabrovskaya, Larisa V. 2006. "Economic Contacts between the DPRK and the Russian Far
East: 1992–2005," *International Journal of Korean Unification Studies* 15(2):95–111.

Zakharova, Ludmilla. 2016. "International Sanctions and Economic Relations with North

Korea." Research presented at a panel of the Korea Economic Institute of America. Washington, DC, March 24. http://www.keia.org/event/international-sanctions-and -economic-relations-north-korea.

Zarate, Juan C. 2013. *Treasury's War: The Unleashing of a New Era in Financial Warfare*. New York: Public Affairs.

Zhang, Hui. 2009. "Assessing North Korea's Uranium Enrichment Capabilities," *Bulletin of the Atomic Scientists*, June 18. http://thebulletin.org/assessing-north-koreas-uranium -enrichment-capabilities.

Zhang, Yong-an. 2010. "Drug Trafficking from North Korea: Implications for Chinese Policy." *Brookings*, December 3. http://www.brookings.edu/research/articles/ 2010/12/03-china-drug-trafficking-zhang.

Index

Page numbers followed by "f" or "t" indicate material in figures or tables. NK = North Korea.

Studies in Asian Security

Amitav Acharya, Chief Editor, American University
David Leheny, Chief Editor, Princeton University

SPONSORED BY THE EAST-WEST CENTER, 2004–2011
MUTHIAH ALAGAPPA, FOUNDING SERIES EDITOR

Dangerous Deterrent: Nuclear Weapons Proliferation and Conflict in South Asia. By S. Paul
Kapur. 2007

Minimum Deterrence and India's Nuclear Security. By Rajesh M. Basrur. 2006

Rising to the Challenge: China's Grand Strategy and International Security. By Avery Goldstein.
2005

Unifying China, Integrating with the World: Securing Chinese Sovereignty in the Reform Era.
By Allen Carlson. 2005

Rethinking Security in East Asia: Identity, Power, and Efficiency. Edited by J. J. Suh, Peter J.
Katzenstein, and Allen Carlson. 2004